TROUT
FLY FISHING
AN EXPERT APPROACH

TROUT
FLY FISHING
AN EXPERT APPROACH

Martin Cairncross
& John Dawson

Illustrations by
Charles Jardine

Lanham and New York

ACKNOWLEDGEMENTS

Although we are presenting our own interpretations, they have been gleaned over many years by fishing with proven experts from home and abroad, and tested over a wide variety of waters. The list is enormous, but we would like to register our particular appreciation (in alphabetical order) to: Bryan Archer, Bob Barden, Brian Bowsher, Geoff Clarkson, Graham Dean, Andrew Donaldson, Dave Grove, Colin Harvey, Jeremy Herrmann, Phil Hooper, John Horsey, George Inglis, Martin Introna, Graham Knowles, Chris Ogborne, Mike Perrin, Frank Schlosser, Dave Shipman, Omri Thomas, Tim Tollett, Paul Wakeham, Neil West, Alan Williams and Davy Wotton. Andrew Donaldson and Tim Tollett deserve special thanks for supplying some excellent photographs, and we feel privileged to have the benefit of Charles Jardine's superb artwork.

Although our experiences cover waters from around the world, our long apprenticeships were served in the British Isles. In this respect, our appreciation goes to the staff of many reservoirs – but in particular to those of Chew, Blagdon and Rutland. Paul Knight at Langford encouraged us to develop an interest in the smaller lakes. The Gliffaes Hotel beat of the Usk has repeatedly provided excellent sport on a rain-fed river. And with Jeff Smith, of the Middleton Estate, we have consistently enjoyed the cream of chalkstream fishing.

Finally, the greatest vote of thanks must go to our wives, Chris and Linda, for putting up with our fishing exploits and the undoubtedly monotonous stories about the ones that got away.

Both authors wrote the previous best seller *Success with Trout* in conjunction with Chris Ogborne. They enjoy sharing their knowledge through guided tours, tuition days and corporate parties. They also want the knowledge imparted in this book to be kept up to date, and to encourage feedback and dialogue. Those wishing to keep abreast of developments, or to contribute their own ideas, should consult www.corporate-flyfishing.co.uk.

THE DERRYDALE PRESS

Published in the United States of America
by The Derrydale Press
4720 Boston Way, Lanham, Maryland 20706

Distributed by NATIONAL BOOK NETWORK, INC.

First Derrydale Edition 2001

Copyright © 2001 Martin Cairncross & John Dawson
Illustrations copyright © 2001 Charles Jardine

First published in the UK in 2001
by Swan Hill Press, an imprint of Airlife Publishing Ltd

ISBN 1 58667 066 2

CONTENTS

INTRODUCTION

It was turning out to be a dour October morning at Llandegfedd. Earlier in the week the trout had been rising freely to both aquatic and terrestrial flies – but now the activity had ceased. Success was inevitably going to require a lot of effort on a day when both fishermen were feeling rather jaded. They had just returned with gold medals from England's fly fishing campaigns in the world and home international series, and the desire for relaxation had become the overwhelming factor. The immediate choice lay between hard work and a pint of Caffreys in the nearby pub – a decision that was not too difficult under the circumstances.

So it was that two Englishmen entered a Welsh pub, drank Irish beer and started to talk about Scottish fishing experiences. They reminisced about *Success With Trout* – a best selling book on still-water fly fishing in the UK that they had written with Chris Ogborne five years earlier. Since then, they had acquired a considerable amount of additional knowledge on rivers as well as lakes. Perhaps it was time to update and republish it.

Their thoughts then started to take on a more global perspective. In conjunction with their close friends, they had experienced many different waters around the world. This included fishing and speaking with local experts and sharing flies and tactics. It was interesting how the same approach had worked so well and so consistently in all these different countries. On reflection, though, it was to be expected, for there was no logical reason why trout should vary their behaviour when the food chain was so similar.

They could identify several excellent books on fly fishing. Many specialized in either rivers or lakes, and most were restricted to the author's experiences in his own country. Some concentrated solely on techniques, while others focused in great detail on the complexities of entomology or the trout's behaviour. But they had not come across an authoritative book that co-ordinated global tactics from many experts with a simplified description of the underlying rationale. That was what today's trout fisherman needed – and that was what today's trout fisherman was going to get!

CHAPTER 1
THE QUEST

Tim Tollett with a wild brown trout.

After the initial burst of enthusiasm, we began to have second thoughts about writing a single book covering such diverse regions as North America, Australasia and Europe. Different species of insects are often unique to a country, and within the USA, for example, there is a considerable variation between east and west.

However, we soon reminded ourselves that the brown and rainbow trout and the basic fly life are fundamentally the same. Variations in species between countries are usually only due to differences in size or shade. Upwinged and caddis flies dominate the stream fisherman's thoughts from Colorado to the sacred chalk-streams of southern England, and aquatic midges are a staple diet for trout in still waters everywhere. Small fish and terrestrial insects abound, while most regions have their share of damsels, stoneflies, corixae and various crustaceans. Thus, general patterns like the Adams, Royal Wulff, Pheasant Tail and Hare's Ear are proven on a global basis.

Of course, you can always obtain detailed tips from the locals, and sometimes from the most unexpected sources. Customs officials at Auckland were only too keen to offer us advice on where and how to fish in New Zealand's North Island. 'You'll need a selection of cicadas at this time of year, and it's worth having a few brown gold-headed damsels for the lakes. And have you got any nits?'

'Well, we've got some of these. Will they do?', we reply, showing them some tiny black dry flies.

'How the hick are you going to scoop a fish out the water with one of them?'

Back in the northern hemisphere, we were seeing our way clear to producing a book that would benefit fly fishermen across the globe. Most of the world's best practitioners have the knack of focusing on the important ten per cent of all the information confronting them. They have the essential understanding and the ability to apply it, and are rarely led down blind alleys by too much data. These qualities allow them to be successful just about anywhere they choose to fish.

The book would therefore be a no-nonsense approach, which would cut through much of the unnecessary detail and mystique. It would combine fly tying and tactics as much as possible, since the relationship between them is often the key to success. Entomology would have a clear focus towards the goal of deceiving the trout, rather than being a compendium of academic facts. Detailed descriptions and artificial flies for very specific or localized species would be out. The use of trigger points and general patterns that covered several different families of insects would definitely be in.

Then we had to consider the balance between running and still water. In streams, the current conveys the food, whereas in lakes the trout has to forage. Although the tactics must vary accordingly, the trout is the same creature in both environments, with the same survival instincts and dietary requirements. To reinforce this point, trout that have grown to a large size in a lake will sometimes remain in an adjoining river, after migrating there to spawn.

Thus, while it was inevitable that the different tactics would have to appear in separate chapters, we have aimed to unify the approach wherever possible to encourage a cross-fertilization of ideas. Those who do have their feet firmly in both camps usually find that their overall skills benefit immensely. Yet many stream fishermen choose not to bother with still-water fly fishing at all – and vice versa. Sometimes the two parties will build up their own expertise in complete isolation, almost as if they were stalking completely different fish. We would make one plea to these specialists. Just occasionally, cross the divide and give the other branch of the sport a try. You may even enjoy it!

After some careful consideration, we decided not to cover tactics specifically designed for competitions. Although we have obtained a great deal of pleasure from these events, we wanted to focus on fly fishing for its own sake. There is, however, one point to be made about competition fishing that is very relevant to anyone who is genuinely interested in becoming more proficient.

At the end of the day, each competitor knows exactly how well he has done relative to everyone else. This can be quite a painful experience, but it presents a golden opportunity to learn from those who have been more successful. Thus, the enquiring and self-critical fisherman becomes progressively more competent. The eliminating rounds to progress to the English team are now so keenly fought that you simply have to increase your proficiency to succeed. Indeed, the experiences we have accumulated over many years from qualifying for, representing and captaining England, have added substantially to our skills as all-round fishermen.

THE PLAYERS

Our eccentric friend Reggie, who professes a love of red ink, volunteered with gusto to review an early version of the text.

'Mmmm,' he remarked in his own inimitable style. 'Good stuff – a veritable landmark – but it reads a bit like a PhD thesis. You'd better get the shops to supply a flask of black coffee with each copy!'

Reggie did not realize the implications of what he had just said. The obvious way to lighten the text was to intersperse it with true stories (in italics) about his own exploits and his love of 'taking the Mickey'. But over the years, he has not been alone in adding colour to our fishing trips. There is Humphrey, an irredeemable showman who delights in deceiving his fellow anglers as much as the trout – and he is an expert at both! Denzil is another top-grade fishermen, who pushes the fishing rules as far and as secretly as he dare – but has two major weaknesses in good wine and bad women. Alex is both knowledgeable and intelligent, but lets his frustration overcome his logic all too easily when things go wrong. Finally, there is the pedantic and highly political Wesley, who remains a mediocre angler because he cannot cut through the superfluous detail to the tactics and flies that really matter.

'Mmmm – but you're giving all our secrets away,' was Reggie's parting comment. We hope to be proved guilty. You will be the final judge of whether we have been successful in a quest that may never have started had the Llandegfedd trout been more co-operative on that crisp October morning.

CHAPTER 2

A BETTER UNDERSTANDING

A cutthroat trout moves between the shadows.

Enthusiasm goes a long way, but what discriminates an expert from the ordinary practitioner is an enquiring mind. Those who simply accept things as they find them from one trip to another inevitably waste a lot of time and effort in trial and error. On the other hand, those who try to understand why a particular method does or does not work gain the knowledge to tailor their tactics correctly to the prevailing conditions. They become more consistent, which then increases their confidence to develop tactics further to even greater effect.

This chapter gives a few perspectives into areas that will provide the foundation for many of the tactics described throughout the book. These ideas should help you to decide, for example, when it is better to use a nymph or wet pattern, even though the trout may be preoccupied with dry flies. They should give some clues into the trout's feeding habits. They will also help you to form your own considered opinions on the best choice of rod, line and leader.

Too much detail makes it difficult to sort out the wood from the trees. For that reason we have taken as many short cuts as we dare in an attempt to ensure that the understanding is properly focused towards an angler's paramount objective. In basic terms, we want to tell you how to catch more fish. Those who require detailed technical descriptions of the underlying phenomena should read *In The Ring Of The Rise* by Vince Marinaro, *The Trout And The Fly* by Brian Clarke and John Goddard, or Gary Borger's *Presentation*.

THE TROUT'S VIEW OF ITS SURROUNDINGS

Alex was feeling rather embarrassed. He was a newcomer to the sport, and had quite logically assumed that the trout's window was something to do with its field of view from the eyes on each side of its head. To have made this faux pas publicly was bad enough, but to have done so in front of the

fastidious and self-important Wesley was the worst mistake of all. Wesley was a retired headteacher, who took delight in exerting his authority at every opportunity, and lecturing to his unfortunate fishing colleagues on any subject under the sun. In this instance, Alex realized that he was about to receive the full works.

'It is all really very straightforward. Consider light approaching the surface from below at an angle (let us call it theta) to the normal. The principle of rectilinear propagation allows us to consider either direction with the same conclusion. Light is, of course, a wave that travels with a greater velocity in air than in water. So from a simple consideration of the wave-front, it has to bend further away from the normal in the medium with the lower refractive index. I hope that you are paying attention. There comes a point, therefore, as theta increases to 48.6 degrees, that the exiting light is bent so far that it can no longer leave the surface. At this point all the light is reflected back into the water. This produces a cone of light when viewed from below with a diameter of 2.269 times the depth at 15 degrees Celsius. Inside the cone, everything is visible just above the surface. Outside the cone the surface is a mirror, which is usually a dark green or brown since it reflects the wavelengths of the weeds or gravel below the surface. I can explain it more succinctly with a little bit of mathematics . . .'

At this point, Alex could take no more. He had a PhD and could have gone into much greater detail about the properties of electromagnetic radiation than Wesley, had he too wanted to show off. But he was also very much admired for his skills of riposte and witty repartee, and on this occasion decided to use the more sophisticated approach to restore his sense of pride.

'B*gg*r off, Wesley.'

We have met many people who have not really grasped the implications of the trout's window because the description was too complex. This is a great pity, because anyone who can at least grasp the way in which it affects the trout's behaviour will become a much better all-round fisherman. This calls for a more down-to-earth explanation. Those requiring more of a challenge may wish to decipher Wesley's pompous, yet technically correct, ramblings.

A Simple Explanation of the Window

First of all, the trout's window has absolutely nothing whatsoever to do with its eyesight. Any submerged creature looking up towards the surface – be it a fish, otter or scuba diver – will see a circular window of light. Within this window, directly overhead, everything on or above the surface is visible. This, of course, includes dry flies resting on the surface.

Dry flies outside the circular window are not directly visible to a trout. It is well worth observing this for yourself by looking into a large glass bowl from below. The area outside the window looks just like a mirror – and that is exactly what it is. It will reflect the colours and features of the sub-surface world. In order to be seen directly by a fish, a fly in the area of the mirror has to be submerged. Thus, nymphs are always visible. So too are those parts of an emerger, such as the emptying shuck case, that penetrate the surface film.

The trout's window.

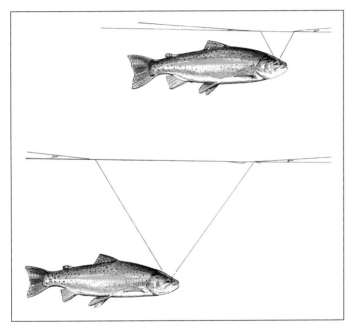

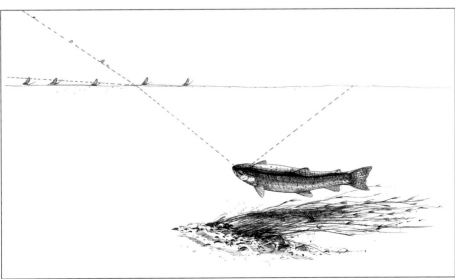

The radius of this circle of visibility is roughly the same as the trout's depth in the water. There is no need to be any more accurate than this due to the uncertainties in estimating distances and depths. So when a fish moves up from 4 ft to 1 ft, its view in any direction of flies resting on the surface also decreases from about 4 ft to 1 ft. A dry fly that was well within the circle at the previous depth has now disappeared, whereas an emerger in the same location would still be visible. Thus nymphs and emergers are often much more effective for catching fish cruising high in the water.

The effect of depth on the number of visible dry flies is greater than you might at first imagine. As every schoolboy should know, the area of a circle is pi times its radius squared. This means that a fish at 4 ft will be able to see 16 times as many spinners, for example, as one cruising only 1 ft below. Consequently, unless there is an abundance of surface food, the trout's interests are best served by keeping well down in the water. This may partially explain why fish often lie near the bottom of a stream, although it is also to take advantage of camouflage and the slower currents.

Finally, a trout that is cruising just a couple of inches below the surface becomes transfixed on the tiny zone in front of its nose. Thus, a successful cast is likely to require extreme accuracy and perhaps more than a little luck, irrespective of whether the pattern is a dry fly or emerger. It is often more productive to distract it from its feeding with a fly that disturbs the surface or to use a hideously bright sub-surface pattern that flashes enticingly outside its zone of concentration.

Imperfections in the Mirror

There is a small, but important, complication to the simple picture. It is possible for a fish on the look-out for food to detect that something is resting on the surface outside its window. Its shape, size or colour may be indeterminate – but something is there, and it is worth closer inspection because it might be edible.

Although the legs of an insect do not penetrate the surface film, they do produce six tiny indentations. Even the featherweight body of a caenis or trico will cause some local distortion. When looking at a small fly from below in a glass bowl, it is impossible to discern too many details outside the window, but its presence is unmistakable. Some large insects distort the surface film sufficiently to allow light to penetrate immediately adjacent to them, which may provide clues to their shape and colour. Trout will therefore inspect the mirror for the presence of surface food. They have a greater chance of success in calm conditions for two reasons. First, any distortion of the surface will be highly conspicuous. Second, more insects are likely to become trapped in the unbroken film.

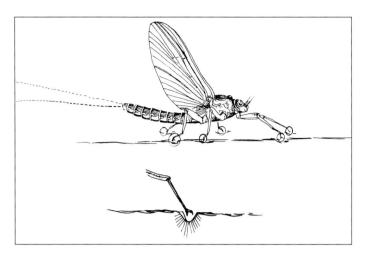

An insect's footprints in the surface film.

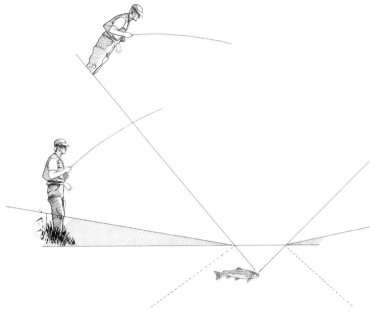

The ten-degree line – plus angler.

In windy conditions or in rough parts of a stream, the ripples will constantly change the angle of the surface. This is good news for the angler since the fish are less capable of discerning his movements or detecting imperfections in the artificial fly. A big swell will move the window from one side of a fish to the other, whereas a tiny ripple will expose transitory windows in the mirror and dark patches in the window. The onset of a slight breeze on a hitherto calm surface can therefore be a mixed blessing, and we have known the fishing either to improve or deteriorate on many occasions. Sometimes in lakes you will encounter areas of both calm water and light ripples. It is then an excellent tactic to position yourself in the ripple for concealment, while casting your fly just beyond it to the calm patch. Here, it will be clearly visible in a region where the fish might expect to find more food.

There is the added factor with most artificial patterns of a hook that penetrates the surface film. It is not very realistic, but it may just attract the trout's attention towards a fly outside its window that otherwise would have gone unnoticed. Silver hooks are worth a try, because they are conspicuous while bearing some resemblance to a gas-filled shuck.

Finally, it would be wrong to give the impression that nymphs are always more visible than dry flies. We have been describing one specific case where the trout are high in the water so that their window of vision is severely restricted. In clear water, trout that are lying deep are able to search over a wide circle of vision for flies on top of the surface. They are far more likely to notice a bushy dry fly, which stands as a silhouette against the sky, than a nymph just below the surface.

Glare – The Angler's Accomplice

When sunlight hits water at a shallow angle, it produces glare by bouncing off rather than penetrating the surface. You can observe this phenomenon by kneeling on the ground with your head low while looking into a river or lake. Irrespective of the water clarity, you will be able to see very little beneath the surface – and, by the same argument, anything beneath the surface will be unable to see you. Thus, an angler whose profile

is below the 'ten-degree line' is unlikely to be spotted.

The Trout's Field of Vision

In order to discern depth, distance and a sharp image, a fish needs to use both its eyes. This means that its food has to appear in a narrow 30 degree cone of binocular vision in front of its head before it is sufficiently confident to take it.

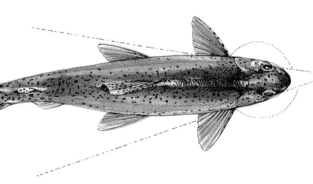

The trout's vision.

Nevertheless, a fish has monocular vision over a much wider area on both sides of its body. Although it can pick out little detail, it is acutely tuned to detecting anything out of the ordinary. It can spot an approaching insect and then turn towards it to get a proper look. More importantly, it can sense any movement of a potential predator. A fish's requirement to survive is usually greater than its desire to feed.

Although a fish's eyes are capable of wide-angled vision, its body gets in the way. This prevents the detection of anything in a 30 degree arc immediately behind it. This cries out for approaching a fish from behind at a narrow angle. The closer you get to the fish, the greater the advantages become of wading rather than casting at a wider angle from the bank.

COLOUR AND VISIBILITY

There is plenty of evidence from both scientists and anglers to demonstrate that fish have the ability to differentiate between colours. Selection of the right colour is therefore important – and for three good reasons. First, there is the obvious requirement to imitate the natural food. Second, certain colours seem to provide trigger points that exploit a trout's aggression or curiosity, or which simply increase its desire to feed. For example, oranges and reds in dry flies and emergers sometimes induce savage takes, whereas the combination of black and green on sub-surface patterns will often kick non-feeding fish into commitment. Finally, different colours show up better than others under certain water conditions.

The Diving Manual of the British Sub-Aqua Club recommends two colours that stand out in water of low (about 5 ft) visibility. They are fluorescent orange and (as a silhouette) black. Not surprisingly, anglers often choose these two options in coloured water to attract the fish's attention, even if there is no correspondence to the natural food. We have found that trout will often show a marked and unpredictable preference for either black or orange, so it is worth experimenting with both until you are certain of the current favourite.

When fishing in deep water, there is another factor to take into account, as illustrated clearly by a friend's experience. While learning to scuba dive, he knocked his hand on a structure that was about 15 ft below the surface of a clear freshwater lake. At first, he did not believe that he had cut himself, since all that he could see was some 'gunge'. But on reaching the surface, he noticed that his hand was bleeding quite badly, without any trace of the gunge. This was a clear demonstration that red objects are not recognizable as such at quite modest depths in even the clearest of water. At the same depth, a bright Soldier Palmer would become a nondescript grey.

We have subsequently spoken to several divers and examined diving references. As a rule of thumb, in a clear water lake, the intensity of red light will halve after passing through 6 ft. So at 12 ft, the 'redness' will only be one quarter of what it was on the surface. The remaining red light also has to penetrate from the fly to the fish. If the fish is a further 12 ft away, for example, the redness will have reduced sixteen times overall. More generally, although red provides a superb trigger point at short range, it is unlikely to attract a trout from 15 ft away, irrespective of the depth or water clarity.

The real deep-water specialists might be interested in the following numbers from diving references. In clear water, the approximate distances at which different colours have effectively disappeared to the (human) eye are 15 ft (red), 25 ft (orange), 35 ft (yellow), 60 ft (green) and 75 ft (blue). Water conditions will affect the overall transmission and the relative behaviour of different colours, but can never increase the absolute values above those for pure water. For example, peat-stained waters dramatically reduce the transmission of the shorter wavelengths of light, to the extent that blue is absorbed more rapidly than red – hence their reddish-brown tinge.

RISE-FORMS

Rise-forms give away more information than just the presence of a feeding fish. They may also provide clues to the food-form, and it may be possible to deduce the direction and depth of a cruising trout, although this is more relevant to lakes than rivers. It is important, though, to treat all conclusions as rules of thumb rather than gospel. A trout's behaviour may depend on other factors such as confidence, familiarity, previous experiences with artificial flies or simply individual preference.

Clues to Diet

One of the most common and misinterpreted rise-forms is the **sub-surface boil**. A natural reaction on seeing any movement in the water is to reach for the dry fly box. But if there is a highly conspicuous swirl without any breaking of the surface, it is a sure sign that the trout is taking some sort of sub-surface food, such as a nymph.

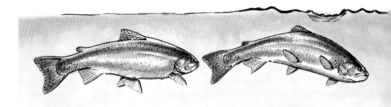

Sub-surface boil.

The movement associated with a **head and tail** rise is not very different from the sub-surface boil, except now the fly is so high in the water that the trout cannot help breaking the surface. The head will appear first as it takes the fly, followed by the body as the fish turns downwards with its prey. This suggests that the food is a nymph that is very close to the surface – most probably at some stage of emergence into an adult.

Head and tail rise.

There is no reason why a trout should not exhibit the same head and shoulders rise to a fully fledged adult on top of the surface. However, a fish will expend less energy by sticking just its nose (or neb) out of the water. A trout exhibiting a **nebbing** rise intercepts an adult fly quickly.

Nebbing rise.

If an insect has no chance of escaping, the trout may want to conserve even more energy. Spent spinners or trapped terrestrial flies are not going to leave the water in a hurry, so the trout can afford to sip the fly gently from below the surface. Often this will produce the merest dimple, and sometimes there will be no sign at all other than the fly being sucked downwards by an invisible vacuum cleaner. Sometimes there is an audible gulp, which has led to the term 'gulpers' in North America. The trout will close its mouth on the fly immediately, so the **sipping** or **dimpling** rise requires excellent reflexes.

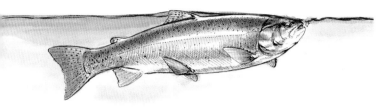

Sipping or dimpling rise.

If trout remain high in the water when taking dry flies, it is invariably a sign that there are great numbers of tiny insects on the surface. This **smutting** behaviour, which is more prevalent in still water, occurs because the most efficient manner to feed is to go into 'vacuum cleaner' mode. Such fish have a tiny window of surface vision, but that is all they need when the food is so abundant.

Smutting behaviour.

Finally, there is the **splashing** rise. This happens when a trout has to act quickly before its prey can escape, and may indicate a chase after scurrying caddis flies or small fish. In the latter case, there is usually a tell-tale sign of several fry scattering near the surface to escape the marauding predator. In still water, it is worth looking for other evidence of fry to avoid misinterpretation. For example, trout will often splash through

the surface to intercept fast-moving nymphs, such as caddis pupae and corixae. In hot, breezy conditions, the wings of emerged insects dry out more quickly. This sometimes results in splashy rises, since trout have less time to intercept them before they fly away.

Fry bashing.

Clues to Depth and Direction

A cruising trout that breaks the surface usually gives some clues to both its depth and direction – providing the water is fairly calm. The behaviour is most relevant in still water, but it also applies to the slow gliding stretches of some rivers, where a trout may forage before returning to its favourite lie. For example, we have often observed cutthroats moving substantial distances in running water in search of food. It is not easy to differentiate between the different signs, but it is worth persevering since anticipation of the direction of a moving trout makes a tremendous difference to success. It also requires some care in both the observation and interpretation, because a wrong conclusion about the cruising depth may also lead to a false estimate of the direction.

The inference is easier if a trout is cruising high in the water. This normally happens when there is plenty of food on the surface, and the rise-forms will only be a few feet apart. As the trout breaks the surface to feed, rings will spread out around it. Those in front will be more closely spaced than those behind, since they are travelling in the same direction as the trout. So you should cast in front of these closely spaced rings.

Clues to direction of a surface-cruising trout.

It is more difficult to predict the direction of a deep cruising fish. This will normally occur in clear water, when the insect life is sparse, with rise-forms from 10 to 20 ft apart. When a trout approaches the surface, it moves with quite a steep trajectory that produces bulging rings in front of it due to the displacement of water. The ripples that form behind are much smaller and consequently more closely spaced together. So you should cast in front of the bulging, widely spaced rings. Most importantly, when casting in anticipation of the next rise, remember to allow for that movement of 10 to 20 ft.

Clues to direction of a deep-cruising trout.

These techniques are only really applicable to calm conditions, since it is very tricky to make out the ring spacing or the presence of a bulge in rough water. This should not matter for high-cruising fish, which will generally be moving up wind, but the deeper fish could be moving in any direction.

FEEDING HABITS

Fly fishermen around the world concentrate their thoughts on representing the insects and small fish that fall victim to the trout's requirement to feed. Their main objective is to recognize the features and behaviour of principal species and then to select an appropriate imitation. This approach is generally sound, but it is not quite the whole story. It is worth taking a couple of steps back to think more generally about the trout's behaviour, because this can have quite a strong influence on tactics.

Progression of a Rise

Unless they are hungry and scanning their horizons for anything that might pass by, trout will not usually start rising until quite a few insects have appeared. Before this happens, it is arguably better to try to attract their attention by a fly that is big, bright or bushy – perhaps with a small natural imitation trailing just behind it.

When a rise first gets underway, trout tend to be quite catholic in what they will accept. At this stage, it is possible to get by with patterns that may not match the hatch very well. But once set in a rhythm, they become extremely selective. As a rule of thumb, they concentrate on the most abundant species, to the

bafflement of many a frustrated angler. They will feast on smuts to the exclusion of nourishing upwinged duns, or ignore a juicy midge pupa in favour of a tiny caenis or trico.

The Induced Rise

Denzil would never miss a trick, to the extent that the kindest verdict on the legality of some of his tactics would be 'borderline'. He was an expert on every aspect of the sport, including fish psychology. He would often carry a large number of creations that, on casual inspection, resembled small dry flies in the prevailing local colours. A closer look would reveal that the patterns had no hook. Some were no more than the stalks of tiny tomatoes or selected items from plants in the appropriate colour. Others involved a concoction of fur and feather that he had learned to tie in as little 15 seconds.

With supreme stealth, he would proceed about twenty yards upstream of the fish, wade into the water and drop them one at a time so that they floated over his quarry. Sometimes, after a good number of specimens had floated past, one or two fish would start to rise. Inevitably, this would result in a rejection, but it had served the purpose of getting the hitherto disinterested trout to look towards the surface. Moreover, there was nothing to put them on their guard – no drag, no leader and no sudden lift-off of a fly line. Denzil would then reposition himself downstream, cast a properly tied version and enjoy some marvellous dry fly fishing, while his unsuspecting colleagues elsewhere had to persevere with nymphs.

We have often covered rising trout and grayling to no effect for the first dozen or so attempts. Suddenly, fish will start taking the same fly in successive casts. A rise does not have to be initiated by a hatch of natural insects, as is so often assumed.

The Sub-surface Intercom

Humphrey was hosting one of his famous stream-side barbecues by the hatch pool. No expense had been spared in the provision of fillet steak, shell-fish, exotic cheeses and – of course – several cases of his favourite red Rioja. Attendance at these events was one of the bailiff's perks, and he was not holding back in his consumption of the superb wine. After three or four ample glasses, he somehow found himself suggesting an experiment on Humphrey's behalf to the rest of the group. This enabled our friend to defend himself against the pompous, formal and obnoxious Wesley when later accused of bringing fly fishing into disrepute.

'What! Me? It was the bailiff's idea.'

The experiment involved throwing some raw steak into a high concentration of fish that were unaccustomed to such delicacies. At first, they ignored the alien food, but soon one or two of the braver members had a go. Almost immediately, the whole shoal was swimming around in eager anticipation to grab anything that landed on the water. It did not matter when the food changed from meat to cheese to bread. The feeding spree continued unabated.

Then Humphrey knowingly threw some small slices of cucumber into the pool. A trout grabbed the first piece before spitting it out in contempt. After only a couple of fish had tasted it, there was no further feeding until the cucumber had been replaced. The entire population got the message within seconds that it was not worth eating.

There is undoubtedly some form of sub-surface intercom that has obvious implications for fly selection. If a particular fly pattern is not working after a prolonged spell, either change it or move elsewhere. This sub-surface intercom is just as effective at transmitting danger signals. The sport will often deteriorate after losing or returning a fish to the water, irrespective of whether it is a trout, salmon or perch. This is one of the reasons why coarse anglers use a keepnet, and why game fishermen should release their captives at least 20 yds away.

Finally, we must add some strong words of warning. Humphrey had the charm, know-how and ability to get away with just about anything. You should never take the risk of throwing food into a fly-only water without prior permission, and you might find the latter difficult to obtain without the right choice of inducement. Full-bodied red wines are consistently effective with fishery managers, although an expensive Chardonnay will occasionally bring spectacular results. Never offer them lager! Without proper attention to detail and wine selection, you are likely to be suspected of ground-baiting, chumming – or worse – and banned from future visits.

Natural camouflage.

The Effect of Weather

Even the best planning can go awry when there is a change from dull to bright conditions – or vice versa. Whether this is for better or worse depends on the local fly life. The sun will keep the wings of insects dry, and the wind will blow airborne flies on to the water. Thus, on 'terrestrial' lakes and rivers, anglers may rub their hands together in anticipation of good sport on hot, windy days. The same is not true of still waters where the predominant fly life is aquatic. Daphnia blooms will descend to the depths in bright conditions and take the feeding trout with them. Sun and wind tend to be a lethal combination for surface fishing, especially if they come from the same direction. Although we have caught many surface-feeding trout in bright sunlight, they seem to be very reluctant to face the sun during a prolonged upwind feeding spree.

Upwinged 'drakes' often hatch freely in sunny conditions. Trout will quite happily brave the brightness and come to the surface to take them, but they could be feeding on the emerging insects rather than the adults. This is because the adults' wings will dry out very quickly, sometimes giving the trout only a couple of seconds to intercept them. In contrast, emergence from the nymph in the surface film may take considerably longer. These factors vary considerably from one species to another.

Dull days will generally favour hatches of Baetid upwinged flies and midge pupae. In spite of potential problems in drying their wings, they will continue to hatch quite happily in drizzle. Irish Lough fishermen often look forward to rain to 'bring the olives up'. 'What species are they?', we asked Jim the gillie (the term used in Scotland and Ireland for a guide). 'Oh, to be sure, just olives', was the inevitable reply. That, and the fact that a wet Greenwell's Glory was a good general pattern, was all that anyone needed to know.

Artificial Cockabully.

In rivers, large streamers imitate a variety of sub-surface species including sculpins, crayfish and leeches. You might not expect their performance to vary much with the degree of sunlight, since the food should always be available. We have found this to be largely true when fishing Cockabullies in New Zealand, but we have experienced consistently better sport in North America when the sky has been overcast. We are not sure whether it is the flash of nylon or the propensity of the natural prey to remain inactive when it is bright, but it has happened too often to be coincidence.

Although the quality of fishing will vary with the degree of brightness, the fact that it has recently and suddenly changed may not be important. This is rarely the case with wind or temperature. A sudden increase in wind strength or direction – or perhaps more fundamentally in barometric pressure – can ruin the fishing for a couple of days. All species are affected by sudden changes, but browns seem to be more tolerant than rainbows. After a sharp frost, trout may hug the bottom of the stream or lake. We have often been frustrated by seeing fish feeding avidly during thunderstorms, while we lay low with our rods horizontal on the ground. (A fisherman with a vertical carbon fibre rod makes a splendid lightning conductor!) Yet a sudden downpour may also kill a previously established rise stone dead. As one old cynic frequently remarks: 'Trout hate getting wet!'

Trout with L-Plates

We much prefer to stalk wild, educated trout, and therefore take the opportunity to fish in the less populated regions of the world such as Montana and New Zealand. Nevertheless, angling pressure has made stocking a fact of life in many areas. Additional stock are necessary to replace trout removed, or – in extreme cases – to supplement those that have been caught and returned so many times that they have become frightened to feed.

Throughout this book we will advocate the importance of stealth and camouflage, because the greatest fulfilment in fly fishing is to succeed with educated specimens. But for completeness, we will mention 'stockies' that have not yet learned the wisdom of caution in their new, spacious environment. In fact, advertising your presence can sometimes be an advantage. They recognize humans as a source of food. Thus, although they may move away on sensing an intruder, it will not be very far. He may be carrying a bucket of pellets.

They are also eager to investigate anything that catches their eyes, and have a love for red and orange. They also have a tendency to nip at a fly rather than turn on it like their more experienced brethren. Anglers who strike at these nips, rather than waiting for the line to tighten, are more likely than not to miss or lose the fish.

Denzil used to do a lot of his fishing from a motor boat in the local reservoir. Near one of the bays there were a few cages for acclimatising the stockfish to the water prior to release. Every day a ranger would take food out to the fish in a high speed launch, and they would be up in the water and waiting as soon as they heard the noise.

Most experienced fishermen travel in a wide arc away from their intended drift when motoring up the wind. But if there had been a recent stocking, Denzil would motor right up the middle. This would ensure the fish knew that an assortment of tasty goodies was about to hit the water. At least one of his flies would be a drab brown nymph 'to imitate caddis larvae'. Another would incorporate some orange wool or fur 'to simulate the transitory glow of a hatching midge pupa'. Finally, he would appear at his most graceful when striking into a fish with a slow, measured lifting of the rod.

THE TROUT'S REACTION TO TIPPETS

So far we have focused on understanding the behaviour of the trout itself. However, fly fishing exists because trout are quite readily deceived into taking an artificial fly. The knowledge for achieving this deception counts for nothing if a fly is presented clumsily. So the second part of the chapter focuses on fairly straightforward, but sometimes misunderstood, aspects that an angler has to get right to be able to fish with confidence. It should help to make leader selection and design less random, and point to the features that really matter about lines, rods and casting. A proper understanding of these aspects really does increase confidence by removing common but unnecessary doubts about tackle choice.

You can buy expensive lines, exorbitantly priced reels and rods that require a mortgage, but it is the humble leader than matters most – because that is the most likely item to give the game away. A trout cannot know about the manufacturer of your rod, but the wrong brand of leader material may render an otherwise perfect imitation totally useless. To be consistently successful, you need to pay great attention to choosing the right material for the job in hand.

The Case for Fine Leaders

Trout are rather unpredictable in their reactions to nylon. Sometimes they are not put off in the slightest by something resembling a ship's hawser. It is easy to blame the diameter of the leader when things are not going well, but often a change to the most superfine gossamer will make no difference.

At other times, we have often noticed that the thickness of nylon is crucial. A good example occurs when winter fishing for grayling on rivers such as the Test and Wylye. At first, the grayling are very easy to catch, almost irrespective of the fly or nylon. As the season progresses and the fish become more educated, the choice of leader material makes a considerable difference. Grayling generally congregate in shoals, so there is a good chance of a fish seeing the fly on just about every cast. Switching from a 4X to 7X tippet with the same fly has often converted prolonged failure into instant success.

The choice of a fine tippet, which must be properly balanced against the risk of breakage, has three major advantages. First, it is less conspicuous. Second, it experiences reduced drag, and is therefore less likely to interfere with a fly's motion – whether a dry fly or nymph. Third, a fish is less likely to feel the leader as its mouth closes on the fly. The smaller the fly, the more likely it is that these effects of the leader material will be noticed.

Floating Leaders

A floating leader is highly visible against the sky because it distorts the surface film – and if greased, it will stand out like a sore thumb! It is therefore arguably better to use 3X nylon that is submerged than 5X nylon that floats. Several anglers deliberately use thicker material in flat calms because it requires less treatment and inducement to cut through the surface film. On those rare outings when almost every cast with a dry fly will raise a fish, we have experimented by alternately treating the leader to float and sink. The effect is sometimes dramatic. (Though we have to admit that there have been many occasions when it has failed to make a scrap of difference.)

A day for fine leaders?

Visibility of the Leader

We strongly recommend submerging any new leader material in water to check its visibility. Since a nymph-feeding trout often sees its food against a background of weed or gravel, the experiment is best carried out against the bed of a river or lake – although an appropriately coloured basin is adequate. You will immediately see that many claims and opinions do not stand up to the test. Strongly tinted materials really advertise their presence, but even more subtle shades of green, grey or brown can be quite conspicuous. Some clear monofilaments take on a whitish hue in the water, which makes them surprisingly visible. Other candidates, which may be acceptable in the shade, shine like a beacon in bright sunlight. Finally, some brands vary noticeably from batch to batch.

Conventional nylon tends to be quite forgiving of clumsy use. It is therefore ideal for the thicker sections towards the butt of a leader that might remain in place for several outings. But for a little extra money and attention to detail, you can really steal an edge on difficult fish by using hi-tech material for the tippet. Several brands have an impressively low visibilty which is enhanced by a fine diameter.

Fine-Diameter Leader Materials

Innovations in leader material seem to be never-ending. While some are good, many more end in disappointment. Yet some anglers change repeatedly to each new product in an attempt to stay that little bit ahead of the game.

Even Humphrey could not resist trying most new products and sharing his initial enthusiasm with fellow anglers. But he was equally quick to throw away 90 per cent of the spools after discovering that all was not well with these wondrous new materials. Unfortunately, others lacked his clinical powers of evaluation. Like sheep, they persisted simply because if it had been good enough for Humphrey, it was good enough for them. In consequence, over the local reservoirs, gullible anglers were not getting much action on the matt black monofilament that was guaranteed to be invisible to fish. Others were trying to improve their knot-tying skills as just about every decent take ended in a 'ping'. Elsewhere the air turned blue as befuddled anglers repeatedly tried to untangle 'birds' nests' of nylon, only to give up after ten minutes to start again with a new leader.

Modern technology is producing many refinements. These include reduced visibility, higher density to assist the leader to sink and increased abrasion resistance. Most importantly, some co-polymers offer up to twice the strength for the same diameter. This sounds a convincing argument for discarding ordinary nylon, but it is important to spell out just what it means. Any nylon with a nominal static strength of 4 lb, for example, will eventually break when the weight it is supporting is very, very slowly increased to this value and above.

Size	Diameter (inches)	Diameter (mm)	Range of Nominal Static Strengths (lb)
8X	.003	.08	N/A – 1.8
7X	.004	.10	N/A – 2.5
6X	.005	.13	2.0 – 3.5
5X	.006	.15	2.5 – 4.8
4X	.007	.18	3.0 – 6.0
3X	.008	.20	4.0 – 8.5
2X	.009	.23	5.0 – 11.5
1X	.010	.25	7.0 – 13.5
0X	.011	.28	8.0 – 15.5

When specifying leader material for presentation, it is more relevant to define the thickness (e.g. 3X) rather than the breaking strain. The quoted (static) strengths can vary enormously, with the top-of-the-range brands being about twice as strong as ordinary monofilament. Normal mono-filaments tend to be not available (N/A) in the very fine diameters. It is worth mentioning that the nominal and actual thicknesses, and presumably the breaking strains, are not as close as they ought to be in some brands.

What the test strength does not tell you is how well the leader material will perform under dynamic loads. These result from the sudden pull as the hook first sets into a turning fish. This is not so important in rivers, since it is the angler that usually controls the strike. In contrast, takes often register by feel when sub-surface fishing in still water, and most breaks will occur on this first, sometimes savage, contact. It is then that the dynamic, rather than static, strength of the line matters, and this is exactly where some materials are at a disadvantage. Pre-stretched nylon, as its name implies, has had much of its 'give' for cushioning against shocks removed during the manufacturing process. Six-pound pre-stretched nylon is almost as thin as three-pound ordinary nylon, but in practical fishing terms it may actually turn out to be weaker. It will also fatigue more quickly after catching a few fish, and is therefore more likely to break unpredictably.

There are other drawbacks. Pre-stretched materials tend to deteriorate more quickly with use – particularly at the knots – so that it is most unwise to use the same leader on successive outings. Indeed, it is a sensible precaution to change a leader deliberately during a successful session. Stories abound of inexplicable 'smash takes' on pre-stretched leaders, such as: 'I didn't strike any harder than I had on the previous six fish'!

The outcome of all these considerations is the importance of thinking about what you are doing. Hi-tech leader materials are essential for fine tippets, but demand extra care. For example, we have found that Rio Powerflex is resilient to repeated takes when using a water knot only if it incorporates (at least) four turns. Before settling on a brand, it is worth carrying out your own tests on visibility, strength and resilience to understand how to put it to optimum use.

Fluorocarbons for Sub-surface Patterns

At first we suspected that fluorocarbons were just another innovation that would not stand the test of time. We could appreciate that there was plenty of 'give' for resisting breakages, and a lack of memory that enabled kinks to disappear after removing a tangle or wind knot. But these hardly justified the high cost. The other claims appeared to be more dubious. It was not until several good nymph fishermen claimed that their catch rates had increased substantially, that we took the new material seriously. A few simple experiments convinced us, for two good reasons, that fluorocarbons should be the first choice of leader material for sub-surface fishing, especially at depth. From that moment onwards, we have never looked back.

The most compelling reason is the low visibility. Fluorocarbons have a refractive index closer than nylon to that of water. This reduces the number of internal reflections, making the leader less conspicuous. Unless the two refractive indices are identical, the surface finish is also important in determining the amount of shine. In our tests, the visibilities varied considerably from brand to brand. Orvis Mirage and Rio Fluoroflex virtually disappeared from view, whereas a few were actually more visible than the better nylon monofilaments. Others were hard to see in dull conditions, but stood out in bright sunlight.

The second advantage to the wet fly fisherman stems from the fact that fluorocarbons are considerably denser than water. Once submerged, they will sink typically four to five times faster than conventional nylon, thereby helping to get a fly down to the feeding depth. This may be insignificant for heavy patterns, but it is crucial for slim, unweighted nymphs.

It is important to recognize that fluorocarbons may cause lightweight nymphs, intended for fish feeding close to the surface, to sink too quickly. Moreover, tests in a transparent glass bowl, to simulate open water, show that fluorocarbons are not significantly less visible than some brands of nylon. The latter may therefore be more appropriate when fishing nymphs just below the surface.

Fluorocarbons for Dry Flies and Emergers

The case for fluorocarbons for dry flies is less obvious. The visibility of a floating leader is easy to investigate by looking into a glass bowl from below. When silhouetted on top of the surface film against the sky, slight tints of colour and the refractive index become less significant. The most important consideration is now the diameter. Fluorocarbons have only a reasonable, rather than exceptional, diameter for their strength, and consequently may be more visible from below than some state-of-the-art nylons. Nevertheless, since they are more resistant to fatigue, a fluorocarbon tippet is arguably more reliable for a day's fishing than its nylon equivalent of the same diameter, even though the latter may have a higher (static) breaking strain.

Of course, the visibility reduces if the leader breaks through the surface film. However, claims that the higher density helps a fluorocarbon in this respect are questionable. Density is much less important than the effects of surface tension – as illustrated by the old party trick of keeping a greased steel needle afloat in a tumbler. Some brands of fluorocarbon are notable for their downright obstinacy to sink in calm conditions.

Once a fluorocarbon leader has cut through the surface film, its greater sink rate will drag the dry fly under the water more quickly than nylon. This is seldom a problem for river fishing or for covering rising trout, but is detrimental when leaving dry flies on still water for prolonged periods.

Overall, many dry-fly experts claim increased catch rates when using fluorocarbon leaders, and we certainly favour them whenever conditions permit their use. But the huge variations in characteristics between different brands of both fluorocarbon and nylon, as well as in an individual's fishing style and surroundings, demand an enquiring mind.

The right balance?

LEADER DESIGN

Fly line manufacturers go to a great deal of trouble to design their products with gradual tapers for good, and quite complex, scientific reasons. It suffices to say that anyone who has ever tried to cast an untapered fly line will need no further convincing. The tapering is essential for getting the line to turn over rather than landing in an uncontrolled heap.

The advantages of a progressive taper are just as valid for the leader, which, after attachment, becomes an integral part of the system that is presenting the fly. So there is no point in possessing the best fly line that money can buy if, for example, it is attached directly to a single thickness of monofilament. Such a leader will only turn over properly with assistance from a favourable wind or a suitably weighted fly.

At the other extreme, some anglers strive for perfection using the most complex formulae, but even these designs may be inappropriate. Other factors, such as wind, flies or individual casting technique, are also important contributors to success or failure.

The Need for Fly Line to Leader Transition

Energy does not get transmitted efficiently across a sudden change in diameter, and it does not matter whether this is gas flow in a pipe or the straightening of a fly line, so the transition from the tip of the fly line to the butt of the leader should be smooth and gradual. Attachment of even 0X nylon, for example, directly to the tip of a fly line typically gives a sudden six-fold step down in diameter, which will hinder the smooth transfer of energy. It is the design of this transition point that is often the most crucial ingredient for achieving good turnover.

There is also a good deal of debate about whether to use a braided or monofilament section. Braided leaders are more popular in England, where there is a greater emphasis on still-water fly fishing, than in the stream-rich areas of North America and New Zealand.

Braided Leaders for Fly Line to Leader Transition

Braided leaders are used much more widely in the British still waters than elsewhere in the world. They have absolutely no memory, irrespective of thickness, which helps to create a tight loop and avoid any of the coiling associated with thick nylon. They will also outlive most fly lines, and it is possible to engineer a very tiny loop for connecting the rest of the leader. They are excellent for presenting a team of flies without tangling in front of a drifting boat. We have always used the Orvis braids, since they are longlived, with a construction that gives minimal problems with wind resistance or twisting.

Most commercially available braids are far too long – sometimes up to 10 ft. This increases the length of a typical leader to the point where control of the flies becomes extremely difficult. Such a set-up is often hopeless where accuracy is required at close range, and increases the risk of snagging on bankside vegetation. Although a very long leader does help when stalking shy fish, braided nylon is more visible than

ordinary monofilament and therefore defeats the object. When fishing a deep nymph, a floating braid will hinder the descent of the fly. Thus, the floating braided section should be no longer than is necessary for optimum turnover – and this corresponds typically to about 4 ft.

You should choose the shortest braided leader that will fit the line size, irrespective of any attached tippets, which are irrelevant. Rather than trying to explain this when placing an order, you may as well opt for an easy life by asking for 4X (or whatever comes to mind). The tackle dealer does not need to know that you are going to throw away the tippet and mutilate his product by cutting 4 ft out of the most tapered section. This will also remove the two loops at either end, which are always unnecessarily large.

The thick end of the braid will fit neatly over the tip of a fly line, and can be secured with either special connectors or, more neatly, whipping thread and Superglue. The thin end requires a very small, neat loop for attaching the rest of the leader. There is no reason why it should be much larger than the eye of a hook, unless you want to keep the option open of looping in a sinking braided section. The loop is formed by threading the thin end through the eye of a needle. The needle is then inserted back through about half an inch of the braid before trimming and securing with Superglue. (This requires a surplus length of about 6 in, so the original section should be cut with the necessary allowance.)

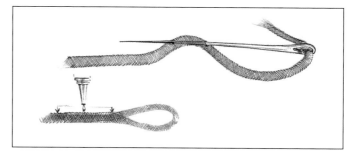

Braided leader construction.

Sinking Braided Leaders

The advantages of a braided leader for presentation are less clear cut for sinking lines. A fast sinking line has to be as thin as possible right along its length, so there is less scope for designing an optimum taper. Fortunately, by the time the fly reaches the trout's feeding depth, neither the line nor leader will have much memory of alighting on the water. Thus, the principal role of a sinking braided leader is simply to get the flies down. The same argument can sometimes apply when fishing floating lines. For example, after casting a team of wet flies across a river so that they swing round in a downstream arc, all memory of the initial presentation may have been lost by the time the flies reach the fish.

This reminds us of our friend, Denzil, who has always been a first-class floating line fisherman on still waters. He used to pay far more attention to presentation than most of his peers, taking a great deal of care from the action of his rod down to the precise dimensions and taper of his tippet. He was one of the first fishermen to adopt a braided leader, and his labours soon bore fruit when covering rises from the better educated fish. Unfortunately, at the same time, his results on the sinking line deteriorated quite markedly. Others assumed that this was due to his unquestioned lack of enthusiasm for the sinking line. It took Denzil some time to realize that the (floating) braided leader was affecting the way in which his flies fished below the surface. It slowed down their descent and caused them to fish higher in the water.

If you really do want to go to the trouble of attaching a sinking braid purely for presentation, then it must match the sink rate of the fly line. However, there are much better applications. A fast sinking braid on a floating line will force the flies to reach the fish's depth quickly, and then to remain at a fixed distance below the surface. This is just like a ready-made sink-tip, but with the advantage of a lighter construction that gives increased sensitivity for detecting takes. It can be a very useful item in fast flowing rivers, since it will get the flies down to the fish before the current can sweep them past at too shallow a depth. The same leader on a slow-sinking line will allow depths to be explored in still water, starting from a few feet below the surface.

Monofilament for Fly Line to Leader Transition

There are three good reasons for constructing leaders purely out of monofilament for river fishing. First, braided leaders have a rough finish and large surface area. This means that they do not cut through the wind so well as their smooth, nylon counterparts. This disadvantage is equally true for lake fishing from the bank where you do not have the same luxury of positioning as you do from a boat or float tube. (In spite of this resistance, some anglers still find that they can cast better into a head wind with a braided leader. Other factors, including individual styles, often make an important contribution.) Second, they have a tendency to become waterlogged. This will drag a fly under the surface in strong currents, although it is possible to reduce the problem by treating the braid with mucilin while it is still dry at the start of the day. In some instances, the trapped water may be sprayed during the cast and thereby create a surface disturbance. Third, river fishermen often need shorter leaders to avoid surrounding obstacles or to control the fly in a small pool. This increases the risk of spooking the fish, so as much of the leader as possible needs to be transparent.

Monofilaments do tend to coil, so you have to take the trouble to stretch them from time to time. Under no circumstances should you try to avoid the memory problem by using limp nylon, because it is the stiffness that helps to turn over the leader. This is especially important when using long leaders or bushy flies, for which a butt section of Mason nylon is ideal. A 3 ft butt section, with a diameter of about 0.5 mm, is a good choice for a short, 9 ft leader. At the other extreme, a 20 ft leader may need about 6 ft of 0.6 mm nylon to help it to turn over. Intermediate lengths should scale accoordingly.

The conventional method of attaching a butt section to a fly line is to use a Nail or Needle Knot. We prefer a system that allows us to change butt sections more easily without any progressive shortening or damage to the fly line. This involves removing about 15 mm of plastic coating from the tip of the line to reveal the braided core. Nail varnish remover is excellent for this purpose, but it does need care to prevent it spreading further up the line. The exposed braid then needs folding back and whipping together with ultra-fine fly tying thread, so that it is flush with the plastic fly line, before finishing with Superglue. (The thread should match the colour of the line, because trout will occasionally nip at this joint if there is a lot of contrast!) The aim is to create a tiny loop that is just large enough to attach the butt section.

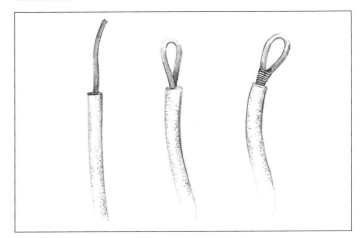

Loop at end of fly line.

We are increasingly using Airflo Polyleaders, which are available at a low cost in tapered 5 ft sections, as a modern alternative to conventional butts. Such 'poly-tips' have many of the advantages of a thick monofilament without any problems from coiling. The thick end can be knotted directly into a small loop at the end of the fly line. At the thin end, we pass about an inch of braid (with a tiny loop at the business end for connecting the leader) over the 'poly-tip' and simply add Superglue.

Choice of Tippet

If you try the academic exercise of casting with no fly at all, you will have great trouble getting the end of even the most perfectly tapered leader to unfurl. The nylon just cannot get enough momentum to turn over completely, and the last couple of feet will usually end up in a snaky mess. There needs to be a little bit of weight on the end to straighten it out, depending on the thickness of the nylon. A slim size 12 nymph will comfortably turn over a 3X tippet, whereas a size 20 fly has no chance at all. This is very convenient, for such a small fly would be conspicuous and move unnaturally on such a thick tippet – not to mention the difficulties of threading the nylon through the eye.

Whereas it is quite feasible to use 3 ft of 3X monofilament, similar lengths of much finer material will usually steadfastly refuse to turn over. Moreover, fine nylon is very limp and more likely to result in wind knots, which are likely to prove fatal. Sometimes, incomplete turnover due to an extra-long tippet may be desirable – for example, when trying to eliminate drag during a long dead-drift. However, when covering a specific fish, an accurate cast with a straight leader that does not turn back on itself is a real advantage. So it may be necessary to use only 18 in for a 6X tippet. This length should be sufficient to keep the more visible, thick nylon away from the trout's area of inspection, and to provide adequate stretch between the fly and the first knot. The choice of fly and, of course, the wind both have key roles to play, so some trial and error may be necessary.

The Intermediate Section

Finally, there is the connection between the two ends to consider.

Attention to detail brings its reward for JD on the Owen.

We could quote many experienced fly fishermen who have claimed, with total authority, that one particular leader construction was the best (and sometimes the only) option. Unfortunately, the diversity between the quoted formulae is so great that they cannot all be uniquely correct. These differences may reflect genuine variations in individual casting or fishing style, or it could just be that there is too much complexity that would not yield any measurable benefit if put to the test.

We would make two observations. First, no one should criticize a fisherman's leader construction if it enables him to achieve a good presentation. Second, we have been privileged to meet some of the best fishermen in the world, and the overriding theme is one of keeping everything as simple as practicable. To this end, we prefer to connect the butt and tippet by a single length of tapered nylon. This saves time, at a small cost compared with the price of a day's fishing, and minimizes the number of tangle-inducing knots. The diameter of the thick end should roughly match the butt connection. At the other end, you can step down by about 2X at the tippet if necessary. If the change is greater than this, especially for a fine tippet, you should consider inserting 1 to 2 ft of an intermediate section.

Many top still-water fishermen opt for an even simpler approach. They will invariably use a proper braided or monofilament butt section, but then will attach three or four flies, each separated by several feet of level nylon. This is usually quite good enough with a favourable wind or with a properly balanced team of flies. Moreover, still-water trout tend to move around a great deal, so the uncertainty in position, coupled with the increased coverage from three or four widely spaced flies, leaves some margin for reduced precision. But when casting to a wily river trout, settled in his favourite lie, you will need every bit of help from the leader that you can possibly get.

Flies and Droppers

Even a perfect leader will fail to give adequate turnover with the wrong choice of fly. Bushy patterns have a great deal of air resistance, which slows them and the point of the leader down – irrespective of the taper. Heavily weighted flies will keep on going under their own inertia, and make the most appallingly constructed leaders behave respectably. (Taking an extreme example, who ever heard of tapered nylon for beach-casting?) So for ultimate presentation, a fisherman using a slim, and perhaps slightly weighted, nymph has a distinct advantage over his counterpart casting a buoyant and air-resistant dry fly. It follows that a dry fly fisherman should make the most of his chances by avoiding unnecessary protrusions and using a pattern that is as slim as conditions will allow.

Although a weighted pattern helps to turn over a leader, it is not easy to control on a badly balanced outfit. The end result is sometimes a fly hitting you in the face at high speed, which is both painful and dangerous. It is advisable to use a steeply tapered leader that is as stiff and short as practicable, but it is essential to allow that little bit longer for the back cast.

Droppers affect turnover by adding weight or air resistance part way down the leader, so improvements in presentation are invariably possible by positioning the flies correctly. A heavily weighted fly would normally go on the point. This provides momentum to turn over the whole leader, as well as allowing the weighted fly to reach a greater depth than it could on a dropper. It is not simply a question of weight, however. The heaviest fly may have a lot of air resistance due to hackles or wings, and in this case a lighter fly with a slim profile may be more suitable for the point. The most bushy fly should usually go on the dropper nearest the fly line, since this will slow the butt of the leader down relative to the tip.

There are occasions when you need a bushy fly on the point, so you will need to make a judgement on the relative merits of turnover versus effectiveness of the tactic. The need to cover a rising trout usually favours presentation, whereas other tactics often take precedence when fishing blindly.

There are distinct advantages to stepping down the leader diameter from one fly to another. A large bushy fly on the dropper may need some stout nylon to turn it over, whereas a small fly on the point will require a fine tippet. Since a knot is required for each fly, there is no inconvenience in using progressively lighter nylon to assist with the turnover. Moreover, the amount of stretch in the nylon increases with its length. There is far more 'give' to cushion a sudden pull from a trout on the end of 12 ft of nylon than there is on a dropper that is much closer to the fly line. This means that you can take advantage of finer nylon to the point fly without significantly weakening the strength of the overall leader.

The Effect of Wind

A favourable wind masks a multitude of casting problems, since it is then relatively easy to get a level length of nylon, connected directly to the fly line, to turn over adequately. Moreover, when using three or four flies on a leader, casting a fairly open loop produces fewer tangles. This is why many still-water boat specialists get quite a surprise when they first visit windy areas, such as the South Island of New Zealand. If they fish with a local expert, they will see him achieve perfect turnover when casting directly into a strong wind – something that they had previously believed to be impossible. Believe us – we have been in that position too, and it caused us to rethink our own techniques.

You will need every bit of help from your tackle. For surface fishing, it is better to choose a line that will just about float rather than one with a thick profile that will catch the wind. In fact, sinking lines are even better in this respect, and are acceptable for dry flies when covering a fish that is likely to accept or reject the offering within a few seconds. One of our friends occasionally uses a greased-up Hi-D! It is also possible to buy fly lines with steep tapers to combat such conditions. Presentation with such a set-up may not be perfect, but it is the best that can be achieved under the circumstances.

So much for the fly line, but that is the easy bit! The leader will still get blown back towards you. It is extremely difficult to get 20 ft of nylon to turn over – unless you are experienced and brave enough to use a weighted fly with enough momentum of its own to cut through the wind. You therefore need to take a few risks, making the leader as short and as stiff as you dare. Windy conditions provide some latitude by rippling the surface to conceal both line and angler. Flies with a slim profile and a bit of extra weight will cut through the wind more easily. A strike indicator must be as sparse as possible (which should be the case, anyway, to disguise its presence), and positioned much closer to the tip of the fly line than normal.

In spite of all these adjustments, casting technique is paramount. It is easy to demonstrate this when two people of differing ability exchange rods for a while – usually to no avail. There are three factors to keep in mind. First, even if the leader straightens perfectly a couple of feet above the water, the wind will have blown the fly back a considerable distance by the time it lands on the surface. So you should aim the cast as near to the surface as you dare. Second, a double haul will give the line extra momentum to cut through the wind. Third, you should reinforce the double haul by tugging on the line at the last moment to straighten the leader at this critical stage.

Ironically, a flat calm is also a good time to double haul, particularly when casting to moving fish. This technique, used in conjunction with a sudden stopping of the fly line, will catapult the leader forward, and provide a quick and clean turnover.

Power Gum

Many anglers dismiss power gum for taking away control of the strike. When fishing sub-surface, it is very difficult to set the hook with so much give in the line. It is hopeless for nymphing in running water when the most rapid of connections between rod and fish is essential. Power gum should therefore be the exception rather than the rule, but it is always worth having some on hand because it does have its uses. For example, you may have miscalculated the tackle requirements and arrived at a new stretch of water that requires a light leader with a more delicate rod than you possess.

One application for power gum is when trout are taking dry flies at distance, and turning on them rather than sipping or nebbing. There is longer to set the hook with a leisurely lift of the rod, so that any delay due to the stretch does not matter. Normally there should be enough stretch in the line and leader, but fish taking at long range sometimes break the leader purely against the resistance of the line on the water. This can occur without any over-reaction from the angler, making the use of an ultra-fine tippet a dangerous tactic. It does not matter how soft the rod is, because for these conditions all the stretch needs to be right at the business end.

The enforcement of a delayed strike is sometimes an advantage for trout feeding on large flies. We found by experimenting that 4 ft of power gum between the fly line and a leader was by no means too long. We would never have believed that it was possible to set the hook properly with such an outfit, but as we progressively lengthened the power gum there was no detectable deterioration in hooking power. It turned out to be perfect for the task. We were able to set the hook into 3 lb rainbows that took our flies savagely and sent the reels screaming. Moreover, we were able to do this with a 7X leader.

Finally, there has to be a word of warning. After using power gum for a protracted period, it is important to take extra caution when returning to normal setups. It is easy to become accustomed to getting away with an over-zealous strike.

KNOTS

Knots for Leader Connections

Knots are invariably the point of weakness in a leader, although the reason for failure is often misquoted or misunderstood. No good knot will actually slip at the loads encountered in trout fishing. Knots fail due to breakage as two pieces of nylon are forced across each other. Just as a piece of nylon will cut into your finger, it will cut right through itself if given the opportunity. This problem is most severe when joining two lengths of nylon rather than when attaching a hook, since steel and nylon will not cut into each other.

The best knots, therefore, are those that do not allow all the cutting force to concentrate at the same point. The Water (or Surgeon's) Knot, which is a simple and very strong means of joining two lengths of nylon, provides a perfect illustration. The spare strand that points down the line is extremely strong for attaching a dropper, providing there are at least three turns, since the load is spread evenly. Use of the upper strand will force the nylon back across the barrel of the knot. All the load will concentrate at this single pinch point, and quite an innocuous little pull from a taking trout may result in a breakage and a lot of unpleasant language.

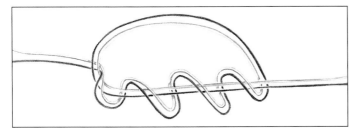

Water Knot.

The Water Knot exemplifies a fundamental problem for droppers. Any strand that has the desirable characteristic of standing out from the line is liable to be pulled back against the barrel of the knot at a single pinch point. In contrast, any strand that spreads the load is likely to have achieved this condition by lying along the leader. This produces a double strand which increases its visibility, especially if twisting occurs.

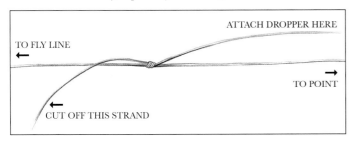

ATTACH DROPPER HERE

TO FLY LINE

TO POINT

CUT OFF THIS STRAND

Water Knot plus dropper to (i) upper and (ii) lower strands.

Incorporation of a half-hitch, which makes the dropper stand out a little, reduces this problem without weakening the knot significantly. It is still stronger than the popular Blood Knot. A Water Knot plus a half-hitch is sometimes called a Snitch Knot, because it also provides an indication of the (almost) successful fly after missing a take – providing it is a solid pull to a dropper. When a fish hits the fly without sticking, it distorts the knot slightly so that the dropper strand now lies parallel to the main leader above it, rather than at an angle. All you have to do is pull on both ends of the main leader to reset it.

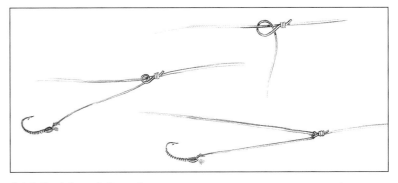

Snitch Knot before and after a take.

Knots for Attaching Hooks

One of the oldest, simplest and most reliable methods for attaching a hook is by means of a Half-Blood or Clinch Knot. Moreover, it can be unpicked by gripping the turns between thumb-nail and forefinger and pulling away from the eye. This little trick is very useful on those days when you end up changing dropper flies, since it allows more changes before the dropper becomes too short. The knot needs five turns to prevent slippage with typical leader diameters, but is unreliable on nylon finer than about 4X. This is because the slippage is greater on fine leaders, which require the strand to be tucked through a second loop. The Tucked Half-Blood (or Improved Clinch) Knot only requires three turns for any thickness of leader material.

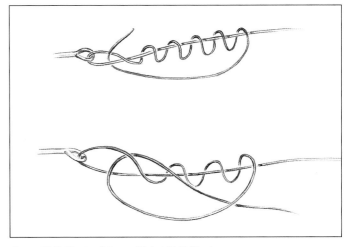

5-turn Half-Blood and 3-turn Tucked Half-Blood.

The Half-Blood Knot allows a fly to hinge over a range of angles. Often this does not matter, but there are occasions where it is important to ensure that the line projects directly forward in line with the hook shank. For example, this helps to ensure that an emerger will cock into position immediately after landing on the water. Hinging is less likely if the line passes straight through the eye before gripping the hook shank, as in the Turle Knot.

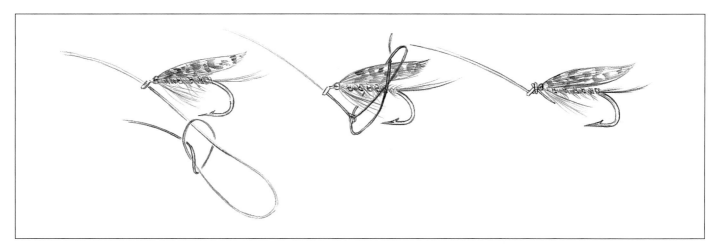

Turle Knot.

The Use of Glue on Knots

Some careful and patient anglers strengthen their knots by applying special quick-setting glues. With properly tied knots, this should not be necessary to stop slipping or breakage. At worst, though, it does no harm, and may allow you to capitalize on special situations. One advantage is to smooth the profile of the joints, in order to reduce tangling or to ease the passage of a leader through the rod rings.

THE FLY LINE

Weight Forward versus Double Taper

In order to guarantee the best possible turnover at large distances, you should aerialise the full casting length of the line and leader rather than allowing it to shoot over the water. This maintains control of the line, and ensures that it is not shooting forward when landing on the water. At least, that is the theory supporting the use of double tapers for better presentation, which seems to be enshrined in fly-fishing folklore.

In practice, though, the difference is, at most, quite marginal. The thin running line of a weight forward exerts enough drag on the belly to help the tip and leader to turnover as the line shoots forward. (Such a drag is absent on a shooting head, and accounts for the very poor presentation. A skilled caster will compensate for this by stopping the backing line with his fingers just before the end of the shoot.)

When judged against this perceived inadequacy, the advantages of a weight forward are so compelling that it is our only choice for rivers and still waters. Taking the issue of presentation first, there is no point is achieving perfect turnover if you have already spooked a fish by excessive false casting. Then, there are the opportunistic arguments. You can reach areas where obstructions limit the back-cast, or cover a 'one-chance' trout quickly before it moves away. (There is also a negative point here. It is not easy to lift a weight forward directly off the water if more than a few yards of running line are outside the tip ring. If this is a frequent requirement, then a double taper – or a longer-bellied weight forward – does have a role.) Finally, when casting large distances for prolonged periods,

it is far more relaxing to use a line that shoots.

If the required distance is no more than about ten yards (a typical length for the belly of a weight forward), then the choice makes little difference. Those who fish the smaller streams exclusively might prefer a double taper, which can be reversed on the spool when the business end wears out. It is also possible to have two different leader constructions at each end, since it only takes a couple of minutes to reverse the line. The light tackle devotee may use half a double taper, which will fit on to a smaller and lighter reel.

Line Colour

Humphrey had a special white sinker to deceive his fellow anglers into thinking that he was using a floater. He also used a dark floating line in big competitions. His prize possession, though, was a bright intermediate line from a well-known manufacturer – and therefore immediately recognisable as such – that sank like a stone due to prolonged use and his own special additives.

Wary trout will usually disappear or go off the feed when they see a fly line – and they will see it whatever the colour. At various stages of our careers, we have spooked them with white, grey, green, peach, brown and goodness knows what else – though we have never been foolhardy enough to try fluorescent orange. So for many years we tended to take the view that, within limits, colour was not too important. Then we began concentrating more on the difficult fish of the chalk-streams and spring creeks, where direct observation made evaluation of the effects of line colour much more reliable.

Our views were reinforced after fishing in New Zealand with experts who had concentrated on these wily trout for much of their lives. The majority selected dull-coloured lines, having learned from bitter experience to avoid a reflective surface or any bright colour that has 'beware – I am an unnatural phenomenon' written all over it.

A light-coloured line has a significant advantage in being more visible to the angler. This helps to estimate the position of a small dry fly or emerger, or to detect when a trout has taken a sub-surface pattern. The need depends on an angler's tactics, eyesight and ability, but in most cases the colour can still be quite natural and subdued. The light grey Air-Cel XPS, for example, is a line that we have used repeatedly and successfully on the most difficult fish.

There is a good technical case for *dull*, light lines that do not flash in bright sunlight. Trout are extremely good at sensing any sudden changes in features outside the water. Thus, the time that a fly line is most likely to cause alarm is when it is moving through the air. So it makes a lot of sense to choose a colour that blends in with the sky – like the under-sides of many (though by no means all) fish-eating birds. It is true that objects appear partly in silhouette against the sky, but differences in colour are still usually discernible.

Green or brown lines are arguably more appropriate when casting against a background of trees or rock. They also blend in with the mirror under the surface film. Lines of any colour will attract a trout's attention, due to the sudden disturbance of the surface film, when landing on the water – but the effect is minimized by choosing a natural colour that matches the surroundings.

The debate will undoubtedly continue for many years to come, but we are clear about our own approach of favouring dull natural colours, such as light grey and olive green. We admit that in many circumstances, line colour does not actually make a tremendous difference, but there is no point in deliberately advertising your presence. Completely clear lines tend not to float quite so well as the conventional alternatives, and will sometimes drag a dry fly, or even a strike indicator, under the surface during a drift. Nevertheless, they have the

MC enjoys success on the Ahuriri.

obvious advantage of blending in with the surroundings, and are a good choice when stalking individual fish that will either take or reject the fly within a few seconds.

The argument for sinking lines is less critical on how the line appears in the air, since the choice of such a tactic generally implies that the trout are unlikely to be looking towards the surface. The choice should therefore be a dark colour to blend in with the surroundings. We can only assume that some of the hideously coloured intermediate lines are purely a marketing gimmick. Some colourless lines, which virtually disappear from view, are an excellent choice if available in the appropriate sink rate.

RODS AND CASTING

When selecting the right tackle, the rod is one of the most difficult decisions of all. There are multitudes of models available for the same length and AFTMA rating. Even brand names with good reputations bring no guarantee of success, since many manufacturers produce several ranges, and each one is likely to have its own characteristic action. Top fishermen will often select completely different actions from each other under the same conditions. Some still-water fishermen perform much better with an outfit designed for rivers – and vice versa. Rod selection often is a case of one man's meat being another man's poison. It is therefore a good idea to think about your own style – including strengths and weaknesses – as well as the type of fishing for which the rod is needed.

We have made no attempt here to describe the mechanics of casting or the details of rod design. Rather, we have just highlighted a few relevant considerations that have influenced our own choice of tackle.

Reggie would sometimes use a rod that most anglers would find far too sturdy for fly fishing. It had been good enough for his father thirty years ago, so it was good enough for him today. He quite enjoyed inviting jibes from other anglers, because he was always sufficiently quick and witty with his replies to turn the tables. But today he was stuck in a boat with Wesley and there was no respite from the pompous monologue.

'I have to tell you, Reggie, that the energy cannot possibly be delivered with such an ill-designed rod that one can only describe as a weapon. I have been observing its damping characteristics, which I can only describe as . . .'

'Mmmm', interjected Reggie at length. 'You're far too restrictive in your methods.'

He took a small rainbow out of his bass bag that he had intended taking home for supper. Then out of his old school satchel, which habitually accompanied him on his fishing trips, he produced some treble hooks and proceeded to set up a snap tackle. Wesley was aghast – and for once speechless – as he watched Reggie trailing the dead-bait behind the boat.

'Mmmm – nothing wrong with it. The rules only forbid trailing behind the boat for trout. They don't say anything about pike!' True to form, in his never-ending quest to poke fun at anyone and anything, Reggie had scrutinized the rules for loopholes. And according to the strict legal interpretation, he was absolutely right – but this did not appease the puritanical Wesley.

'I have to tell you, Reggie, as a friend, that there are senior people in the angling world who will look most unfavourably on your behaviour. If they were to get to hear of this, your international career would be ruined.' Wesley would always try to put the blame on others, but in this instance he realized that there was only the one witness to what he judged to be Reggie's inexcusable lack of etiquette. 'And, moreover, they could hear of it, because I might have no choice other than to report you to the fishery management, lest they should infer that I am an accomplice to your Philistine tactics.'

Wesley thought about the next committee meeting. He would introduce the incident with a statement along the lines of: 'How can we help Reggie?' This was his usual procedure to give the impression that he was both whiter than white and a philanthropist. It would also bring the inevitable questions that would force him – as a dutiful officer of the committee – to reveal the details.

What Wesley did not realize was that the chief ranger had always been amused by Reggie's eccentric ways, and made allowances. More importantly, he appreciated the frequent gifts of that excellent red Rioja.

'Mmmm', remarked Reggie to the ranger at the end of the day. 'Pike fishing's off today!'

'No wonder,' came the reply. 'You were at the wrong end of the lake. Try that weedy bay to the left next time you come.'

A Relaxed Style

It is the speed of the rod tip, rather than the butt, that projects the line. The rod, rather than the angler's right arm, should therefore be doing much of the work. Yet one of the commonest and least discussed faults is the one of trying too hard to achieve extra distance. Arms move too quickly, backs arch, bodies rock from side to side and limp wrists abound. These factors impair the performance of the rod, create tangles in the leader, disturb the water and play havoc with accuracy. The best approach is to fish with a relaxed style and minimal movement, forgetting completely about distance and concentrating just on technique. Distance will progressively increase as the style improves.

Weighted Nymphs

Extra time must be allowed when casting a weighted nymph, otherwise the result may be a bump on the back of the head as well as poor turnover and tangles. It is worth taking the effort to look over your shoulder to ensure that you have made the correct allowance.

Fast-actioned Rods

A rod with a fast action, usually but not always concentrated close to the tip, flexes over a short distance. It will project the line with a fast speed and tight loop (i.e. less air resistance) so that it travels further. Not surprisingly, fast-actioned rods are favoured by tournament casters who concentrate on getting the split second timing just right. However, for most of us, it is better to perform ten out of ten respectable casts, rather than nine mediocre attempts and one magnificent one where the split second timing just happened to work out.

The avoidance of 'smash takes' is another reason for avoiding such rods, since there is very little cushioning to absorb the impact of a strike. River fishermen often need very fine tippets, and still-water trout will often give the leader an almighty thump.

Slow-actioned Rods

Slow-actioned rods are very forgiving of the strike. There is some sacrifice of distance, but they are more tolerant of timing inaccuracies due to the slower speed giving a greater margin for error. An angler *has* to relax his style, because such rods will not perform at all if thrust through the air at too high a speed. This is good training for over-zealous casters and adds to the enjoyment of a relaxing day out. However, quite often the wind, trees and other obstacles will not allow all the time you may need. You need to be able to dictate to the rod, rather than vice versa.

Different rod actions.

Progressive Action

Whether using a soft rod with a delicate tippet on rivers, or a stiffer one to set a hook at distance in still water, we will opt for a rod with a progressive action. As the name implies, such a rod will flex increasingly from the tip downwards as the load increases. This gives a better 'feel' as more line is aerialised during casting, and allows more control over how much pressure to apply when playing a fish. It cushions the strike as energy is progressively absorbed down the length. Finally, a progressive action allows the same rod to accommodate a considerable range of line sizes

Several good brands exist, but Omri Thomas's Carbotec range takes some beating. The first time that we used one, we were casting out full lines while seated in a boat without thinking about it. These rods add a new dimension by incorporating up to five steps in the taper. As you aerialise more line, successive steps take over. Moreover, they use hi-tech resins which make them exceptionally light.

The Double Haul.

Matching Rod to Line

For ultimate accuracy, the line should match the rod. This may sound obvious, but it is very often overlooked. Rods are rated on the assumption of 10 yds in the air, with a reduction of one in the AFTMA scale for every 2 yds under this figure (and vice versa). This means that the ideal rod for aerialising, say, six yards of an AFTMA 5 line will be a model rated AFTMA 3. An AFTMA 5 rod will still throw the line, but it will not give its optimum performance. So the dedicated brook fisherman, for example, can use a moderately weighted line while maintaining an ultra-light rod. For general river fishing, we usually use a line that is one AFTMA rating higher than that quoted for the rod.

Sinking fly lines put less strain on a rod when being aerialised, since their finer diameters result in considerably reduced air resistance. So you can use a line weight that is one size heavier than you would for a floater.

The end result – a glorious Irish brown trout.

CHAPTER 3

FLY TYING TO CATCH FISH

Providing you avoid getting carried away by too many exotic materials – and this is easier than it sounds – fly tying saves a lot of money. This is especially true in the USA where commercial flies cost about twice as much as they do in Europe, while many materials are considerably cheaper.

The other reason – and the focus of this chapter – is that an expert fly fisherman generally prefers flies that he has tied or specified himself. Knowledge, experience, tricks learned from others and an individual's own tactics call for sophistication and features that are not available in commercial patterns. However, the danger is that it is easy to get carried away at the bench with a wide choice of materials and an open-ended range of possibilities. It is therefore important to be sufficiently self-critical to ask yourself one simple question. Are you really concentrating on those aspects that will catch more fish – or are you becoming too preoccupied with creating a fly box that 'looks the part'?

In our formative years, we used to spend a great deal of time during the winter filling our fly boxes for the coming season. We would think carefully at the bench about the most appropriate tying for each pattern, and then produce ten or more identical copies. So right from opening day, we were ready to go with 'this year's models', thereby saving precious moments during the summer for more fishing time. But the performance of the patterns often varied from nothing out of the ordinary to downright disappointing. In our enthusiasm to be properly prepared, we had let the desire for a full box and the whims of the moment dictate the strategy for the whole season.

Experience has taught us to be more realistic in our expectations. Winter still presents a good time for tying large numbers of flies, but only those patterns that are already well established as proven fish takers. These flies form the backbone of our selection. We treat any novel ideas with a certain amount of caution, and tie only one or two prototypes until they have been properly tested. In practice, most of the successful ideas for innovation arise during the season, either from our own experiences or from tips given by other anglers.

There are many fishermen who dislike tying flies – from considerations such as dexterity, eyesight or just plain boredom – and prefer to buy their patterns off the shelf. This leaves less scope for experimentation, although sometimes this is a blessing since it forces them to concentrate on what they already know to best effect. But they still need to maintain sufficient knowledge to judge whether a fly is up to standard in the trout's eyes. For example, the hackles may be too stiff to give any movement or inadequate to set the fly at the right angle in the water, or the wings may not look right when viewed from below.

There are many good books, videos and articles that describe the basics of fly tying. Taking all these skills for granted, we intend to focus on just a few areas that enhance many patterns. The emphasis, though, is very much on the trout's reaction rather than winning prizes in fly dressing competitions.

THE ART OF IMPRESSIONISM

Denzil was arguably the best fly fisherman in the locality – and he wanted to keep it that way. After a while, the other anglers stopped asking to see his successful fly patterns, since those he professed to use were too crude and too ill-fashioned to be taken by any self-respecting trout. No one actually got to look directly into his favourite fly box, and so it was that he developed the reputation of being a bit of a 'wide-boy'.

It was some time later that he was drawn to share a boat with Humphrey in a social get-together on Chew Valley Lake. Denzil came armed with his single rod and floating line – for he hated using sinkers – and a solitary fly box. Humphrey could not take the risk of getting beaten in front of so many other competitors in this pairing of the Titans. He therefore brought with him that most enjoyable aid to fly fishing – the red Rioja. This rather fine wine from northern Spain works wonders for calming the nerves and debilitating the other angler.

'Have another glass, Denzil.'

'Don't mind if I do, Humphrey, old chap.'

As Denzil's conversation became progressively more slurred and repetitive, the resilient Humphrey gained sufficient Dutch courage to ask for a peek into that famous fly box. 'Of course, old chap, old chap, seeing as I've partaken of so much of your excellent wine, I think I'll let you into my secret.' At first Humphrey could not believe his luck, then his eyes.

'But this is the same old tatty rubbish you've been showing everyone for years!'

'I know, old chap, old chap, old chap – but that's the irony. No one knows what flies I use, because no one believes me when I show them the genuine article. But I'll tell you this – they don't half catch a lot of fish.'

This encounter illustrates one of the most important concepts in fly dressing. A quick glance at Denzil's 'tatty' patterns could not do justice to all the thought and experience that had gone into their creation. He was not bothered about a neatly tied head, the precise number of body segments or Grade A cock hackles. What his patterns did portray was the correct profile, colour and weight. They incorporated carefully selected materials, which combined to give each fly that essential ingredient of appearing to be alive.

The sober angler might discover a few trade secrets.

A trout has much less resolving power in its eyes than a human. It can discern colour, profile and movement much more readily than precise details, so there is a strong case for concentrating on patterns that give the correct overall impression. They are much less likely to be rejected than an amateurish attempt at exact imitation, which can all too easily appear false and lifeless. There is an analogy here with the French impressionist paintings, which impart stunning realism while ignoring much of the fine detail.

HOOKS

Sometimes a perfectly tied fly is wasted on a completely inappropriate hook. It may be too heavy, too narrow in the gape or just plain blunt. The choice of hook can be just as important as the choice of materials, so it is important to get it right. It needs no special skills – just a little extra thought.

Points

In still water, trout often announce themselves obligingly by a sharp tug on the line. Many years ago, we used to miss a fair proportion of these takes and accept it as a fact of life. Then the situation improved dramatically due to innovation by the

Japanese, who have very little native trout fishing of their own. They introduced chemically etched hooks made of high quality steel, with points that were so sharp that they would scratch a finger nail with very little applied pressure.

Chemically etched hooks will also set into a trout's mouth with a more delicate strike. So the use of lighter leaders is possible. Slowly but surely other manufacturers followed suit, and now chemically sharpened hooks fashioned out of higher quality steels are universally available. There is no excuse for tying a fly on any other form of hook. It also follows that there is no reason why you should pay good money for a commercial fly that has been tied using the old technology, even if the dressing is perfection itself.

However, the sharp points of chemically etched hooks are prone to 'curling' after striking an obstacle – including the bony region of a trout's jaw. When this happens, they become much less effective than traditionally sharpened hooks, and it is not uncommon for anglers to miss several takes in a row before they realize what has happened. It is therefore advisable to inspect a hook after any contact with a fish, especially if it was just a tug on the line which might indicate a collision with a hard object. If the point has become curled, you should either replace the fly or sharpen the hook. For this purpose, it is a good idea always to carry a small diamond sharpening tool attached to a zinger.

Hooking Angle

In order to obtain a good purchase, the pull from the leader on a hook should be along the line of the point. Attaching the leader to the eye will therefore have some tendency to pull the hook out of a fish's mouth. In theory, therefore, a reduction in the angle by lengthening the shank or reducing the gape will improve matters. Similarly, a down-eyed hook should gain a slightly better purchase than an up-eyed hook.

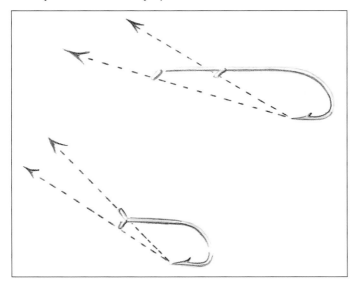

Hooking angles: Long-Shank versus Wide-Gape and D/E versus U/E.

Gape

In practice, we have never noticed any great difference in hooking power within the normal range of conventionally shaped hooks. Thus, a narrow gape or long shank should not take precedence over other more important factors, such as avoiding obscuration of the point or the need to tie a small fly on a stout hook to hold a large trout.

Tiny flies do not always need the narrowest possible gape, since it is the length of the shank that determines their size. An excellent wide-gape hook is the Kamasan B160, which in a size 16 is equivalent in length to a typical size 20. The larger gape makes the point more prominent and adds an intrinsic weight that will help some dry or emerger patterns to cock into position. It also provides more space for the addition of weight to nymphs. The hook is made of a reasonably strong wire, with a bigger eye than a size 20 that will allow the use of thicker nylon. Both of these factors are a real advantage if the fish are large or need to be bullied away from weed.

Profile

Historically, up-eyed hooks were selected for dry flies and down-eyed hooks for wet flies and nymphs. The up-eyed hook was intended to keep the leader above the water so that it would not pull the fly under the surface. The modern approach, of trying to submerge the tippet to reduce visibility, is quite the reverse. Taking into account the slight disadvantage of the hooking angle and the larger selection of down-eyed hooks, the up-eyed versions do not have a lot going for them.

The one exception is for 'micro-patterns' where obscuration of the point by a downward-pointing eye may become significant with a very narrow gape. An up-eyed hook is beneficial here – but no better than a straight-eyed version – and the use of a wider gape might be more appropriate. It is, perhaps, surprising that a full range of straight-eyed hooks, which represent a common-sense compromise with a direct line of pull, are not more widely available.

We cannot pretend to have noticed any differences in the hooking capabilities of Limerick, Sproat, Round-bend or any of the conventional designs. In all these cases, the point of the hook is parallel to the shank. Some other shapes, which may be very tempting because of their resemblance to a specific nymph, often result in a lot of missed fish. This usually occurs if the hook points away from the line of pull, or if the shank bends downwards to obscure the gape. Realistic they may be, but patterns tied on some grub hooks are strictly for optimists.

However, both the Kamasan 110 Grubber and Drennan Sedge hooks have excellent hooking characteristics. The shanks are curved sufficiently to produce killing, lifelike patterns for a whole range of insects and bugs in addition to caddis. The point of each hook aligns with the direction of pull and is not obscured by the shank, which curves away from the point rather than across it.

The Klinkhammer derives much of its effectiveness from the contoured hook.

Gauge

The gauge of the wire is an important characteristic of a hook. A deep nymph needs a strong wire, irrespective of any additional weighting, to minimize the risk of the hook opening out. But during a rise, you may have to fish the same pattern just below the surface on a lightweight hook, and live with the risk.

A dry fly fisherman usually has more control of the strike and can therefore tolerate lighter hooks and leaders. Fine wire hooks will also increase the chances of the fly staying afloat. However, there are occasions when a little bit of weight will help the fly to achieve the correct posture on the surface. This is especially true of emergers, where only the front end of the fly is meant to rest on the surface film. It is good practice, after tying a new fly, to drop it into a glass of water and watch carefully. It needs to cock into position immediately of its own accord. You may be unpleasantly surprised and have to return to the fly tying bench, but it is better to realize at this stage than to waste precious hours on the water.

Manufacturers

When describing fly patterns, authors often specify a particular model of hook. We have based our descriptions on Drennan and Kamasan hooks, which are widely available in the British Isles and New Zealand – but not in North America. Unfortunately, manufacturers vary significantly in the way they interpret gapes, lengths and sizes in general. Trying to cross-reference hooks is a minefield, but we have included the table as our best shot to help those who wish to use other suppliers, for reasons of availability or preference.

More delicate patterns and sizes demand a greater investment, either in time at the bench or outlay on more exotic materials. Tungsten falls into the first category, being nearly twice as dense as lead and relatively cheap. It suffers from being very brittle, and it is therefore not possible to wind it round a hook. One way of incorporating it is to attach short lengths painstakingly along the shank with Superglue and tying thread.

A simpler way of adding tungsten is to attach a commercially available bead – usually, but not necessarily, at the head. It is arguable that a gold or silver head represents the trapped air within the pupal case of a nymph in the process of emergence. It is much better to add a small tungsten bead to the head of a Baetis nymph, for example, rather than to destroy the slim, tapered profile by incorporating too much lead in the under-body. Wary trout are generally quite prepared to accept a fly incorporating a small (2 mm) gold or silver bead, but in extreme cases – as we encountered in New Zealand – black is a safer

This Book	Description	Purpose	Tiemco	Mustad	Partridge	Charles Jardine	Daiichi	Dai-Riki
Drennan Wet Fly Supreme	Normal shank Medium wire	General wet fly/nymph	5262	9671	SH2	CJ5	1710	730
Drennan Traditional Wet	Short shank Heavy wire	Deep and strong					1530	075
Drennan Sedge	Special shape Med/fine wire	Top-of-water pupa/grub heavier	205BL	81001	K2B	CJ14	1150	
Kamasan B110	Special shape Med/heavy wire	Deep pupa/grub heavier	2457	80200	K4A	CJ2	1130	135
Kamasan B160	Very short shank Med/fine wire	Top-of-water, wide gape for tiny flies					1510	
Kamasan B170	Normal shank Med/fine wire	Top-of-water emerger	100?	94840?	E6A?	J1A?	1170?	305
Kamasan B175	Sproat bend Heavy wire	Mid-water and strong	3769		G3A		1550	
Kamasan B400	Slightly long shank Med/Fine wire	Slightly bigger dries	5212		E1A			300
Kamasan B405	Short shank Med/fine wire	Standard dries	5210				1640	305
Kamasan B830	Long shank Medium wire	Large nymphs	5262	9671	79706	CJ7	1720	710
	Special shape	Klinkhammer	200R	80050	GRS15ST			270

ADDITIONAL WEIGHTING

A few turns of lead wire around the hook shank are adequate for weighting many patterns, providing the body does not become unnaturally bulky. It is possible to obtain lead wire with a rectangular cross-section, which restricts the space for pockets of air. The other solution is to tie patterns whose profiles can accommodate the additional volume, such as woven nymphs or shrimps. On arrival at the water, there are other obvious options such as sinking lines or split shot.

alternative. Many, less educated trout, will happily grab nymphs with colossal gold or silver heads of up to 6 mm.

It may sound like sacrilege to fabricate flies using precious metals, but the industrial platinum wire, used for applications such as thermocouples, is twice as dense as lead. Moreover it is sufficiently ductile to be wound around the hook. It is of course expensive, but the cost for an individual fly is typically only about 40 pence. If you put this into the context of the cost of rods, lines and permits, it is really quite trivial.

'Mmmm', commented Reggie. 'Have you tried depleted uranium?'

RIBBING

The visual impact of ribbing depends very much on the rest of the fly. For example, over a gaudy orange body, the choice between flat gold tinsel and silver wire is unlikely to make any significant difference. It is when a body is fairly drab that the correct choice has the potential to turn a very ordinary pattern into something quite special.

There are no hard and fast rules about the choice of ribbing, but we have taken the bold step of providing some subjective, yet simple rules of thumb based on our own judgement and experience. We make no claims about our system being better than any other, but it has worked well over many years. Having a logical framework increases confidence in the design of a fly by removing an unnecessary source of uncertainty.

Tinsel Colour

Silver is arguably a good choice near the surface, since bubbles of air are highly reflective close to the source of light. Thus it is appropriate for corixae or emerging species that trap air inside the pupal case. As the depth increases, light being reflected from a bubble will take on tinges from the surrounding features in the water. Gold may be more appropriate here, and gold-bodied flies, such as the Dunkeld, seem to give their best on sinking lines in coloured water.

Copper wire is a good material when you want to suggest segmentation without too much glare. Many fishermen prefer to rib Hare's Ear nymphs, for example, with copper rather than the more traditional gold as a safer, less flashy alternative that is unlikely to be rejected.

Very fine dark copper wire is suitable for strengthening patterns with a peacock herl body without destroying their subdued appearance. However, the right choice of coloured copper wire to match the natural insect sometimes adds a bit of enticement. For example, fine green wire round a Stick Fly suggests the vegetation sometimes present in the case around a caddis larva, while fine red wire improves a Diawl Bach when trout are feeding on bloodworm.

Pearl tinsel is affected very much by the under-body. It will subdue the flash of gold or silver, while retaining their features. Over hare's ear, it will give a subdued, flickering green or blue tinge, depending on whether it is first stretched, which provides an enticing yet natural appearance suggestive of some nymphs of upwinged flies. Over a black body, it will glow as a much stronger 'beetly' green. When added to an imitation of a small fish, it will produce an impression of iridescence in the scales.

Segmentation and Impressionism

Soft fur, especially if well teased-out, partially conceals the ribbing and therefore needs a wider tinsel than a firm silk body. A fine wire ribbing will represent the thinner regions between each abdominal segment, whereas each turn of a closely spaced broad tinsel will suggest the segments themselves. A proper imitation requires about eight turns – but sometimes this appears much too fussy. You can usually get away with this when using a fine, subdued wire, but for wider or very bright tinsels, three or four turns often give a better impression.

For difficult fish in clear water, it is worth considering a body that achieves its segmentation from contours – just like the genuine article. Fine strips of latex, wrapped in slightly overlapping turns, are well suited to caddis pupae, though purpose-made materials are becoming increasingly popular. Nylon or very fine wire, wound tightly around a soft latex back, make a pattern that is very suggestive of a shrimp or free-swimming caddis larva. It is possible to achieve some very good imitations by using off-the-shelf materials such as flexi-floss. A single strand, wound in touching turns, will suggest a wide range of nymphs with a uniform body colour. Two different coloured strands, or a single strand wound with spacing on top of a silk body, give an excellent representation of a midge pupa.

Finally, there are instances when even a good natural imitation can put the angler at a disadvantage. For example, a close inspection of some adult still-water midges reveals a greyish body with crimson rings in between the segments. However, when viewed from quite a short distance, they appear as vivid orange dry flies. Artificial patterns tied with grey and crimson flexi-floss, for example, fail to capitalize on this particular feature, so that orange flies, such as a dry Grenadier, often work considerably better. Thus, there is a need for judgement on the relative merits of long-range attraction versus short-range deception.

Trigger Points

One important role of ribbing is to provide a trigger point, especially in bright conditions. The effect is obviously much greater from a flat tinsel than from wire. A fine flat tinsel sometimes provides the best overall compromise between good imitation and flash. There is no doubt that flies tied using such materials, viz the Gold-Ribbed Hare's Ear, have stood the test of time with distinction.

BODY FURS

Hare and Rabbit

Fur from the root of a hare's ear has been a popular material for generations. One of its enticing properties is the lack of uniformity, since it exhibits light and dark regions that are interlaced with spiky protrusions. This all contributes to the overall impression of life, which the early pioneers were quick to exploit. The protrusions may suggest tracheal gills, which are quite prominent along the abdomens of the nymphs of some upwinged flies. They also give a strong impression of emergence when included in a thorax. The natural greyish-brown is a good all-round colour, but sometimes a dyed olive-green is more appropriate. Fur from the flank of a rabbit gives similar variation and spikiness, though individual specimens vary considerably and it is better to select a skin with plenty of dark regions.

Translucent Furs

Genuine seal's fur is now unavailable in some countries. Its advantages over many other materials include life-suggesting translucency and long fibres which can be teased out to aid floatation. It is always worth holding any sample up to the light to inspect the individual fibres. A good batch of fur will almost shine with life, whereas others will appear totally dead. Ironically, even the genuine article often fails the translucency test, having been taken from the wrong part of the body or from an animal of the wrong age. Although there is absolutely nothing wrong with using opaque fibres in a fly, this should be by design rather than accident.

Having selected a good sample, it is important to exploit it properly. There is no point in dubbing large amounts tightly on to the tying thread and then wrapping it in close turns around the body. You might just as well have employed some very ordinary wool, because the compressed mass will not exhibit any translucency. Small amounts of fur, wrapped loosely around the thread, will allow individual fibres to stand out to catch the light. One pertinent piece of advice is to estimate the absolute minimum amount for the job, and then to halve it – twice!

Traditionally, fly tiers have resorted to a dubbing needle to pick out the fur. A simpler and much quicker way is to use a piece of Velcro. If proof were ever needed about the value of the technique, many flies become noticeably more successful after a trout's teeth have mutilated them. It is easier to fish a fly with confidence that has become straggly after taking a fish or two, than a deliberately teased-out pattern straight from the box.

Although seal's fur and its substitutes have the advantage of translucency over hare and rabbit, they do not exhibit any contrast from one fibre to another. This can be overcome by mixing furs of different colours, but if you are after visual impact rather than simply matching an exact shade, you will need to be careful. Two soft colours blend together as if created by a single dye. To obtain contrast – and life – you need to mix colours that will stand out from each other as the natural light catches them. Dark claret and a rich amber will sparkle with contrast in sunlight. A mixture of light crimson and hot orange, on the other hand, will produce a single, unexciting shade of orange.

It is worth noting that nominally identical furs can vary significantly in colour from batch to batch – even from the same supplier. Sometimes this is due to the use of dyes from different manufacturers. It may also arise due to different degrees of bleaching, inconsistent concentrations of dye or an ad-hoc mix of two different shades. Thus, flies tied to the same written specification may perform completely differently from each other. So once you find a winning pattern, keep the fly or retain a sample of the fur for future reference.

Synthetic Living Fibre

SLF incorporates the contrast, translucency and lustre of a living insect by a mix of up to six contrasting fibres, differing in their properties of colour, translucency and sparkle. It is totally reproducible in its appearance. Although teasing will improve the overall impression of life, the built-in sparkle makes this mix less sensitive to the requirement than ordinary furs. It is

therefore capable of producing a compact fly body without losing too much of the natural appearance, providing you take care not to crush it (with a dubbing loop style, for example), or the fibres may lose much of their sheen.

Many furs are inappropriate for hooks much smaller than about a size 14, since the fibres start to appear out of proportion to the size of the fly. SLF Finesse and Midge cover hook sizes down to about size 22 and 28 respectively. There is not the same colour variation between fibres, but it is arguably better to keep the fibres in proportion than it is to strive for the ultimate in visual impact. A fly exhibiting perfect lustre, but with appendages looking like tree trunks, will not deceive any self-respecting trout.

The permutations with SLF – or any furs for that matter – are endless. We have found that 'Martin's Mix' of SLF black, fiery brown and light olive in equal proportions will produce a very good substitute for hare's ear – with added life. The addition of 25% dark green SLF to 75% translucent black fur produces the most striking iridescent green, which is a perfect imitation for many beetles and terrestrial flies.

Dubbing Technique

The commonest mistake while dubbing is to use too much fur. This invariably results in a body that is too thick and unrealistic. Some patterns derive their lifelike qualities from a body that is so slim that it exposes the underlying thread, and teased fibres that stick out from such a body give the fly an enticing appearance. The use of liquid wax, which some tiers use to help stick the fur to the thread, keeps the fibres close to the thread, thereby negating the advantages of the fur.

One problem with a conventionally teased fur body is that the fibres may become detached from the fly, since they are not securely attached to the thread during the dubbing and twisting process. It is possible to tie a more durable pattern, which will survive the rigours of a great deal of chomping, by using, for example, Danvilles's thread which is separated into two strands. This old technique, expounded by Halford, is particularly suited to some modern materials, since it reduces the risk of crushing the hollow fibres. It also produces a more translucent and spiky body than conventional methods.

Start by winding the tying thread down the hook shank to the back of the fly. Tease out a sparse mat of fur that is typically 50 mm long and 10 mm wide. Now separate the tying thread below the hook with a dubbing needle, and hold the two strands apart while you insert the dubbing between them. Then twist the thread in an anti-clockwise direction so that it just starts to trap the material. Finally wind the thread clockwise in touching turns towards the front of the fly, avoiding any overlap that would make the body too bulky.

WOVEN NYMPHS

Many woven nymphs exhibit such an 'insecty' appearance that you really do have to look twice to check whether they are living creatures rather than artificial patterns. The top of the fly partially envelops the narrower underside and gives a definite but natural segregation between the two shades, which is a feature of many natural nymphs. Those with a flattened profile are ideal for imitating stoneflies or stone-clingers. In addition, the added weight along the sides of the hook gets the nymph down in the strong currents favoured by these insects, without any unnatural bulk. During the descent, the contrast in colour provides a trigger point as the nymph twists in the water. It will also swim upside down so that the hook point is on top of the fly away from snags on the river bed.

We do not intend to describe the various complex weaving

Profile and segmentation in a sophisticated woven nymph.

processes in detail. Rather, our objective is to highlight areas where many fly tyers fail to produce a pattern that appears sufficiently realistic to the fish. Many woven nymphs look almost alive in the palm of the hand, yet fail miserably to live up to their expectations on the end of a leader.

The under-body is crucial in determining the shape and realism of the fly. A flat body usually comprises a strip of lead wire bound along the top of the shank, followed by a strip along each side and finally two intermediate strips. Silk may replace the lead wire for unweighted patterns. The crucial factor is to stagger the points of termination at the tail-end to produce a gradual taper rather than an abrupt step. Thus, the top strip alone should extend virtually to the end of the fly, the two side strips should terminate a few millimetres further up the body, and the remaining two strips should be cut somewhere in between the others. There should be a gap of about 2 mm in front of the eye to prevent the head from becoming too bulky.

Many waters do not contain flat-bodied insects, such as stoneflies or corixae. Woven nymphs will often still produce good results, providing they incorporate a slimmer body. The process is the same, but it needs very fine lead wire.

The next stage is to bind two lengths of differently coloured embroidery silk along each side of the shank, so that they extend beyond the tail-end by up to a foot. It is better to use too much than too little at first, to prevent the obvious frustration of running out of silk in the middle of a weave. Embroidery silk typically comprises about six strands. Although all six may be necessary for the larger stoneflies, a couple of strands of each colour are sufficient for many patterns that would otherwise appear too bulky.

It is essential to produce a smooth and hence naturally shaped under-body by binding the tying silk around the shank as many times as necessary. Before starting the weave, whip-finish and remove the bobbin of silk.

It takes quite a lot of practice to weave a nymph properly, and several anglers lack the patience or manual dexterity. There is a popular short cut, using a series of half-hitches, that you can master in a few minutes. Unfortunately, this process will often produce a fly that appears unnatural along the edges due to a bulky criss-crossing of the light and dark silks. However, there are a few steps you can take to minimize the size and visibility of this undesirable effect.

First, wind one of the two strands of the lighter silk round the shank to the eye to produce a conventional silk body. This means that you will use only three strands in the weaving process to minimize the unnatural protrusion at the edges.

When tying the half-hitches, always pass the light strand over the dark strands. Before tightening each knot, separate the two silks in front of the eye of the hook, and push the dark and light silks back along the shank above and below the eye respectively. Each successive weave should be tightened to butt against the previous one. On approaching the eye of the hook, reattach the tying thread and secure the weave, then add any wing cases, legs or hackles as you would for a conventional pattern.

FLUORESCENCE

Fluorescent materials absorb invisible radiation, such as ultra-violet and x-rays, and re-emit it (usually) as the same visible colour as the host material. Thus, while fluorescent red wool remains rather unexciting under dull conditions, it exhibits an added glow when exposed to the sun. This provides a trigger point to the fish or a means for the fly tier to incorporate extra life into a pattern. It also enables the colour of the fly to stand out, rather than appear as a silhouette, when there is a strong source of light behind it. Thus, fluorescent surface flies stand out better against a bright sky – as do those hideously fluorescent fly lines preferred by the more sporting anglers who choose to give the fish a better chance.

Some patterns exhibit so much fluorescence that any self-respecting trout ought to swim away in fright. However, the strong visual impact is often irresistible to uneducated fish, and will occasionally tempt even the most wily trout into an act of uncontrolled aggression. Such a fly can also cause the essential distraction when trout are preoccupied with surface insects. A striking example is our palmered V1 wet fly, which is an unashamed mix of Phosphor Yellow and Fire Orange seal's fur (or substitute). Similarly, takes to the highly fluorescent Carrot Fly – an emerging dry pattern that would make Halford turn in his grave – sometimes almost wrench the rod from your hand.

Those who wish to catch the more educated fish consistently, especially in clear water, need to be frugal in the application of any fluorescent material. A fly should incorporate just enough either to bring it to life or to catch the trout's attention, without raising any alarm signals. A modicum of fluorescence in the thorax of a dry fly or emerger, or in the tail or thorax of a nymph, provides a good trigger point. The thorax of a fly can come alive by exploiting the contrast from a mix of ordinary and fluorescent furs. Nevertheless, a simple woollen tail, as proven by the success of the Green Tag Stick Fly, works consistently well.

Two principal colours – red/orange and green – form the backbone of our fly selection, though there are a few subtleties in the exact choice of shade.

A modicum of red or orange is especially effective close to the surface. This is arguably due to the portrayal of a transitory flash of orange that appears in some species as the wings break free from the pupal case. It is therefore more imitative to incorporate the fluorescence into the thorax rather than the tail, and this is a very safe approach for dry flies and emergers. Fire Orange is a good general purpose compromise between red and orange. Since it exhibits a very bright glow, you should restrict the quantity or mix it with a duller material.

When fishing in deep water, a shift from red to orange will increase a pattern's visibility, but the disappearance of colours beneath the surface is slightly more complicated for fluorescent materials. Although a basic red will not survive below about 15 ft, the fluorescent component will remain if the ultra-violet light penetrates that far. Thus, the colour of a red fly will be greatly reduced, but not completely destroyed. The penetration of ultra-violet rays through water is fairly similar to blue light – that is, very high in clear water, but poor in the presence of algae. This leads to the conclusion that deeply fished fluorescent flies are likely to have more impact in clear rather than coloured water.

Phosphor Yellow is an example of fluorescence at a different colour to the host material. It glows as a seductive bright green when incorporated into a fly, in spite of its name and appearance in the packet. It is a colour that works very well on deep sub-surface patterns, since green light is excellent at penetrating fresh water. In fact, at any depth and water clarity, a green fly will advertise its presence to trout over a greater distance than most other colours. Phosphor Yellow is excellent in low-visibility conditions, though many anglers seem to favour Signal Green in clear water.

We usually avoid Phosphor Yellow and Signal Green close to the surface due to the lack of vivid greens in hatching insects. Nevertheless, there is no logical reason for avoiding either shade if it matches the natural colours. For example, it is an excellent choice when trout are chasing small fish or feeding on some species of grasshopper.

EMERGERS

From the fly tier's perspective, an emerger exists in three separate forms. The first is the ascending nymph just before it reaches the surface. This is the most straightforward, since there is no need to worry about keeping it suspended in the surface film. A standard nymph will do quite nicely, although some adjustment to the thorax helps to suggest the process of emergence. A simple method is to use some fur of an appropriate colour – often slightly brighter than the nymph – and to tease it out to suggest the expanding wing cases or the emerging body. This was the rationale behind our development of Gerald's Midge. Jungle Cock cheeks, as in our Caretaker, give an enticing impression of emergence with an added trigger point. Short wings are appropriate to those species that have the ability to escape from their nymphal skins several inches below the surface.

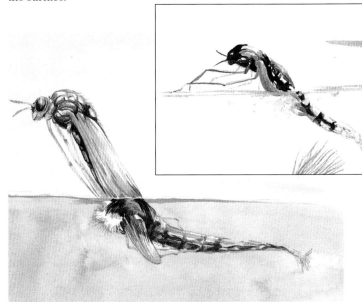

Different stages of emergence.

When feeding on emergers, trout will normally be looking towards the surface, so in still water it is important to tie the fly on a lightweight hook. A heavier hook or added weight is usually necessary in a river to sink the fly slightly before the current takes it out of range. There should, however, be no concentration of weight near the eye that would produce an unnatural diving posture. Any gold or silver beads should therefore ideally be plastic rather than metal.

During the second stage a pupa may hang vertically, anchored by its front end to the surface film. Most of the fly is therefore clearly visible to a trout, even outside its window. Such emergers are often represented by Suspenders, which incorporate a ball of Ethafoam or Plastazote for buoyancy. They hang with the right aspect, but the foam can have an ungainly appearance and feel, so trout often reject them very quickly before there is time to strike.

The modern answer is Cul de Canard (CDC), which quite literally is French for the backend of a duck. The feathers have a very soft texture, so a trout is less likely to spit them out quickly. Since they come from the area surrounding the preen glands, they have a first class water repellence. Thus no additional treatment is necessary, which prevents floatant accidentally coming into contact with a body that is intended to sink. More importantly, the feathers comprise a multitude of fine fibres that grip the surface film with a large area of contact. They dry out very quickly when false casting, and will keep a fly afloat for ages.

If tied as a 'shuttlecock' sticking out in front of the hook, CDC will ensure that the fly cocks into a vertical position every time. The protrusion of these vertical fibres above the surface probably gives the impression of an emerging adult. It is rather unnatural to see an insect emerging from a vertical shuck, which may explain why educated trout will often ignore the fly if the fibres are too prominent. Nevertheless, trout lacking such critical minds often grab these patterns savagely, presumably to intercept the emerging insect quickly before it has a chance to escape.

One trick is to tie a 'size 16' midge pupa, for example, at the base of a lightweight size 10 hook. A CDC shuttlecock at the eye of the hook will suspend the fly several millimetres below the surface, but will not be so evident to a trout due to the separation.

Dyed CDC is available in addition to the natural grey/brown colour, although such a process is bound to remove the natural oils. These can be replaced, or enhanced, by the addition of floatants. Although solutions, such as Gink, are suitable for

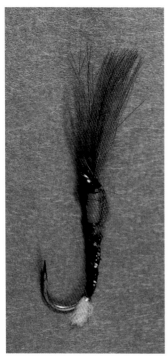

Vertical and horizontal CDC emergers.

many materials, they can cause the very fine fibres of CDC to clog. Some of the less viscous alternatives are no longer available due to fears that they could have been carcinogenic. It is possible to buy the natural oils, but the best compromise is to keep the floatant warm in order to make it less viscous, and to apply it sparingly.

The final stage of emergence sees the pupa moving into a horizontal posture as the case splits open and the adult breaks free. CDC feathers also have a role to play here when tied along the back of the fly as a conventional wing. They then hold the body at a slight angle beneath the surface of the water, representing the pupa as it moves towards its final position. It is possible to tie emergers so that they sit perfectly horizontally just below the surface film, but we will postpone the description of these patterns until we have discussed the representation of duns.

DRY FLIES

Problems with Convention

Traditional representations of duns (and spinners) incorporate several turns of a full cock hackle. The hackles are stiff in some of the more expensive capes, so that the fly stands well clear of the water on 'legs' that are unlikely to collapse or become waterlogged. Such patterns are the very image of fly fishing. They are pleasing to the human eye and, if placed strategically in a display box, will impress non-fly fishing acquaintances.

Unfortunately, trout inspect a dry fly differently. The full hackle appears very fussy, and the lower fibres hold the fly at an unnatural angle, with the front of the body raised in the air while the rear touches the surface. This is contrary to the posture of many natural insects, such as an adult midge or a distinctively arched mayfly, where the tail-end of the abdomen curves upwards away from the water. Some fishermen prefer softer hackles, which lower the front of the body slightly – but for calm conditions, where imitation rules over floatability, there is still too much superfluous feather.

Role of Traditional Dry Flies

While conventional hackles on dry flies are not very imitative, it is important to stress that there are many occasions when they will outperform more sophisticated, modern creations. As a rule of thumb, traditional flies, such as a Royal Wulff, are more appropriate to rough water for three reasons. First, they are less likely to become submerged by the waves, currents and riffles. Second, they are more visible to the angler. Third, unless the trout are cruising high in the water when their window of vision will be small, they are more visible from below against the sky. One way of improving the posture of a fully hackled pattern, for the more discerning trout, is to cut away all the fibres that point downwards, so that the body sits horizontally on the surface. A cut-down Bob's Bit, for example, is an excellent rough-water pattern for the English reservoirs.

Another use for fully hackled flies is when trout are accustomed to feeding on terrestrial insects, which they will have observed alighting on the surface rather than breaking through it. They therefore expect to see their food sitting proud of the surface, and a good way to achieve this posture is to use a pattern with a short, stiff palmer along its full length. Such a fly will rest high above the water where it is clearly visible as a silhouette, and sit at a more natural angle than one with just a hackle at the front.

Parachute Patterns

An elegant way of improving the realism of a dry fly is to tie it with a parachute hackle. It will land on the water with most, if not all, of the hackle points in contact with the surface film, so the fly remains buoyant independently of the body materials. The stiff parachute hackles copy the legs realistically with a footprint that provides a trigger point. There are no unnatural bunches of fibres protruding above the fly or beneath the surface, and the body can be as slim as necessary to imitate the natural without any unnecessary bulk to aid floatation.

So far, so good – but there is just one small problem. The parachute hackle, which the trout will see as legs, rests on the surface film and supports the body from above. The body, therefore, sits on or just below the surface film. In contrast, a natural insect is supported from below by its legs so that the body sits proud of the surface. The parachute-hackled dun is upside down!

Parachute hackle fly.

Improved Representations of Duns

Neil Patterson swept a conventional hackle forward over the eye of the hook to produce a funnel shape. This supports the body from below, in common with the natural insect, on legs that project in front of the fly. The horizontal fibres rest on the surface at a tangent, thereby giving a more natural footprint than conventionally hackled dry patterns. A splayed-out tail supports the other end of the fly. In this respect, it differs from the natural insect where the tail stands proud of the water. By carefully angling the tail so that it points slightly downwards, and by cutting a small V-shape out of the underside of the hackle, the fly will alight upside down. The hook is now inconspicuous to the trout on top of the fly.

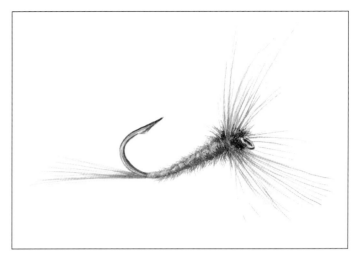

Funnel Dun.

Brian Clarke and John Goddard ingeniously overcame the limitation of parachute hackles with their USD (an abbreviation for *upside-down*) paraduns. They took a parachute fly and tied it in a manner that was upside-down to the normal artificial pattern. Turn an object upside-down twice and it becomes the right way up. So the body of a USD paradun sits above its legs on top of the surface film just like the natural insect, with the hook inconspicuously positioned on top of the fly. Unlike all the previous patterns, the tail stands clear of the water as it does on the natural dun. So the USD paraduns are worth a try for stalking discerning fish that are rejecting all other patterns. (The terminology is slightly unfortunate, because it implies an exclusive representation of upwinged flies. Although adult midges, for example, do not have two distinct stages in their life cycle, they are effectively tail-less duns as far as fishermen are concerned.)

USD paradun.

Importance of the Shuck

In practice, life is never that simple. Although USD paraduns are, entomologically speaking, greatly superior to standard patterns, the average trout does not seem to appreciate them as much as it should. We therefore tie most of our parachute patterns the normal (i.e. wrong) way up and only treat the hackle fibres, with the result that the untreated, horizontal body penetrates the surface film. USD paraduns stay in our fly boxes for special occasions.

The most probable explanation for this paradox is that the submerged body is visible long before it enters a trout's window. So does this mean that trout are totally oblivious to the fact that the artificial duns are the wrong way up? Not necessarily. A dun has to emerge from the nymph beneath the surface, and the trout arguably take these patterns as emergers rather than duns. This theory is supported by the fact that a shuck case on the back of an artificial pattern seems to do its performance no harm at all. In fact, there is plenty of evidence that it will often improve a pattern.

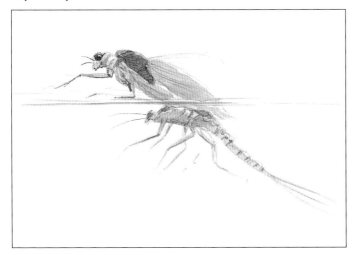

Emerging adult plus shuck case.

This is hardly surprising. During the process of emergence, the shuck is unmistakable as the adult breaks free. Furthermore, the shuck has to be as long as the adult fly. So at the very point of escape, the overall natural fly will be almost twice as long as either the nymph or the adult. The trout are familiar with this rather ungainly looking concoction, which is highly visible as both a dry fly and a nymph. Increasingly, dry flies such as Craig Matthews' Sparkle Dun are exploiting the added attraction. The pertinent question is not whether to attach a shuck to a dry fly, but rather why so many patterns have ignored it for so long!

Importance of the Post

The original and sole intention of the post was to provide a rigid, upright feature around which to wrap a parachute hackle. Rather than trimming right back, many patterns leave a length of the post uncut to provide a sighting point. The tying of such flies requires considerable care to avoid an unnatural appearance from below – especially in calm, clear water. Trout can see the post, and it is possible to exploit this with a small hackle tip to imitate the third and final stage of emergence. If the tip leans slightly forward, it will suggest a hatching adult breaking free from the nymphal case. A small grizzle hackle, with its contrasting shades to represent segmentation and life, is ideal for many species. CDC is an excellent alternative for darker flies. In both instances, the overall impression is one of a body exploding into life on the surface.

The Panacea.

After quite a lengthy development, the end-product is a dry fly pattern with various plus points. They include a submerged horizontal body for visibility, legs with the correct posture, a slim profile with lots of buoyancy, and a trailing shuck and forward-leaning post as trigger points. It is essentially a midge or upwinged dun in the final stage of emergence, and the best time to fish it is undoubtedly during a hatch. This is the basis of our Panacea, which has proved its worth time and time again on both running and still waters around the world.

Tying Delicate Parachute Patterns

It is not easy to tie a parachute hackle around the tip of a delicate feather, which will disintegrate under the tension from a gallows tool. It is possible to trim a large, stronger feather, but this removes the natural taper of the post and destroys the appearance of the emerging adult. There are, however, a couple of different ways round the problem.

Whichever method you choose, the whole process becomes much easier with a long genetic saddle feather that can be gripped between the fingers. The stiff fibres will also cling to the surface film better than an ordinary feather. The legs of the emerging insect must not be too large, so this may require a neck rather than saddle cape for smaller patterns. In this case, a pair of hackle pliers with a good grip will avoid a great deal of frustration.

The first technique involves tying in a few millimetres·of stalk, from the base of a large feather, across the body at the base of the delicate post. The parachute hackle is then wound around the reinforced post, between the stalk and body. After securing with tying thread, it is a good idea to seal the joint with Superglue before trimming the stalk to be as short as possible. The glue must be applied with the point of a dubbing needle, rather than straight from the tube, to ensure that it does not spread to the hackle.

The second method requires slightly more manual dexterity, but produces a neater finish. One of the difficulties in tying a parachute fly is to complete the body and head of the fly without disturbing the hackle. So the trick is to tie the whole fly first – whip finish and all – with just the base of the parachute hackle tied in at the post. Then, very carefully holding the tip of the post between the fingers, the required number of turns of the parachute hackle are incorporated. Rather than securing with tying silk, some Superglue is carefully applied to the base of the post with a dubbing needle before trimming. Such flies hold together surprisingly well.

Wings

Emerging duns are great fish-catchers, but trout will often insist on taking just the fully fledged adults. This means replacing the post by something more representative of a wing.

After experimenting with polythene wings, we came to the conclusion that they did not work particularly well in practice. The outline appears much too stark when compared with the real thing, and this is a classic example of where impressionism is superior to an attempt at exact imitation. This, unfortunately, is an intrinsic problem with a USD paradun, since the polythene wing is necessary to make it land on the surface the right way up (i.e. upside down). With a soft material, there is inadequate air resistance to counteract the tendency for the bend of the hook to point downwards.

CDC wings – an impressionist's delight.

The fuzzy outline makes CDC ideal for many dry flies. Adult insects have a variety of wing shades, such as grey, brown, olive, white and yellow. Although natural CDC is usually grey or brown, it is available in a wide range of dyed colours. The wings may look awful to the human eye, but from beneath the surface they give a very natural impression. The fuzzy outline, and perhaps some movement of the tiny fibres fluttering in the breeze, give an added suggestion of life. They are the purist fly tier's nightmare and the impressionist's delight. They also provide a second line of defence should the rest of the fly start to sink.

WASTE NOT – WANT NOT

Those who are prepared to scavenge can obtain fly tying materials from the wild at no cost. So it was that Reggie, bellowed 'Stop' as we were travelling across Ireland on our way to Lough Conn. Without explaining what he was doing, he took a knife out of his tackle bag and walked back along the road to a mutilated carcass that had been the victim of a passing car. He then proceeded to dismember the dead hare from its ears.

Reggie explained how he had, for years, obtained many of his furs and feathers opportunistically. It increased his enjoyment of the sport by going right back to the natural origins rather than relying on suppliers. For the remaining few days he would keep an eye open for anything by the road-side, ready with all his medical knowledge to execute the next amputation. There was no telling what he might grab next. We were thankful that snakes were so scarce in the Emerald Isle.

A life-long friend later related Reggie's encounter with a heron, which must have been dead for several days, on the banks of the Hampshire Avon. 'You don't want that,' retorted his fishing colleagues in disbelief. They had no wish to share the car with the large, dead bird on the journey back to Gloucestershire. 'What flies can you possibly hope to tie?'

'Mmmm. Wait and see', came the measured reply. 'I know exactly what I'm doing.'

The following week, the fish were not being very co-operative. Whatever concoction Reggie had tied, it was not doing any better than the others' more conventional patterns. It was time for a well earned break for lunch. It was also a chance to talk about the morning's fishing, and to joke at Reggie's expense about his new fly creations and how they had (or had not) performed.

'Mmmm. I don't think there was enough mobility in the feathers', replied Reggie thoughtfully. 'I thought the herls might provide some extra life, but the fly looked completely wrong in the water. Never mind, it was worth a try. Let's forget the morning by drinking this magnificent, full-bodied Super-plonk I picked up the other day.'

The conversation continued into the intricacies of fly tying. One member of the party argued that it was not worth picking up a dead bird or animal just because it was there. That way you could end up with a collection of useless patterns based on the need to utilize the free materials rather than aiming for the best fly design. Reggie accepted the sentiments, but was still very much a believer in the principle of 'waste not – want not'.

'That wine of yours is superb, Reggie, but I have to say that your sandwiches taste a little strange. What's in them?'

'Mmmm. Roast heron.'

For the next few weeks, we would enjoy the occasional chuckle thinking about the reactions of the fishing party on realizing what they had been eating. We also pictured Reggie carefully placing the heron in the oven with seasoning, roast potatoes and who knows what else. On asking him for the precise recipe, he exhibited a blank expression.

'No idea. I got my wife to prepare it.'

'Did she mind cooking a heron?'

'No. Nothing wrong with it – tasted quite similar to beef. Anyway, I told her it was a Lake Pheasant.'

CHAPTER 4
ENTOMOLOGY AND PRAGMATISM

Good enough.

THE ANGLER'S DILEMMA

Sometimes trout are catholic in their choice of food, and will take just about any respectably dressed fly that passes in front of them. This behaviour is usually true of recently stocked fish that have not yet learned from their mistakes, but even established residents will sometimes oblige if undisturbed by fishermen for prolonged periods. On other occasions, they are extremely selective, and the correct choice of artificial pattern will then be crucial.

Unfortunately, entomology is a complex subject, which is confounded by the use of not just one, but two ancient languages. Some authoritative books unwittingly give the impression that recognition of all the minor features is an essential ingredient for even moderate success. This is rarely the case, and prevents many fishermen from persevering to acquire the relatively small amount of essential knowledge. It also causes confusion by producing a state of information overload through which vast quantities of detail hide the crucial facts. A trout has no detailed understanding of entomology, and is only capable of judging an offering by its similarity to a recognisable food form.

We have fished in many different rivers and lakes with experts representing their countries at the highest level. Amongst these proven fishermen, there are undoubtedly some with a passion for entomology who can recognize just about any species at five paces. There is also a sizeable fraction that takes little interest in the fly life – and representatives from this sizeable fraction repeatedly qualify for their national teams by fair selection methods. They have acquired just enough knowledge of entomology to be successful. They are pragmatists who have discarded much of the academic detail and concentrated on the key points that spell success.

Most fly fishermen want to know just enough about entomology to be able to choose the right pattern with confidence. Our approach in this book, therefore, is to take as many short cuts as we dare. Not surprisingly, we favour the more general patterns that represent a large number of different species. In practice it works very well for most of the time, but any rule of thumb turns out to be inaccurate on occasions. Excellent stream-side books already exist to assist with more specific imitations, such as Dick Pobst's pocket guide of *Trout Stream Insects* for the USA, and John Goddard's *Waterside Guide* for the UK.

The ultimate reference will always be the correct entomological classification. So it is worth a brief excursion into the entomologist's world to extract the salient points. We hope to remove the mystique from some of the Greek and Latin names and to highlight those aspects that are important to the angler.

OBSERVATION AND IMPROVISATION

One hot summer's day in early June, JD arrived at the water without a box of dry flies. (At the time MC claimed never to be so forgetful, but more recently has had his moments too!) The trout were feasting on the large dark mayflies known affectionately as *Ephemera vulgata*, and would not look at anything else. So in desperation, a size 10 Mallard and Claret was treated with floatant and cast carefully on to the surface where, thankfully, it remained. Within a minute a large, silly rainbow turned on the fly and sent the reel screaming. Amazingly, seven more equally stupid rainbows obliged in as many casts.

Over the next couple of weeks, spurred on by this experience, we did a lot of experimenting. The trout became progressively more suspicious of improvised imitations. After a couple of days the good old Mallard and Claret would still rise a few trout, but it no longer deceived them into commitment. At the end of the fortnight, an off-the-shelf Brown Drake was acceptable to many of the trout, providing the nylon had been properly treated to sink.

From then on, the number of large mayflies started to diminish rapidly. Feeding fish were still in evidence on the surface, but try as we might we could not catch anything on the most sophisticated mayfly imitations. It was not until we saw a splashy rise under our noses, where we knew there had been no mayfly, that the penny dropped. There were plenty of the brilliant blue adult damsel-flies in evidence, and the fish had to be taking the nymphs as they made there way just below the surface to hatch on the bankside vegetation. On went a lightweight damsel nymph, moved with a lively figure-of-eight retrieve, and the sport recommenced.

There are two interesting conclusions from these experiences. First, although you will achieve a great deal by observing and copying the natural insects on the day, you cannot ignore the broad fundamentals of entomology. You do not need to focus on all the minute details, but you still need to know something about the key items on the trout's menu, such as outline, movement and likely habitat.

Second, it is easy to become preoccupied with the conspicuous adults and overlook details of the nymphs. A knowledge of entomology is arguably more important for nymphs than for dry flies. Dry flies are clearly visible, so that anyone with a good eye can copy them. In contrast, it is difficult to observe what the trout are taking beneath the surface. It is therefore important to be able to deduce the form of the nymphs and to recognize when the sub-surface activity is unrelated to the natural dry flies. You must also have a good idea of the best general patterns to use on unfamiliar waters in the absence of visible clues or local experts.

NYMPH EXPLORATIONS

In our formative years of river fishing, we started collecting our own nymphs from the River Usk in South Wales. We must have looked a right pair of eccentrics, walking down to the water's edge with our little nets and plastic buckets. There were quite a few light-hearted comments from passers-by about grown men acting like little boys. But we resolutely stuck to our task, collecting weed and scooping up stones with our nets. Then we proudly returned home with the prize of our endeavours, only to be met with rather unenthusiastic comments from our wives – something about grown men acting like little boys.

Nevertheless, the little boys were well pleased with the results. Nymphs may be rather drably coloured, but in an aquarium they are far from dull to watch. They move in a variety of different ways, ranging from graceful to clumsy. Some are sleek and elegant, while others are downright ugly. There are predators, victims and those with ingenious ways of escape. The spectacle was mesmerising, and for a while we became quite preoccupied with this new-found hobby.

We have repeated these studies from time to time over the years, and indulged ourselves with a few experiments in macro-photography. The end result has not been the development of patterns that are complex or exciting, because we have approached the task pragmatically as fishermen rather than entomologists. The main pay-back has been the ability to develop and fish nymph patterns with far more authority and confidence than would otherwise have been possible.

We would recommend any serious fly fisherman to do the same. It takes a little extra effort, but you will learn more about sub-surface entomology in three hours than you would otherwise accumulate in three years. Moreover, the information will be tailored to your own local water. It will reveal details of the principal nymphs and provide a good indication of the relative numbers of different species. The nett result will be the correct choice of an artificial fly that both looks the part and represents an important and abundant food item.

For rivers, a net with a very fine mesh is essential. The trick is to find a small boulder and to place the net vertically in the water about six inches downstream. Kick away the boulder and the nymphs, which have become accustomed to the relatively still water afforded by this natural barrier, will suddenly be swept into the net by the current. The net should be square or have a straight rather than curved end, so that it will rest flat on the river bed and stop nymphs being swept underneath it.

You should not become discouraged if the first few attempts result in failure. We soon learned that nymphs do not colonize all areas of a river bed. The local currents and eddies play an important role in their choice of habitat, and this results in enormous concentrations in some spots while large areas elsewhere remain almost barren. Persevere, because if the river holds trout that are not feeding exclusively on terrestrial insects, it must also hold nymphs. Moreover, once you have characterized the local hot-spots for nymphs, you will have identified the most likely places to locate a feeding sub-surface trout.

It is easy for a lake fisherman to collect nymphs that are about to hatch near the surface, or to pull up samples of weed. Any trout that has been despatched should be spooned, and very often some of the nymphs examined by this process will still be alive and kicking. These are the specimens that really matter. Dead midge pupae, for example, will often turn a drab green colour, and it is therefore easy to misinterpret the colours of the natural insects.

CUTTING THROUGH THE MYSTIQUE
The Problem
The logic behind the classification of insects can appear bewilderingly complex, with two apparently similar flies sometimes being categorized into completely different groups. The classical nomenclature also tends to be very precise, to the extent that

minor differences imply totally different things. For example, *Baetis* nymphs are streamlined, agile darters, whereas *Baetisca* are ungainly, hump-backed, triangular specimens. A *Hexagenia* nymph is large and graceful, while a small *Heptagenia* nymph bears a passing resemblance to a tiny frog. Last but by no means least, the frequently encountered terms *Ephemeroptera*, *Emphemeridae*, *Ephemerellidae*, *Ephemerella* and *Ephemera* all have subtly different meanings.

The streamlined baetis nymph.

In spite of its complexity, the classical terminology provides a structured and consistent framework for grouping different species together, and is a final source of reference when the same angling name covers several different species. It allows you to relate an observed adult back to the nymph, noting that the nymphs of two very similar adults can vary considerably in their appearance and behaviour. Finally, it gives a definition of a fly that is not open to any misinterpretation, providing of course that you read the name carefully.

The challenge is to try to cut through much of the mystique and apply it in its simplest possible form – even if this means taking a few liberties by omitting the more precise details. It is usually possible to ignore the Greek and Latin terminology in favour of English terms, but there are times when it helps to find out something more about a specific fly. So in this spirit, we will briefly outline the scientific terminology in a way that should make it a little less daunting for those occasions when it is needed. The large number of anglers with a phobia for classical names need not worry, because this brief digression does not set the tone for the rest of the book.

Importance of the Wings

The first stage of the classification, at least, is fairly straightforward. Many of the most important flies in the trout's diet exist in four orders. The entomological name for each order ends in *ptera*, which is ancient Greek for wings. It is essentially the wings that distinguish these four orders from each other, although the first part of the name does not always translate literally to the type of wing in the description below:

Greek Name	Description	Common name
Ephemeroptera	Upwinged flies	Mayflies, olives etc.
Trichoptera	Roof-winged flies	Caddis or sedge
Plecoptera	Hard-winged flies	Stoneflies
Diptera	Flat-winged flies	'True flies', including midges

Adult upwinged fly.

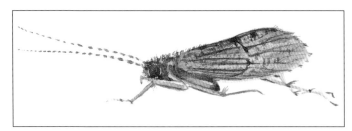

Adult caddis.

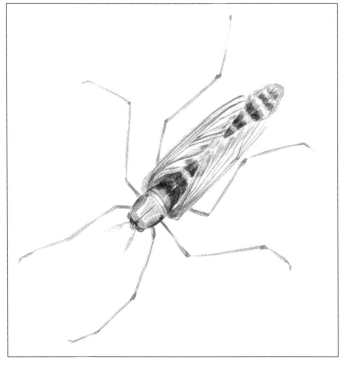

Adult midge.

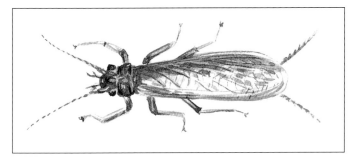

Adult stonefly.

An Example for Upwinged Flies

The adult upwinged flies are ephemeral – a word derived from the Greek meaning 'lasting for one day'. This explains why the order is so-named, and why the same root (*ephemer*) appears so frequently in the subsequent break-down into families and genera. Upwinged flies are very important insects to the river fisherman. They are also the ones that are scrutinized most closely by angling books and – though arguably not to the same extent – by trout!

Each order breaks down first into families. Those upwinged flies whose nymphs cling to stones in fast-moving water are members of the *Heptageniidae* family. The name may be awkward to pronounce, and it is not clear exactly why it is so called. Perhaps it was once considered as a family containing seven genera. Nevertheless, the logic behind the separation into a single family is clear. Incidentally, the plain English terminology sometimes causes confusion here since, apart from being insects and inhabiting similar stretches of water, stone-clingers bear no relationship whatsoever to stoneflies.

The ungainly stone-clinging nymph.

The *Heptageniidae* family then separates into genera. Those stone-clinging nymphs that have only two tails belong to the *Epeorus* genus. This breakdown of upwinged adult, stone-clinger and two tails gives a very clear picture of the classification of order, family and genus. The name of the genus alone is adopted as the first half of the name to describe uniquely each individual species. There is no reference to the order or family.

The species is the final stage in giving a unique identity to an insect. Species within a genus are often, but not exclusively, separated by factors such as size and colour. Often different species will be prevalent in a specific region. For example, *Epeorus pleuralis* is a brown coloured dun of about 10 mm in length which is common in eastern USA. *Epeorus longimanus* is a slightly smaller pale greyish coloured dun which hatches in the west, whereas *Epeorus sylvicola* is predominantly green and brown and is found in mainland Europe.

The Need for Pragmatism

We have deliberately chosen one of the most simple cases for the purpose of illustration. Even within the *Heptageniidae* family, there are at least seven genera of three-tailed stone-clinging nymphs. These are classified by minute details that include the gills, head, mouth-parts and even the genitalia!

Reggie was in fine fettle in the bar on the banks of Lough Conn. The Budweiser, which the Irish barmaid had assured him was cider, did not seem to exhibit the slightest taste of apples – but who cared. He had been the only angler in the party all day to have caught a decent brown trout, and he was celebrating. Moreover, he needed to unwind after suffering Wesley's ceaseless monologue on how to fish the Irish loughs. At first he interrogated the barmaid on the strange taste of the local apples, which he eventually put down to the peat bog. Then he started to describe how he had caught his fish in each and every language that came to hand.

'Mmmm. J'ai jeté le mouche, et le poisson . . .'.

'You mean la mouche, because fly is feminine', responded Wesley, who was always ready to demonstrate his superior knowledge.

'Mmmm. You've got remarkable eyesight. You ought to take up entomology.'

Differences between families, such as minor variations in the veins on the wings, can also be rather too subtle for the non-specialist. It is easy to confirm the degree of obscurity by noting that the entomological classifications themselves have changed considerably over the years. Species have been moved from one genus to another. Genera have been combined, separated or moved between families, and families have been separated into smaller units. Moreover, colour variations sometimes exist within the same species, with a tendency to darken at reduced temperatures. (This is consistent with the rule of thumb to use darker flies in spring and autumn than in summer.) Anglers are therefore justified in taking more than a few liberties to simplify the choice of pattern.

Moreover, it is interesting to note that, give or take a few exceptions, the same genera of insects exist on both sides of the Atlantic. The species tend to be different, but in many cases both the angler and the trout may need very sharp eyes to distinguish them. Good old favourites such as the Ginger Quill, Adams and Pheasant Tail seem to be universally successful. It is therefore possible to draw on experiences and information from across the world to provide a co-ordinated approach to fly fishing. In this book, therefore, we are attempting to give the broad picture, avoiding as much as practicable the precise details of individual species. This ability to focus on the key aspects is an essential ingredient that is shared by experts around the world – experts who achieve consistent success over a variety of waters and conditions.

CHAPTER 5

THE TROUT'S LARDER

Ephemera danica.

Trout feed on a wide variety of items ranging from tiny water fleas to quite sizeable fish. In still waters, where the food supply tends to be more varied than in rivers, they can put on enormous growth. It is easy to make assumptions about their favoured diet, only to find that they will sometimes disappoint the most obvious expectations.

Early one June, we were standing on the road bridge at Castle Combe, admiring some large mayfly duns leaving the surface of the stream. The trout were gobbling up these majestic cream and brown-flecked specimens, until one onlooker started throwing bread on to the water. Brown trout are apt to be selective, and once the 'hatch' of bread had occurred, all interest in the mayflies evaporated rapidly.

Trout need to learn whether something is worth eating – and this process takes some time. The Castle Combe trout had presumably got the message after repeated offerings from passers-by. Wild fish determine what is edible as a gradual process so that, when mature, they will recognize most natural food-forms while ignoring man-made offerings – however nutritious. Recently stocked fish, on the other hand, may take time to adjust to a natural source of food. For example, they often lose weight in lakes teeming with small fish and sometimes go hungry during prolific hatches of midge.

UPWINGED FLIES (*EPHEMEROPTERA*)

We refer to this order of insects as upwinged flies throughout the book. It is a good descriptive term that sounds a lot more friendly than *Ephemeroptera*. It also avoids the confusion that results with the other common terms which differ on opposite sides of the Atlantic. Americans refer to all species as 'mayflies'. Europeans reserve this term for the large 'Drakes', whose nymphs burrow in the bed of the river or lake, and refer to the remainder loosely as olives and 'bloody caenis'.

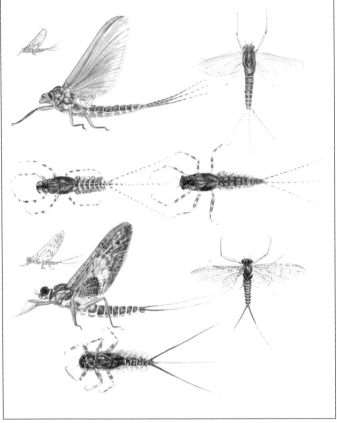

Upwinged flies showing a selection of duns, nymphs and spent spinners.

Adult Upwinged Flies

Upwinged insects epitomize most people's vision of fly fishing. The overall profile of the dun is majestic as it floats on the water, with its sail-like wings and two or three upturned tail filaments. Not surprisingly, many illustrations and logos incorporate its outline in preference to the rather ordinary features of a midge or the moth-like profile of a caddis. Add to that the graceful and dancing flight of the spinners, and it is small wonder that even people with no interest in entomology become spell-bound into admiring them. Unfortunately, they have no mouths through which to eat or drink, so the life-cycle of the adults is very short.

Overall there are about 2,500 species of upwinged flies throughout the world. They are fundamental to river fishing, where typically they may comprise about 50% of the trout's diet – although there are enormous regional variations. Species that can tolerate lower oxygen levels will thrive in isolated lakes, though trout may be less dependent on them due to the many other sources of food.

Prior to emergence, the nymph's wing-cases become increasingly prominent, giving it a hump-backed appearance. When the dun breaks free, its body, which is covered with fine hairs, exhibits a dull appearance. The prominently veined wings are only slightly transparent and often take on a greyish tinge. It is these drab features that originally gave the duns their name from the English adjective meaning dull-greyish brown. Most species have four wings, but the two hind-wings, where they exist, are sufficiently inconspicuous to ignore in any artificial representation. Duns rest on the water, for varying times from a couple of seconds to half a minute, waiting for their wings to dry out. At this stage, of course, they are extremely vulnerable. The waiting period is much shorter on hot, dry days, and may vary appreciably between members of the same family.

Upwinged flies are unique in undergoing a moulting on the bankside vegetation from dun to spinner (so named because of its movement in the air). This moult removes the drabness from the fly to yield a shiny body and beautifully transparent wings – although the veining and any mottling remain. Both the tails and the two front legs, which are noticeably longer than the other two pairs, increase considerably in length. It is at this stage that mating occurs, with the male grabbing the female with his longer front legs and his claspers at the rear. The females then return onto the water to lay their eggs before dying. They lie spent on the surface with their wings and tails outstretched. Male spinners are usually less important to the angler since they fly away after mating, but this is not the case for all species.

Nymphs of Upwinged Flies

It is so easy to concentrate on the adults, given their elegance and visibility, that many fly fishermen remain under-informed about the nymphs. Consequently they do not take full advantage of an important food item. Even some professional fly tiers are ignorant of the appearance of many nymphs. We have collected specimens to convince sceptical river keepers that such species existed in profusion in their stretch of water. We have also shown photographs to many fly fishermen who could not tell whether the corresponding adult was a mayfly, stonefly or whatever – or even whether such a specimen hatched into an adult insect.

For most other orders of insects, the profile and movement of the nymphs does not depend greatly on the genus or species. So once you have identified an adult as a midge or a sedge, you can make a pretty good judgement about which pattern to use for the nymph. This is not the case with the upwinged flies. There is a surprising variation in overall shape and behaviour that cannot be deduced from a straightforward observation of the adult. Even the number of tails can be misleading, because in many species a three-tailed nymph will hatch into a two-tailed dun.

Differences in the adult insects between families and genera are rarely obvious to the non-specialist, whereas the corresponding nymphs display quite distinct features. Oliver Kite's work, entitled *Nymph Fishing in Practice*, classified upwinged flies into six different groups of nymphs. This provides an excellent framework for general patterns and the manner in which to fish them.

In the table below, we have added some of our own descriptions. We have also trawled through European and North American literature to compile a list of the principal genera that are associated with each group. Many of these genera exist in just one continent, and we make no pretence of being familiar with all of them. The aim is simply to provide a means of cross-referencing any species that you may come across with the appropriate form of nymph.

SUMMARY OF KITE'S GROUPING OF NYMPHS OF UPWINGED FLIES

GROUP	OTHER FEATURES	GENUS
BOTTOM BURROWERS	Includes large mayflies (Drakes)	Ephemera, Hexagenia, Ephoron
AGILE DARTERS	Streamlined bodies (often referred to loosely as Baetis or Baetid nymphs)	Baetis, Callibaetis, Acentrella Potamanthus, Cloeon, Centroptilium, Procloeon, Pseudocentroptilium, Siphlonurus, Ameletus Isonychia, Siphloplectron
STONE-CLINGERS	Flat, fat-headed nymphs present in fast-flowing water	Epeorus, Rhithrogena, Heptagenia, Stenomena, Stenacron, Leucrocuta, Cinygma, Cinygmula, Ecdyonurus, Electrogena, Nixe, Uligoneura
MOSS CREEPERS	Sturdy-bodied nymphs	Ephemerella, Drunella, Eurylophella, Dannella, Serratella, Caudatella, Timpanoga Anthopotamanthus
LABOURED SWIMMERS	Dark nymphs with prominent tracheal gills	Leptophlebia, Paraleptophlebia, Habrophlebia
SILT CRAWLERS	Tiny insects – principally for dry flies (Caenis and Tricos)	Caenis, Tricorythodes

Even the most fastidious angler should only need a single pattern for each group, although he may vary the size, colour and weight to suit local conditions. His more pragmatic counterpart may debate whether it is worth the effort of distinguishing between the different categories of nymph at all. A little time spent in the collection of specimens, or examination of the stomach contents of dead trout, should help you to come to your own conclusions.

1 – Large Mayfly Nymphs (Bottom Burrowers)

Bottom burrower.

These nymphs have tusk-like mandibles for burrowing into the river or lake bed, and three short, fringed tails that are only about one third of the length of the body. Just to make life complicated, the numbers of tails on the adults vary according to the genus. *Ephemera* mayflies, which exist in both North America and Europe, have three tails. *Hexagenia*, which inhabit more silt-bottomed waters in North America, have only two. These two genera belong to the same family and correspond to the large mayflies that anglers frequently refer to as Green, Yellow and Brown Drakes. Apart from the obvious clue of size, the nymphs and adults of each species tend to exhibit similar colours, so associating them with each other is relatively straightforward. They are a great asset to any water, but sometimes the trout become so gorged on them that they will 'sulk' for a couple of days and refuse to feed.

Our observations of *Ephemera* nymphs in the aquarium revealed the very pronounced gill movements. The natural nymph spends quite a lot of its time in a static posture or just inching forward – but its gills seldom seem to be still. These mayflies have evolved to survive in slow moving or still waters as well as rivers, so that some action of the gills is necessary to pump water round the body for extracting oxygen. There are series of moving gills along the top of the translucent abdomen, which are most in evident mid-length, suggesting the use of highly mobile material in any artificial representation.

One unexpected finding in the aquarium was the movement of these large nymphs in open water. When they do decide to move, they can really motor. The problem for the fly dresser is that the whole body wriggles like an eel with a motion that is impossible to imitate on a rigid hook. We gave up the use of articulated hooks long ago because the end effect looked even less realistic that the conventional pattern. Instead, we have stuck to our belief in impressionism and teased out the fur to give a blurred effect, or tied a short body with a long marabou tail.

2 – Flat, Fat-headed Nymphs (Stone-clingers)

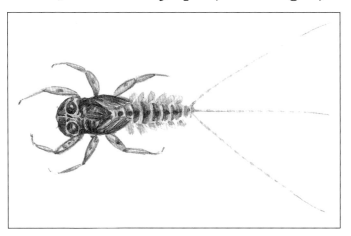

Stone-clinger.

On the first occasion that we collected nymphs, we were fascinated by an ugly specimen with two strange, large black eyes. The overall profile was flat instead of cylindrical, with a large head that appeared to be out of proportion with the body. The legs were also rather strange, appearing to our uneducated eyes more like those of a small frog than an insect. It was only the three very long tails that suggested that it would hatch eventually into some form of adult fly.

We remember trying to identify the species against a variety of possible candidates in reference books. It actually corresponded to a Yellow May Dun – an identification that owed more to a knowledge of the local hatches in the River Usk, and a gradual process of elimination, than to a close study of the nymphal features. Although we could not agree on the exact identification at the time, one startling point was clear. These rather ungainly, fat-headed nymphs would eventually hatch into elegant upwinged duns – a little like the fairy tale of a frog turning into a prince. They correspond to duns like the Cahills and Quill Gordons in North America, the Yellow May Dun and Olive Upright in Europe, and March Browns on both sides of the Atlantic.

Stone-clingers have a requirement for lots of oxygen, and therefore thrive in the faster, and sometimes cooler, stretches of water. Although from a completely different order of insect, they often populate the same stretches of water as stoneflies. The flat profiles, sturdy legs and the use of suction allow them to cling to stones in the fastest of currents. We found that they will grip on to a finger just as securely. They will invariably face upstream, lying in crevices or on the underside of stones during bright conditions to avoid direct sunlight. Only when conditions become more overcast, will they venture – a step at a time – on to the tops of stones to feed on algae that grows on the exposed surfaces. We have observed a very similar shuffling motion from the adults on dry land.

Most stone-clinging nymphs have three tails, without any fibres attached, that are as long as their bodies. The exception is the *Epeorus* genus, which has only two tails – though we do not believe for one moment that any trout will notice! Some nymphs work their way slowly on to the upper surfaces of stones to split their nymphal skins. Nature very cleverly protects the wings by an envelope of nymphal gases, and a buoyant fly, which is half nymph and half adult, drifts upwards to emerge in open water. This is one time when it is perfectly sensible to fish an emerger well below the surface.

The difficulties encountered with identification of that first nymph in the aquarium convinced us that it would only be necessary to have a single pattern to represent the entire group. A good imitation will have a body with a flattened profile, so the lead needed to weigh it down in the fast currents should be tied along the side of the shank rather than around it. Woven nymphs are eminently suitable, but we have known fishermen simply flatten a conventionally leaded pattern with a pair of pliers. Imitation of the nymphs as they cling to stones is obviously impractical, but a dead drift is appropriate to represent a dislodged nymph or emerger. Most references categorize stone-clingers as non-swimmers, but our observations suggest that they are really very laboured swimmers. Some species swagger from side to side, whereas others move with an undulation of the body that is very suggestive of the motion of dolphins. So a little bit of added movement in an artificial pattern will not necessarily come amiss.

3 – Streamlined Nymphs (Agile Darters)

Most agile darters belong to the Baetidae family. Anglers often refer to them loosely as Baetis (rather than Baetid) nymphs, but this term strictly applies to one particular genus rather than the entire family. Their streamlined, highly segmented appearance corresponds quite closely to what one might expect from the shape of the adult, although they have three tails compared with only two on the duns and spinners. The three tails are typically about 40% of the length of the body and are fringed with tiny fibres. In common with many nymphs, there is a very definite

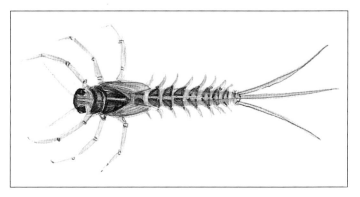

Agile darter.

lightening of colour beneath the body. They tend to live near the edges of weed and, when disturbed, propel themselves in a series of very rapid jerks. We have observed them covering distances of up to a foot with a single sprint in a fraction of a second. This suggests experimenting with a correspondingly fast and jerky retrieve in addition to the more normal dead-drift.

Most Baetid nymphs are small and slim – with a size in the range 5–10 mm – and very fragile. Some of the most important examples are the Little Blue-Winged Olive and Speckled-Wing Duns in North America, and The Pond and Lake Olive, Iron Blue and Pale Watery Duns in Europe. Larger examples of agile darters from other families, which can be as large as 20 mm, include the North American Slate and Grey Drakes and the European Large Summer Dun. Overall, a slim, tapered Pheasant Tail is an excellent general pattern for the nymphs, and an Adams, Panacea or Sail-Wing will do nicely for the adults.

4 – Sturdy Nymphs (Moss Creepers)

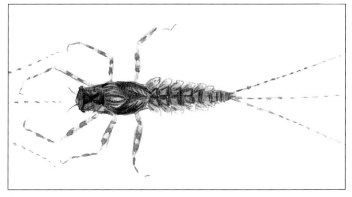

Moss creeper.

This group includes the classic, three-tailed upwinged flies of the *Ephemerella* genus, such as the Blue-Winged Olive (not to be confused with the Little BWO), Hendrickson and Pale Morning and Evening Duns. Unfortunately, to make life more complicated, entomologists have now separated this single genus into six! We will ignore this distinction.

Ephemerella nymphs tend to be rather inactive, creeping around the mosses or stones in a river. They tend to have a fairly sturdy profile that is intermediate between the elegance of agile darters and the ungainly appearance of stone-clingers, but there is considerable variation between these two extremes. Due to their stocky appearance, it is possible to incorporate lead wire around the hook without detracting from the natural shape. The tails, on average, are just under half the length of the body, although they can be as much as two thirds, and on some species they are fringed with hairs.

Ephemerella nymphs usually hatch in open water, and since their wings also take quite a time to dry out, trout are able to take them in large numbers. Another important feature for the angler is the ability of some species to escape their nymphal skins while several inches below the surface. This behaviour gives further justification for fishing weighted emerger patterns – wings and all.

5 – Dark Nymphs with Prominent Gills (Laboured Swimmers)

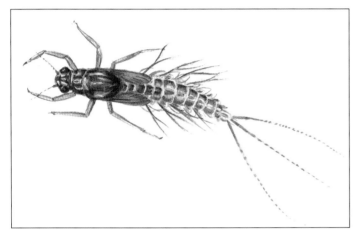

Laboured swimmer.

Nymphs of the *leptophlebia* and *paraleptophlebia* genera are also crawlers, but they tend to swim from place to place in a rather laboured fashion. Examples are the Black and Dark Blue Quills in North America, and the Claret and Sepia Duns in Europe.

The second of the two genera is slightly more streamlined, but both resemble the sturdy nymphs of the previous group with two exceptions. First, to a variable extent, the nymphs of upwinged flies have tracheal gills along the sides of their bodies. This is perhaps one reason why the fur from a hare's ear, with its projecting spikes, has proved to be such a successful material. In these two genera, though, the gills are very pronounced, and make them instantly recognisable when swimming. This suggests the use of a long-fibred herl or a great deal of teasing-out of the fur in an artificial pattern. Second, the nymphs and adults are very dark in colour.

6 – Silt Crawlers

The separation of tricos and caenis into their own group as silt crawlers is of minor importance to fishermen, because mostly it is the adult insects – rather than the nymphs – that are relevant. An important feature is the tiny size – typically a size 20 or smaller. Success with these dry flies is the sign of a true expert,

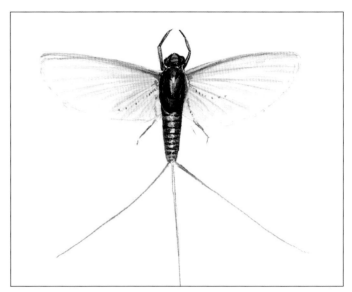

Adult trico

but even the best fishermen often fail with imitative patterns. This is not because of any lack of skill, but because the statistical odds are stacked so heavily against them.

Tricos are common in many parts of North America from July to October. The life-cycle from dun to spinner is rapid, varying from a few minutes for the females to a couple of hours for the males. The duns, which often provide the most productive fishing, may be hatching up to mid-morning. Favourite patterns include a Size 20 to 24 white-winged, black-bodied No-Hackle, but we have enjoyed plenty of success with a tiny Adams or Panacea. Sometimes you will cover the same fish several times without success. This is partly because trico-feeders will remain high in the water and move in all sorts of directions, so that accuracy and anticipation are essential. But if you feel your fly is being ignored, rather than missed, it may be worth making a few subtle alterations. These include a change of size or pattern, degreasing the leader or simply drying the fly with powder so that it rests higher on the surface film.

Caenis are often referred to as 'the angler's curse' – and with good reason. The basic problem is that they tend to hatch in such enormous numbers at the same time just before sunset or at dawn. You can almost set your watch by the event, and very often trout will be up in the water in anticipation. Right at the beginning of the hatch, they will pick out the isolated specimens. A considerable number of fish may be up and looking for the small number of natural insects that have started to hatch, and the odds will temporarily be in the angler's favour. It is then quite possible to be successful using imitative techniques.

The numbers soon increase dramatically, and in a few minutes it is not just the water that is covered with caenis. You will find yourself coated from head to foot by the tiny creatures, and will probably be spitting them out of your mouth. The transformation from nymph, to dun to spinner can all take place in a matter of minutes. It is when the hatch really gets under way that the odds reverse dramatically against the fisherman, with thousands of duns and spinners available to each trout. At

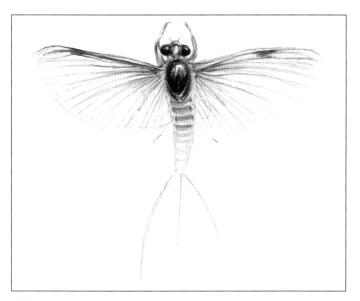

Adult caenis.

this point, a perfect imitation of the natural has only a one in a thousand chance of being taken, unless it lands with pin point accuracy directly in front of a trout's gaping mouth.

The trout stop rising to individuals and go into 'vacuum cleaner mode'. They appear totally mesmerized, moving slowly in a zigzag motion across the top of the water with their mouths wide open to mop up the feast. Even a perfect cast just in front of a gaping fish is by no means guaranteed to be successful, because its zigzagging motion is so erratic that it is more likely to move to the side. The trout's window of vision for dry flies is virtually zero right in the surface, so the chances of seeing even a perfectly cast fly is very small. It is not going to expend unnecessary energy by turning to take one particular fly when it is already mopping up large quantities of insects in one go.

Alex was becoming more and more irate. The fishing had not gone well that day, but now that the trout were at last feeding right on the surface, they were untouchable. To make matters worse, he was covered from head to foot by these 'bloody caenis'. His language was starting to become rather colourful. 'It's a waste of time trying for these bl**dy fish', he shouted, spitting out caenis from his mouth and trying to brush hundreds of them from all parts of his body. The angler's curse was turning out to be a very accurate description.

He was also having great difficulty with the bargain rod that he had just picked in the local auction. Apparently, it had belonged previously to Humphrey, so it had to be good! (Had he done his homework, he would have discovered that Humphrey had won the rod in a competition, used it once and disposed of it at the first available opportunity.) The rod seemed to oscillate in the air before projecting the line and leader into a heap on the water. Proper presentation of a small dry fly was really out of the question.

Alex started to blame himself. He obviously had to adapt his casting style. Since he was failing to catch anything, he might as well avoid the tangles and use a stronger leader while getting the feel of the new rod. But the thicker nylon would not go through the eye of the tiny flies, so – after a few more choice swear words – he delved into his fly box for something larger. By now, he had lost all patience and picked the largest pattern he could find, which turned out to be size 8 Viva. He was not at all happy with his first

cast. In mounting frustration, he ripped the line back at full speed, only to see a bow wave behind the fly and then to feel the rod bending fiercely.

He tried it again, this time without the swearing, and picked up two more fish during the next fifteen minutes while the rise to caenis continued. If he had not been so honest in admitting that it had all been a fluke, he could have told quite an impressive story. He could have explained how he had caught the preoccupied trout off balance with a sub-surface attractor pattern that they could actually see, as opposed to a proper imitation that they would have been unlikely to notice. There would have been the skilful choice of a black and green pattern that was likely to promote a response by appealing to the trout's instincts of aggression or curiosity.

We are not advocating the routine use of enormous attractor patterns during a rise, but this experience does illustrate an important point. Fish are sometimes deceptively difficult to catch during prolific hatches, causing the frustrated angler to blame his fly patterns for the failure. Sometimes, the lack of success is simply due to the low odds of an artificial fly being noticed against the large number of natural insects. It then pays to depart from the laudable tactic of aiming for the best imitation possible, and to try something that increases the chances of the pattern being noticed. Options include a larger size, the addition of a fluorescent tail or thorax and submerging or moving the fly to make it more noticeable. This will usually increase the catch, even though the chances of the fly being accepted – once seen – may actually decrease considerably.

An Illuminating Experience

It is possible to divide the nymphs of upwinged flies into several key groups, but it would be wrong to be too dogmatic about the differences. Just when we thought we had sorted everything out in our early days of collecting specimens, we had quite a surprise during one afternoon in early April. We had wanted to photograph some adult March Browns, and arrived at the water eager for action with our newly purchased macro lens and ring-flash.

Unfortunately, there was a cold north wind blowing down the river and, true to these conditions, there was very little fly life and not a March Brown in sight. So we decided to make the most of the trip and collect a few nymphs. At the time, we had already obtained quite a few agile darters and lots of 'fat-headed' stone-clingers, but we had not managed to collect a single *Ephemerella* nymph.

This occasion turned out to be different, since we captured about half a dozen specimens with our first few scoops of the net. They exhibited an undulating swimming motion, and the pronounced humped-back appearance, due to the wing cases prior to emergence, contributed to our perception of their sturdy profile. We were proudly showing off our knowledge to each other, pointing out the ease with which we had identified members of the *Ephemerella* genus, when one of them swam to the surface and hatched into a March Brown! This seemed impossible. We knew March Browns to be stone-clingers. We even knew that they belonged to the *Rhithrogena* genus. But we had failed the most basic practical test in the field of being unable to identify the living nymph when it was in front of our very eyes. We had not only mistaken the species, but also the genus and family.

Adult March Brown.

We mentioned earlier that the identification of our first fat-headed nymph owed a great deal to elimination, and this outing was part of that process. With the benefit of hindsight, it was very easy to tell that these nymphs were March Browns. They had three tails, which were almost as long as the body. They had flat bodies and fat heads, but they were not as exaggerated as the previous stone-clinging species that we had observed – and they were concealed partly by the growth around the wing cases prior to emergence. What had really thrown us from the start was their ability to swim, in spite of what we had read. This experience proved that there is no substitute for your own observations at the waterside. It also added more evidence to support general patterns for representing a whole range of nymphs.

It brought another message firmly home to us. The discarded shuck case retained its shape, and with a sideways glance you could be forgiven for mistaking it for the nymph itself. During the final emergence, all of this shuck case was still attached to the dun. So there is no need to restrict the tail of a pattern to just a short length of antron or feather fibres. The attachment at the back can be as long as the fly itself.

CADDIS OR SEDGE (*TRICHOPTERA*)
Adult Caddis

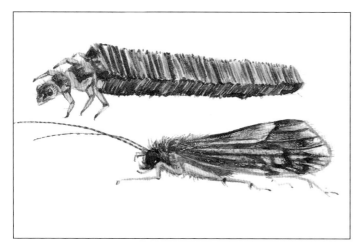

The caddis family.

Many beginners have mistaken adult caddis flies for moths. Entomologists recognize the close similarities, since the Greek name *Trichoptera* literally means 'hairy wings' to distinguish the order from the moth's scaled wings. The vital difference for anglers, of course, is the aquatic rather than terrestrial life cycle, which makes the caddis accessible to trout. Like moths, many species are nocturnal, but there are thankfully plenty that choose to hatch at more sociable times of day, with a definite inclination towards late afternoon and evening. The roof-shaped wings vary in colour from a pale fawn, through a reddish brown to black. Very often they are marked or mottled with a dark colour, and this makes a hen pheasant centre tail feather a suitable all-round material for their representation.

Although there are important exceptions, such as the huge Irish Murragh and some gigantic Scandinavian specimens, many important species correspond to a hook in the size range 10 to 16. Imitations of the smaller sizes should employ a short-shank (i.e. wide gape) hook to prevent the chunky body obscuring the point. Many fishermen capitalize on the chunky profile to produce buoyant patterns that will stay afloat in rough water, irrespective of the occurrence of any natural insects.

Strictly speaking, a true imitation ought to include the two prominent antennae, which are up to twice the length of the body, but trout are seldom as fussy about this as one might expect. There are no tails to consider, and no transformation from dun to spinner. So although there are over six thousand different species across the world, the pragmatic angler can get away with a single dry fly pattern for the stationary adult in a variety of sizes and colours.

The adults often emerge in open water. Some species hatch quickly and fly away almost at once, while others skitter along the surface for considerable distances before taking off. In the latter instance, a very splashy rise may occur as a trout dashes to capture its quarry before it can escape. Sometimes the natural insect makes a great deal of commotion in hatching and leaving the water, which attracts the trout's attention. This explains the success of moving buoyant flies across the surface to produce a wake. Sometimes you can provoke an almighty bow-wave followed by a savage pull on the line if you rip the flies back as quickly as possible.

Although incapable of consuming solid food, the adults can take in liquid which enables them to live for a few weeks. They may return to the edge of the water to drink, and in so doing they sometimes get swept into the river by the current. Therefore, river trout may be expecting the arrival of an isolated adult caddis at any time of the day, irrespective of whether there is a hatch in progress.

Specific patterns such as the Elk Hair Caddis, G & H Sedge and Richard Walker's Sedge are all respectable fish takers. But so too are some of the more general patterns such as Hoppers (UK) and 'Ginked-up' Muddlers. (UK is used throughout the book for the popular British fly to avoid confusion with the same term used in North America for grasshoppers.) Any palmered fly that vaguely matches the hatch will disturb the surface and probably capture its share of trout. The Wickham's Fancy is a

G&H Sedge.

consistently successful pattern, and has fuelled our speculation about the role of gold in fading light conditions when many caddis tend to hatch. The simpler wingless version will often work just as well. If the naturals have any tint of red in them, the Soldier Palmer is worth a try, since it capitalizes on the attraction of this colour near the surface. As its name suggests, the Solwick combines the features of the Soldier and Wickham's to provide simultaneously the advantages of gold and red. Our own palmered White Sedge relies on its fluorescent white body for attraction as much as imitation, with that little bit of added bite from the orange tail.

One of the oldest and yet most successful imitations of the hatching caddis is the Invicta, which was invented many years ago by James Ogden. The hen pheasant centre tail wings and yellow fur body contrast to give a deceptive impression of the adult fly. It is quite a complicated pattern, but the hatching caddis is a very messy concoction, with skittering legs, long antennae, big wings and a chunky body and shuck. The red game (i.e. red-brown) palmer disturbs the water to attract the trout and the golden pheasant tail gives an impression of the pupal case. Even the blue jay throat hackle gives a subtle flash of colour that adds to the overall impression of life. It is a good idea to vary the body colour to match the natural insects, with shades of green, red, cream brown and black being the most useful. Going a stage further, the replacement of the fur body by a flat silver tinsel produces the Silver Invicta. This fly may not at first sight appear to be such a good representation of the natural insect, but it is one of the most devastating wet flies in any fisherman's armoury for a whole range of food forms and conditions.

Greek and Latin names seem to appear much less in angling literature for caddis flies (and all other orders) than for upwinged insects – though the terms *Rhyacophila* and *Hydropsyche* have found their way into the river fisherman's repertoire. Rest assured, though, that a horrendous compilation of such detail still exists in the entomological textbooks. We suspect that only

the upwinged flies were of real interest on the hallowed chalk-streams in bygone years when the Classics were taught in the exclusive English schools. Once you have recognized an adult fly as a caddis, you will have a pretty good idea about the form of the nymph – though, unlike the upwinged flies, there is a full life cycle that includes separate stages for larva and pupa. The nymphs all have the same general shape and behaviour with only one important exception – the tendency for some larvae to be free swimming rather than to build themselves a mobile home.

Caddis Larva

The larva is well known for its habit of constructing a case out of materials from the river or lake bed, such as gravel, sand, twigs or leaves. We have often marvelled when looking down a microscope at the way that particles of sand fit together in a beautiful mosaic. The caddis larva is indeed a master builder, cleverly joining the materials together and sealing the inside with its own secretion. The home is cunningly constructed to allow for future development, since the larva can lengthen its tapered case from the (wider) front to accommodate its growth. Although the construction of the case may give some clues to the species, the choice of materials will depend on what is available in the vicinity. John Goddard reports observing some caddis larvae in an aquarium that partially ate their homes, previously constructed from leaves, only to rebuild them out of various small shells. Lake species may favour lightweight materials to increase their mobility, whereas river species may build a gravel-based case to help anchor them against the current.

The cased larva moves very slowly in search of food by means of legs that extend with the head outside the front of the case.

Cased caddis larva.

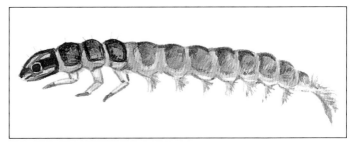

Free-swimming caddis larva.

The use of a short-fibred hackle at the front of any imitation is therefore very important. The larva can quickly retreat back into its case, but for all the trouble in construction, the case affords little protection against large predators. This is bad news for the caddis, good news for the trout and even better news for the nymph fisherman. So perhaps the free swimming species, which tend to be more common in running water, save themselves a lot of unnecessary effort.

Many fly dressers make good copies of the caddis case using shells, twigs and gravel on a long-shank hook. We have had quite a lot of success on the rivers by glueing sand over a coiled lead under-body. In order to get a better imitation of the prevailing natural insects on our favourite beat of the River Test, we coloured the sand a light olive green with a fibre-tip pen. When we experimented by adding a few differently coloured particles to the sand to improve the mosaic, Reggie reminded us – in his own subtle manner – that we might be getting carried away by exact imitation.

'Mmmm. Why don't you engrave c-a-d-d-i-s on the side just to make sure.'

'Sorry to have to tell you this, Reggie, but grayling can't read.'

'Mmmm. Maybe not where you've been fishing – but try the stretch by the school.'

The more impressionist imitations do, of course, work consistently. One of the most popular is the good old Stick Fly. It is simplicity itself to tie from peacock herl and a red game hackle, and is sufficiently general in its appearance to represent a wide range of bugs. The addition of a fluorescent green or red tag may not please the entomologist, but it certainly makes the trout aware of its presence.

You need to be patient to imitate a cased caddis properly in still water, because it moves so slowly at about an inch per minute. Retrieving an artificial fly correctly after a long cast should therefore take all day! This is obviously not practical, but it does reinforce the need to retrieve very slowly and perhaps to allow the fly to remain static for extended periods.

Although the majority of caddis larvae build cases, several important running water species spare themselves the effort. Much as we would like to avoid the terms, many anglers seem to prefer the classical names for the two principal genera. The free-swimming *Rhyacophila* are mostly green and prefer cool, fast-moving streams. *Hydropsyche*, which form nets to trap food at the entrance to their shelters on the river-bed, are more widely abundant and exist principally in shades of green and brown.

Apart from their curved appearance when moving, the bodies of the free-swimming caddis are not significantly different from those of the cased larva – it is just that they are not constrained and concealed. They are long, slim, clearly segmented and distinctively lighter underneath. The contrasting colour might suggest a representation by woven patterns. However, slimmer flies, such as the Czech nymphs which maintain contrast and segmentation by the use of a ribbed latex back, tend to be more consistent. Those wishing to simulate the eel-type motion of the natural larva may face quite a challenge, but the addition of a sparse, soft hackle will imitate the hard-working legs.

Whether cased or not, 'Genghis Khan' the caddis larva is a merciless carnivore. It will try to grab anything that happens to pass within reach of its powerful front mandibles, including other nymphs of twice its size. Quite a few corpses in our aquarium were the work of these rather unsavoury creatures.

Caddis or Sedge Pupa

Caddis pupa.

A week or two before emergence, the caddis larva becomes attached to a suitable underwater feature and encloses itself in a cocoon. The main features of the adult become progressively more evident during pupation through the skin, which is almost transparent. The colours therefore match those of the adult very closely, and include cream, green, orange, brown and black. The pupa swims in open water to emerge into the adult, although a few species emerge via reeds or any other obstacles that break the surface of the water. At this stage it is highly visible and provides a tasty mouthful, particularly if it is one of the large bright green or orange coloured species. It is therefore small wonder that fishing a caddis pupa is a deadly technique at the right time of year.

The pupa is quite a strange looking beast with two prominent dark eyes. The body is slightly arched and rather chunky over most of its length, with a pronounced tapering at the back end. The segmentation is not very obvious, and so the ribbing should not be overdone. The wing cases are about half as long as the body and point slightly downwards, thereby accentuating the effect of the arched profile. It is no surprise that manufacturers produce specially shaped hooks to create more realistic imitations, which happen to work very well for midge as well as caddis pupae. Although tucked underneath the body, the legs are easily visible, and the sturdy hair-lined middle pair act as efficient paddles for propelling it through the water. It can move quite quickly, which sometimes results in savage takes and splashy interceptions when close to the surface. The antennae are tucked under the body, although they may be wrapped round the abdomen or trail behind the pupa. In some cases, they are twice as long as the pupa itself.

The wing cases, legs and antennae are relevant when it comes to imitating the caddis pupa. Many artificial patterns have quite long hackles swept back along the sides and underneath of the hook to represent these appendages. The legendary Dr Bell, who was a pioneer of still-water nymph fishing in his local Blagdon reservoir, was responsible for an early successful pattern. Today, better flies exist from a simple Amber Nymph to Davy Wotton's sophisticated SLF Emerger.

Amber Nymph.

Weighted caddis pupa.

In rivers, a thin band of latex wrapped around the shank in slightly overlapping turns gives both translucency and realistic segmentation. It also maintains a compact profile that helps the pupa to sink, although due to its chunky nature, the caddis pupa lends itself very well to the addition of extra weight. During a rise, it is worth attaching the pupa a couple of feet behind a dry caddis. Rather than fishing the combination in a dead-drift, it is often more productive to work the dry or palmered caddis imitation to make an attention-grabbing disturbance of the surface that is characteristic of a skittering adult. Trout are just as likely to grab either fly.

For still waters, we prefer translucent furs because they are more suggestive of life. The body of the Amber Nymph incorporates a translucent fur that is not too bulky, but well teased out and ribbed with fine flat gold tinsel. A darker thorax of brown fur or peacock herl, for example, provides some enticing contrast. A soft, speckled brown partridge hackle gives a blurred picture of the brownish wing cases, antennae and light coloured legs.

AQUATIC MIDGE (CHIRONOMIDS)

Adult Midge

Aquatic midge belong to the *Diptera* order, which literally means two wings in ancient Greek. There are actually four, but the hind-wings are so minute as to be virtually non-existent. In everyday English, the descriptive terms of flat-winged or true flies are more common. There are over a hundred thousand species around the world, including a good number to which trout are quite partial. These include many well known insects such as house flies, crane flies, mosquitoes and dung flies.

Entomologically speaking, most aquatic midges of relevance to the fly fisherman belong to one rather insignificant genus called *Chironimus* in this enormous order of insects. Nevertheless, they form the staple diet of trout in many still waters throughout the world. They are also more common in rivers than many anglers realize, although the species are often considerably smaller. Sometimes the adults make a distinct buzzing noise, and this has led to most anglers in the UK referring to both the adults and nymphs routinely as buzzers. They are noted for emerging mostly at dawn and dusk, but there are healthy hatches right through the day on many waters. They vary considerably in size from microscopic dimensions to a length of about 25 mm. There is also a wide variation in colour, from a vivid orange through crimson to almost jet black – plus several shades of green and brown. There is so much similarity between the different species that you can easily rationalize your fly selection. It is arguably more important to have different patterns to exploit varying water conditions than it is to cover different species.

Of course, Wesley frowned on the use of the term 'buzzer', and would frequently correct anglers in their misuse of the terminology. He once gave the group a good telling-off, informing them that – at best – the term could only be applied to the adults, since he had never observed any such noises from the pupae.

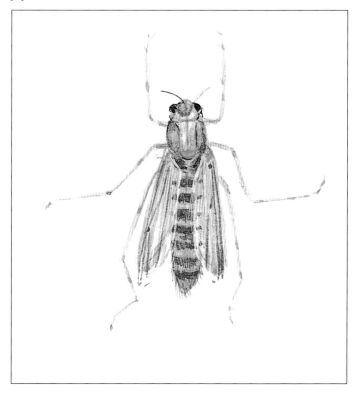

Adult midge.

'Mmmm – but they do when they're breaking wind', replied Reggie.

Humphrey seized on the experience to refer to chironomids as 'buzzards' for ever more in Wesley's presence, taking great delight in the thinly disguised irritation that it so obviously caused.

Denzil tried to debate the irrelevance of the issue, but after fifteen minutes of banging his head against a brick wall wished he had never opened his mouth.

And Alex simply referred to Wesley as something that sounded similar to 'you pompous, fat buzzer', and walked away.

The adults are easily recognisable by their short flat wings, which fold down the body. Other give-aways are the six splayed-out legs, two short antennae and the absence of a tail. The temptation is to include all these recognition points in an artificial pattern – but exact imitations are rarely necessary. One of the simplest flies to tie is Shipman's Buzzer, which is just a body with a couple of white tufts fore and aft as sighting points. The adult does not have these white tufts – and the pupa only has them at the front end – but it does not seem to bother the trout. It is also a good pattern to use when trout are mopping up shucks after a rise. Shipman's Buzzer takes impressionism just about as far as it can go.

Midge pupa shucks.

In lakes, Bob's Bit, which has a full hackle and simple feather fibres for the wings, works well as a dry fly in rippled water. Even though natural midges usually remain static before taking off, the pulling of a palmered wet fly may produce a lot of fish. Sometimes trout will turn on the palmer, whereas on other occasions they may reject it but then grab a more imitative nymph on the dropper below. The combination of a Soldier Palmer, Gerald's Midge and Cruncher, for example, is a deadly team when midges are on the menu. The additional resemblance of a Soldier Palmer to a Caddis makes it a trusted all-round pattern.

When the adult females return to the water, their bodies take on a hooked shape due to the weight of the eggs that they are carrying. This very familiar sight may be another reason why too many fly tiers are tempted to tie their midge pupa patterns right round the bend of a conventionally shaped hook. They are copying a shape that may be very attractive to fly-eating birds and bats, but which has little relevance to any hungry trout beneath the surface.

Midge Larva (Bloodworm)

The larvae hatch from eggs, where they wriggle around amongst aquatic plants or tunnel into the mud. They will exist at a range of depths from a few inches down to about 20 ft. Sufficient numbers venture out from the mud to make them worth imitating – and we have caught trout that were stuffed to the gills with them. Although the head section is quite detailed under a microscope, they may be represented as small worms with no features, other than perhaps faintly segmented bodies. The red bloodworm is the best known and most imitated form of the larva. It derives its name and colour from the haemoglobin in its blood, although green and light brown species are also common.

Bloodworm.

In observing these creatures, the most striking effect is their wriggling motion. It is therefore not surprising that some of the best patterns are those that incorporate as much of this movement as possible. Arthur Cove's Red or Green Diddy uses a coloured rubber band that is tied along the hook so that the curve of the band bends back from behind the hook over the shank. Another pattern employs a length of flexible floss. This is folded into two lengths that are twisted around each other to produce a segmented tail. One of the two strands at the front end is whipped to the shank of a wide-gape hook, before winding the other round it to form a short, profiled body. Although lacking any movement in the body, the San Juan Worm is an excellent general pattern that works well when trout are feeding on midge larvae.

Since the segmentation of bloodworms is not very pronounced, the ribbing must be fine. If the body material is in any way compressible, a tight winding of tying thread of a similar colour will produce a realistic effect. A heavyweight hook will help to get the fly down to the bottom, but any further weighting needs care to avoid making the body too bulky. It is best fished in a series of very short twitches to try to emulate the wriggling motion of the natural larva. In still water, a long leader on a floating line will give the best control, since the bloodworm will usually move slowly, close to the bottom of the lake or stream.

Midge Pupa

The pupal stage usually lasts for a few days before the final ascent to the surface. It is this ascent in open water that makes the pupa vulnerable to trout, and is the reason why it is generally more important to anglers than the larva. It moves slowly upwards in the water to hatch in the surface film, but sometimes in lakes it will move downwards again if it encounters a surface layer chilled by a cold wind. On such occasions, a slow-sinking line or a fast-sinking fly can be beneficial. Even during a rise, its ascent can be copied very successfully by casting the fly on a sinking line and then lifting it back towards the surface.

It is easy to recognize midge pupae by their white breather filaments, or tracheal gills, which extract oxygen from the water. These gills are attached to the head rather than the abdomen (as is the case for upwinged flies). Any soft white feather fibre, such as ostrich herl or the base of a cock or hen hackle, will provide a good imitation. The translucent shuck gives the pupa a similar colour to the adult, albeit somewhat subdued. This suggests a layer of a material such as polythene over the chosen colour of silk. Without due care, though, the overall effect can be rather dead, and the fly will not work nearly as well as teased out fur. It all comes back to impressionism in fly tying.

Midge pupa.

This does not mean that you should not coat the body of a pupa with glue or varnish to imitate the shuck case. A fine, ribbed silk body coated with Superglue produces a universally successful pattern. There is no right or wrong technique in the choice between fur and rigidly coated bodies, but there is a rule of thumb. The translucent fur-bodied pupae give their best in the brighter conditions close to the surface. The slim, varnished patterns sink more quickly for use in deep water.

The clearly segmented body suggests the importance of ribbing artificial patterns. However, eight turns of wire, although anatomically correct, can appear somewhat overdone – unless you use a very fine or rather drab ribbing material that is not too conspicuous. Patterns with just a few turns of wire – or fine oval or flat tinsel – all seem to work quite well enough.

The thorax, which tends to be characteristically dark, is often represented by materials such as peacock herl or mole's fur. A closer look will reveal small wing cases at the sides of the thorax. It is not essential to imitate them but, if applied properly, they will provide a good trigger point. Some patterns try too hard to imitate the wing cases with a very unrealistic, overdone effect. What is needed is a subtle addition of colour.

In the coated silk patterns, a thin strip of fluorescent or luminous material, tied down and across each side of the thorax, will glow strikingly yet realistically from under the coating of glue. Towards the evening, white shows up better. Fur patterns may benefit from the simple but effective addition of an orange thorax or small Jungle Cock feathers. Jungle Cock is an impressionist's dream, and the trout seem to love it. Our own Caretaker is an excellent general pattern, which works for midge pupae as well as for the emerging nymphs of some upwinged flies.

A tiny amount of the same white feathers that copy the breather filaments will suggest the white-tinged tail that helps a

pupa to move through the water. This is too often overdone in the mistaken belief that the breather filaments exist at the tail as well as the head. Nevertheless, such patterns will still take their share of trout as shown most pointedly – albeit as a dry fly – by Shipman's Buzzer.

Last, but by no means least, there is the body itself. The overriding objective, whether using fur, silk or whatever, is to keep it slim. It is possible to create some excellent imitations using the modern flexible flosses. Two differently coloured strands, such as claret and green, are wrapped around the hook in a single layer from the tail end under tension. The two strands need to be wound together (but not twisted round each other) in touching turns to produce a flat ribbed body with a very natural contrast. Reducing the tension towards the front of the fly on a tacky hook produces a gradual tapering effect. Alternatively, a single winding of green-olive or golden-olive flexible floss on top of a black or red silk body will give a realistic segmentation. In this case, a coat of Superglue or nail varnish will help to blend the materials and colours together.

When swimming through water, the pupa's body moves from a curved to a straight posture. For this reason, the use of some sedge or grub-shaped hooks will improve a pattern considerably – but check the hooking characteristics before making your selection. A rigid, abruptly curved nymph appears to be somewhat unnatural, and it is preferable to have no curvature at all rather than too much. A sproat bend is a suitable choice for conventional hooks, since its curvature is relatively gentle.

A buzzer nymph needs to be fished very slowly to imitate the natural, either with a figure-of-eight retrieve or by a long draw of the line. During a hatch the trout are invariably looking towards the surface, so any heavyweight hook will quickly sink below them. In running water, a relatively heavy pattern may be essential to get the fly down just a few inches, but still water demands the lightest of hooks during a rise.

One of our oldest direct imitations is the Perfection Buzzer. It incorporates the key points of the natural in a subdued manner, which raises very few alarm bells to the trout. The body is a very sparse dubbing of the dark fur from the root of a hare's ear on a fine wire size 12 hook, ribbed with a few turns of fine gold oval tinsel. This blends into a mole fur thorax. The sparse white breather filaments come from the fluffy base of a white cock or hen hackle. It has proved itself time and time again in taking many a fine residential specimen, including a magnificent 7¼ lb brown trout for JD from Chew Valley Lake which fought for 35 minutes.

Emerging Midge

Before hatching into an adult, the pupa hangs enticingly in the surface film. At first it is usually vertical, but it then adopts a more horizontal posture with the thorax just breaking through the surface before splitting down the centre. One of the most striking features among some species is the transitory orange appearance of the wings as they emerge from the thorax. Trout are naturally attracted by light at the red end of the spectrum, and any appearance of red or orange in the natural fly should be fully exploited. This is probably a reason for the success of

Emerging midge pupae.

our Gerald's Midge. In addition, it has a long tail that gives some semblance of a shuck.

In rough or broken water the nymphs can emerge relatively quickly, and the trout will be looking for them a foot or two down as well as on the surface. Retrieving them back slowly through the water is then a fairly straightforward affair. In calm conditions, the emerging pupae become trapped in the surface film for some time. This presents easy pickings for the trout, which will be focusing their concentration on the top few inches of the water. Artificial nymphs therefore need to remain close to the surface, and flies such as Gerald's Midge require the lightest weight hooks possible. An excellent tactic is to place the lightweight fly on the middle dropper between two dry flies so that is can remain stationary just below the surface. Alternatively, you can tease out the thorax and treat it with floatant to suspend the top of the fly in the surface film with the vertical abdomen submerged.

There are purpose-made emergers that are better at staying afloat. These are the patterns that incorporate materials, such as CDC and Plastazote, to grip the surface film. Midge pupae are perfect for this application, because their slim bodies help to ensure that the fly cocks vertically into position after alighting on

CDC variations.

the water. It is only necessary to attach some forward-projecting CDC or a foam ball to the front end of your favourite buzzer pattern to represent the vertical stage of emergence. The application of CDC as a conventional wing covers the final horizontal stage.

It is possible to improve the original tying of a Suspender to make it more buzzer-like. Black Plastazote, which is more buoyant and durable than Ethafoam, gives a reasonable representation of the dark thorax. It then resembles our Perfection Buzzer, providing you use a smaller ball diameter than for the conventional Suspender. Our diameters range from 4 mm on a size 12 to 2 mm on a size 16, and always incorporate the lightest weight hooks. These factors are essential to prevent the ball appearing too unnatural. For those who wish to be more technical, the volume of the Plastazote should be nearly ten times that of the steel in the hook to keep the fly just afloat.

STONEFLIES (*PLECOPTERA*)

Adult Stonefly

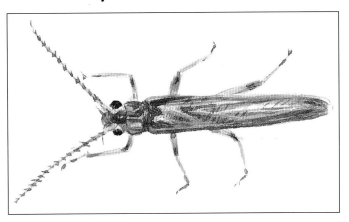

Adult stonefly.

This order of flies comprises about 3,000 different species world-wide. The adult's hard, shiny wings partially wrap around the body in many species. The four wings stack so neatly that there is no way that even the most suspicious trout would be able to differentiate them. Thus, only a single wing should be necessary in any artificial pattern.

As a rule, trout do not feed extensively on adult stoneflies, which on average contribute less than 5% to their diet. There are, of course, localized exceptions, such as the Western Golden Stones and the giant Salmon Fly of the western United States at the end of June. In the northern English rivers, stonefly imitations, such as the Needle Fly, bring consistent success. But on alkaline waters that support a whole host of insect life, the gourmet trout tend to be more accustomed to mayflies, caddis or midges in preference. It is in the more acidic or high altitude waters that stoneflies become more important food items, since they tend to be more tolerant of hostile environments.

Stoneflies prefer cool, running water and therefore often exist side by side with the stone-clinging upwinged flies. They emerge by crawling on to waterside stones, and at this time trout may follow them right to the edge of the water. Some of them lose their footing, so it is often worth fishing a static adult in mid-stream. However, since emergence takes place out of the water, the most important adult to the angler is the female as she returns to lay her eggs. The eggs are already attached to the outside of her body as she alights or crawls on to the water, and she then flutters across the surface to detach them. This is a good natural trigger point for attracting a trout's attention, which is easy to exploit by twitching the dry fly.

Stonefly Nymph

Stonefly nymph.

Large stonefly nymphs are very juicy morsels to any hungry trout. Although they do not ascend to the surface to emerge, they quite frequently become dislodged from stones in the heavy currents. A dead-drift is therefore a very productive tactic. We have mentioned the giant Salmon Fly (or Pteronarcys Nymph) of the western USA, but other varieties that grow to a fair size are common throughout the world. We have come across European specimens of 30 mm in length, excluding the two tails and two antennae which are all typically half as long again.

The bodies have a very stark profile, with no softening from tracheal gills or hair-fringed tails. There is often a great deal of contrast between the dark top and lighter under-side. These features make them ideal for representation by woven nymphs. The thorax is about the same length as the abdomen, and is quite prominent in having three clearly distinct segments, with a pair of sturdy legs attached to each. The segmentation and legs present obvious recognition features. Although other insects also have three segments, you would have to try very hard to pick them out – and so would a trout. The segments vary from being spherical to almost half-moon shaped, and are quite similar in size and shape to the head. Stonefly nymphs tend to have a substantial body weight (presumably as a survival aid in the strong currents), so the addition of lead is a more integral part of the dressing than for many other aquatic creatures.

In spite of the scope for tying realistic imitations, simple patterns using fine chenille over a lead under-body can be very successful indeed – providing they include a set of rubber legs. These seem to be the most important recognition points of all due to their enticing movement in the water. Suitable varieties

Artificial stonefly nymphs.

are those that are soft for mobility and translucent to suggest life. A mottled chenille, such as brown and olive green, gives a little more subtlety to the a body than a single colour. With care over varying the tension, it is possible to align the mottling of some chenilles to achieve the effect of segmentation. A 3X long-shank size 8 hook is by no means too large. It is a good idea to tie a small Pheasant Tail or Hare's Ear nymph about eighteen inches behind it as a hedge-bet tactic. The Prince Nymph will imitate a stonefly as well as providing a more general pattern for a wide variety of waters.

OTHER AQUATIC FOOD
Shrimp or Scud

Shrimp.

Europeans call them shrimps, Americans talk of scuds, and in-tellectuals around the world refer to them as *Gammarus*. Trout, irrespective of nationality, treat them as very accessible and nourishing food. During many of our expeditions to rivers for collecting nymphs, they would outnumber all the other species by quite a large margin. It is therefore not surprising that they form a staple diet for trout in many areas. They prefer water with a fairly high oxygen content, but can be prolific in still water as well as in rivers and brooks. Their coloration is normally rather drab and ranges from a fawn grey to olive green.

Some of the Irish Loughs, for example, hold such enormous numbers of shrimp that the trout eat virtually nothing else and remain on the bottom for virtually all the year. They have no need to look to the surface, and such waters have sometimes gained a poor reputation. But beneath the surface lurk large numbers of massive wild brown trout that have one weakness – a large dry *Ephemera* mayfly. This results in the most fantastic dry fly fishing for a couple of weeks each year at the beginning of June.

To the river angler, *Gammarus* is a friend indeed. First, it is present in great numbers in many different waters. Second, due to its convenient shape, it is easy to create a heavily weighted yet natural looking specimen that will sink quickly in fast currents. Third, it exists in temptingly large sizes in the range 10-20 mm. Very often we have observed a male carrying the smaller female underneath his body. This is a doubly nutritious meal for any trout, and an indication that the fur body can be teased out a great deal to form a very chunky specimen. Finally, it sometimes exhibits a pink-red hue – a colour to which trout respond very positively. This occurs when the female carries her brightly coloured eggs, or during the late stages of disease. Under some conditions, they will take on a similar colour when they die – which is when they will drift in front of the trout. An artificial shrimp should therefore qualify as a key pattern in any fly collection. The tying of one of our own favourites, the Scrimp, appears in the chapter on *Great Fly Patterns*.

Damsels and Dragons

Damsel and dragonflies are prevalent in still waters throughout the world, although occasionally they are found in the slower-moving reaches of some streams.

Adult Damsel and Dragonflies

For any budding entomologist, both damsel and dragonflies belong to the *Odonata* order of insects. You would be forgiven for expecting this to refer to the long bodies or characteristic wings. In reality, it refers to the teeth or mandibles, which the larva will use to grab any unfortunate victim that happens to come within range. In common with the caddis larva, it is another Genghis Khan of the sub-surface world.

Adult damsel and dragonflies may appear to be similar at first glance, but there are two dead give-aways that make identification easy. First, the two pairs of wings are of equal size on damsels, but quite different on dragons. This may be largely academic, since it is not so obvious from below the water. The second difference is far more relevant. Damsels hold their wings virtually closed over the top of their bodies when at rest, whereas a dragonfly's wings remain splayed out. Trout therefore see a different profile between the two sub-orders, and artificial patterns should take this into account.

Life cycle of damselfly.

Trout rarely feed on adult dragonflies, but this may be at least partially due to difficulties in catching these jet-propelled insects. Anglers are much more familiar with the brightly coloured damsels, which we have observed in various shades of blue, green and red. The size, which is typically from 20 to 30 mm, provides a real feast which will enable trout to grow quite rapidly.

It is easy to dress the long, slender body of an adult damsel on a long-shank size 10 hook. A combination of bright blue fur and a stretched pearly rib works well for the blue species that is prevalent in the UK. Since the wings fold neatly on top of the fly, there is little need for too much detail and CDC does very nicely. However, there is one little problem in that a damsel's front legs keep its body well clear of the surface. It is for this reason that many patterns have a stiff conventional hackle. Some fly dressers tie a hackle at the back as well, but this does little for the natural appearance – even if it does hold the body at the right aspect. A better solution is to tie the body on a stalk of material, such as braided nylon or specially produced foam extensions, away from the hook. This is not easy to do, and may result in a lot of failures and possibly a few frustrated utterances. But if it works, it is the sort of challenge that really enriches the sport.

As the female damselfly re-emerges from the water after laying her eggs, the attendant male, who has been waiting patiently, plucks her from the surface. We have observed brown trout that have become totally pre-occupied with these paired adults as the male carries the female a couple of inches over the water, ignoring any dry fly on the surface – whether artificial or natural. On such occasions, the only hope of modest success is to cast a fly immediately to a trout that has just risen in the hope of catching it off balance.

Dragonfly Nymphs

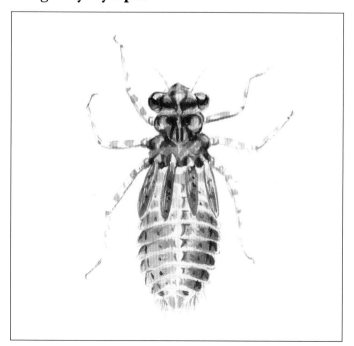

Dragonfly nymph.

Dragonfly nymphs are rather chunky in both body and thorax. They reach lengths of up to 75 mm in some parts of the world. Their colours are rather dull, blending in well with the surroundings to provide camouflage against predators and intended victims alike. They are the arch-villains of the sub-surface world, which will grab unsuspecting prey – even tiny fish – by extending a pair of strong claws from the head. Although they can move in fast bursts, they tend to crawl slowly among the mud and stones for most of their existence. When the time arrives to emerge into adulthood, most species will crawl along the bottom towards the shore or up some vegetation to the surface. You should fish an artificial pattern as slowly and as close to the bottom as conditions will allow. There are several specific patterns, but a bulky version of the trusty old Stick Fly will often work as well as many more exact copies.

Damsel Nymphs

Damsel nymphs are slimmer and more graceful in movement and colour, although they too can be demons of the deep with their powerful front claws. They spend much of their time clinging to sub-surface features such as reeds, and we have observed their bodies exhibiting a range of shades from golden-olive to dark green in the same locality to blend in with the gravel or weeds respectively. In spite of this natural camouflage, evolution has not been so kind to them. In order to emerge into the adult, many species have to swim in open water just under the surface towards the land in broad daylight. They are strange-looking nymphs as they wriggle their way towards the shore, and it is a fascinating experience to watch them transform into the adult on the bankside vegetation or even on a wader.

At the same time, very splashy rises occur as the trout feast on the less fortunate individuals that are never going to reach maturity. There is often such a commotion that it is easy to assume that the trout are feeding on anything other than nymphs. Small fish, crane flies, adult damselflies and large mayflies may all be the suspected victims. This stresses the importance of careful observation and perhaps some systematic trial and error.

Artificial damsel nymph.

A key feature for a damsel nymph is the long, slim, tapering body. Irrespective of the bright colours of the adults, the nymphs usually exhibit less exciting shades of olive. A size 10 or 12 long-shank hook is ideal for representing specimens that are about to emerge into adults, but there will be plenty of much smaller, immature nymphs living amongst the weeds. In New Zealand's Lake Otamangakau, for example, where thousands of quite large adults were present, we found the most successful all-round size for the nymph to be a normal shank size 10. One of the guides, Graham Dean, gave us a simple gold-headed pattern with a matching marabou body and tail, which had been consistently effective, although the best colour varied in different years from brown to olive green.

A lightweight hook is more suitable for a nymph on its journey to the shore, but extra weight may be necessary in flowing water or for getting down to weed beds. The three tails, which are actually tracheal gills, and the six legs are all prominent features with the same colour as the body. Three mobile marabou fibres give a good representation of the tail, although a bunch of hackle fibres also works in giving a blurred image of motion. The legs are quite prominent, but we avoid the temptation to use thick and hence rigid materials. A soft olive green hackle, such as dyed partridge, or simply a teased-out fur thorax, brings the fly to life.

Some anglers prefer articulated patterns to enhance the wriggling motion, but this seems to be one of the many good intentions that have limited success in practice. The natural nymph moves with such a fast and pronounced wiggle that you cannot possibly hope to imitate the effect with a simple articulation. A short body with a long marabou tail is a better option. It is again a question of balance between impressionism and the dangers of insufficiently exact imitation. Several authors suggest retrieving the fly with long slow pulls, but we much prefer a slow figure of eight that is more in line with the natural movement of the nymph.

Corixa

This is one example of a trout fly that keeps its Latin name in preference to the rather long-winded English term of lesser water boatman. There are lots of different species, but trout are rarely selective on the basis of minor details. It is simply necessary to focus on a small number of general key features. Generally, corixae inhabit still waters rather than rivers.

Corixae breath air rather than taking in oxygen from the water. They therefore prefer shallow water and margins so that they can easily travel to the surface to replenish their air supply. This suggests that a corixa pattern should be a serious consideration when fishing in shallow water. It also gives the obvious clue of where to look for a concentration of fish should you suspect corixae of being a likely item on the menu.

Although anglers classify them as nymphs, corixa are capable of flight, which enables them to migrate – often in large numbers – from one region of water to another. Prominent wing cases, which cover the back of the fly, should be a key feature of any pattern. They are usually quite markedly patterned, with brown, green and yellow being the most common colours. The mottled fibres from a cock or hen pheasant centre tail make an ideal material for this purpose – although most trout seem to find brown tapestry silk, which is more robust, acceptable for both the back and legs

Corixa.

Corixae maintain their oxygen supply by trapping a bubble of air between the wings and body. They are completely exposed near the surface away from the weed bed, and have to move very quickly during this manoeuvre. They are more vulnerable during the descent from the surface, since the newly acquired bubble slows them down by making them more buoyant. Thus a trout may follow a corixa to the surface before making its interception, and will be pre-occupied with this single specimen. This explains one of the most important, yet neglected, aspects of fishing the artificial pattern, which is to avoid covering a rising fish. Keep your head down, resist the temptation and retrieve patiently for long periods.

Although species may vary in colour from white to cream or yellow, they will often exhibit a pronounced silvery tinge due to the trapped bubble of air. Many patterns therefore incorporate a white, cream or yellow body with a prominent silver ribbing.

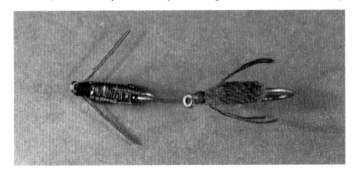

Artificial corixae.

Some of the more successful tyings dispense with the normal body colours altogether and just rely on the silver, because it is the glistening bubble of air that is the most striking feature. The Silver Invicta, with its hen pheasant wing that resembles the mottled wing case, is an excellent general pattern that will often take its share of corixa-feeding trout.

Many patterns tend to be rather too plump. A flat body gives a more realistic impression as it shimmers from side to side through the water. It is therefore not surprising that woven nymphs can be very suitable imitations. Davy Wotton's creation, comprising a weave of brown silk and silver tinsel over a flat lead under-body, has scored consistently over the years. Because of its added weight, it works best in 'deep' water, bearing in mind that for corixae this is seldom much more than 3 ft. Short sharp pulls seem to be the best way to exploit the shimmering effect.

We have enjoyed some of our best corixa fishing in water that is no more than 1 ft deep. In such conditions, a weighted fly is completely inappropriate since it hits the bottom too quickly. The under-body should therefore incorporate strips of silk in place of lead wire. Although woven patterns look the part, a simple body of flat silver tinsel with a pheasant tail back is usually adequate. This pattern should be retrieved in short twitches, separated by a couple of seconds.

Sometimes, a dry corixa pattern turns out to be more effective than a slow sinking wet imitation. An excellent fly for these occasions is a small CDC 'emerger' in the prevailing colour with a silver rib. Paradoxically, the shuttlecock versions seem to work better than those incorporating a flat CDC back, even though the latter would appear to be a better imitation of the natural. In stronger winds, you may need to use more conventional dry flies that will not become submerged under the waves. Alternatively, a Suspender on the point will keep a couple of lightweight nymphs on droppers high in the water. The only problem with this method is that the Suspender needs quite a large ball of Plastazote to stay afloat, and although it will raise a lot of fish, it may hook very few.

The two hind legs are prominent and heavily lined with fine hairs. Many patterns employ two quite bulky fibres, which are tied in at the head of the fly. These include mallard grey wing, pheasant tail and goose biots. Other patterns simply rely on a light coloured cock or hen beard hackle. We have tried all these variants, and none stands out as being significantly better than the others. It is more important to concentrate on the other features.

Finally, it is also productive to imitate a natural corixa when it is inching around the bottom. The textbook method suggests a weighted pattern that is moved very slowly with, for example, a figure-of-eight retrieve. But if you are lucky enough to find corixae in an area that is free from too much weed growth, there is a more deadly method as first proposed by Dave Collyer. It avoids any weighting and uses instead a fly with a buoyant white Plastazote under-body. The fly is twitched along the bottom on a six inch leader attached to a sinking line. The built-in buoyancy makes the fly bob up and down in the reverse way to a sink and draw. It moves downwards on the 'draw' from the sinking line resting on the bottom, and upwards during what would have been the 'sink'. Furthermore, it will always remain just where it is needed – close to the bottom.

We cannot begin to estimate how many trout have fallen victim to this type of method, since it has an added dimension over and above imitation of the natural. Trout seem to become mesmerized by buoyant flies that bob up and down beneath the surface, whatever the details of the tying. It is exactly the same for Suspenders and Boobies. Yes, in case you are starting to wonder, this is still a book about fly fishing. We did not invent the names!

Daphnia

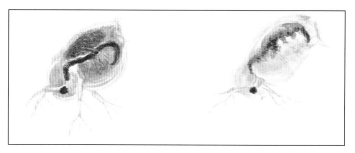

Daphnia.

Daphnia are small water fleas that are prolific in many still waters throughout the world. They conglomerate in large blooms that provide fish with a ready made soup of nutritious morsels. Once trout have located a daphnia bloom, they will feed on them avidly and put on a great deal of weight in the process. It is easy to tell whether a trout is feasting on daphnia, since there will usually be quite a few of the little fellows sticking to the inside of its throat. If so, it is a pointer to a specific set of fly patterns and a different set of rules for locating the fish.

It is, of course, not practical to imitate a single water flea. Even if it were possible on a size 30 hook, the chances of it being noticed amongst the millions of other daphnia would be minute. This is a classic case of needing a fly that stands out from the crowd – and fortunately, daphnia-feeding trout are usually only too willing to oblige. Although totally preoccupied, they are easily distracted and will often grab anything that takes their eye. They tend to be quite catholic in their choice of an artificial fly, but are more likely to notice something that incorporates bright colours – such as fluorescent green or orange. Daphnia often exhibit either a slight orange or green hue, and on occasions we have noticed that trout have a preference for patterns of the prevailing colour. This occurs in spite of the artificial fly being orders of magnitude brighter and larger than the tiny natural creatures.

If you intend taking no prisoners, a large fluorescent attractor pattern will be much more visible amongst the blooms than more conventional flies. The orange Vindaloo and the green and white Light Bulb are both killing patterns, but there are times when trout will avoid excessively bright flies altogether. More modest attractors such as the Christmas Tree – in spite of its name – therefore tend to be more consistent. Sometimes, trout will grow wary of even this trusty old pattern, after a bombardment from large numbers of anglers, and require more sophisticated flies. A normal shank size 10 is the perfect all-round size for this purpose, since it is neither too large to rouse suspicions nor too small to be missed in the daphnia soup. The main trick is to make sure that it incorporates that little bit of colour. Our own favourites are Dave Grove's Monty, Dunkeld, Clifton and a Green or Orange Thorax Pheasant Tail. We will quite often fish one or two of these patterns on a dropper with a more flamboyant attractor on the point.

There is an alternative approach when the trout become suspicious. Instead of toning down the flies, it is sometimes better to use a single pattern on a very long leader. Spooked trout are just as likely to associate danger with three flies, having a co-ordinated movement at the end of a thick fly line, as they are with a bright pattern. It is worth mentioning that Jeremy Herrmann won the coveted Brown Bowl – awarded for the highest weight in a Home International – on a single, highly fluorescent Light Bulb and a 30 ft leader!

In general, the main skill in catching daphnia-feeding trout is simply the location. Daphnia are largely at the mercy of the currents and will normally end up towards the down-wind shore. A strong wind overnight can completely change the hot spots from one end of a lake to the other, since the trout will automatically follow the food supply. The effect can be dramatic and very rewarding to those who have done their homework. Those who have not realized the significance of the food supply will waste several hours fishing barren water on the basis of yesterday's information.

Location is a three-dimensional challenge since daphnia will move up and down in the water at a moment's notice. Bright sunlight will send them down, particularly if the water clarity is high. As soon as clouds block the sun, however, they may move right up to the surface. An embarrassingly large percentage of fishermen will interpret the sudden movement of trout as a hatch of insects and will waste the precious opportunity with dry flies and emergers. We can all be caught out by this phenomenon, so it is important to consider the possibility of daphnia whenever conventional flies fail to work. It is often possible, with a pair of Polaroids, to see the blooms in the water.

A perfect illustration of the need for accurate location arose in the final of a major competition in the basin area of Rutland Water. About 20 boats spent the day there under tough conditions, with each angler averaging just under three fish. Late in the day, Neil West and Michael Heritage spotted a concentrated plume of daphnia about 6 ft below the surface, and concentrated on positioning the boat so that they could cast right into it. Every time a fly landed right in the narrow plume, a fish took. They succeeded in landing 20 rainbows in under three hours. (In spite of this, the prize for the day went to Tony Curtis who caught a magnificent brown trout of over nine pounds.)

One of the favourite angling jokes is to talk about upwind daphnia. The daphnia in some lakes are so strong, apparently, that they can actually swim up-wind. The irony of this story is that the concept of upwind daphnia is not as far-fetched as one might imagine. In bright conditions they may be lying very deep. The wind blows the surface water to the downwind shore, but this has to be accompanied by a movement of deeper water in the opposite direction – otherwise all the water would pile up on one side of the lake! So under these conditions, the daphnia will actually move upwind. Their location in bright, windy weather may therefore need a little more care and a lot more luck.

When using a sinking line, various speeds of retrieve from fast to dead slow will work well. Surface feeders are usually more likely to turn towards a bright or bushy pattern that is moved quickly past their noses. This can provide great sport as a bow wave follows the fly across the surface.

Snails

A sophisticated dressing for an aquatic snail once appeared in the angling press. Its originator had become an acknowledged expert on small waters by using it almost exclusively. He had the knack of being able to locate rising fish that every one else had seemingly missed. He was also famous for his large cigar, but eventually people started noticing that it was never lit. It turned out to be a blowpipe for propelling trout pellets into the water. There were quite a few red faces from anglers who realized that they too had been catching trout on an excellent imitation of *Pelletus vulgaris*.

Snail.

Snails are present in many rivers and lakes in considerable numbers and provide a ready source of food. Trout will often find them by grubbing around the reeds or stones. Occasionally, snails will migrate to the surface in large numbers, where they will cling to the underside of the film in the same way that terrestrial species will fix themselves to a wall. When this occurs, trout may feed on them exclusively – but it is not a frequent occurrence, and many anglers do not realize what is happening. The clues can be gentle sips at the surface, as if taking a spinner, or a head and shoulders movement as if taking emerging duns or midges. To make matters worse, the feeding may take place in the early morning or evening when there is a hatch of such insects. Every thought process will be targeted towards imitating these observable flies rather than towards the humble, unseen snail.

We cannot give any hard and fast rules on how to spot when this is happening. It is most likely to occur in high to late summer when oxygen levels in the water are low. The only advice we can give, therefore, is to keep the snail in mind at this time of year. Do not wait too long before giving it a try when conventional flies have failed to tempt a rising fish. These migrations to the surface can last for several days. So once you have identified the phenomenon, you are likely to enjoy very good sport for some time.

The size of migrating snails can be difficult to determine, since you are unlikely to see them without looking down directly from above the water. Species vary from less than 3 mm to a massive 60 mm, though the largest that we have observed trout devouring is about 20 mm. If in doubt, start with a small pattern on a size 16 hook, which will not raise any alarm signals, and work upwards in size.

The most important feature of any artificial pattern is its ability to float low in the water, since the natural snails cling upside down to the bottom of the surface film. Materials, such as cork or Plastazote, trimmed to the right shape, provide perfectly adequate representations with the added convenience of never requiring treatment with floatants. However, they need some additional weight to compensate for the excess buoyancy, so that no more than a very small fraction is above the surface.

TERRESTRIAL INSECTS

The importance of terrestrial insects depends to a considerable extent on the water quality. If it is acidic, or low in aquatic fly life for any other reason, then land-based insects may form a substantial fraction of the food chain. Even in the rich and hallowed spring creeks and chalk-streams, trout will sometimes become preoccupied with insects that are blown on to the water by accident. On many occasions we have observed them completely ignoring the most tempting and aristocratic upwinged flies in favour of very ordinary little ants or beetles.

You should, therefore, always carry a balanced selection of terrestrial flies. Although two adjacent rivers or lakes may contain significantly different aquatic species, the same terrestrial insects are likely to exist over a wide area. It is usually worth a visit to the local tackle shops to look at the popular artificial flies that are specific to the region, but there are a few patterns worth carrying everywhere. Our collection is not totally comprehensive, but it does provide a good starting point. It includes ants, beetles and non-specific flies to cover a multitude of different insects. There are also a few specific patterns that we expect to encounter on our travels, such as grasshoppers for North America and cicadas for New Zealand.

There is one ingredient to success that dry fly fishermen often overlook. Some terrestrial insects, although trapped by the surface film, remain supported by their legs clear of the water. In other words, they maintain a high profile. The same is, of course, true of most adult aquatic insects, but there is an essential difference. Just prior to the adult stage, aquatic insects will have broken through the surface during the process of emergence – so the trout will expect to see them below and within the surface film, as well as resting on the top. Thus, an aquatic pattern may take its share of fish, irrespective of whether it is clear of the surface or partially submerged.

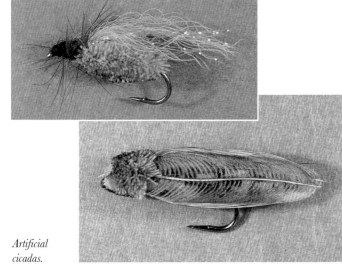

Artificial cicadas.

For this reason, those used to dry fly fishing on rivers or lakes with plenty of aquatic fly life sometimes come unstuck when tackling unfamiliar 'terrestrial' waters. Trout close to the bank from which the insects have been blown may expect their food to be stationed clear of the surface film. Expressions of disbelief abound as to why a beautifully tied Heather Fly, with its orange and black legs meticulously impersonated, performs significantly worse than a 'common or garden' Bibio. Apart from any other factors, such as impressionism versus exact imitation, a Bibio, when treated with floatant, sits proud of the surface on its palmered hackle tips.

Trapped terrestrial insects may try to break free of the surface, so trout will be used to seeing some form of commotion and a twitched dry fly may prove to be effective. After a while, the struggling insects will become progressively submerged. At this point, patterns that penetrate the surface film, as well as conventional wet flies, will often take their share of fish. We must also mention that many terrestrial insects, such as large grasshoppers, do become partially submerged after landing on the water.

Flying Ants

From middle to late summer, ants develop wings as part of the breeding cycle. Although terrestrial in nature, large numbers will often alight on water and remain trapped. On some rivers and lakes, they will arrive predictably at the same time

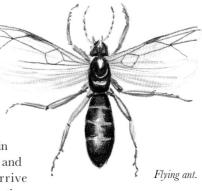

Flying ant.

each year and provide superb fishing for long periods of the day. Elsewhere, years may elapse between occurrences until they become all but forgotten. Being terrestrial and mobile, they can arrive on any stretch of water, and sometimes when least expected. When they do appear, trout will feast on them – often to the exclusion of everything else. We have encountered this on lakes and on the hallowed chalk-streams. Charles Jardine has enjoyed a lot of success with para-ants on Henry's Fork, where the aquatic insect life is so rich that the fish live in a 'bug soup'. It is therefore important to carry a couple of patterns in the fly box just in case, because an incorrect imitation is unlikely to work. To the trout, ants are like caviar.

As well as sometimes arriving unexpectedly, ants may re-semble small upwinged flies to the casual or preconditioned observer. It is therefore not surprising that many fishermen make the wrong diagnosis and become totally perplexed and frustrated. This illustrates the importance of routinely scooping up flies from the surface for a closer inspection when artificial patterns are failing to tempt any trout. Once you have made the correct diagnosis, success should be relatively straightforward. Imitations on a short-shank size 16 hook in black or cinnamon will cover most eventualities.

Difficulties do arise, however, when ants are present on the surface in large numbers. This happens predominantly on still water since there is no current to carry them away. Trout prefer to feed by expending the minimum amount of energy. Thus, since their quarry is not going to escape, they will often cruise slowly across the surface with their mouths gaping open. This 'vacuum cleaner mode' can really test a fisherman's skill and patience, since the surface-feeding trout have a tiny window of vision and frequently change direction. This phenomenon also occurs with several other types of insect such as caenis. We first observed it with ants on a small, crystal-clear lake in Montana where we had been advised by a local guide to be watchful for callibaetis. On this occasion we managed to catch a few good trout by avoiding the 'vacuum cleaners' altogether, concentrating instead on the fish that were rising in a more conventional manner. Even this approach required accurate casting and a good deal of patience.

Beetles

Beetle showing iridescence.

Beetles can be either aquatic or terrestrial. The former may be present at any depth, but even wind-blown terrestrial species often remain fairly low in the surface film. Although many different species exist, our standard fly box contains only a single black beetle in sizes ranging from size 12 to 16. Rather than using a straightforward black dubbing, our Iridescent Terror incorporates a mix of 75% black seal's fur (or substitute) and 25% dark green SLF. This provides a very realistic sheen that many natural beetles and flies exhibit. For variation, it is not a bad idea to incorporate a little red, since it occurs naturally in some species and provides a trigger point.

Dung Flies

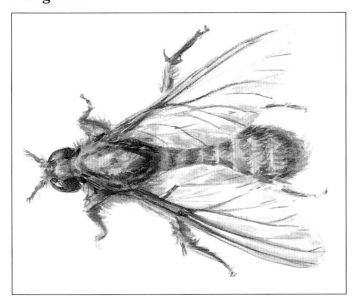

Dung fly.

Artificial dung fly.

Any water surrounded by grazing sheep or cattle in the British Isles is likely to see its share of dung flies, which will be blown onto the surface in windy conditions. We have never found that trout take too much notice of the precise details. (*'Mmmm', said Reggie, 'perhaps it's the smell that stops a close inspection.'*) Thus, general patterns, such as a golden-olive Bob's Bit or an Amber Hopper (UK), will usually work acceptably well. When fishing sub-surface, it is worth putting an appropriate wet fly, such as an Invicta, somewhere on the leader to represent the drowned insect.

Crane Flies

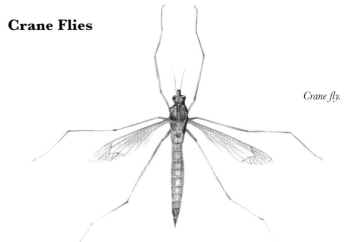

Crane fly.

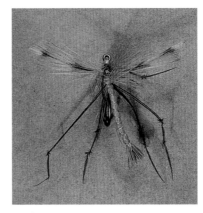

Artificial crane fly.

Crane flies, which are nicknamed 'Daddy-Long-Legs' in the UK, are familiar to many as the large, gangly creatures that often arrive in large numbers during late summer. They are poor fliers, and often get blown onto the water where they sometimes make quite a commotion in their fruitless efforts to escape. When this happens, you can capitalize on an artificial pattern that presents a small banquet to a hungry trout with added attraction through disturbance of the surface. Some patterns concentrate on representing the natural insect and may be fished statically, while others incorporate stiff hackles or rigid horse hair fibres to advertise the fly's presence when moved across the surface. A Hopper (UK) with its dangling, knotted legs will often provide an adequate imitation.

The larvae vary from being semi to fully aquatic. Gardeners in the UK are familiar with the leather-jackets which inhabit damp areas of ground, while other species live in shallow or muddy margins. There are also many species that thrive in rivers and lakes and feature strongly in the trout's diet – especially in the western USA. Since they can be up to three inches long, patterns such as the Fur Crane Fly Larva (or any large, curved worm-like pattern) are sometimes extremely successful when fished close to the bottom.

Although crane flies pupate outside the water, this often takes place in the

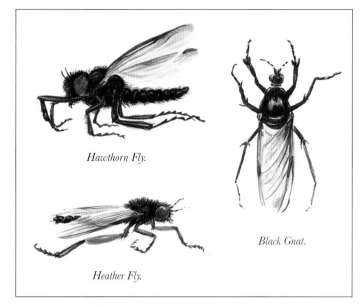

Hawthorn Fly.

Black Gnat.

Heather Fly.

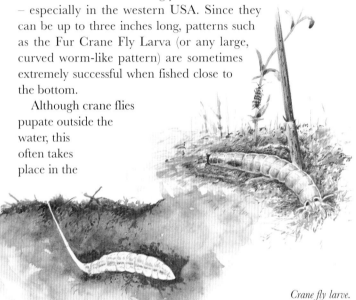

Crane fly larve.

muddy banks just above the surface. Some may pupate in the river bank below the water-line, or some may fall into the water – but whatever the explanation, trout grab an artificial pupa at the right time of year as something they definitely recognize. The fantastic fishing provided by the adults and pupae is one reason why late summer trips to Montana have become an almost annual event for JD and Andrew Donaldson.

Assorted Black Flies

Many terrestrial flies are predominantly black. These include Black Gnats, Hawthorn Flies, Heather Flies, House Flies and numerous other species. General flies in a variety of sizes often outperform the more precise imitations. Successful dry patterns include the Black Hopper (UK) and our Black Catch-All. Our Iridescent Terror and a Bibio on a floating or intermediate line will also take their share of fish by suggesting drowned terrestrial insects.

When Heather Flies are present, it is worth trying a Black Hopper with dyed red or orange legs with black tips. In spite of its unnaturally large size, a size 10 often works well, but you should always be prepared to use smaller sizes if unsuccessful.

Artificial Hawthorn Fly.

Fly that has been consistently successful on Llyn Brenig in North Wales. It is tied on a normal shank (B405) size 10 hook with a black seal's fur (or substitute) body and a false (beard) hackle of dyed red golden pheasant tippets. The front third of the body has a red palmer and the rear two thirds have a black palmer, which keep the fly suspended well clear of the surface film.

Grasshoppers

Any European fisherman who visits some of the grassland areas of North America in August or early September cannot help being impressed by the abundance, size and colours of the grasshoppers. They are much larger and more numerous than their European counterparts. Any specimen that is unfortunate enough to alight on the surface of water holding trout or whitefish is likely to be gobbled up very quickly indeed. In one gulp a fish can take in more food than may be possible during an entire Baetis hatch. In reality, there is not a great deal of

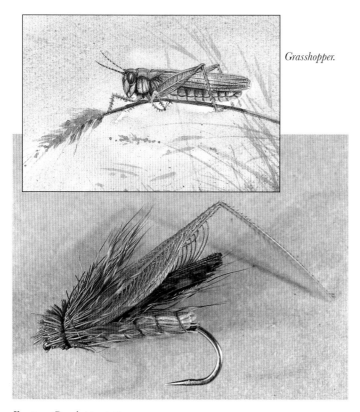

Grasshopper.

European Grasshopper pattern.

Dave's Hopper.

nourishment in a grasshopper – but to the trout's eyes, it is a large T-bone steak, arriving at a time of year when there may not be a great deal of other choice on the menu.

Grasshoppers become more active when it is hot, and are blown on to the water in greater numbers on windy days. Consequently on visits to the USA in late summer, we welcome the days that are a fly fisherman's nightmare back home. Often trout will not switch on to Hoppers until late morning when most of the natural insects start to appear on the water. This does not mean that artificial patterns are not worth a try earlier in the day or when the weather is unfavourable. Trout become preconditioned to their 'T-bone steaks', and sometimes they will grab one at a time when a better educated and more patient fish might know better – even when conditions are cold and wet!

On his visits to North America, Denzil routinely used to kick the grassy banks by a river, or catch individual grasshoppers and throw them on to the water. By watching their progress as they were swept by the current, he could ascertain whether the fish were feeding on the natural insects and – more importantly – determine the exact position where trout would intercept them. On really windy days, when the water became alive with hoppers (without his intervention), he would follow them at a respectable distance downstream. Even on a spring creek, the ruffled surface would disguise his presence sufficiently from the preoccupied trout for him to cast his artificial fly downstream into the boil created by the feeding fish.

There are several different patterns available, and in practice it is worth having two or three to choose from in the fly box. This is not simply a matter of being able to match a pattern to the natural species. We have known trout favour one pattern to another for reasons that are not apparently obvious. Trout on two similar

stretches of the Lamar, only 200 yds apart, consistently showed opposite preferences between Dave's Hopper and a Para-Hopper. On Flat Creek, several large trout that rejected imitative hoppers from a foot away took Guy Turc's Red Tarantula with supreme confidence. And on one pool on the Buffalo, trout would only respond to an enormous tarantula that was at least twice as large as any of the naturally occurring insects.

Thus, there is good reason for having a selection of patterns. Trout soon learn to associate such large and conspicuous flies with danger after a few of their number have been caught or pricked, but sometimes they will accept a different profile, colour or size. The dangling rubber legs of a Madam X or Tarantula will often entice trout when other patterns fail. We have often caught educated fish that have gobbled up a Royal Wulff, after rejecting all our specific hopper imitations. Sometimes it is worth fishing smaller Hoppers for wary trout, but on other occasions it is worth going up a couple of sizes to provoke a response.

As the names suggest, both Dave's and Whit's Hopper were created by Dave Whitlock, and designed to maintain a low, visible profile. If we had to draw

Madam X leg arrangement.

any conclusions from our experiences, they might point to the coarser outline and buoyant features of Dave's Hopper being better suited to rough conditions. Its visible yellow body is certainly an advantage for attracting trout – especially in coloured water. It has brought us a lot of success, but the more realistic outline of Whit's Hopper, which sits lower in the surface sometimes makes it the better choice for selective fish. One of our favourite patterns is a Henry's Fork Hopper, which loosely resembles a Whit's Hopper with yellow rubber legs. The rear pair, which are knotted, dangle enticingly to create a superb trigger point.

Dave's Hopper will usually alight on the water more or less the right way up, but the straggly deer hair that trails behind the head plays a key role in keeping it afloat at just the right angle. It is worth checking any commercial patterns before buying them to make sure that there are sufficient numbers of these fibres in place along both sides of the fly. It is also worth checking that the legs do not affect how the fly sits on the water. If necessary, do not be afraid to cut them back slightly.

We have known Para-Hoppers land on the water sideways for no apparent reason, and sometimes the only solution is to replace the offender with a new fly. A commercially tied Whit's Hopper started to do the same due to partial deterioration after taking its eighth large trout in 30 minutes! Both of these patterns have clear sighting marks of a white post and red top respectively. It is essential to make sure that the sighters are visible on top of the fly – and thus invisible to the fish below – because these flies are useless if they fail to land properly.

Under ideal conditions, trout like to take large, stationary insects in a leisurely manner, 'drowning' them before closing their jaws. When this happens, a rapid strike is unlikely to be successful. When fishing the lake that we mentioned above, we pricked the first fish, which showed us its enormous flank before disappearing, due to reflexes brought about by seven consecutive days of stream fishing. After that, and a few customary expletives, we settled into a proper rhythm with a very high percentage of hits.

River trout are less obliging. They can spit even a large Hopper out so quickly that it is quite common to miss many takes in succession. On some occasions, the more honest anglers will admit to a good fraction of their hits occurring accidentally during the lift-off or an over-zealous mend. This is more likely to occur on a stream where heavy fishing has made the trout ultra-cautious, such as with the highly stressed cutthroats of the Lamar. The only visible sign may be a local movement of water or the fly just disappearing vertically downwards without any wake. Sometimes they will follow the fly just under the surface for a few moments before deciding whether to commit themselves. The temptation to strike may be irresistible, especially if several fish have already been missed through being too slow. There is no foolproof method, but if a lot of fish are being missed, it is worth thinking about waiting for an extra half second before blaming poor reflexes.

In contrast, we have observed larger trout behaving very differently. They may not be so easily tempted to rise to the artificial fly, but when they do there is often total commitment. This calls for a split second delay in the strike to allow the fish to close its mouth on the fly as it turns away.

Due to its large size and buoyancy, a Hopper also makes a good strike indicator for a nymph or a small dry fly that is difficult to see. There are few better hedge-bet tactics.

THE LAST WORD

Entomology needs taking seriously, but not overly so. The good fisherman will have an enquiring mind and will sort out the important facts from the esoteric information. The challenge of entomology to the fly fisherman, rather than the academic specialist, is the ability to differentiate the wood from the trees.

You need to know enough to be able to judge what is likely to be on the trout's menu, and to adjust your ideas accordingly from observations on the day. You need to be able to relate artificial patterns to the trout's food, and to recognize the key features. The important aspects to the trout may not necessarily be the most obvious to the human being. For example, the way the fly rests on or in the water may be more important than minor differences in body colour. A fuzzy outline may turn out to be far more realistic than a slightly imperfect attempt at exact imitation. Sometimes, a dry palmered pattern that stands proud of the water can be an absolute killer, whereas on other occasions you might as well fish with no fly at all.

It is interesting how some of the best known fishing entomologists often rely on general patterns for much of their sport. They have learned from a position of authority that entomology is a bonus that can only help their fishing provided the detail does not obscure the importance of presentation, movement and overall fly fishing 'nous'.

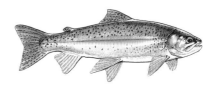

CHAPTER 6
TACTICS FOR RUNNING WATER

Hooked! Andrew Donaldson on the Whanganui.

Success on a river involves an appreciation of the type of stream, an understanding of the trout's behaviour and a focused rather than fanatical knowledge of entomology. This chapter explores these factors and the way they relate to tactics. Those who carry out the ground-work, keep their eyes open and think about what they are doing before casting a fly, are likely to reap the greatest rewards.

Many fly fishermen enjoy catching grayling as much as trout. Sometimes, grayling turn out to be more difficult to deceive, since they are truly wild fish in rivers where browns or rainbows may have been stocked as fully grown specimens. They are also beautifully marked – especially the species in English rivers with their red dorsal fins. From an angler's perspective, the main differences are the later spawning cycle, the inclination to gather in large shoals and the diet, which largely excludes small fish. Apart from occasions where differences are important, we have not pedantically added the words 'and grayling' after every reference. In our view, they fully deserve their treatment as honorary trout.

UPSTREAM VERSUS DOWNSTREAM TACTICS

At last we had arrived at the legendary Henry's Fork of the Snake River for a drift through Box Canyon. We had gone to the expense of hiring a guide for the day because much of this stretch is virtually inaccessible from the bank. He was worth every cent for his hard work in wading behind the boat so that we could drift very slowly through the rapid waters of the canyon. In between netting the hard fighting rainbows, and spitting out the chewing tobacco to which he was more than a little partial, he told us of a little known hot-spot on the Madison River. If we went there, all we would have to do would be to move downstream with a Hopper.

'Surely, you mean upstream.'

'Nope. (Spit).'

'But they're more likely to see you with a downstream cast.'

'Not if you wade carefully downstream, keeping a low profile and a reasonable distance. And they don't see the line before the fly. (Spit). It'll give you Limeys a chance to broaden your tactics.'

This was a complete contrast to some stretches of the English chalk-streams where downstream fishing is banned – let alone encouraged. But we were not challenging him on etiquette. It was because we believed that upstream tactics were more productive – especially for dry flies.

This stretch of the Madison turned out to be a big disappointment for all tactics, although we did manage some success a few miles away with (you guessed it) an upstream dry fly. This was followed by a couple of excellent days on the Lamar for cutthroats. Here we would experiment with Hoppers in both directions, but it was invariably the upstream tactic that caught the large fish. Perhaps we needed to spit in the water. The next stop was Poindexter Slough, and there were no surprises about the successful tactic on this fascinating spring creek, which closely resembles our English chalk-streams.

Interspersed with the delicate tactics on Poindexter Slough, we spent a few days on the faster moving waters of the Beaverhead. The quality of the fishing turned out to be as good as any we had experienced. We can thank Tim Tollett, owner of the Frontier Angler in Dillon, for sharing a few local secrets – even though it did involve us all getting up at 5 am! It was worth it, because we caught over a hundred large brown trout that fought like salmon in the torrents. Moreover, there was one inescapable fact. Over 80% of the fish had come to downstream tactics!

The upstream versus downstream debate contains a great deal of dogma and prejudice. The English undoubtedly favour upstream methods, whereas the western Americans and central Europeans have more of a tendency to cast downstream. This geographical difference is not fortuitous. Much of it arises from the different characters of the rivers – upstream for slow glides and downstream for raging torrents. In spite of this separation of tactics, it is often a good idea to work the flies downstream after an upstream cast. This hedge-bet technique encourages a more flexible approach that sometimes leads to pleasant surprises. Upstream tactics often turn out to be more successful in some stretches of fast-flowing rivers. Others may say that downstream tactics are occasionally more productive on the slow-moving chalk-streams of southern England – but we could not possibly comment!

When to Use Upstream Tactics

The most important reason for casting upstream is so fundamental to a trout's behaviour that we hesitate to mention it. Trout face the current to breathe, thereby giving an angler the perfect opportunity to approach them systematically from behind. To be visible, an upstream caster has to be positioned to the side of the fish, which partly explains why wading can often be more effective than walking the banks. The need for upstream casting is obviously more acute on those rivers where the fish can get a good view of an angler. These tend to be streams that are clear and slow-moving with an unruffled surface.

In slow currents, upstream tactics are also more amenable to fishing a dry fly or nymph in a dead drift to imitate a motionless insect borne by the current. This is because it is much easier to retrieve line from upstream than to pay it out downstream without interfering with the movement of the fly.

When to Use Downstream Tactics

Although it is better for a trout to see the fly before the line, we do not believe that this is nearly as important as a trout seeing the fly before the angler. On many occasions we have watched trout stay in position as a line is cast over them repeatedly. Their suspicions may have been aroused so that they will no longer feed, but their behaviour bears no comparison to the way they will often bolt for cover on seeing movement above the water. The real case for downstream tactics arises from causes other than camouflage.

In fast flowing rivers, it is almost impossible to retrieve slack line quickly enough after an upstream cast. Responding to a take is therefore virtually out of the question. However, for once, Murphy's Law seems to favour the angler. Fast currents produce rippled surfaces that distort a trout's view of the outside world. Moreover, the force of the current is sufficiently strong to allow you to pay out and mend the line for quite a distance without the effects of drag being too apparent. Thus, downstream fishing is likely to be the most suitable tactic.

At the end of a downstream drift, it is worth allowing the line to move round in an arc. This will sometimes provoke a savage take. It may be due to the impression of a nymph rising to hatch into an adult, a dry fly skittering across the surface, or simply a reaction to stimulus. At the expense of achieving a prolonged dead drift, this effect can be exploited by casting more directly across the stream.

Since it is possible to pay out line, the distance downstream is not limited by an angler's casting ability, as it is with upstream tactics. He can let the fly drift down towards the fish, irrespective of any bank-side obstacles that would obstruct casting. He can also use the technique of 'slotting', which involves pulling the fly back against the current to position it perfectly before allowing it to drift down over the intended target.

At the end of a drift, the fly will cover a considerable section of the stream as it moves round in an arc. 'Down and across' tactics are therefore capable of exploring a much greater area of the stream. This implies that they are suited to a systematic search for fish in featureless rivers that are sparsely populated.

Finally, paying out line enables flies to drift under bushes where direct casting is impossible. It may be worth a try, even in the calmest and clearest of streams. Occasionally it really does work – and these locations often hold the largest trout.

FEATURES OF THE STREAM

Rivers obtain their water either from underground springs or from rain and melting snow. These two principal sources create quite distinct types of stream, which produce corresponding differences in a trout's lifestyle and its response to anglers. Nevertheless, it is dangerous to decide on tactics purely from a rigid classification of the water source. Local features, such as changes in terrain, dams and confluences, may result in a spring-fed stream bearing a closer resemblance to a rain or snow-fed river – and vice versa. Moreover, some tiny brooks and the margins of larger rivers have a character all of their own that require specialized tactics.

It is important first to appreciate the essential characteristics of each type of stream, such as water clarity, fly life and current, in order to understand how they affect the choice of tactics. Having accomplished this, you can then tailor your methods to the large number of waters with hybrid features.

Spring-fed Streams

The sedately flowing chalk-streams of southern England and the spring creeks of North America are prime examples of this category. The former were the prime haunts of the classic fly-fishing authors, such as Halford and Skues – and the latter would have been, had they crossed the Atlantic. Wherever they happen to be, spring-fed streams entice anglers with three important characteristics.

Davy Wotton lands a grayling on the River Itchen.

First, the water passes through porous underground rocks before reaching the source of the stream. Such rocks are rich in minerals, and this makes the water slightly alkaline. Most aquatic insects and fauna thrive in these conditions, so that the streams are rich in both abundance and variety of fly life. Such a wealth of food may cause the trout to become very finicky about what they choose to eat. This gives an angler ample opportunity to cover rising fish and to hone his fly selection skills to perfection. Therefore, before travelling a long way or paying a lot of money, it is worth doing a little homework to arrive properly equipped with a suitable range of patterns. It is easy to focus on the rich aquatic food chain and forget about terrestrial insects – and this can be the greatest mistake of all. Even these aristocratic trout sometimes forsake the most beautifully tempting upwinged flies in favour of the humble ant or beetle.

Weed growth is often prolific in the mineral-rich waters, so that syndicates and river-keepers may have to reserve a few days each year for weed cutting. (This practice is much more widespread in England than in North America.) Usually, there is a healthy mixture between weeded and bare areas. Due to the lack of natural camouflage over areas of gravel or silt, it is often possible to stalk individual specimens in the clear, slow-moving water and watch them intercept a fly. Bare patches adjacent to

weed beds are always worth scrutinising for fish lying in wait for passing food. Grayling will often haunt patches of gravel (the 'redds') towards the end of the year in search of trout spawn, and it is no wonder that a small, round orange pattern works so well.

Geoff Clarkson returns a grayling on the Test.

Second, the source of underground water is usually large and well established. This means a sedate flow with levels and clarity that are not affected significantly by heavy rainfall. There are no spate conditions to change the profile of the stream from one year to the other, and no extremes of temperature in summer and winter. Thus, it is possible to book a day well in advance and remain 99% confident of the right water conditions, irrespective of the weather. You can never be totally confident, because even the best-laid plans can go amiss. In 1996 spring melts caused the mighty Yellowstone River to alter its course, and in the process to wipe out the exclusive De Puys spring creek.

Third, the passage of underground water through porous rocks removes fine suspended particles. Thus, spring-fed streams tend to be crystal clear, and offer superb opportunities to gain insights into trout behaviour by first hand observation. You will get a marvellous chance to watch every move of a trout as a dry fly or nymph approaches from upstream. You may see takes to the nymph that are so subtle that they do not register, even on a strike indicator. You may see a fish adjust its position slightly towards your nymph, only to turn away as it recognizes an impostor. It is a chance to experiment with different weights and leader constructions to reach the right depth at the right time, and thereby to get a real feel for this essential aspect of nymph fishing.

There is, of course, a downside to the clear water and the unruffled nature of the surface. Trout get a good view of an angler and will often disappear into cover with great speed at the slightest movement. They seem to react far more timidly to an angler's motion on the bank than to his presence in the stream. The lower profile and the smaller angle of approach are crucial factors, but it is also true that the most feared natural predators are those that appear without warning from outside the water. One of the tricks of chalk-stream fishing is therefore to wade rather than to cover fish from the bank. In addition to the camouflage, this reduces line drag by lessening the casting angle. It is not uncommon, after remaining motionless in the same spot for a few minutes, for trout or grayling to appear next to your feet. Sometimes they will almost brush against your legs – completely oblivious to your presence. Once established in a stationary position in the water, it is also possible (apparently) to deceive fish with downstream tactics.

Wading has its problems, though, when stalking really spooky fish. Most obviously, it creates vibrations in the water, particularly when moving into position. In addition, it is quite easy to disturb an unseen fish that darts upstream amidst the intended quarry. This can put all the fish on their guard. They may still remain in position, but be totally disinclined to feed – whatever the offering. This becomes an increasingly common problem towards the end of the grayling season on well-fished chalk-streams such as the River Test. We have also noticed the tendency for shoals of fish to dart downstream past a wading angler. It is as if they have learned that they are safe as long as they do not remain upstream of this strange, two-legged intruder. Under these conditions, it is arguably better to fish from the bank, while kneeling to achieve the lowest possible profile.

It is not surprising that demand for such waters is high. The better known stretches tend to be primarily the haunts of the wealthy, the well connected or those who are able to book a year in advance. They tend to be rather localized, and for many this will involve a great deal of travelling. Nevertheless, it is quite possible to experience many of the features of this type of water if you make the effort to enquire and look around.

In England, rivers like the Wylye and Frome are cheaper to fish than the more famous chalk-streams. It is possible to fish stretches of the celebrated Test and Itchen for grayling outside the trout season, usually from October to December. Grayling will quite commonly reach 18 inches in the chalk-streams, take nymphs freely and rise to sporadic hatches of Baetis right through to the end of the year.

Many publicly accessible waters in North America have the essential characteristics of spring creeks, even though some do not derive their flows from underground sources. Streams such as Poindexter Slough in Montana, Flat Creek in Wyoming and Slough Creek in Yellowstone Park will test any angler's ability to stalk visible fish with the right selection of fly. It is also worth taking the trouble to find out about lesser-known waters. For example, McCoy Springs, near Dillon, Montana, provides really exciting sport at an affordable cost. And at the opposite scale, stretches of the Missouri resemble a 100 yd wide chalk-stream, with large visible trout.

Freestone Streams

The sources of most rivers come from rain draining off the land or from snow melting off the hills. If the water has passed over a suitable rocky terrain, the river may be rich in nutrients and support a wide range of fly life. On the other hand, if the river is surrounded by acidic vegetation, such as pine forests, the fly-life will be scarce. The trout may not then be so choosy about what species they will accept, but this does not mean that you will get away with a bad imitation. It simply indicates that the fish will be unlikely to reject anything that they recognize as a naturally occurring insect, unless there is a substantial hatch in progress. A reduced abundance of food often prevents the trout from reaching the same dimensions as in alkaline waters, but this is only a rule of thumb. Some of the world's largest specimens come from freestone rivers where they forage for small fish or large crustaceans.

It is usually more difficult to spot fish in freestone rivers. Sometimes this is due to coloration from pigments picked up from the land. At other times, the gin-clear water from melting snow passes over a river bed of large pebbles that provides perfect camouflage. Such rivers often have a ruffled surface that helps to conceal both fish and angler from each other. If you try to watch a trout after returning it to the water, it is miraculous how quickly it may disappear from view.

Thus, one negative aspect of such rivers is the difficulty of locating the fish. In addition to the greater degree of camouflage, there may be fewer give-away rises due to the reduced fly life. To be successful, an angler may therefore require a great deal more experience than on the spring-fed streams to identify the likely lies. Moreover, in some rivers, old haunts are likely to disappear, since rising water levels from heavy rain or melting snow may change the character of the stream considerably. We spoke to a passing guide, who was complaining about having to 'work for his clients' after the Lamar had changed its course during the spring. Even expert local knowledge needs refreshing from time to time.

The corresponding positive feature is that the fish have greater difficulty in seeing an angler, but this must not give rise to a dangerous complacency. When approaching a chalk-stream, you are fully aware of your own visibility, because the fish will punish any false move by swimming for cover or totally ignoring the most perfectly presented fly. In a coloured river, you are unlikely to observe the fish's reaction to your presence, but this does not necessarily mean that they have not seen you. A ruffled surface will distort the view of an angler, but will not conceal his clumsy movements. If the water is clear and calm, trout in a freestone

A fast-flowing stretch of the Yellowstone.

river will spot you just as easily as will the aristocrats of the chalk-streams.

A ruffled surface also helps to disguise the features of less sophisticated flies and leaders. Moreover, flies that are tailor-made for the slower flows of spring creeks and chalk-streams may not float or stand out sufficiently well against the riffles of the faster currents. Thus, unsophisticated hackled flies such as a Royal Wulff or Humpy may turn out to be just what is needed.

In spate conditions, trout stay well down in any slack pockets they can find, such as behind rocks or submerged tree trunks. Coloration by suspended silt may impede their vision and make them less cautious than normal. They will not have had a chance to experience settled conditions, and are therefore much less likely to notice anything outside the ordinary. It is an opportunity to take full advantage of the natural camouflage by exploiting downstream tactics. Several different morsels of food may have been disturbed by the increased flows, and a wide range of patterns will usually be successful. In particular, they may be feeding on larger items such as worms that have been washed down and small fish that have been driven into the slacker pools. Larger fish-imitating flies, such as the Peter Ross or Butcher, and streamers can therefore work well.

The most important ingredient for sub-surface fishing under spate conditions will be the added weight – and perhaps a sinking braided leader – to get the fly down to an increased depth against the stronger currents. If the water is coloured, it is

worth adding a small amount of fluorescence to increase the visibility of the fly as it rushes past. The trout are often most likely to make their move – or at least you are most likely to feel the take – at the end of the cast as the line straightens and the flies rise in the water. They are unlikely to be too particular. General nymphs such as the Pheasant Tail, Hare's Ear and Prince, and traditional wet flies such as Mallard and Claret, Wickham's Fancy and Invicta, may all do the trick.

As the water subsides and clarifies, the fishing can improve dramatically. The trout will have spent a few days during which their prime motive has been to shelter from the strong currents, and food may have been virtually inaccessible. They are now ready to make up for lost time. It is a time to take full advantage of a period when all upstream and downstream methods may be appropriate. The fish tend to be bolder than they were at low water, and the sport can be spectacular if they start feeding.

Stony Brooks

A visit to some of the remote brooks amongst the hills, moors or mountains might involve a great deal of walking, sometimes up some fair old gradients. You will want to make life as easy as possible by travelling light with a single rod set up with a floating line. The fish may not be large, but the pleasures of stalking wild trout in such tiny streams can really take some beating, and you will want to return.

Brooks, such as the East and West Dart in Devon, are quite common in Europe as well as in North America. The conditions can also occur on the edges of some of the larger streams. We had great fun one evening in the canyon area of the Gallatin in Montana. Although the river can scarcely be described as a brook, there were several tiny pools on the edges that were largely protected from the main flow. A fly dropped into virtually every pool brought an immediate response from a hungry rainbow. They were no great size compared with the trout holding in the main pools, but they were still great fun on a day when the larger residents were disinclined to co-operate.

The pools can be tiny – sometimes only a few feet across – but any area of water that produces additional depth or slackening away from the shallow rapids is likely to hold fish. In some cases, the only way to present a fly in such a tiny area will be to dap it onto the surface. A fisherman, who may be quite experienced on the larger waters, will often walk the entire length of a stretch on his first visit and decide that there cannot possibly be any decent trout in such shallow and inhospitable conditions. In many cases, it is only when he has seen respectably sized fish caught that he acquires the necessary faith to approach the water seriously.

Trout inhabiting these tiny streams can lead a pretty hard life. There may be precious little cover in the shallow, clear water to shield them from predators, especially under the low water conditions of a dry summer. They therefore have to be constantly on their guard. Stealth is always important, but when stalking timid creatures in such a tiny area, it is paramount. The fish must – rather than should – be approached from downstream, and the cast made upstream from behind them.

Since it is unlikely that any offering will be missed, it is always the first cast into a new pool that has the best chance. After that, the trout will become increasingly suspicious. They will see an artificial fly, which they have already rejected, pass over them several times. Changing the fly is unlikely to bring success, because the fish will have been frightened by the repeated commotion of the fly line and leader passing over them and being lifted off the water. So it is advisable to limit the number of casts into each pool to half a dozen at the very most, and then to move stealthily upstream to the next likely fish-holding spot. If a few pools have failed to bring any response, then it is obviously worth changing the fly – but invariably in a new stretch of water rather than one that has already been fished.

Most of the food tends to be funnelled into the faster water. A trout's eyes will therefore concentrate on the point at which the most rapid section of current first enters the mouth of the pool. It expects to see everything arrive through a tiny area of perhaps a few inches square. Any fly that lands too far to the back or side is therefore likely, at best, to be missed as outside its field of concentration. At worst, the fly will be rejected as being unnatural and put the trout on its guard. It will be obvious that the achievement of first time casting accuracy is a great advantage. In many instances it is quite possible to reach the fish by dapping rather than by conventional casting.

Since a trout will be focusing on such a tiny area of quite fast moving water, it will grab a fly within a second or two of

Dave Grove covers successive pools on the East Dart.

landing. Any undue delay will mean a missed opportunity. Thus, there is not a great deal of time for the leader to exert any drag on the fly. Drag is also mitigated on a narrow brook, since most casts will be more or less directly upstream rather than across the currents. So it is not worth trying to throw a slack line if this in any way impairs the precision of the cast. Accuracy must not be compromised.

Hatches of insects can be rather sparse, so there is often not a great deal of visible surface activity. You will have to take it on trust that there are fish in these pools. Food is seldom abundant, so the trout are likely to be hungry. Their eyes will be scouring the surface of the pool for anything – aquatic or terrestrial – that happens to pass by. Thus dry flies are likely to be the most appropriate under normal conditions, although sub-surface tactics might excel after heavy rain. The trout will not be too fussy about the precise details of the fly, providing it is generally representative of likely food items. Moreover, in many stretches the current will take the fly past so quickly that there will not be sufficient time for a detailed inspection.

Such waters are therefore tailor-made for general patterns. As a first line of attack, there is no need to carry more than about half a dozen favourite patterns which, if properly chosen, will form a fully comprehensive selection. If you are casting into the rapids at the head of a pool, bushy flies that ride the water well are preferable. Although the pool may be tiny, the flies do not have to be correspondingly minute. Sizes 14 and 16 are usually quite small enough. We have had consistent success in riffled water with an Adams, Elk Hair Caddis and Wingless Wickham's. All traces of fluorescence or unnaturally bright materials should be removed, since a trout is guaranteed to see a properly cast fly, and can only be put off by anything that is too gaudy. In the slower water, our Panacea takes a lot of beating.

MARCH TO SEPTEMBER

We would not even think about listing the multitude of different insects that might hatch in the various streams of the world. Our aim here is simply to outline the important trends that exist throughout the season (referring to months in the northern hemisphere). Even then, we are well aware that such a generalization will contain large regional exceptions. For example, while those living in lowland areas can fish quite comfortably in March and April, others fishing rivers fed by melting snow from the mountains may have to wait until June or even July.

Early season trout tend to be relatively forgiving of poor fly imitations. They will have spent a trouble-free winter without any untoward experiences, such as flies that bite back or an unexpected force that moves them towards the river bank. They may have forgotten the previous year, when they had been lifted from the water and displayed to onlookers before being returned. In short, they will have lost a lot of the caution that had been instilled into them by the end of the previous season. Nevertheless, over-wintered fish will have learned the art of survival in the wild and are likely to react suspiciously to any unusual movement. The sudden arrival of hordes of hopeful fly

fishermen in a remote spot may fall into this category. With care, they may catch the prize over-wintered fish. Otherwise, heavy footsteps and clumsy casting will limit their catches to the smaller or recently stocked trout. 'Stockies', which are often introduced during the close season, are used to disturbance and often associate approaching humans with food rather than danger.

Throughout March and April, sub-surface tactics are likely to be more consistent. The fish are not too fussy about wet fly patterns, and so a team of dark, general flies and nymphs is the order of the day. It may pay to search for the fish that have spent the winter grubbing around the river bed in the deeper, gentle stretches. Downstream tactics will often work better, since they cover more of the river at a time when the trout may be less suspicious after a winter's rest from angling pressure.

No fish may break the surface during the early morning, but towards midday – when conditions are warmest – the river can come to life with some sporadic hatches. Apart from the aptly named March Brown, the predominant flies are likely to be the darker versions of upwinged flies. With fish that may be both innocent and hungry, it is worth trying your luck with any general, dark-coloured dry pattern.

May signals the start of prolonged surface activity, when the fish move to the shallower, slightly faster reaches of the stream. Aquatic flies grow lighter in colour, although black terrestrial flies will also be in evidence. At the end of the month the large mayflies, often referred to as drakes, may start to appear and be taken in total abandon. In the British Isles the first two weeks of June are often called 'Duffers' Fortnight', because the trout are so much easier to catch on these tempting big morsels. Syndicates will often not allow guests during these two weeks so that the members can exploit the stream to the full.

By June, a whole feast of different aquatic and terrestrial insects will be on the menu. Sufficient food will float by with the current for the trout to look to the surface rather than grubbing around the bottom. At times it may be essential to match the hatch, but with such a diverse choice of food, general patterns such as the Adams and Pheasant Tail should work consistently. Those fishing the Western rivers of the USA start to look forward to great sport from the middle of the month as the massive salmon fly appears.

Although trout may be feeding avidly in June, they will also be learning to be more cautious and become more difficult to deceive. Repeated angling pressure will almost certainly have educated them. By July stealth will be a prerequisite, and bright conditions will make any movement more noticeable. Flies with the incorrect profile or posture in the water may be worthless, and all but the lightest tackle and longest leaders may give the game away. In North America, the tiny tricos provide a good test of an angler's ability.

By now you may know exactly where a trout will lie, but the trick is to manoeuvre yourself into such a position that you can cover it without being noticed. During the really hot 'dog days' of July and August, it is worth looking for shady spots under bushes, and persevering in the deeper pools with a heavy nymph. The bigger fish will often take refuge in such areas before moving out at dusk to feed on hatching insects, such as caddis. Late evenings are generally the most productive times to fish, although early mornings are spectacular on some rivers if you can summon up the energy to get out of bed.

Some localized hatches may occur throughout the day, but terrestrial insects could now be the most important surface food. August marks the arrival of grasshoppers on the North American rivers. These are most active on the hottest days and provide magnificent sport in high summer. Crane flies become an increasingly important source of food towards the end of the month. In our experience, the importance of these two classes of insect is hard to overstate.

Alan Williams with a brown trout on a Hopper from the Yellowstone.

By September, fish will be feeding avidly to build up strength for the winter months and rigours of spawning. The insects tend to be similar to those in spring, both in their overall profile and dark shading. Terrestrial insects such as grasshoppers, crane flies, ants and beetles can still be very important. In some regions, quite large drakes may emerge that are best imitated on a size 12 or even a size 10 hook. Otherwise, smaller patterns for both dry flies and nymphs tend to be necessary. This is partly due to the nature of the hatch and partly due to September trout being better educated and less forgiving of flies that are too large. In spring a larger fly may have been successful by advertising its presence, but now the same pattern can give a danger signal. Clumsily tied and unnecessary hackles, floating tippets and even the slightest drag might now render flies virtually useless. Once spooked by poor presentation, late season fish can go off the feed for some time.

There is another angle that is well worth pursuing at the end of the season. The fish will have become well educated in all the usual angling tricks. Sometimes fishermen are very predictable, and like sheep they will all use the same flies, the same techniques and even share the same hot spots. Although trout will respond to correct imitations of their natural food supply, they are still creatures that will react to stimulus. So you should cultivate ideas for trying something different. These may include unusual tactics that they will not have seen before, or a visit to less popular places where the fish, although less numerous, remain unmolested.

In their attempt to put on weight for the winter, September trout will increasingly turn their attention to small fish. Cock fish, in particular, will become more aggressive near the mating season. Large gold-headed nymphs progressively outperform the more sophisticated patterns such as Pheasant Tails. Lures and streamers can become deadly towards the end of the month and into October. Woolly Buggers, for example, representing large food items like sculpins and crayfish, become increasingly deadly. These large sub-surface patterns are more forgiving of heavy leaders, and the effects of drag are immaterial when imitating a fish rather than an insect. The large fish that are especially partial to these offerings tend to live right under the bank. Thus, relaxation in the delicacy of tackle must not be an excuse for clumsy footsteps or careless wading.

Woolly Bugger.

You cannot *be serious!', wrote one of our reviewers across the text. Brian is very much a traditional devotee of the English chalk-streams, and was rather taken aback by some of the American expressions and techniques. But Woolly Buggers were just too much for him. From then on his comments took on a more sarcastic tone. 'Why not use ECU?', when we quoted prices in dollars and pounds in the same chapter. 'You'll be recommending worms next!', he wrote as we discussed strike indicators. And the simple word 'Philistines' appeared against a section on downstream tactics. Finally, when we were describing upstream tactics with the ill-chosen expression of 'the approach from behind', he wrote the simple words: 'I suppose this is where Woolly Buggers come in useful.'*

A PRAGMATIC CHOICE OF TACKLE

Fly fishing on a stream is often associated with a short, featherweight rod and an ultra-light line. This produces maximum delicacy, minimum drag, the most sensitive feel to any pull on the line and the ability to fish a fine leader without breakage. It also creates a fantastic sensation in landing even quite a modestly sized trout. It is sometimes easy to misconstrue such tackle as being associated with the pinnacle of experience and success. Such light tackle does have its place – perhaps on a small, slow-flowing brook on a windless day – but many successful fishermen will tailor their tackle to the prevailing conditions. Frequently this means adopting more man-sized equipment.

The Pragmatic Line

It is predominantly the line that determines delicacy, distance and the ability to handle bushy dry flies or heavily weighted nymphs. The choice is usually a compromise. There may not be a great deal of point in achieving the ultimate in delicacy if the slightest breath of wind blows the fly off course. Paradoxically, this makes the lightest of lines unsuitable for some of the tiny brooks, where the fly has to land first time on an area no bigger than a pocket handkerchief to be accepted. The first choice for a specialist on such a brook may therefore be a surprisingly meaty AFTMA 5.

The same line is the first choice for many fishermen on most types of stream, and is the one that we would choose if restricted to a single weight. The need for accuracy may not be quite as demanding on a moderately sized river as on a tiny brook, but any effects of the breeze are magnified when casting a greater distance. A 'five-line' allows effortless casting over considerable distances, and will handle a wide range of flies from a tiny midge to a meaty Hopper. As distance and wind strength increase, life becomes easier by changing up to an AFTMA 6 or 7. It may not be fashionable to admit it, but with careful casting such lines will catch even the more sophisticated trout of the chalk-streams and spring creeks. We do not advise the routine use of such unnecessarily heavy tackle, but it does emphasize that you can get away with it for covering fish that would be otherwise out of reach. To press the point further, the right line for casting a heavily weighted streamer or giant stonefly to the far bank may be an AFTMA 8 or 9.

The Pragmatic Rod

At first sight, any casual observer would think that Reggie was a traditionalist with his vintage built cane rod that he uses on the chalk-streams. Then comes the realization that the top section is made out of a totally different material – probably greenheart. But on closer inspection, it turns out to be the top half of a Japanese carbon fibre reservoir rod. The attachment between the two sections is a length of dowelling, lovingly tapered by Reggie's own fair hands.

'Mmmm. Nothing wrong with it. Broke the top section of my Hardy river rod when I walked into a tree, and closed a car boot on the butt section of the Shimano.' On this hybrid contraption, Reggie catches as many trout and grayling as the next man – and makes us question our own qualifications for recommending a pragmatic approach to tackle. (He also carefully protects each one of his antique reels in an old sock.)

A short rod, which is so often associated with river fishing, is perfect for use along overgrown banks, under trees or on small brooks. It cuts through the wind easily, casts accurately at short range and, due to its lightness, is more enjoyable to use. These undoubted advantages have caused short rods to become enshrined in river fishing lore to the extent that other factors tend to get overlooked. The normal range is from about 7–9 ft.

Lake fishermen, on the other hand, use longer rods for two valid reasons. The first, which is not necessary on many streams, is the ability to cast farther. The second, which loch style fishermen exploit, is to work the flies close to the surface. This is not very far removed from the requirement in running water to work the line to eliminate the effects of drag. It is therefore not surprising that a longer rod gives the stream fisherman much better control over movement of the fly and mending of the line. Thus, we never use rods of less than 9 ft unless there really is a problem with overhanging vegetation.

A rod of 9.5 ft is quite manageable, and gives that extra bit of length for clearing obstacles and line control. Longer rods will give even better performance – providing your wrist can take the strain. You should not be afraid to go against convention if you are happier using a longer rod, because in many circumstances it may help you to catch more fish. Moreover, do not necessarily believe everything that the tackle trade may preach.

Line control on Henry's Fork.

JD was unfortunate enough (his words) or stupid enough (the consensus opinion) to break his 9.5 ft, AFTMA 5 rod in Montana. He needed to buy a replacement, but not one of the six local shops stocked a lightweight river rod over 9 ft long. 'There's no call for them out here – and the visitors from the East Coast think that 9 ft is far too long. You certainly shouldn't be using anything longer.' So 9 ft had to do. A few days later, he bumped into one of these tackle dealers on the banks of the Madison. He was using a rod that was 10 ft long!

The Pragmatic Leader

It is easy to follow doctrine and use a leader that is unnecessarily long. A total length of 9–12 ft, including the tapered butt section, is usually quite long enough when using a single fly for the 'average' trout in the 'average' river. It is quite easy to control, and minimizes the chances of wind knots and snagging on the back-cast. Moreover, a total length of much more than 9 ft, including the butt section, can seriously impair accuracy when casting very short distances. Trouble-free casting helps to maintain confidence and concentration, which in turn leads to better catch rates.

Of course, special situations require longer leaders. Getting a nymph down deep in a fast current may require a lot more nylon. Trout in heavily fished or gin-clear waters grow wary of fly lines, and it may be worth increasing the leader to as much as 20 ft – providing you can handle it. However, it is always preferable to cast a 12 ft leader that straightens than a 20 ft one that lands like a heap of over-cooked spaghetti.

The Pragmatic Waistcoat

One of the golden rules of river fishing is to keep moving. This is more easily accomplished by carrying everything in a waistcoat with a short landing net hanging from the back. The waistcoat needs to be short to avoid items such as flies and nylon becoming wet when wading. It also needs to have a comprehensive range of pockets, zips and attachments to accommodate the average angler's requirements. Some designs, though, are too complex for their own good.

Reggie used to carry all his equipment in an old school satchel until incessant peer pressure eventually persuaded him to invest in a waistcoat. At first he could not come to terms with the multitude of features, but took comfort after writing to the manufacturer.

'Mmmm. Nothing wrong with it. I'll be all right as soon as they send me the instruction manual.'

CAPITALIZING ON THE RIVER

Local Advice

Whenever visiting a new area without the benefit of any local knowledge, the tackle shops are a good port of call. Most of them will give genuine advice, but they will, of course, give the same information to everyone else. Thus, you are likely to end up fishing a stretch of water where many of the trout will have been either removed or spooked. The shopkeepers will probably know of more select areas, but if they offer a guide service they are unlikely to give away too many trade secrets. It would unfair to paying customers if they did not get some exclusivity for their money.

If your budget will stretch to it, we would therefore recommend paying for one day's guided fishing at the start of a stay in a new area. We have never been too proud to use guides when visiting unfamiliar areas in North America and New Zealand, and neither should anyone else. Once you have paid up, your guide – who may be expecting a tip at the end of the session – will be more likely to share a few local secrets. In certain parts of the USA, the best use of the money might be a float trip. You really do then get something extra for your money. There will be 10 miles of bank covered in a single day with drag-free fishing. You can make a note of the hot spots that may be accessible from the bank for future visits. Last but not least, there will be a guide trapped between you and your colleague who cannot escape a barrage of questions on all the local information – and a couple of glasses of wine or Jack Daniels will invariably loosen his tongue.

A float trip down Box Canyon.

To get away from the crowds completely and enjoy some superb fishing in Yellowstone Park, we were once advised to go on an eight mile hike (each way) across two large meadows. 'And whatever happens, don't take any food or you might attract the bears'. We were just about to start the hike when a group of six other anglers turned up to do the same thing. There were also quite a few parked cars, and it was not clear how many others we would eventually meet on arrival at our destination. Ironically, the usually popular stretch of the creek by the car park was virtually deserted, because everyone now seemed to be following the same advice. It was a blazing hot day, and we did not need much of an excuse to stay put by the local stretch where we had an adequate supply of cold drinks. We were able to enjoy some virtually uninterrupted fishing for good sized cutthroats that were sporadically rising to terrestrial insects.

Fan-casting

It is very tempting to make your first cast straight into an area that looks the most 'fishy' – perhaps where riffles enter a deeper stretch of slow-moving water in the middle of the stream. This is fine if there is a visible fish to cover, but very often it is not the most sensible approach. In many rivers, there are trout – and sometimes very big ones – that are lying almost at your feet. Any wading or casting of a fly line on top of them is likely to advertise the danger and waste a golden opportunity.

The simple and obvious tactic of covering a stretch systematically is easy to forget or ignore due to impatience, but it will often make a major contribution to a successful outing. The meticulous angler may therefore start with a very short cast along the bank. He will then carry out a series of 'fan casts' over the same distance, increasing the angle so that each successive cast is directed more across the stream. After that, he will increase the distance slightly and repeat the process, ensuring that each successive cast covers new fish that have not had a fly line cast over their heads.

There are some occasions when it does pay to go straight for the most productive area. In tiny pools, for example, a trout may be anticipating the arrival of food in one very specific area. Any exploratory cast may then cause an unacceptable disturbance. It is advisable to assume from the outset that there is only going to be one casting opportunity in each pool – an assumption that too often turns out to be true.

Keeping on the Move

We often find that our catch rates improve when we start exploring for ourselves and use our own initiatives. We are not trying to imply that our judgements are better than the majority, but rather that we are more likely to find the less popular places where the fish have been left well alone. Our maxim is quite simply that you may achieve more success by covering ten 'virgin' fish than a hundred that have seen every conceivable kind of artificial fly. It is not just a case of covering the easy prey. Deserted stretches allow you to work your way leisurely along the stream to cover a large expanse of water, showing your fly methodically to different trout.

One of the more spectacular outings occurred one September afternoon on the Yellowstone River a few miles south of Livingston. The local advice had been to ignore this large and unpredictable river for wade fishing, and to concentrate instead on smaller rivers such as the Gallatin. However, JD and Andrew Donaldson had already been on a float trip and come to two important conclusions. First, there were plenty of accessible trout from the banks. Second, all the bank fishermen seemed to congregate around the access points. This meant that these few areas were getting a real pounding, while the majority of the river was untouched apart from the passing fishermen drifting down in boats.

Starting at 2 pm, JD and AD worked their way upstream along opposite banks, out of sight from each other due to a long island in the middle of the river. They had agreed to meet back at the bridge four hours later. It was cloudy with some rain and, although there was a respectable hatch of Baetis, there was initially no rise. JD then noticed some activity in a pool, tied on a size 14 Panacea and caught over 30 respectable trout in the next 90 minutes. If there had not been an agreement to meet back at the bridge by 6 pm, who knows how the total might have grown.

JD felt a certain satisfaction while walking back to base, knowing that he had chosen the better bank. Arriving at the bridge, the two stationary fishermen had managed only one rainbow between them all day. The satisfaction increased to smugness. There was AD, back at the car already.

'How many did you get, Andrew'.

'I'm not sure', was the reply. 'I stopped counting after fifty! That Panacea is one hell of a fly.'

'B*st*rd!'

Whereas the fish on the left bank had been rising steadily, there had been a feeding frenzy on the opposite side. More importantly, in two separate areas of the river, excellent fishing was available if you were just prepared to walk to undisturbed water.

Resting the Swim

Although our preferred approach is to move upstream to cover new water and undisturbed fish, there are sometimes very good reasons for staying in the same stretch of the river. It does not make a lot of sense to leave a good head of fish that is feeding avidly, or to disappear from an area where a hatch of insects can be predicted to occur like clockwork a little later in the day. Access problems may give you no choice. Large numbers of other anglers may severely restrict the availability of new water, so that any move carries a major risk of being unable to find another good stretch. The one thing that can be guaranteed is that someone else will take your spot soon after it becomes vacant.

The trouble with fishing the same stretch repeatedly is that the fish will soon grow aware of your presence. Insects with the wrong feel, flies that bite back, or the strange behaviour and disappearance of fellow trout will all increase awareness and decrease the propensity to feed. Thus, if the fishing goes off it is not necessarily an indication that the natural food supply has stopped. The fish may simply have had enough hassle for the time being. Changing the fly or the tactic is usually worth a try, because sometimes trout will only associate danger with the specific pattern that has been passing their noses time and time again. On other occasions, they will even ignore the natural insects, which is very reassuring.

In tiny brooks you may have no option other than to move on, but trout in the larger streams can have very short memories. Thus it is always worth resting the stream for a while. If a hatch is underway, the will to feed may result in a return to normal conditions quite quickly. During hatches, we have known the rise to natural flies to start again after as little as a couple of minutes. Otherwise, it may be necessary to wait for perhaps half an hour. It can take some will power to put down the rod and do nothing for a while, but more often than not it will result in an increased catch over the session. A bottle of wine will help to pass the time and temper the eagerness to start again too soon.

In heavily fished rivers, it is quite common to raise a fish as soon as you cast a fly into a new stretch of water, only to miss the opportunity. This is because such fish have become familiar with the dangers of feeding and can reject a fly in an instant. Even in the larger streams, two or three early chances are all you will get, after which you may as well carry on without a fly on the end of the leader. It is time to move on, but a return after an hour or so will often provide the same opportunities all over again.

Water-craft

Water-craft is sometimes easy to overlook in the excitement to start fishing. Half an hour for proper reconnaissance might seem like an eternity, but it is usually only a small fraction of the total session and will usually be worthwhile. Unless you are already intimately acquainted with a river and its lies, the initial investment is likely to pay for itself several times over.

Expert anglers will assume instinctively that they are fishing for truly wild creatures and conceal their presence accordingly. Careless anglers may catch several trout on large, coloured and turbulent rivers, but could still be missing out on the larger, educated specimens. Moreover, a lax approach here will only instil bad habits that may be punished ruthlessly on other waters.

Stealth can be much more important than technique or choice of fly. The smaller the stream, the clearer the water and the lower the level, the more the trout will be preconditioned to react defensively to the slightest unnatural movement. Even a rambler or grazing cattle may put the fish off the feed for quite a long time. One improper cast may be the only chance you get before a wily old 'trophy fish' is sent fleeing.

A Systematic Approach

Whether using upstream or downstream tactics, your flies should reach the fish before you do. In other words, never put the fish on their guard by avoidably walking past their lies before casting to them. This means walking continuously upstream or continuously downstream, depending on the chosen approach.

For example, you may want to fish upstream, but know that the better or less fished water is downstream of an access point. Avoid the temptation to start fishing straightaway. Estimate how far you will want to walk during the session, and proceed downstream for that distance – away from the water if possible. If, for whatever reason, you have to work your way downstream while fishing with upstream techniques (or vice versa), it is worth trying to spot the likely looking stretches from a distance. Then, move from one spot to another in a wide arc, keeping a low profile and a good distance from the water.

Reconnaissance

One of Humphrey's favourite party tricks was to head straight for a pool that he knew would always hold a good stock of trout and grayling. He would then succeed in landing several fish before they started to grow wary of the artificial flies that kept drifting past. At this point, he would offer to

move on and – very considerately – let another angler into his stretch of prime water. Walking upstream past the fish that he had already spooked, he would stop at some good virgin water and continue to catch fish. Inevitably, the lucky angler who had taken over his previous swim would experience very little action. Humphrey's reputation grew for both his undoubted skill and his generosity in offering less able anglers a chance to fish in the best water.

An important way to increase catch rates is to carry out a proper reconnaissance of the water before starting to fish. If two equally competent fishermen tackle up identically with the same fly, the one fishing his 'home water' will do better nearly every time. This is simply because he knows where the fish are likely to lie and exactly the right vantage points from which to tackle them.

The need for reconnaissance may appear to be little more than good practice straight out of a textbook – but it really does make a tremendous difference on the chalk-streams and spring creeks. An angler walking the beat for the first time is unlikely to know exactly where the trout are holding until he is level with them. At this point it may be too late, depending on his profile and angle of approach. Quite often, an isolated fish at the tail of the holding area will dart upstream as an angler draws level. This will alert the rest of the shoal to the imminent danger, even though they may be many yards away, and prevent them feeding.

Thus, we will invariably carry out a brief reconnaissance on arrival at any chalk-stream, however familiar we may be with the stretch. We also tend to spend a significant fraction of our time on such waters observing rather than fishing, in order to get to know all the favourite hot-spots for future visits. This is an ideal tactic for the early afternoon to consolidate existing knowledge while simultaneously working off the effects of any excesses of wine.

Once the holding positions are known, you can approach the fish slowly and methodically, casting into their midst before they are visible – and, more importantly, before they can see you. Of course, it would be nonsensical to ignore rising trout in favour of a reconnaissance. But if nothing is showing, the angler with the patience to walk the length of the beat, taking due note of the landmarks, is likely to reap the highest reward.

A Low Profile

We were enjoying some splendid dry fly fishing on the Lamar River. There was a very high bank opposite, and two passing anglers sat on the top of it about 20 yds upstream of the fish. They had no wish to encroach on our stretch, and sat there – motionless – for about ten minutes. During this period the fishing went off completely, until they climbed down from the bank to the water's edge to continue their foraging upstream. Almost as soon as their silhouettes disappeared from the skyline, the fishing picked up again – even though they were now closer to the water. The high bank behind them now provided cover.

Denzil had encountered a shoal of fifty large grayling in a deep pool on a feeder stream into the River Test. His instincts and experience told him from the start that with such a tiny, clear and slow-moving stretch, he had to use the maximum amount of stealth. Quite literally crawling on all fours, he worked his way past them before casting an upstream nymph. Since they had not sensed any danger from the bank, their suspicions were not aroused, even after ten had been caught (and returned well downstream).

Then along came Wesley.

'Get on to all fours, or they'll see you,' pleaded Denzil.

'Denzil. I have to tell you that when you have been fishing for as long as I, you will know instinctively when you are below the ten-degree line. Providing my torso is horizontal, taking due account of the water level, I know that I will not disturb the shoal. Moreover, you cannot expect someone of my seniority to get down on his hands and knees without proper cause.'

Wesley later claimed that he had based his assumption on a previous visit when the water level had been higher. The more popular opinion was that he had deliberately ruined Denzil's chances out of a long-held jealousy of an immeasurably better angler. Whatever the explanation, from that moment the fish disappeared and did not return for the rest of the day – and Denzil could not help murmuring an assortment of words that included git, fat and pompous.

The bending of light in passing from air to water (or vice versa) helps trout to see objects at a lower height than would otherwise be the case. Fishermen do not have to stand on top of high banks to be visible. The fish may notice anything more than a couple of feet above the water – or, more precisely, above an angle of ten degrees to the surface. Even the rod may be visible as it moves through the air, and the normal varnished finish sends an alarming flash as it catches the sun on a bright summer day. Shorter rods are arguably less conspicuous, but it is possible to reduce the problem by a side-casting when there is sufficient space that is free from obstructions.

Wading

Although it is imperative not to make any avoidable commotion by unnecessary wading, river trout tend to be more tolerant of an angler's presence amongst them than their cousins in still water. They seem to sense danger much less if it exists inside rather than outside their watery world. This should be exploited because of two other major advantages that wading can offer. First, moving into the centre of the stream keeps the drag on the line to a minimum. This is because it reduces both the angle of the cast and the variations in current that the line has to cross between the angler and the fish. Second, wading helps to conceal an angler by reducing his profile above the water and his angle of approach.

Before wading, the route should be properly planned. It pays to enter the water well downstream (or upstream) of the intended area, and then gradually to work your way towards the fish. It is always worth locating the likely holding areas in advance to avoid wading directly through them. Large numbers of fish may be hugging the bank at exactly the point you might choose to enter the stream, and even experienced anglers continue to be surprised on occasions. Before entering the water, it is therefore a good idea to cast a few times over the proposed wading area. On some stretches the centre of the stream is shallower than the edges, and this is a prime opportunity for wading into the middle and casting towards both banks.

Other Factors

It is a good idea to capitalize on the cover offered by bank-side features. This inevitably means wearing drab green or brown clothing as most anglers do out of habit. Due to the ten-degree line, the colour of a jacket is more important than the colour of trousers when casting from the bank. There is also no sense in wearing a totally camouflaged outfit if it is topped with an orange hat, perhaps with an inscription saying 'Top Rod'. It might as well say 'Here I am'!

MC exploits bank-side camouflage on the Itchen.

Sometimes you may have got everything else right, only to be throwing an enormous shadow across the water that will advertise your every movement to the fish. This is a very frustrating experience. It is worth thinking about the direction of the sun before deciding which bank to fish, but there may be other factors such as access rights that are completely out of your control. Moreover, the river may twist and turn so that no bank is consistently better. On these occasions, it is worth looking for crossing places well away from the areas that you wish to fish.

THE LIKELY LIES

One of the most fundamental skills of stream fishing is the ability to locate trout when they are not giving themselves away by rising. If the water is reasonably clear, and the fishing dour, it is often quite rewarding to take a little time off and walk carefully along a mile or so of bank. This allows you to mark where the best fish are lying in preparation for improved conditions later in the day.

Polaroids are a necessity because, even on the dullest of days, there is still plenty of glare that will obstruct sub-surface vision. It is arguably worth investing in an additional pair with a higher light transmission for these occasions – even though such versions are only partially polarising. (You can never remove all the glare, unless your glasses are at just the right angle when direct sunlight bounces off a mirror-like surface.) A pair that extends around the side of the head, or one with attachments on each side arm to cut out extraneous light, will improve sub-surface vision considerably. You only have to look into the water and then block the light entering through the sides of an ordinary pair with your hands to be convinced. In exactly the same way, a peaked or brimmed hat will restrict the amount of extraneous light entering your eyes from above.

A greater challenge arises when the water clarity is too poor to make any direct observations. This may arise from coloration, a highly rippled surface or sub-surface features that provide camouflage. Fortunately, it is possible to make some pretty informed guesses about the likely haunts because trout are quite predictable in their choice of a lie. This predictability stems from a fish's three primary motivations.

First and foremost, it needs to survive against predators from the air and land, and occasionally from the water. It is therefore unlikely to stay for too long in the most fertile area of the stream if it is totally exposed – except at night. Thus, areas under bushes, bridges, weed-beds or boulders are all likely to be holding stations. They also help to fulfil the second criterion which is, of course, the necessity to feed. Bushes are a constant source of terrestrial insects in the warmer months, and weed-beds are likely to hold aquatic nymphs right through the year. Bridges are a source of food if the area holds its quota of residential *Homo sapiens* – a universally abundant species that is likely to drop bread and other goodies into the water to feed the fish and water birds. The third and final requirement is an easy life – for the bigger specimens at least. Just as humans tend to be more restful in later years, so do the older statesmen of the stream. They prefer the more sedate areas where they do not have to work so hard to fight against the current. Privilege comes with age and brawn, and the larger trout are thus able to secure the best lies that combine slow currents with an ample food supply and seclusion from predators. The smaller trout are driven out into the faster areas of current, but just like children they seem to have the endless energy necessary for the task. It is very often these youngsters that are constantly on the feed, and they can easily create an unwanted distraction from the larger specimens in the slower areas of the stream.

The flow can vary quite dramatically across the stream, from slow glides to rapids. Insects on the surface tend to get sucked across into the faster flows, often resulting in a fairly narrow conveyor belt of food. Unfortunately, these faster currents are not ideal for the trout's conservation of energy. It will therefore try to find a spot out of the main current that is close enough to the flow for it to see and intercept the food. Such a spot may be immediately obvious from a submerged obstacle, but the real trick is to look for the less visible signs.

The speed of the current varies with depth as well as position across the stream. Water next to the bed will be moving more slowly than on the surface, and sudden changes in depth or width will cause all sorts of local variations in the current. The same number of gallons per second of water have to flow along the entire length of the stream, otherwise the water would accumulate in some spots and empty in others. Therefore, any deepening or widening has to signal a reduction in the speed of the current somewhere in the immediate vicinity.

You would need a PhD in fluid dynamics even to attempt to work out all the likely variations, but suffice it to say that all sorts of complex three dimensional behaviour exist beneath the surface. In very localized areas, some of the water will actually be flowing up the stream, to such an extent that trout sometimes face 'the wrong way'. The existence of such variations, back-eddies and stagnation points means that there may be plenty of slack holding areas with a good food supply quite close to some of the most inhospitable surface currents.

The identification of such holding areas will increase with experience into a 'sixth sense'. If you fish the same water frequently, the signs of rising fish will, of course, help to build up an accurate picture of all the best holding spots. But a thinking fisherman will do more than simply register the good lies in his local river. He will try to understand why these areas are so productive in terms of the features of the stream. Once he has grasped all the reasons, he will be in a much better position for tackling new and unfamiliar waters.

The Bank

Many anglers have a psychological difficulty in imagining that there is a good fish right beneath their feet. It is perhaps the fishing equivalent of the grass being greener on the other side of the fence, for there can be an overwhelming desire to cast farther than necessary. Yet the same anglers on a float trip will constantly cast their flies so that they are almost touching the

JD hooks a good trout close to the bank on the Beaverhead.

bank – and if they do not, they are more than likely to receive some friendly nagging from their guide.

The bank satisfies two out of three of the trout's criteria for the perfect home. First there is comfort since the current is usually slacker than it is out in the stream. Second, there is often quite a respectable concentration of food. This arises partly from the proximity of terrestrial insects, and partly from the abundance of aquatic life that exists in weed growth close to the margins. Small fish often seek the sanctuary and calmer waters close to the bank, and such places are therefore very attractive to large, predatory trout. Even the most careful anglers will occasionally disturb large specimens, which could not have come any closer to the edge without leaving the water.

The third criterion is security, which is put at risk by land-based predators. So any overhanging bush or deep undercut is a prime area. In stony rivers, a trout's camouflage is so good that it may quite happily rest in a tiny pocket that is only a foot or so deep – safe from all predators until it gives its presence away by rising. Sometimes trout will visit shallow areas to feed, while spending most of their time in deeper water nearby. As long as such deeper water is close at hand as a bolt-hole, they may feel quite secure in an exposed stretch of water. They will feel even more secure if there is a layer of scum on the surface, and such localized areas therefore merit very serious attention.

Rocks and Large Boulders

Barriers to the flow are always likely to hold fish. Rocks and boulders offer sanctuary against the current for species such as caddis and shrimps, and are a natural habitat for the nymphs of stone-clingers and stoneflies. They therefore harbour an ample supply of food right through the year. They also provide a substantial amount of camouflage, especially if there are any pockets beneath them. It is not just the obvious boulders that attract the fish – larger than average stones that are almost inconspicuous on the river bed might hold a resident trout. It is worth scouring any stretch of water for such features, because they are real hot-spots. Without any exaggeration, it is not unusual to raise a fish with the first cast to every rock in some stretches of river.

First thoughts might suggest that trout will always choose the shelter and comfort behind boulders. Certainly, plenty may exist there, but others will actually remain more or less in front of the obstruction. The continuous pounding by the currents will often produce deeper pockets, and 'stagnation points' of stationary water will exist as the flow separates round the sides of the obstruction. From this position the trout is right next to the conveyor belt of current-borne insects. Furthermore, it is often the bigger fish that take up these prime locations.

We have already explained our preference for keeping on the move to cover new water, since fish soon become aware of an angler's presence. On some streams, one cast is the only chance

MC with a nice trout from the boulders on the Whanganui.

you will get. But in 'pocket-water', which is strewn with large boulders, it is worth persevering in any 'fishy-looking' swim for as long as your patience will allow. A trout lying under a large rock is less likely to detect the disturbance of the line, especially if he is not looking to the surface for food. A nymph is therefore the logical approach. On many occasions, though – sometimes after 15 minutes of fruitless casting over the same small area – a large trout has eventually spotted a dry fly and taken it with total confidence. Thus, an excellent tactic is to use a bushy dry fly, such as a Royal Wulff, with a nymph 3–4 ft below it.

Deeper Runs

Deep or wide runs contain sedately moving water, which is an ideal home for weed and comfort-seeking fish. Slow, weedy water will harbour a wide variety of nymphs and provide plenty of cover.

In many cases, the runs do not have to be that deep. In stony waters, where the natural camouflage is so good, a deepening from (say) 1–2 ft can make all the difference between a barren stretch and a hot-spot. We found one such run on the Lamar River almost by accident. The banks of the river were lined with fishermen in every known hot-spot, and we had to make do with what was left. It was not until we started fishing, more through the mechanics of being there than out of any real expectation, that we noticed a very subtle deepening in the middle over a stretch of about 100 yds. The fishing turned out to be spectacular, with numerous cutthroats between 15 and 20 in.

Riffles

Shallow water does not offer a great deal of protection from external predators, but the reduced visibility through a broken surface provides some compensation. Riffles also stack the odds in the angler's favour by offering camouflage, disguising the leader and impeding a fish's ability to inspect the fly. Some rivers, such as the Madison, flow for miles as virtually one continuous riffle.

Fish need to expend a lot of effort to stay in the current, and the faster riffles are therefore the likely habitat of smaller trout. Nevertheless, uneven flows may channel a lot of food into selected areas, and any deeper and therefore slower stretch to the side will attract the larger specimens.

It is often difficult to identify sub-surface features beneath the riffles, so it is always worth methodically working a fly through and around them. One key area to try is the point at which the riffles start to die out, since this may signify the entrance to a deeper stretch or pool. More importantly, it will be where the comfort-loving trout in the deeper water will be expecting their food to arrive. In the tiny pools of stony brooks and creeks, it is often essential to allow the dry fly to enter the pool along the flow of riffled water.

Pools

When referring to pools, anglers usually think of a wider or deeper area of the river, but the term also covers less obvious features. In stony brooks, pools may be the tiny pockets of habitable water that hold nearly all the trout. Elsewhere they may be no more than the slightly deeper glides and holes, or the sanctuary offered by the calm area behind a rock.

Ironically, the large pools that appear at first sight to be the most tempting spots often hold disappointing numbers of trout. In some cases this may be due to over-fishing of the most promising water. They do, however, often offer sanctuary to the better specimens. There is one 'fishy-looking' pool on the River Wylye that we used to try for short spells on every outing for a couple of years. In all this time we only took two brown trout, but both of them were comfortably over 3 lb. In some instances, the larger fish may drive out their smaller brethren, preferring to keep such prime locations to themselves. The fact that such places contain larger and more educated trout may also account for the reduced success in such areas. Many pools with a poor fly fishing record will sometimes yield trophy-sized trout to worm fishermen.

Unless there is a good rise, success in such pools may require a dedicated and patient approach with a heavily weighted nymph. It may be necessary to keep pounding away at the same spot for some time, until the nymph just happens to land in the right pocket of water with the appropriate trajectory. You should not neglect the edges, where food may be funnelled by the currents and where bank side vegetation offers sanctuary from predators and provides a source of terrestrial insects. Moreover, very deep areas may not be so conducive to weed growth that supports the aquatic food chain.

Sluices

The 'hatch pool' just below a sluice or weir tends to be deeper than average and well oxygenated. There is often a combination

of currents bringing in food, with a substantial amount of slack water where fish can hold station with minimal effort. These features make the area a highly desirable residence that is likely to hold large specimens. In fact, providing the pool has not been over-fished, it is quite likely to be the most productive location for a nymph anywhere on the river. The trouble is that such hot-spots are also visited frequently by anglers.

Apart from the potential for high concentrations of sizeable trout, the ruffled surface increases the chances of success by distorting a fish's view of the outside world. The requirement for stealth is therefore somewhat reduced, and downstream tactics may be quite productive on what is otherwise a slow-moving, shallow stretch that demands an upstream approach. Nevertheless, the fish are likely to have become especially wary due to angling pressure, and may decide to move away. Thus, hatch pools may become devoid of fish quite early in the season, although they are likely to prove irresistible dwelling places to any new arrivals.

Wherever possible, always start well downstream with short casts to the tail of the pool. These areas of relatively slack and shallow water will often hold a lot of fish that you can reach with dry flies and conventional tactics. Then – and only then – should you work your way up to the head of the pool. At this point, the most important requirement is probably sufficient weight to get the fly down as close as possible to the sluice. A really heavy rolled nymph can be deadly. It is also worth experimenting with different retrieves as if fishing in still water.

A hatch pool on the River Test.

Impossible Locations

The fact that large specimens tend to favour the unreachable locations may be more an act of chance than a conscious decision by the fish. Once a trout has taken up residence in such a place, it will be free from anglers and be able to put on weight, perhaps over many years, without interference. Examples include large bushes that completely overhang the water for several yards, and the far banks of large rivers where access is forbidden by land and the middle of the stream is too deep for wading.

Those seeking a specimen fish could do worse than look for such locations purposely and then explore ways round the problem. It may just be possible to cast under a bush from an upstream or downstream position by side-casting close to the surface of the water with an ultra-short leader. The required casting distance may be too great for conventional stream tackle, but a longer rod and better-shooting line might just do the trick. A really heavy and (perhaps) ungainly nymph may be necessary to get down to the fish quickly in the confined space. Good presentation with such tactics may be impossible, but there is the chance that the trout will have lost some of their survival instincts through continued protection.

One afternoon MC made a two mile hike through awkward terrain to reach the far side of the River Usk, which was hardly ever fished. An 18 in brown – not enormous by many standards, but a monster for this river – took the size 14 Panacea on the very first cast. Although a trout of this dimension would have become very firmly established as an educated resident, it had no reason or opportunity to have grown suspicious of artificial flies.

DRAG

The Problem

Imagine a stream where the current was the same all the way across, and an angler could walk down the bank at an identical speed. The fly, leader and line would then all move down at exactly the same speed independently of each other. The angler would not influence the line, the line would exert no pull on the leader, and the leader would not drag the fly. We were able to do this with considerable success by walking downstream with the fly on a very gentle 200 yd stretch of the Lamar. Those taking a float trip on a large river also experience the enormous advantage of drag-free fishing while moving with the stream. However, such occasions are the exception rather than the rule for any one of two very good reasons – a stationary angler and varying currents.

An educated trout will see large numbers of flies. Colour, size and profile may vary considerably, but the trajectory past its lie will always remain the same (providing the water conditions do not change). Not even a strong cross-wind will cause a natural fly to divert from its downstream passage. Any pattern that moves in just a slightly deviant direction will be immediately obvious as an unnatural phenomenon. In some rivers we have noticed large trout holding position just beneath an artificial fly

as it moves down the stream, only to disappear the instant that any drag occurs. It is a matter of conjecture whether they are sufficiently intelligent to do this as a means of sorting out the impostor from the real thing, but it sends out a very clear message. Drag is bad news.

There are exceptions to exploit, such as a hatch of caddis when the adults will sometimes skitter across the water, or the deliberate lifting of the fly at the end of a downstream cast. However, for most of the time it is important to take the problem very seriously indeed. An extra second of drag-free fishing after a fly has landed on the water may be the vital ingredient for success.

Mending the Line

Even with a perfectly uniform current across the entire width of the stream, a bow will form in the line and drag on the leader and fly. This arises because a stationary angler constrains the line close to the bank, whereas the rest of the line is free to move faster with the current and overtake it.

When fishing upstream, the line will tend to bow belly first down the current, increasing the speed of the fly relative to the stream. It is therefore important to pre-empt this condition by throwing an 'upstream mend'. This is simply a flick of the rod tip in the upstream direction to create a bow. This deliberate bow, which should not exert any drag on the fly, will introduce a delay while the line straightens before it can curve again in the unwanted downstream direction.

Mending the line will inevitably create some disturbance, even though practice does bring a lot of improvement. It is therefore a good idea to incorporate an aerial upstream mend into the casting technique to reduce the need for any adjustments on the water. This involves a curve cast (or shepherd's crook) with a movement of the rod tip just before the line alights on the water, and should come as second nature to any experienced river fisherman.

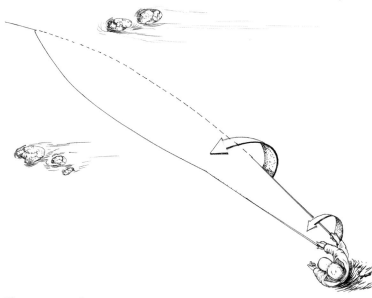

The upstream mend.

When fishing downstream, the belly of the line will form a bow that drags behind the fly and slows it down relative to the current. A 'downstream mend' will delay the onset of this drag. The drag can also be alleviated by paying out extra line and moving the rod round to follow it so that both point in the same direction.

An excellent description of mending and casting can be found in *The Cast* by Ed Jaworowski.

Varying Currents

Not all stretches have nice, uniform currents. Very often depths will vary across the stream, giving rise to large variations in flow from slack water to fast moving riffles. Large rocks may introduce further complications. The net result is that these effects can completely dominate the drag experienced by the fly.

For example, suppose that you cast a fly upstream and it lands in fast water in the middle of the river. The flow gets slower towards the bank. The end nearer the fly will be moving much faster than the rest of the line, so that a bow will form pointing up the current. Thus, the normal upstream mend would have made matters worse. The mend needs to be in the opposite direction.

Whenever the current varies greatly between an angler and the fly, it is worth trying to wade out as far as possible to get

A case for wading.

closer to the fish. The other tactic is to hold the rod high with the arm outstretched to reduce the amount of fly line that has to make contact with the water. If all the line can be kept clear, drag will be virtually eliminated. Moreover, the end of the line, which is slightly bowed, is sufficiently free to move and register the slightest take to a nymph. Long rods obviously have a big advantage here.

Snaky Lines

When casting directly up or down the stream, the line experiences very little sideways force, and a large arc will therefore be unlikely to develop. Drag is therefore less of an issue, but local variations in the current may still cause some problems. A tight line between angler and fly has no 'give' in it to absorb these disturbances, so that some amount of drag may eventually occur. A snaky line takes time to straighten in the current, thereby giving the fly more time to flow freely, and a nymph longer to reach the required depth.

All sorts of complicated routines exist to achieve this objective. One of the most popular tricks is to aim to cast a little bit too far, and then to check the line between your fingers at the last moment. The line and leader will then spring back slightly. A better method is to waggle the rod tip from side to side a few times during the final forward cast before releasing the line. The technique only takes a few minutes to master, and you can actually see the waviness forming in the line during its flight through the air. A few large sideways waggles will produce correspondingly large S-shapes in the line. Faster, smaller waggles produce a greater number of smaller S-shapes. Both outlines will go a long way to achieving the required objective.

The snaky line.

Positioning and Observation

There is more to combating drag than a perfect mend or a masterful control of the rod. Even with the best available techniques, currents may play havoc with the motion of the fly. It is worth positioning yourself so that the line does not cross an area where the current varies too dramatically. This is very important when casting to the far bank, since the fly line in the centre of the stream is likely to be moving considerably faster than the leader. The solution may be to wade into the water rather than standing on the bank, and casting up or downstream rather than across it.

Unfortunately, trout in well-fished rivers may become spooked by a line landing on top of them – or even passing over their heads. This will often cause them to move away or to stop feeding altogether. The obvious remedies are to use a longer leader or to cast with expert precision. An easier solution is to stop casting directly along the current, and to reposition yourself to cover the fish at a slight angle of about twenty degrees. This will avoid most of the drag, while reducing the risk of lining your quarry.

One of the most useful pieces of advice for avoiding drag is simply to make maximum use of observation and common sense. A careful watch on a dry fly or strike indicator close to a bubble (or any small item floating on the surface) will reveal just how quickly the paths of the two objects diverge. This may be a little depressing, but it provides the opportunity to experiment with the best combination of techniques on the day. It is by continued observation, experimentation and practice that experienced anglers are able to combat drag almost as second nature.

FISHING THE DRY FLY

Specific versus General Patterns

Trout are sometimes very finicky about accepting a dry fly, to the extent that they will ignore everything except a suitable imitation of the naturally occurring insect. It is often assumed that this is because they will be suspicious of anything that does not resemble the natural food currently on offer. More often, though, the problem is one of fixation once they have embarked on a determined feeding spree. We have often observed that they become totally preoccupied with the most abundant food form. This is particularly true when there are large numbers of tiny flies on the surface. Given the choice between a large, juicy pupa and a tiny caenis or trico in isolation, they might opt for the larger meal. But once they have embarked on a feast of particular insects, they will often continue to the exclusion of everything else. This is why it is often much easier to succeed with the 'wrong' patterns right at the start of a hatch before the rise has become properly established. Browns seem to be particularly susceptible to this form of selectivity.

There are definitely some insects that trout will usually take out of preference, and others where the selection is rather less predictable. Fish are not so different from humans in this respect. Confronted with lots of stewing steak and a few pieces of sirloin, most of us would completely ignore the inferior meat – although our preference for sirloin or salmon may change with our mood. Thus, trout of the fertile spring creeks and chalk-streams are sometimes spoilt for choice and can be ultra-selective. In contrast, their counterparts in the 'Third World' of the more acidic rain-fed rivers may have to take what they can whenever the chance arises.

The need for careful fly selection varies according to the type of stream, the time of year and the hatch conditions. The number of liberties that you can take with general patterns will also vary with the education of the trout and the proximity of any neighbours. This latter point is simply a statement of the competition element. A trout may put aside its natural caution if it thinks a rival will get to the prize first. Thus, those sharing a pool may always be in a position where they will have to compete. On the other hand, a resident with its own private lie will have no difficulty in intercepting any fly that it sees, and can afford to be more cautious about what it will select.

Even when trout become preoccupied, the predominant or most visible species might not be the one that matters. There may be plenty of duns on the water, but the trout may be insisting on the less numerous spent spinners if they are easier to intercept. Flies in the surrounding air may not be those being taken on the water. Dancing spinners, for example, are probably a cloud of males which are most unlikely to return to the water to lay their eggs! Even female spinners may not be returning to the water immediately in front of you. Many an angler has suffered from a mind-set and mistaken ants for small upwinged flies. Even if you watch the water like a hawk for every visual clue, it is still possible to go astray. In the presence of an ample supply of tempting upwinged flies, the trout may have become preoccupied with virtually invisible species such as migrating snails.

Identification of the 'dish of the day' by watching individual flies on the water calls for a lot of patience and concentration, and may require exceptional eyesight. So you should take full account of additional clues from rise-forms. An unhurried sipping or nebbing will suggest a fly, such as a spinner, that is unlikely to escape in a hurry. A pronounced head and tail movement is more likely to point to duns or emergers. A splashy rise may indicate a skittering caddis or a large species such as a crane fly.

Those who come prepared with imitations of the right species have a head start, but this does not necessarily need a deep knowledge of entomology. All the studying and preparation in the world often cannot prepare you for your first encounter with a new water. Local species can vary considerably over distances of a few miles, let alone continents, and the collection of all possible variations will be a very expensive or time-consuming task. If you want to match the hatch precisely, you may have to be prepared for some observation at the water before returning to tie or purchase the right patterns. It is worth remembering that the choice between a dun and a spinner may be far more important than identification of the exact species.

Before visiting a new region, we will do a little bit of research to get a broad picture of the predominant flies. On arrival, we will try to get more detailed information from the local tackle shops and anglers. We are never too proud to ask others for advice or to let them do most of the talking. Having obtained a set of local patterns, it is then possible to supplement or modify them progressively throughout the stay from our own experiences and observations. Above all, we will make sure that we arrive with a comprehensive supply of general patterns that have served us consistently well in the past over a wide range of localities and conditions. They are almost guaranteed to get us off to a respectable start.

We usually managed to schedule fishing trips to coincide with events in Wesley's calendar that he could not — or would not — miss. Often, these were committee meetings that would allow him to indulge himself (and others) in his own importance. Such matters were of far higher priority to him than the diverse streams of Montana or the wild six-pounders in New Zealand — and of course, we would give him every encouragement. The organization of fly fishing depended on someone of his intellect and experience.

Eventually, he managed to impose himself on an unsuspecting party visiting Alaska. His wife took the opportunity to travel out with him via Seattle, where she had arranged to visit a friend for the duration of the trip. Since he would be travelling out in a small plane to remote areas of wilderness, and she would be touring the west coast, there would be ten glorious days (her perspective) when contact would be impossible. Northern California turned out to be a break made in heaven.

Wesley, on the other hand, did not have a very good holiday. The fishing was fantastic, but the mosquitoes seemed to take a particular dislike to him. They would bite him in every conceivable place – even through his shirt – and he had to resort to a combination of thick clothing, face nets and a risky amount of DEET. On a couple of days, he chose to remain at the lodge, unable to contact his beloved wife who would be sure to sympathize with his predicament more than the uncaring fishing party.

He was quite relieved to return to Seattle, but there was no sign of his wife or her friend to meet him at the airport. Perhaps there had been a traffic jam or accident, because he had clearly and pedantically typed out all the details of his flight arrival – in triplicate. He consulted his copy, and everything was correct. So he phoned his wife's friend, but could not get through due (it transpired) to one of her sons surfing the internet. He was in a dilemma, because if he caught a taxi he might miss them when they eventually arrived.

Eventually, after two hours, several coffees and an unwanted snack, he managed to get through. There had been no error in his details, no bad news and no traffic hold-ups. They had quite simply and genuinely forgotten all about him!

We are not going to pretend that a general pattern will always work as well as a purpose-tied imitation, but anglers who carry a comprehensive range of general patterns tend to do consistently well. They get less bogged down with unnecessary detail, and focus their concentration on fishing the flies properly under the prevailing conditions. They exude an air of confidence, and soon develop a sixth sense of when their failure is due to the patterns themselves rather than other factors. Thus, when they opt for precise imitation, there is usually a very good reason. In contrast, their precise-imitation-only counterparts may try a couple of dozen different patterns when the reason for failure may be due to entirely different causes, such as inadequate presentation.

We can recall one outing on the River Usk, when we shared the beat with Jeremy Herrmann who is a very competent fisherman – in fact, an ex-world champion. The medium olives started to hatch and, as often happens, the trout became very selective. Jeremy mentioned casually that the wild brown trout were not at all impressed with any of his dry flies – and he was right!

After we had netted a considerable number, he pleaded for our successful pattern – so we gave him the size 14 Adams. 'But I tried that', he exclaimed, 'along with a dozen other olive patterns!'

Our simple approach had told us that the Adams was a good general pattern for copying the hatching olives. There was a choice of a conventional or parachute hackle, but the former was more appropriate in the rough water – and it needed to ride high. Thus, we were meticulous in keeping it high in the water – first by adding Gink, and subsequently by using a 'Shake and Dry' powder. This simple technique of inserting the drowned fly in a drying agent made the fly sit up on top of the surface film, which was precisely where the trout wanted it.

We gave some of the powder to Jeremy, who immediately started to catch fish. It was a classic example of how, with a proven general pattern, you can concentrate exclusively on the most productive way to fish it.

Basic Dry Fly Collection

The broad categories of insect for rivers are upwinged, terrestrial, caddis and stone flies. Terrestrial flies, unlike the other categories, may belong to various different entomological orders and exhibit quite different forms. Thus, there will be enormous differences between some fly patterns – an ant and a grasshopper, for example. Variations within each of the other three groups in the list, however, are sufficiently limited to allow a proper exploitation of general patterns.

Our basic collection of general river flies is outlined below, and followed by more detailed descriptions and tyings in the chapter on *Great Fly Patterns*. We tie this small nucleus of flies in a variety of shapes and sizes to cover a wide range of conditions. Some of the flies are our own developments or those of fishing acquaintances, while others are already well established patterns. The latter have the distinct advantage of being thoroughly proven by perhaps hundreds of thousands of fishermen. The former, being that little bit different, may provide that extra edge on a heavily fished stream.

Specific imitations definitely do have a role to play for maximum success. The variation of species within Europe and the USA is so large, however, that any attempt to cover them all is outside the scope of this book. Our aim is to concentrate on up-to-date tactics and techniques, with a restricted selection of reliable general patterns that will suffice for most rather than all situations. Many excellent books already exist that describe more specific representations.

For upwinged duns and emergers, we have a nucleus of only three patterns – though they span a good range of colours and sizes. If our first choice fails, we will try the remainder before considering specific imitations – unless, for example, there is a hatch of something special, such as large *Ephemera* mayflies. The CDC Flat-Backs represent insects in an early stage of emergence, and being so simple and unfussy are ideal for tiny flies. Our own pattern for the emerging upwinged dun with its shuck attached has become affectionately and deservedly known as the Panacea. For duns, the Sail-Wings cover the range of fully formed adults that have become detached from the shuck. They perform very well in this role, but often they will obstinately disobey all the rules of natural imitation and perform spectacularly well if fitted with a shuck. A CDC Spinner completes the selection.

Next come the often neglected terrestrial insects – essential on the less fertile streams, but often surprisingly effective on the chalk-streams and spring creeks. They may contribute a substantial proportion of a trout's diet of adult flies in a typical river. These include ants, beetles, black gnats, (in the USA) grasshoppers and (in New Zealand) cicadas.

Caddis representations are also essential, being universally present and more tolerant of water conditions than upwinged flies. If we had to restrict ourselves to only one basic pattern, it would have to be the Elk Hair Caddis. We make no apologies for selecting such a well-known fly. It has three useful properties of representing the natural, staying afloat in rough water and being easily visible to an angler.

Adult stoneflies usually form only a small fraction of a trout's diet, and a comprehensive set of general patterns will probably get you by on most occasions. However, Stoneflies are a prime example of the need for a little bit of research in advance. Needle Flies are essential for some of the northern English rivers. You might also miss out on a lot of fun without patterns to represent Western Golden Stones and the gigantic salmon fly in the western USA.

Last, but not least, we would never go anywhere without a Royal Wulff. It covers a range of large insects, will pull trout up from their lairs to investigate, and act as the perfect strike indicator with added attraction.

Visibility versus 'Floatability'

The natural flies on two streams may be identical, but the best patterns to represent them are sometimes quite different. This is because the angling priorities for the two waters are not the same. On a slow moving and clear stream, the trout has a clear

MC has success with an Orange and Green Woven Nymph on the Whanganui.

view and plenty of time to make up its mind. The imitation therefore has to be very good indeed. On a fast moving river, a perfect imitation may be too slim to ride the currents. It may also be invisible to the angler and possibly to the trout. It is therefore a matter of choosing the right balance between two opposite requirements. At one extreme, you may use an otherwise perfect pattern that is rejected before you become aware that it has been taken. At the other, you may be able to observe a fly perfectly that no self-respecting trout will touch.

One key factor for success is to understand where the balance lies under the prevailing conditions, and how and why to adjust it.

On small, slow-moving chalk-streams and spring creeks, the emphasis leans towards a proper imitation. For example, the post on a parachute fly should be as inconspicuous to the trout as possible, or comprise a hackle point or other feature specifically chosen to improve the representation of a natural insect. One of the most common mistakes is to worry too much about whether a fly will stay afloat or be visible from a distance. The result is inevitably a pattern that has too much bulk, too many unnatural appendages, overdone full hackles or too much floatant in the wrong places. This is a fly that the wary, educated trout will not even consider intercepting, because it has 'inedible' or 'danger' written all over it.

Slim flies, providing they are treated with floatant to prevent them becoming water logged, will stay afloat for a surprisingly long time on slow moving streams. Normally they need to be pulled beneath the water to sink. The most common cause of sinking is a sideways pull from the leader as the current drags the nylon. Once this drag starts to occur, a fly that remains afloat is unlikely to be taken as it moves unnaturally – but a drowned fly might arguably have a chance of being taken if it bears sufficient resemblance to a natural sub-surface species. Although drag is bad news, it is not quite so serious for nymphs that can propel themselves to some extent across the current. We have quite often caught fish when a submerged dry fly experiences this type of movement, especially towards the end of a retrieve when it is about to break upwards through the surface.

An obvious problem with a lightly dressed fly that has no sighting point is the detection of a take. Those with good eyesight will always have a distinct advantage. Nevertheless, any angler can improve his skills to differentiate between surface features and a dry fly. It needs practice, concentration and patience from the moment the fly lands on the water. If you can spot the fly at this point, it is usually possible to track its passage downstream. It is a good idea to try to focus on a nearby bubble at the same time. In addition to increasing the chances of keeping an eye on the right general area, it provides a measure of when the fly starts to drag. Another trick is to position a strike indicator within a couple of feet of an inconspicuous dry fly.

Reflexes are usually that bit faster if you can see the fly rather than spreading your concentration over the immediate area. On many occasions, simply watching the right general area may not be enough. Sometimes a trout – and it is often one of the larger specimens – will suck a fly under without any visible rise-form or disturbance of the surface. The only way of hitting such takes is to watch the fly itself.

The balance changes towards visibility and 'floatability' on the faster flowing streams or in poor light conditions. This may call for a large, conspicuous post in a parachute fly or the use of flies with more visible wings. Long Microfibbet tails will help the flies to stay afloat better than hackle fibres. The faster the water, the more advantage there may be in choosing flies like the Royal Wulff or Humpy. Whenever using such patterns, we will remind

The high-floating Grey Wulff.

ourselves constantly that some of the features may not be sufficiently realistic. So the absence of a response may be a sign to tone down the fly. This does not necessarily mean removing all traces of visibility. A shortening or thinning of the wings or post is sometimes quite sufficient.

Graham Dean with a victim of the Royal Wulff on a fast-flowing stream.

Striking

River trout sometimes call for lightning reflexes before they reject a fly. The strike is transmitted more efficiently at distance by pulling with the left hand at the same time as lifting the rod. The instant that contact is felt with the fish, the left hand should stop to transfer all the striking force to the rod. Such rapid striking requires good co-ordination and a forgiving rod that will comfortably absorb the impact of the strike against a delicate tippet.

A delayed strike is appropriate when a confident trout turns on a large pattern, such as a Hopper or crane fly. This usually calls for a delay of perhaps up to a second for its mouth to close around the large morsel. This does not necessarily apply to heavily fished catch-and-release rivers, where the trout seem to learn to reject a large artificial fly more quickly. A slight delay is sometimes imperative when fishing a dry fly downstream. This allows a trout to turn, so that the strike will set the hook into the side of its mouth rather than pulling it straight out of the front.

The Kick-start

It was a miserable afternoon towards the end of September in the Rockies. The temperature had dropped, there was a continuous drizzle and there were rumours of snow only twenty miles away. The Baetis did not seem to mind, hatching in their thousands, but not a trout was rising. The grasshoppers had now all but disappeared for the year, and in any case there would have been no activity of the natural insects in such overcast and wet conditions. Nevertheless, we managed to pull out a few trout by breaking all the rules and mismatching the hatch with such a pattern.

If trout are not rising to a multitude of natural flies, there is no way that an exact imitation of the same species is going to work. Under such conditions, the trout need a 'kick-start'. They may react to a stimulus of added size, colour or movement, or may just have sufficient memory of a larger pattern that they enjoyed eating earlier in the month. It is better to give yourself a 'dog's chance' than no chance at all.

The same technique is often useful, even when trout are rising, if there is a surfeit of natural food. It is worth reiterating that the odds of a perfect imitation being taken when surrounded by a thousand natural insects must be one in a thousand. Under these conditions it is (99.9%) essential to do something slightly different. You can appeal to their greed by using an imitation that is a couple of sizes larger, to their impulse by trying something brighter, or to their aggression by ripping a fly past their noses. A good fisherman has to be flexible and diverse in his thinking.

FISHING THE NYMPH

It was lunch time during a float trip on the Beaverhead. We had tied up the dinghy to the side of the stream and were taking a well-earned rest. Since this was our first visit to this magnificent river, we had hired the services of Tim Mosolf – an experienced local guide with an enormously long beard and an uncanny ability to spot fish. After a while, Tim walked progressively upstream with the air of a man on a mission, stooping while he scanned each area of water. Ten minutes later, he called over. 'Cast your nymphs about 10 yds from here. There are two good browns, and one of them is about 28 in.'

We needed little encouragement and crept up to where Tim was standing. It was difficult to make out any details on the stone river bed beneath the rippled surface. Nevertheless, in the interests of international diplomacy, JD went along with the instructions and covered the area exactly as instructed.

'You're a foot too far out,' advised Tim. 'Cast upstream another 2 yds to let the fly sink a bit further. Lift off *now*, or you'll get the smaller fish and ruin your chances of the big one.' And so the charade went on for about ten minutes. Then, on what seemed like the hundredth cast: 'That's spot on. You should get . . .' – and at that moment the strike indicator twitched, JD struck, and a monstrous fish charged across the stream to the far bank.

The battle went on for about ten minutes. JD tried to re-position himself downstream from the fish, but this turned out to be impossible in the strong currents and locally deep water. Then, as feared, the fish charged 100 yds downstream. The reel screamed, the leader caught some weed and the size 18 Serendipity pulled out of its mouth. (This was one of many experiences that led to our preference for a short shank size 16 hook.)

Apart from highlighting our guide's ability to spot fish, this experience showed the advantage of working as a team, with one angler watching from a more advantageous angle while the other fishes. We could not have asked for a better example to confirm the need to get a nymph right in front of a fish's nose. It also illustrated the importance of distance, depth, drag and the avoidance of smaller fish. Some dry fly practitioners may not enjoy nymphing – and that is their prerogative – but any fisherman who claims that there is no skill in it is not a fisherman at all!

Confidence and Dogma

An angling guide once told us how many of his clients were surprisingly reluctant to use a nymph on the spring creeks, even when there was not the slightest chance of catching anything on a dry fly. This was often due to a lack of confidence. Dry fly fishing is arguably more enjoyable, and there is the inevitable temptation to try it first. If the trout are in any way responsive, you will stay with the dry fly. If nothing happens, then you might as well give the nymphs a try, but you are doing this in tough conditions – and half-heartedly without any commitment. Successful nymph fishing demands concentration. Half an hour without a fish, and the subconscious belief will start to develop that nymph fishing is both ineffective and boring – quite for-getting that the dry fly would have fared no better.

Historically, nymph fishing has always been the poor relation to the dry fly. To this day, it is only allowed on some of the English chalk-streams for a limited part of the season, and then it has to be upstream-only. We agree whole-heartedly that there have to be rules and etiquette to maintain fly fishing as a skilful pastime, but nymphing is arguably at least as challenging as the dry fly. It may be possible to take a few more liberties with presentation, but there are the added dimensions of depth, movement and bite detection. The emphasis moves to getting the fly to the required depth before it is too late, imparting just the right amount of movement (which may be none at all) and reacting to the most subtle of takes.

When discussing their observations on fly life, many river anglers talk mostly about duns and spinners, because their knowledge of nymphs will be far less. Apart from the larval cases left behind by stoneflies at the water's edge, it is quite rare to observe nymphs that lie buried under stones or hidden in weeds for most of their life. If you make a casual effort to lift a stone, the nymphs dart away so quickly that it is almost impossible to catch them to get a closer look – unless you take the trouble to go to the water properly armed with a micro-mesh net. It is small wonder that dry patterns receive far more attention and scrutiny, even though nymphs make such a major contribution to a trout's diet.

The Case for the Nymph

For the benefit of any dry fly-only fishermen, we would like to make one simple point. The average trout in a fertile stream will eat perhaps five to ten times as many nymphs as dry flies.

The complete river fisherman has to be as skilled with the nymph as with the dry fly, because there are many occasions when nothing will tempt a trout to rise to the surface. Even during a rise, trout can become preoccupied with the pupa to the exclusion of the adult. If a hatch is heavy there may be so much choice on the surface that a pattern may be needed that stands out from the rest. In achieving this there is often an advantage in a sub-surface fly because it removes any restriction to visibility outside the trout's window.

Bite Detection

On several occasions when fishing in clear water, we have observed a trout intercepting a nymph without any indication on the fly line. Although a river trout may not always be quite as fastidious as its still-water cousin in what nymph passes for the natural, it can spit out an impostor so quickly that the take will hardly register to the keenest eyed angler. It is therefore unavoidable that you will miss a fair number of takes, but any trick that you can possibly play will be worth the extra effort.

There is a significant advantage in fishing at close range in gin clear water because you can observe directly the sub-surface activity and a trout's manner of feeding. If it moves up in the water to intercept an ascending pupa, you will need to wait for the turn or the whitening of the mouth before striking. If it is resting stationary in the stream, apparently oblivious to anything that might be happening towards the surface, it is very unlikely to swim any significant distance to intercept a passing nymph. You should therefore strike immediately at the slightest unusual motion of the fish, whether it is upwards or sideways.

Such sub-surface visibility tends to be the exception rather than the norm, and even then you will invariably do better with a strike indicator. This assumes that such aids are allowed by the fishery rules, because some owners consider it unsporting and akin to float fishing. They have a point, but it is difficult to know where to draw the line. It is even more difficult to police since a bushy dry fly on a dropper will fulfil the same function. An indicator is closer to the fly than the tip of the fly-line, and is therefore more sensitive to the take. It can be as visible as you want it to be, and places fewer demands and strain on the eyesight than trying to watch any part of the leader.

During a dead drift, it is essential to watch the strike indicator for the slightest unusual movement. It requires some experience to differentiate between a taking trout and the erratic movements caused by the current, especially in fast flowing rivers. Our 'spitting guide' on Box Canyon introduced us to the use of two strike indicators about 6 in apart, so that we could watch for any sudden motion of one relative to the other. It turned out to be a useful tactic.

This does not mean that you should advertise your presence with an unnecessarily large indicator. It also needs to be as sensitive and hence as small as practicable to register the slightest take. It is worth striking at any suspicious change from a slowing down in the current to the merest quiver. The experienced river fisherman becomes so attuned to the slightest departure from normal that he will often lift instinctively into a fish without really knowing why he did it.

There are two other good reasons for a strike indicator. First, it can and should be used to maintain the nymph at a fixed distance below the surface. One and a half times the depth of water is a good all-round distance from the fly on an average stream, but be prepared to experiment. If the fly frequently snags on the bottom, shorten it. If it never snags, and there is no action from the fish, increase the separation to let the nymph travel deeper – or increase the weight of the fly. Heavy flies will soon drag a small float under the surface. Thus, it is the weight of the fly, rather than the ability to see it, that will often dictate the minimum size.

The second reason is to obtain some clues about whether the nymph is drifting downstream at the same rate as the current. This is easy to check by comparing the movement of the indicator with any small object floating on the surface. If the trajectories of the two objects diverge, it is almost certain that there will be some drag on the nymph. Trout are far better at noticing this unnatural phenomenon than we are. So this is a signal to try to improve the presentation by additional mending of the line or repositioning to narrow the casting angle.

There are several different types of strike indicator on the market. An adhesive patch that can be rolled into a very slim cylinder on to the leader is simple, visible and very sensitive to the take. Unfortunately, once in position it will not move easily up the nylon, and once moved it is likely to come unstuck. It is cheap enough to replace, but when changing weights or depths frequently, the use of a movable float may save considerable frustration.

Many purpose-built floats will not pass through the rod rings, and are therefore inappropriate for fishing with long leaders. More importantly, we have seen spooky fish in the chalk-streams move out of the way as soon as a float hits the water. Increasing numbers of nymph fishermen therefore use a buoyant yarn that passes through the rings and makes less disturbance as it lands. This is easy to tie on to the line with a simple knot that will disappear from the leader once the yarn is removed. One trick is to fold the yarn into a U-shape before attaching it to the leader, so that it is easier to remove later by pulling one of the two free ends. A buoyant yarn allows maximum flexibility in the size of

the indicator and in the choice of colours. Fluorescent yellow and orange are good all-round colours. In dull light conditions magenta can be considerably easier to see, whereas black is a good choice when there is a lot of glare on the water.

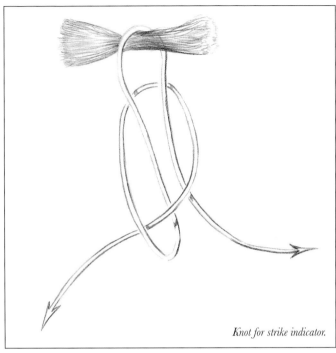

Knot for strike indicator.

Trout that have become educated on over-fished streams sometimes learn to associate even a buoyant yarn with danger. The problem is more severe in shallow water that requires a separation of perhaps only 18 in from the fly. When helping a local fisherman to stalk individual fish in New Zealand, we observed trout move away from an otherwise perfect cast the instant that his coloured yarn fell on the water.

Trout are not used to seeing fluorescent blobs floating down the river. There are, however, plenty of innocuous and diffuse white objects that pass by at one time or another – feathers and seeds, for example. Our friend Colin Harvey first took some of the hollow white filling out of his duvet. This has worked consistently on the chalk-streams towards the end of the year when the grayling become severely spooked by angling pressure. It also caused no detectable problems with the suspicious trout in New Zealand's shallow rivers.

We use this white filling material exclusively, except under the occasional awkward light conditions that can make it difficult to spot. It is then worth trying black yarn before resorting to fluorescent colours. For spooky fish, we will use the absolute minimum that will stay afloat during the duration of the drift. This is usually a very small piece indeed, and typically five to ten times less than you might first estimate. A small amount is also less prone to being blown off course by a strong wind.

Even with an indicator, takes will go unnoticed. This is evident with educated grayling towards the end of every season when we catch progressively increasing numbers by fluke while lifting or mending the line. Sometimes missed fish are unavoidable due to the gentleness of the take and the speed of the rejection. On other occasions, the hit rate can be improved. One common occurrence is when the indicator stops for a fraction of a second rather than twitching to the side. This may be difficult to spot when fishing directly upstream. It calls for total concentration and, if possible, some slight repositioning sideways. There is also a good argument for the shortest possible separation that the required depth will allow between the nymph and strike indicator.

General Nymph Patterns

At any time of year there is usually an abundant selection of different life-forms tucked away under the stones or in the reeds. While collecting nymphs, we have seldom failed to catch several completely different species at the same time. A typical session will produce a few agile darters, a few stone clingers and crawlers, several cased and free-swimming caddis, a large mayfly and lots of shrimps of various sizes and shades. When there is no hatch to preoccupy its thoughts, a trout will have no reason to reject any one of these specimens. It follows that in many instances there will be a wide choice of artificial flies and no need for careful selection.

A sound strategy, therefore, is to concentrate on a few nymphs in different sizes and weights. It is more productive to get to know a few patterns well – understanding their characteristics, strengths and weaknesses – than to dilute expertise and add unnecessary confusion. Fly selection can be a very subjective affair, but we will give a brief outline of the patterns that have pride of place in our own boxes. The dressings and additional information appear in the chapter on *Great Fly Patterns*.

Frank Sawyer's Pheasant Tail has proved itself consistently over decades, and if anything has overtaken it, it has to be the same fly with a gold head! It is a good first choice on most rivers, but since every man and his dog will be using it, it might just arouse suspicion on heavily fished waters. It may therefore be worth trying something slightly different, such as Flashbacks or a woven nymph. Apart from its novelty value, it is easier to add weight to a woven pattern without making it appear too bulky.

Shrimps (UK) or scuds (USA) are very common in many rivers. Our Scrimp pattern is consistently successful and is perfectly suited to the addition of lots of extra weight within the arched back. Even a size 16 pattern will hold quite a respectable amount of lead.

Czech Nymphs provide a superb imitation of free-swimming caddis larvae, which are abundant in rivers throughout the world. A weighted version of the good old Stick Fly – a pattern that no self-respecting English lake fisherman would ever be without for the cased varieties – will work in rivers too. Finally, Davy Wotton's caddis pupa in green or cinnamon presents a juicy morsel to any trout and, when fished just below the surface, will sometimes tempt preoccupied trout away from a prolific hatch.

Stonefly nymphs make a greater contribution to a trout's diet than the adult insects. The artificial patterns are sufficiently large for including a lot of added weight while maintaining a natural profile. Stoneflies are also well suited to woven patterns,

but a simple representation incorporating a mottled chenille body and rubber legs to provide some added stimulus takes a lot of beating. The Prince gives a respectable overall impression of a stonefly nymph, and is a good all-rounder for exploring any water where the fly life is uncertain.

Bright nymphs stand out like a sore thumb in clear water, and any imitation should not have colours that are unnaturally bright. It pays to experiment a little if the trout are ignoring drab-coloured flies, but this should be done delicately with the merest hint of fluorescence. A size 10 Hare's Ear Gold-Head is an excellent pattern for provoking a response, especially with a touch of orange towards the end of the season as the trout become more aggressive. In coloured water, a fly may need to be more visible with some added brightness.

For downstream techniques, wet flies such as a Greenwell's and Wickham's, and hackled nymphs such as spiders or hare's ear variants, should provide sufficient choice when teamed with the nymph patterns mentioned above.

Achievement of Depth

It is no exaggeration to state that achievement of the correct depth is often much more important than the choice of pattern. The currents channel all sub-surface food into localized areas, so trout soon learn at exactly what point the morsels are likely to pass by. The interception of a passing nymph is often a leisurely affair, with just a slight flick of the tail to move the short distance into the 'conveyor belt' supplying the food. A trout may be disinclined to move to intercept a nymph, and will be very suspicious of anything that does not conform to the normal delivery route. In clear water we have sometimes seen a trout adjust its position to look at a nymph moving past, but without any attempt at interception. This is just as likely to be a signal that the fly is incorrectly positioned in the water as an indication of the wrong pattern.

It is important to look carefully for clues to the feeding depth, such as a sub-surface boil or a flicker of gold or silver. If the disturbance is clearly visible, it is unlikely that the trout will be taking nymphs very deep down. Lightweight nymphs may then be necessary to remain fairly high in the water, rather than sinking to the river bed beneath their intended quarry. The obvious time is during a hatch, but sometimes there may be other reasons. Unweighted nymphs are often ideal for low water conditions on slow-moving stretches of the chalk-streams when trout may hold station on top of the weed beds.

The usual requirement, though, is to get the flies down. Before discussing the obvious ploy of adding weight, which will inevitably add bulk to a fly, there are three other features to consider. First, the rate at which a fly sinks depends not only on its weight, but also on its profile. A slim nymph, comprising tightly packed materials wrapped around a reasonably meaty hook, sinks at a surprisingly fast rate in quite a strong current. It is also important to avoid unnecessary appendages that will slow the descent, such as teased-out fur or full hackles.

The second tactic involves the choice and treatment of leader material. A leader clings to the surface film and slows the descent of a nymph. The effect may be negligible for a fully weighted size 10 shrimp, but with a size 18 Pheasant Tail it becomes quite a problem. So for small patterns, it is worth taking extra care. The leader needs to be as fine as possible to minimize the drag as it sinks with the nymph – as well as disguising the nylon, which is more prominent when attached to a tiny fly. It is just as important to degrease it from time to time to help it to cut through the surface film as soon as it lands on the water. Fluorocarbons are considerably more dense than water and are perfect for helping to get small or lightly weighted flies down quickly, providing you can get them to penetrate the surface film quickly.

Third, the length of leader will influence the ultimate depth of the fly. However, it will do little to increase the speed at which it descends, and by the time it has reached this equilibrium position the fly may have travelled too far downstream. More often, the requirement is to get the fly down quickly to a relatively modest depth. For example, trout will frequently hold position just behind a weed bed that forms a formidable barrier to any nymph that has been cast upstream.

Additional Weighting

The choice of fly is often dictated by the weight that it will accommodate. The existence of large sub-surface species in the stream is ideal for a nymph fisherman because there is plenty of scope for creating realistic imitations that will sink quickly. This is where stoneflies, woven nymphs and our old friend *Gammarus* the shrimp are such valuable assets. In addition, the last two patterns have the advantage of sinking upside down, thereby helping to keep the point of the hook clear from obstacles on the river bed.

Bead-heads offer another opportunity to conceal weight in the bubble of air that they represent. Tungsten beads are perfect for submerging a nymph quickly in strong currents. In many patterns, a layer of thick lead around the hook shank will be relatively inconspicuous given the prominent and dominating profile of the head.

Often, however, the trout's principal food will be much smaller nymphs. At first they may seize the larger offerings as manna from heaven, but they will soon realize the associated danger after a few of their number have been caught. Inevitably they will return to a diet where small is beautiful and safe, and ignore anything that is even slightly on the large size. This presents an obvious problem because, even with the most exotic tying techniques, a size 18 nymph may not sink quickly enough.

One trick for submerging a small nymph, such as a Pheasant Tail or Serendipity, is to place it on a dropper with a heavy pattern on the point. The larger pattern is there principally to add weight, but it may also attract fish to the smaller nymph or even take its own share. A size 10 Hare's Ear Gold-Head, incorporating a subtle red-orange tag, is one of our favourite all-round patterns for this purpose, although it might put the fish on their guard. Another heavyweight nymph, with drab colours and without a gold head, should therefore be kept in reserve. In fast-flowing stony rivers, a large leaded stone-fly nymph with enticing rubber legs might be an ideal choice, as both an anchor and a natural attractor. The appearance of two closely spaced flies moving in tandem does not seem to bother the majority of trout, but it may appear sufficiently unnatural to the more educated specimens. Thus, if the large nymph is unlikely to catch anything, there is a good case for replacing it with an appropriate amount of split shot, which is also less likely to snag on weeds.

Nymphs attached in the New Zealand style.

A fly never moves as naturally on a dropper as on the point, and any twisting of the leader around itself will be apparent with a tiny fly. A long dropper will improve the chances of success, but it may also increase the number of tangles. It is therefore better to fish the team the other way around, with the larger heavy fly on the dropper and the small nymph on the point. An ideal way to achieve this, and reduce tangles, is to attach the nylon from the small nymph directly to the bend of the heavy pattern (New Zealand style).

Success for JD with an upstream dead drift on the Lamar.

The Upstream Dead Drift

Whenever water conditions allow, this is arguably the most consistent line of attack. First, there is the camouflage afforded by stalking the fish from behind. Second, the movement of an artificial nymph in a 'dead drift', without any influence from the fly line, imitates many natural species when they are at the mercy of the current. This may occur after a nymph has become dislodged from weed or stones, or during its deliberate ascent to the surface to hatch.

The achievement of a dead drift needs a considerable amount of care, skill and practice. It is essential to retrieve just enough slack line to keep up with the current. Too much speed will give an unnatural motion to the fly, whereas too little will allow the line to go slack and delay the effect of the strike. On top of this, it is usually necessary to mend the line as soon as any bow starts to form, or at the instant the strike indicator starts to diverge from surface features such as bubbles. Drag may not be quite so undesirable on a sub-surface nymph as it is on a dry fly, but it is sometimes more difficult to control. The speed of the current will usually decrease with depth. Thus, even with a cast that is directly upstream, the line on the surface could be pulling the submerged nymph at too fast a speed. This makes a snaky line all the more advantageous.

At the same time, it is essential to watch the strike indicator like a hawk, responding with lightning reflexes to the slightest movement that may indicate the take prior to rejection. Contact with a fish is more difficult when there is any slack in the line – slack that may be deliberately created to allow the fly to move as freely or as deeply as possible. If there is the slightest suspicion of anything the slightest bit different, then strike.

The Induced Take

Sometimes trout will not respond to nymphs that simply drift past their noses with the current. On these occasions, a little twitch at the right moment can make all the difference. It is often claimed that this is because they are used to seeing some life in the naturals. An agile darter, for example, moves in a series of very distinct jerks, with a 'dead-drift' pause in between. Nymphs ascending to the surface to hatch into adults will often do so in a series of small undulations. Most nymphs will make some sort of movement, whether or not they are capable of swimming.

There is arguably more to the success of this method than pure imitation. We have observed trout responding to a stimulus far too often to discount it, and suspect that the induced take is exactly what its name implies. The balance may vary considerably between different times and locations, but any technique that embraces both features

The induced take.

has to have a lot going for it. Furthermore, the slack in the line will disappear at the time of moving the nymph, so the chances of registering a take at this point increase considerably.

A careful lift of the rod will impart the correct upwards trajectory, and it is a good idea to combine this deliberate movement with the mending of the line. When fishing at a distance, it may be necessary to give an additional short, sharp pull on the line. The aim is to get the nymph to move upwards by just a couple of inches in the water, followed by a pause of a few seconds. Nymphs rarely travel from the river bed to the surface with sufficient speed to justify a more vigorous lift. Although a trout's interception may be one of reaction to a stimulus, its survival instincts will usually tell it to turn away if the motion is too unnatural. If the lift is overdone, or if the retrieve between the lifts is too fast, an educated fish will not only ignore the artificial nymph but may also remain on its guard for future drifts.

After arriving at a new stretch of water, it is usually worth starting with a dead drift to get the feel of the stream. This tactic will help to get the baseline right before superimposing the subtle, additional movements. Attempting induced takes straightaway in unfamiliar currents is like trying to run before you can walk, and may cause an unnatural motion that arouses suspicion. Moreover, you should never forget that a simple dead drift is often the best method.

Sometimes trout may follow an artificial fly, which is a sign that they are interested but still very suspicious. They can sometimes be persuaded to commit themselves as the nymph is about to escape from the water at the end of the retrieve. It is therefore always worth making the effort to incorporate a few twitches into the line just before and during the final lift off from the water. FTA, which is discussed in the chapter on *Tactics For Still Water*, occasionally works on rivers as well as the lakes for which it was intended.

In water of sufficient visibility to cover an individual trout, it is best to lift the rod when the nymph is about a yard upstream. This will help to signal its arrival before the final little twitch when the fly has almost reached its target. Whether successful or not, such experiences are invaluable in obtaining immediate feedback on the motion of the nymph due to the lift of the rod. The weight of the fly and the speed of the current may also be crucial in obtaining the right movement. Actually seeing how the nymph responds works wonders for the confidence.

Concentration

We cannot over emphasize the need for concentration. When the fish are responding well, adrenaline will keep the brain active and on full alert for long periods. But the longer you fish without results, the more difficult concentration will become. At this point the retrieve starts to become very mechanical, which adversely affects the trajectory of the nymph. Any problems with the movement or orientation of a dry fly are clearly visible, but a tired nymph fisherman may suffer from the syndrome of 'out of sight, out of mind'. Drag will gradually creep in, and previously subtle lifts of the rod may now turn the nymph from an agile darter into a sub-surface high jumper.

One of the most important points we can make, therefore, is to restrict fishing under difficult conditions to short periods. These may be as short as ten minutes, after which you put down the rod for an equal period to relax and dream of better sport to come. You can use this period to look at different areas and to identify the likely looking lies.

The Downstream Dead-drift

Some river purists scoff at this tactic, but their response probably implies that they have not experienced the glorious fishing on some of the world's faster flowing rivers. Controlling a downstream dead-drift requires more skill than its upstream counterpart, and there is the need for greater stealth since you are now face to face with the fish. You need to make every use of background camouflage and keep movements to a minimum above and below the surface. The rough water will provide some disguise, but any unnatural disturbance of the water will carry downstream to the fish. A greater separation between angler and fish will help the camouflage, although it will hinder control of the fly. A little thought may be necessary to balance the two factors, tending towards a greater separation in clear water but risking a closer encounter when the river is coloured.

Denzil had volunteered with other syndicate members to cut the reeds on their stretch of river. On arrival, his first reaction was to give up since he was the only person who had bothered to turn up for duty on this rather miserable day. He was more than a little irritated, but since he had already got this far he decided to continue. There would be some pretty sharp words at the next committee meeting, and he would not be tricked into this thankless task again.

After a while he noticed some sub-surface boils about twenty yards downstream of his position, but by the time he had set up his rod, the feeding had stopped. Grumbling to himself about a missed opportunity, he continued with his task, only to see the trout reappear. He grabbed his rod, which was now ready for action, cast his favourite Pheasant Tail Nymph into the water, and immediately connected with a superb brown trout. The trout were feeding on the nymphs that were being removed from the cut vegetation, and from the stones dislodged by the reed cutter's waders. They were also attracted to the slightly coloured slick of water caused by the upstream commotion – and being a day reserved for weed cutting, there were no other anglers on the water to take advantage.

In the event, Denzil did not complain about the absence of other volunteers. He told the committee that he thoroughly enjoyed the task, and would happily do it all by himself in future. Other fishermen observed that

MC enjoys downstream success on the fast-flowing Wairau.

he now tended to favour downstream nymphing techniques. He had also become more restless, constantly shuffling his feet in the water. They put it down to a form of stress.

Carrying out some of the actions for a downstream dead-drift can be very difficult to describe and even more difficult to achieve in strong currents without a good deal of practice. It is therefore worth spelling out the two basic principles of achieving a dead-drift – whether upstream or downstream. First, the strike indicator should always travel in front of the flies. If it does not, it will be unlikely to register a take. Second, there should be no drag from the line on the flies.

The first objective is easy to attain by attaching a second small strike indicator about a foot above the main one. This should always remain in front (downstream) of the main indicator. If it moves upstream, this signifies that there are adverse currents that will prevent you from detecting a take. It is a signal to cast into a different part of the stream.

In achieving the second objective, it is essential to cast upstream to allow the flies to sink to the required depth in a drag-free environment before they continue on their journey downstream. Sometimes this is helped by an immediate and large upstream mend of the line, but from then on there should be no interference until the strike indicator starts to move downstream from your position.

At this point, you need to mend the line so that it forms a narrow V-shape, as close to the indicator as possible, that points downstream. This takes a lot of practice, and is perhaps best achieved with a careful roll-casting action. There will be a great deal of trial and error – and possibly some colourful language – before you get it right! Once this shape has formed, any minor disturbance, such as paying out more line, is unlikely to produce a significant amount of drag. Fast currents will buffet the flies and thereby help to conceal imperfections in their trajectory.

It is important to have your wits about you to convert a take into a bending rod. The direction of the strike over the appropriate shoulder is crucial and possibly contrary to your intuition due to the existence of the downstream loop. The best way to get this right is to experiment towards the end of the first few drifts to see which striking action moves the indicator *downstream* most effectively. It is sometimes argued that downstream takes are easy to miss, because the strike is tending to pull the fly straight out of the fish's mouth, rather than setting it into the scissors as the 'upstream trout' turns back towards its lie.

At the end of a drift the line will move round in an arc and the flies will rise in the water. This is just the type of movement that you may have been trying to avoid for most of the time to give the flies a fair chance of drifting naturally with the current. Nevertheless, it is at this point that takes sometimes occur. This may be another form of induced take, or the trout may interpret the upward movement as an insect that is about to emerge. Some takes are so savage that it is advisable to remove your hand from the line and allow the fish to hook itself against the check on the reel.

Since the first part of the drift is arguably more suited to a nymph, and the final lift to an emerger, the downstream technique may usefully employ two or more flies on the leader. A weighted nymph on the point is perfect for a dead drift and provides an anchor to the other flies. A dropper fly will ride higher in the water, and the most suitable patterns are arguably those that represent an emerger or a drowned adult fly. It is probably for this reason that the traditional winged wet flies have proved themselves repeatedly for the last hundred years. A small Greenwell's represents many of the smaller upwinged flies. Other good wet patterns are a Wickham's Fancy and a Mallard and Claret. These three flies by themselves comprise bodies in olive green, gold and claret. Supplementing them by, perhaps, one of the many variations of Hare's Ear nymphs or Yorkshire Spiders, provides a fairly comprehensive starting collection for most circumstances.

Down and Across

A cast straight across the stream will immediately cause the flies to move round in an unnatural arc right in front of you. You may still have some good sport, but usually such a tactic will pick out the smaller or less well-educated fish. What is needed is a systematic application of fan-casting over various angles and downstream distances. The amount of line paid out before letting the flies swing round may also be systematically increased. This will cover a large area and is perfect for searching a sparsely populated river for trout.

If a hatch to caddis is in progress, for example, the movement of the line in an arc can be deliberately exploited from the outset to imitate the adults skittering across the surface. A palmered fly, such as an Invicta or Soldier Palmer on the top dropper is ideal for this purpose, with a caddis pupa beneath. Some of the most exciting river fishing we have ever experienced has involved working a large crane fly to create a wake with the corresponding pupa trailing a couple of feet behind it.

When trout are not responding to a surface disturbance, it may be difficult to achieve the required depth with a 'down and across' tactic on a floating line in strong currents. Sinking lines are not usually a good alternative because mending a submerged line is virtually impossible, and there is little chance of detecting any movement as a means of bite indication. A sink-tip line will allow mending of the floating belly, but there is limited sensitivity to a taking trout and the thick floating section is not ideal for attaching a strike indicator.

A sinking braided leader or 'poly-tip' overcomes all these problems. Unlike their floating equivalents, which exist purely for the achievement of turn-over, they are there solely to get the fly down quickly. It is a good idea to attach the sinking leader directly to the end of a short floating butt section. This provides a few inches of thin line for attaching most forms of strike indicator. A wide variety of densities are available, but for the most imitative fishing the sink rate should match that of the fly. This prevents the fly being pulled down at an unnatural angle by an invisible force. Nevertheless, in strong currents this may not matter too much, and the need to get the fly down before it reaches the fish may be the most important factor. It is very much a case of trial and error, and it pays to carry a full range of leaders in your pocket. They occupy very little space.

The rate of descent of a fly can be increased further by using a tuck cast, which stops the shooting line suddenly so that it springs back upon itself. This enables the weighted fly and leader to drop vertically below the line tip to get a head start. This obviously needs to take place when the line is well above the water so that the leader has a chance to drop. Ideally the rod should halt at eleven o'clock on the forward cast, with the casting arm held as high as possible in the air.

For fishing larva imitations close to the river bed, the nylon between the end of the sinking braid and the fly should be short – typically about 3 ft. If it is much more, the descent of the fly may be too slow. A short tippet, however, provides very little cushioning against the strike. This is a disadvantage at the best of times, but when trying to set the hook against a strong current it can almost guarantee a smash take. It is therefore important to use a very strong leader or to incorporate a few inches of power gum between the sinking leader and tippet. Six inches is a good compromise between shock absorption and contact with the taking fish. When fishing ascending pupae in fast streams, it is preferable to use a slower sinking braid attached to a longer nylon leader of about 6 ft. This allows the flies more freedom to move at a natural angle in the water.

The Rolled Nymph

The Eastern Europeans are experts at working nymphs along and just above the river bed at close range. Although they exploit the technique on the fast-flowing rivers of central Europe, it often works well in the deeper pools of more sedately flowing streams. The essential ingredients are a very heavy nymph on a dropper, which hugs the bottom, and a small imitative pattern that moves enticingly in the current about 18 in behind it. Some anglers put another small nymph on a dropper above the heavy pattern.

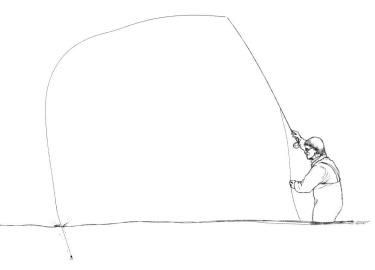

The tuck cast.

The angler will normally be wading right next to the fish, so unless there is a feature such as a gully, the water will not be much deeper than about 3 ft. Since the nymphs are 'rolled' under the rod tip, they are sufficiently close to the angler that the fly line need not touch the water. The leader has to be long enough to allow the heavy nymph to reach the bottom of the stream, but sufficiently short for maintaining control. Typically it will be one and a half times to twice the depth of the river, which in many situations implies a leader only about 5 ft long. The margin allows for a slight angle up, down and across the current, plus any curve that the current may introduce.

A simple under-arm pendulum swing, using the weight of a very heavy fly on the dropper, deposits the nymphs far enough to be just slightly upstream of the angler by the time they reach the bottom. Once in the water, the heavy nymph 'rolls' slowly along the river bed with the current. There is no attempt to move the flies. The rod follows the leader round as the flies travel downstream, and is held at the appropriate angle (10 or 11 o'clock) to keep a slight bow in the fly line. This helps to avoid any drag, and enables the tip of the slack line, which is about 6 in above the surface, to serve as a strike indicator. Everything now relies on watching the tip of the line and striking at the slightest movement, since you are unlikely to feel anything.

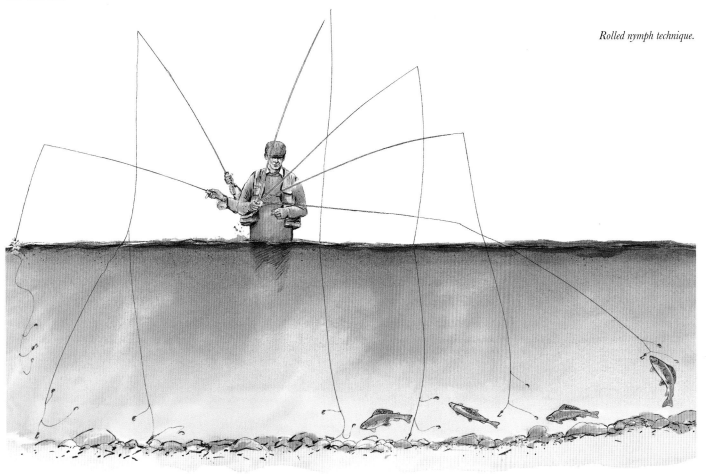

Rolled nymph technique.

When the flies have swung round it is time to raise them slowly to the surface, while intermittently holding them stationary for a few seconds. Trout may follow any of the flies as they leave the bottom and commit themselves at some stage of the ascent. Detection of the take at this stage can come from sight or feel.

MIXED TACTICS

Just occasionally, a trout will rise to a strike indicator. (Before becoming too critical of this apparent village idiot of the stream, we must admit that we have succumbed to the reflex action of striking!) After the initial surprise comes the thought that the trout are probably looking up to the surface for food. If they are still responding to nymphs, it may be worth replacing the strike indicator by a 'buoyant' dry fly to fish the two different methods simultaneously. Mixed tactics are ideal when there is any uncertainty in which method to use. They will instil extra confidence on dour days and increase the chances of locating pockets of fish when searching large areas of a sparsely populated river.

It is important not to attach the dry fly to a long dropper, since this could result in a delay in detection or even the failure to register a take. It is preferable to use the New Zealand tactic of dispensing with the dropper knot altogether and tying the nylon directly to the bend of the dry fly hook.

In clear, slow water, the disadvantages of a dry fly on a dropper become more apparent. Nylon only appears at one end of a fly on the point, so it is less visible and less constrained in its movement. The fly is also further from the tip of the line. Thus, mixed tactics may compromise the effectiveness of a dry fly, especially when fishing for the more educated trout with small patterns on clear, slow-moving streams. Although the dry fly does little to interfere with the presentation of a nymph, it is unlikely to perform as well as a purpose-built strike indicator. Moreover, from bitter experience, the additional fly may snag in weed and result in the loss of a good trout. When any of these factors are important, we prefer to keep things simple and stick to one method at a time. It takes very little time to change from a single nymph to a single dry fly and back again to explore the different tactics.

However, there is much more to mixed tactics than simply fishing two methods at once. A bushy dry fly will often attract a trout's attention to a nymph, which it might not ordinarily take. We can recall many occasions when the addition of a dry fly has dramatically increased the effectiveness of the nymph.

This is often the case when fish are sheltering amongst weed or rocks, largely hidden from view and in a position where it is impossible to place a nymph in front of them. Even though they may be suspicious, and ultimately disinclined to take the large, bushy dry fly, it will often draw them to within a few inches of the surface. It is a fascinating sight to see a large trout rise to the surface to intercept a grasshopper, for example, only to turn away at the last moment and take a tiny Pheasant Tail nymph that would otherwise have gone unnoticed.

Mixed tactics are ideally suited to large dry flies. Our favourite all-round pattern has to be a size 8 or 10 Royal Wulff due to its 'buoyancy', visibility and unquestioned effectiveness in drawing fish to the surface in a wide range of rivers. In slow-moving streams, where the current exerts less drag and the nymphs require less weight, it is possible to use more sedate patterns, such as a size 12 or 14 Para-Adams. Yet even in chalkstreams and spring creeks, it is surprising us how many fish will sometimes rise to a large Wulff.

Mixed tactics with a dry fly and nymph.

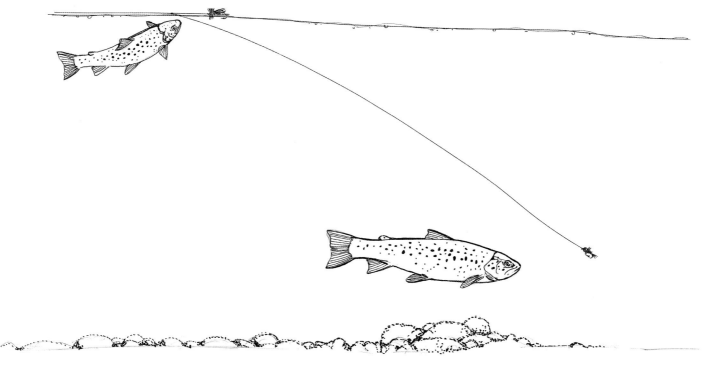

THE ONE-SHOT SPECIMEN

Attitude

Stalking a large, wild trout is arguably the greatest challenge in fly fishing. Trout that have grown to such a size in a natural environment will have learned all the tricks of survival. In well-fished rivers, they may have been pricked by artificial patterns, and possibly caught and returned. They will also have grown fat by well defined feeding habits, so that they know exactly what food to expect and the manner in which it should arrive. This inevitably means that their suspicions will be aroused by the slightest occurrence that is outside the normal run of events.

Tim Tollett prepares to release a large brown trout.

A proper attitude is essential for stalking fish in any water, but we know of no better training ground than the clear, stony rivers in the South Island of New Zealand. There are plenty of truly wild trout of over 5 lb that seem to have a sixth sense when it comes to noticing an intruder. It calls for a keen-eyed, camouflaged approach just to spot a specimen without being noticed, because if you are seen first, you will have wasted the opportunity.

We were fortunate to spend three weeks in New Zealand with Tim Tollett, who runs the Frontier Anglers shop in Dillon, USA. His commitment to large specimens stems from a life-time spent stalking wild fish and animals in Montana, and if necessary he is quite prepared to spend hours stalking a single specimen trout. His patience and attention to the finest detail produce a consistent success rate that is, to say the least, impressive. This motivated us to improve our own stalking techniques to the level where we could catch trout that we might previously have dismissed as uncatchable.

A healthy approach is to aim to catch a single, large trout in a day's fishing. This instils the right attitude from the start. It helps to overcome the urge to cast before all the conditions are in your favour, and prevents too much disappointment if you end up with nothing to show for your efforts. Moreover, you do not have to fish in exotic places to experience the satisfaction of stalking a specimen trout. The ultimate thrill is (almost!) as great after catching any wild trout that is large for the local river, such as a one pound fish in a mountain stream.

Stealth

Wild creatures will spot an intruder at surprisingly large distances. As a rule of thumb, if you can see the fish, then it has a chance of seeing you – unless you are suitably camouflaged or approaching from behind outside its field of vision. It is notable how quickly they can differentiate a human being from creatures they have learned to accept, such as grazing sheep or cattle. We have observed the most spooky trout in New Zealand take no notice of low flying birds, which they recognize as harmless. In North America, however, where fish-eating eagles abound, it is quite another story.

Trout are sensitive to any sudden change in their surroundings. This means that any unavoidable movement that might fall into their range of vision should be painstakingly slow. Even a sudden flash from a varnished rod in bright sunlight will put a fish on its guard. It is ironic that expensive rods should be treated deliberately to reduce their fish catching capabilities – but that is exactly what the manufacturers do in the interests of marketing. It takes will-power, but if you intend stalking wild fish in bright conditions, you will need to give your pride and joy a good rubbing down with fine steel wool.

Items attached to the outside of a waistcoat, such as scissors and forceps, should be black rather than silver. The leader should be as long as you can handle, and the fly line must blend in with the surroundings rather than advertising its presence. Green and brown are appropriate colours for clothing against a background of trees and bushes, but blue and grey blend in better against the sky when fishing in open water. Soldiers – whose lives depend on camouflage – often wear mottled battle dress in preference to a single colour to break up the contrast against the natural surroundings. The same advantage applies when stalking trout.

A spooked fish will often swim away or head for cover. Sometimes, though, they will swim downstream past you to get a good look – almost as if they are letting you know how incompetent you have been! Quite often, they may hold position and ignore everything on offer, as if they know they are safe as long as they do not feed. We have observed them moving casually to the side of their holding spots to avoid an approaching artificial pattern. If a fish has become even slightly suspicious, it is advisable to move on and come back again an hour later.

Locating Fish

To be consistently successful, you have to be very good indeed at spotting fish. Polaroids and a hat to keep out extraneous light are essential, but so is the acquired skill of being able to recognize the slightest sign in the water. Often it is just the most subtle contrast against the sub-surface terrain, or the merest hint of movement as a fish intercepts a nymph. Sometimes, without warning, a fish will move out from the weeds or boulders and start feeding in an exposed position. These factors point to a slow, patient approach to ensure that you allow ample time for spotting the fish before unwittingly moving in front of it.

Given the choice, it is worth selecting the bank that is more appropriate for stalking, taking into account shadows and glare. A high bank offers a useful vantage point for spotting fish from a good way downstream, but you should keep as low as possible to avoid standing out against the horizon. Wary trout are capable of using the very last degree of their monocular vision to detect anything that is not immediately behind them.

The cast to a 'one-shot' trout has to be very accurate and made at exactly the right moment, otherwise the opportunity may be lost. Thus, having spotted the fish, it is highly desirable to keep it in sight. If it disappears, you should wait until it comes into view again. Teamwork is very productive; one volunteer lies low on the bank, preferably behind an obstacle, where he can see the fish. He can then inform the angler exactly where and when to cast.

A trout will often remain in a fixed position for long periods. If the holding spot is easy to pin-point from bank-side features, you should be able to cover it blind from a considerable distance. This is the right approach to adopt if you believe that you cannot catch sight of the fish without being seen yourself. Even if it disappeared on detecting your presence earlier, it will often return to its favourite haunt. When you come back later in the day, you need enough faith to assume that it is in the same position, rather than risk giving the game away by a closer inspection just to make sure.

Feeding Habits

You should always look for fish that are showing signs of feeding. A trout that is taking nymphs will twitch its tail from time to time as food comes into view. Sometimes, it will feed predominantly on one side, giving an obvious clue to the direction for the cast. A fish lying motionless in the water, however, is unlikely to feed. It may be worth trying to arouse it with the plop of a heavy nymph, but often this will simply put it on its guard.

Large trout will often switch from dry flies to nymphs (and vice versa) in a matter of minutes. This is very frustrating when you have been waiting patiently for your opportunity with a nymph, only to see the trout concentrating on dry flies as soon as it comes into range. Thus, even though a single fly is better for presentation, it is often advisable to use a dry fly and nymph together.

Observation of when and where a trout spots a natural insect will help to assess the most suitable place to cast a dry fly. A deep-lying trout will need a greater upstream allowance, since it will see the fly sooner due to its larger window of surface vision. Grayling will sometimes drift backwards with the current for up to 3 ft during their ascent to intercept a dry fly, and may therefore require an even greater allowance. Ideally, the

Camouflage, observation and positioning.

fly should land just outside the fish's window with the smallest possible margin. This will minimize the time during which drag can occur before it intercepts the fly, and – if the leader is sufficiently long – keep the fly line out of its vision.

Whether using a dry fly or nymph, a well-educated fish may become suspicious after very few attempts to cover it. This suspicion may arise from errors made during an earlier cast or inadequacies in the fly itself. So any initial period of observation to ascertain the correct natural insect could be crucial. Having decided on the right choice of food, you should ensure that the artificial pattern is sufficiently small and slim. On no account should you compromise the natural dimensions in order to increase the visibility of a dry fly, or to provide extra confidence that it will stay afloat. Nymphs also need to be appropriately slim, with the least conspicuous strike indicator.

Position and Casting

You should plan your casting position in advance and, if possible, avoid any obstacles. It is usually better to cast from the bank, since these wily trout are exceedingly sensitive to any unnatural motion in the water. This means that you are likely to be more visible, so extra care is necessary to keep low and to use all the camouflage that you can. Surprising as it may seem, even a clump of grass will help. This is because the trout will be accustomed to seeing a broken horizon at that point, without paying too much attention to the detailed shape or size.

If a trout is facing directly upstream, you will probably be able to cast when it suits you. Nevertheless, the best time to attack is immediately after it has taken a natural fly when its confidence will be high. If it takes two or three natural insects in quick succession, you will know that it is really switched on to feeding. You should then cast as quickly as you sensibly can while the opportunity exists.

In slow-moving stretches, you may observe a trout cruising around looking for food. This may require a great deal of patience while waiting for it to move into the right position – i.e. within range and swimming away from you. While waiting, you must always keep your rod down. You should also make sure that the running line is suitably positioned on the ground so that it will not tangle during the cast. Sometimes, this may involve uprooting twigs and other vegetation.

In still water, you can cast out and leave a fly on the bottom, and then give it a single, slight twitch as a trout approaches. The movement, plus any stirring of the mud, will help to attract its attention, as long as it is not over done.

When casting, you need the minimum amount of movement. If you can cover a fish with a switch cast, which essentially uses the tip of the rod, then so much the better. This is easier to achieve with a rod of at least 9.5 ft. A long rod also increases the chances of clearing obstacles behind you.

If your cast is unsuccessful, but has not spooked the fish, you should leave the line on the water until it is well out of view, before lifting it away gently with the minimum amount of commotion. Sometimes a big fish will not move for a fly unless it passes right by its nose, and you may need many casts before getting the position exactly right. However, if you believe it noticed but rejected the fly, you should change patterns immediately, because something is not quite right. You should also consider using a finer tippet.

JD with a one-shot specimen deceived by a Sail-Wing.

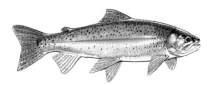

Blagdon Reservoir.

CHAPTER 7
TACTICS FOR STILL WATER

JD with a large wild Rainbow from Lake Otamangakau.

In the British Isles there is a greater choice of publicly available fly fishing on still waters than on rivers and brooks. A major factor has been the creation of many large reservoirs for water supply. The number of river-only specialists has therefore gradually declined over the last couple of decades, but this has brought an influx of traditional fly fishing skills to the lakes. Although techniques vary due to the different food forms and behaviour of the trout, much of the traditionalism and etiquette has remained. For example, most fisheries strictly forbid the trolling or trailing of flies behind a boat. Furthermore, there is a tendency spawned from competition rules for many flies to be tied to a maximum length of just under an inch – fifteen sixteenths to be precise.

In many other parts of the world, less restrictive tactics are practised as a matter of course. As a result of this custom, many local fly fishermen specialize on rivers and sometimes look down on still waters as a poor relation. This is an unfortunate interpretation because there is enormous scope for traditional fly fishing on lakes, and the trout can be every bit as challenging. There is a wide range of different tactics and plenty of opportunity for experts to exploit their skills to maximum effect. There are more dimensions to explore in still water, including a greater variety of food forms, holding depth and locations. The principles of fly fishing are just the same; it is only the emphasis that is different.

We have to admit that we tend to favour river fishing when travelling to other parts of the world, but this is largely to redress the balance from what is available in the British Isles. Nevertheless, we still try to put in a respectable amount of time on the lakes. We have sometimes had to use special flies to match local insects, such as cicadas and grasshoppers, but the same tactics have been universally effective. Moreover, general patterns have consistently produced results. Shipman's Buzzer and the Panacea brought good results in North America, and many locals in New Zealand asked for the dressings of Superglue Buzzers and OB's worm, which had been so effective on Lake Otamangakau.

Bank fishing tactics are the same across all continents, apart from the use of much larger lures and streamers where trout grow to enormous proportions on forage fish. Approaches differ, however, in open water. Many fishermen troll with streamers, lures or spinners. This is a tactic that we have not included for the simple reason that we are unqualified to comment with authority. When fishing abroad, we have tended to concentrate on the approach that gives us most pleasure, which is to use small flies. The craft have varied enormously, from small boats and float tubes to quite large seafaring vessels, but the fly fishing methods have remained unchanged.

Rules vary in different parts of the world.

WATER-CRAFT

Trout behave in a fundamentally different manner in still water. In some ways they can afford to be more lazy since they do not have to wrestle constantly against the current. Nevertheless, they cannot completely rest on their laurels and wait for the food to come to them, because often they will have to move around and forage for it. As a result it is rare to find lake trout in exactly the same spot for very long. Some of the larger browns may have a favourite little hole where they spend most of their time, and only venture forth occasionally to gobble up a few small fish before returning. But when feeding, the majority of lake trout will be continuously on the move. This adds a further dimension

to consider for any fly fisherman visiting the larger lakes. Not only does he have to choose the right fly and tactics, he also has to summon up all his skills to locate the fish. Areas can change overnight from containing large shoals to being virtually barren.

Since a still-water trout seldom remains in the same pocket of water for very long, it is never quite as familiar with the immediate surroundings as it would be in a river. Thus, it is less likely to notice any subtle change in the horizons caused, for example, by an arriving angler. Moreover, as often as not, it is the trout that will be moving towards the bank angler who is already stationary and in position – rather than the other way round. This sometimes leads to a degree of complacency which may be a grave mistake, since the still-water trout has the same primeval instinct for survival. Scare the fish of a lifetime and you may not get another chance as it scurries away to forage elsewhere. Moreover, it is far less likely to return to the same spot than its cousin in the river.

One of the most common mistakes is unnecessary wading. Whereas river trout are used to movements in the water induced by currents, still-water trout sense any intrusion as a more alien phenomenon – especially on calm days when there is no ripple to disguise it. They may also be more wary of aquatic predators, such as pike.

The best advice is not to wade unless there is a very good reason. That reason may be to reach more fish, but often this is at best no more than an assumption. Without disturbance from man, trout will often favour the fertile margins in shallow water close to the bank. You should start with your feet on terra firma and cover the margins first before progressively lengthening the cast. The exception is when you are surrounded by wading anglers who will have already driven fish away from the margins.

Wading essential – but disturbance inevitable.

Many wading anglers will drop the retrieved line on to the water at the side of them. On the subsequent cast, the shooting belly has to drag this line from the water. The resistance is serious for floating lines, but disastrous for sinkers where the retrieved line has to be pulled upwards through a couple of feet of water. It reduces the casting distance considerably – sometimes to the extent that it would have been possible to get the flies further out by casting from the bank. With practice, it is possible to bunch all the retrieved line together in the hand without tangling. A less sophisticated, but very effective solution, is to use a line tray. Those who feel a little self-conscious with such a contraption strapped to their midriffs – and that includes us – can get by with a landing net on a long, spiked handle. The spike should be pushed into the lake bed at an angle so that it is possible to drop the retrieved line into the frame of the net. The mesh should be folded around the frame so that it holds the line above the surface of the water.

CAPITALIZING ON THE WIND

It is not uncommon to watch trout moving upwind from one end of a lake to the other taking dry flies or nymphs close to the surface. They will then swim back downwind at depth before re-embarking on the same feeding spree. To experience this phenomenon it is usually necessary to be fishing from a boat or float tube away from the bank. The speeds at which trout move upwind are sometimes deceptively fast, and it very easy when covering a fish to find that the flies have landed several yards behind it. It is essential to give the fish plenty of 'forward lead', casting perhaps as much as 10 or even 20 yds in front of where it last broke the surface. If in doubt, give it more rather than less, because it will eventually be heading in the right direction. Underestimate, and the opportunity may be lost.

Even when travelling upwind, trout will often swim with a good deal of random motion from side to side. In calmer conditions they may have no upwind direction at all, but simply cruise from one surface fly to another. This is when the truly observant fisherman can capitalize on the information by estimating the direction of the next move from the bulge in the water (see Chapter 2). Very few fisherman are proficient at this technique, but it is worth persevering because it will pay handsome dividends.

The direction of the sun gives another clue. Trout may be tolerant of bright conditions, but we have observed on many occasions that they choose to move away from it. So if the sun is shining from right to left across the ripple, there is a fair chance that they will move towards the left. If the sun is directly behind a strong wind, they will be reluctant to move near the surface at all. One of the worst conditions for the still-water fisherman is a bright and windy day with the sun and wind in the same direction. There has even been a very bushy fly invented called Sun and Wind for use under such conditions, but it is usually a better idea to switch from a floating to a sinking line.

Trout are quite happy to remain high in the water on bright days if there is an abundance of food on the surface. However, in the absence of such an incentive, they will descend to a depth that depends on both the brightness and water clarity. In clear lakes, you would expect them to be much deeper than they would be in coloured water, where the sun's rays will be filtered out within a few feet of the surface. It is not just the trout's response that matters. Daphnia move down in bright conditions, and the fish will follow them to continue mopping up the delicious 'soup'. Finally, during prolonged hot spells in high summer, the temperature and stratification of the water are often the key determinants to depth, since trout will seek the cooler water that is richer in oxygen.

Local features surrounding a lake will funnel the wind to give lanes of calm water. These lanes act as a trap for emerging insects that have difficulty in breaking through the surface film. Flies are also more amenable to inspection in the absence of ripples. Trout therefore gather in large numbers beneath these 'calm' or 'wind' lanes to capitalize on the local abundance of food. They often move upwind in the rippled water right on the edges of the lanes. Any alert boat fisherman will keep his eyes open for a wind lane, and every experienced bank fisherman will pray for one that extends to the edge of the lake.

THE RETRIEVE

In still-water fly fishing, there is one simple statement that cannot be over emphasized. The style and execution of the retrieve is fundamental to success.

In the absence of a strong current, it is often – but by no means always – necessary to impart some form of motion to a fly to make it appear alive. River fishermen have to retrieve line purely to keep up with the current. The superposition of any further motion to a nymph to suggest life may then be optional. In still waters, a much greater part of the retrieve will normally translate directly into a movement of the fly, so that any irregularities become readily apparent. Moreover, the trout have much longer to make up their minds. So the manner in which you pull the line is crucial, and demands careful consideration rather than mechanical repetition. Master the retrieve, and you are well on the way to becoming an expert.

Alex was getting more and more frustrated. Try as he might, he could not get the trout to take, and yet Humphrey at the side of him was catching fish after fish. Admittedly, this was the first time he had fished here, but he was

Scum lanes on Chew Valley Lake.

using the same line, the same nylon, the same flies and he was casting just as far. It had to be the position. His companion, although only twenty yards away, was obviously over a localized shoal – unless he was using some new secret fly. And now he was into another!

Totally deflated, he cast out his line again and continued to retrieve in a purely mechanical manner. At the same time, he muttered something about lucky flies, lucky rod, lucky position and the lucky b*gg*r who seemed to have all three. 'Why don't you have my lucky position', was the immediate reply, 'and you can use my lucky rod as well if it'll give you more confidence.'

Alex did not need any encouragement to accept Humphrey's generous gesture as he rushed over at break-neck speed, leaving his own rod on the ground with the line extended in the water. Now he was going to catch some fish – and he'd inspect the flies later! Humphrey strolled lazily over to pick up the rod on the ground, gave the line a couple of gentle pulls, paused while he had a sip of Rioja, and then beamed with satisfaction as he lifted into another fish. Alex gaped in disbelief. He took off his hat, threw it on the ground, and started jumping up and down on it making utterances that are better left untold.

Most of us will have experienced days with a companion when one or the other has taken nearly all the fish. This is in spite of the successful angler doing absolutely everything in his power to help his less fortunate colleague – giving him the same fly, swapping positions on the bank or in the boat, or even exchanging rods – and all to no avail. With an expert and novice this would be expected, but often it happens with two anglers of comparable skill and experience. It occurs frequently when there is not a fish to be seen, so that accuracy of casting cannot be the cause. But it seldom happens when the successful fisherman is retrieving his flies quickly, and this provides the vital clue.

We have all been on the receiving end, so we can grit our teeth and think back to our thought processes at the time. 'What am I doing wrong? I'm using the right flies, I'm covering the

same area of water, I'm using the same leader, so what can it be? I'm copying his hand movements so I must be retrieving the flies in the same manner.' But are you? Patience seems to go by the board, and it may require a Herculean effort to steady your retrieve – but steady it you must. For on those occasions when you are the successful angler, fishing with a perfect rhythm and moving your flies with total confidence, you can see quite clearly that your companion is retrieving his flies in a purely mechanical manner. There is an artificial jerkiness, which is the inevitable consequence of frustration, and try as he might, he cannot relax into the same rhythm.

In such frustrating circumstances, it is advisable to take a break from the fishing for a few minutes and relax with a cup of coffee or a glass of wine. Then, aim to fish the flies as statically as possible. In front of a drifting boat this will require concentration to make sure that the retrieve does little more than compensate for the boat's motion. The aim is to take all possible steps to remove the jerkiness that seems to propagate down the line to the fish. It only needs a single tug on the end of the line from a trout to let the adrenaline take over and put you well on the road to recovery.

For many years, Humphrey fooled his rivals in competitions by catching trout with a very fast retrieve. Instead of concentrating on their own methods, too many anglers could not resist copying his movements even though their flies may have been totally different. If only they had stopped to think, they might have done a lot better by choosing a retrieve based on their own experiences and flies. More importantly, if only they had used their powers of observation, they would have noticed that there were long periods between each of Humphrey's casts. He was letting the line slip through his fingers so that the flies were almost static!

However, even the more astute anglers who timed his retrieve could be caught out. Sometimes, when using a sinking line, he would find that takes would occur predominantly on the drop during the first few seconds. So after using slow pulls during the short productive period, he would rip the line back to avoid wasting time – and grin with amusement at the widespread misinterpretation.

On balance, a slow continuous retrieve is probably the most consistent over all conditions, although it is by no means the whole story. There are a numerous possible techniques to exploit. Sometimes you will only find the successful method by trial and error on the day, but often you can make some pretty informed guesses from a knowledge of the water and, of course, the trout. We will now try to take some of the mystique out of the subject and give a few pointers to different types of retrieve and when to use them.

The Slow Retrieve

At times, nymphs dart amongst the reeds and pebbles at a speed that is quite impressive for their size. Although a few inches per minute may be really motoring for a bloodworm, it is frustratingly slow on the human scale. It is well worth timing how long it takes to recover the line during a typical 'slow' retrieve. A couple of minutes may seem like eternity, but for a 20 yd cast this translates to an average speed of 6 in per second! You may think that you are retrieving the line slowly, but the

trout sees an Olympic gold medallist rushing past its nose. So if you are really serious about natural imitation, you will need to fish at a speed that appears slow to the trout – and that means dead slow or virtually static to the human.

One way to move a fly slowly is to give repeated little pulls of an inch or so at a time on the line. In the first instance these should be as smooth as possible, because a jerkiness that arises out of impatience or frustration may kill the fishing stone dead. Then be prepared to experiment with the movement. Lengthen the draw, speed it up, even make the retrieve deliberately jerky to simulate the motion of a darting nymph – until you find the most successful formula for the time and place.

Perhaps surprisingly, a slow retrieve often works with the most gaudy flies that bear no resemblance whatsoever to any living form. The most killing patterns seem to be those with a marabou wing or tail. The most likely explanation is that the tiny fibres move more enticingly when the fly is almost at rest than when it is sprinting through the water. You can exploit this tactic by fishing a couple of nymphs (say) on droppers in front of a less inhibited attractor pattern. This adds to the confidence that comes from fishing two different types of method at the same time – and confidence breeds its own success.

The Static Retrieve

The ultimate in slow retrieves is obviously no motion at all. Often this is the only successful method, particularly when the trout have become spooked by repeated bombardments. At this point, they are likely to reject anything that moves faster than the natural insects – most of which hardly move at all. At the same time, it is important to use patterns that are as slim as the flies they intend to imitate. Still water is seldom totally still, and the effect of the surface drag on the line will often give the fly a considerable amount of motion – and that little bit of motion may be quite a lot in the trout's eyes.

MC with a wild river trout caught on a lake pattern (Cruncher).

It is easy to achieve a static retrieve from the bank, but a drifting boat requires more skill and concentration. The retrieve must just remove the slack from the line and no more. This is similar to the requirement for an upstream dead-drift on rivers, except that a fisherman is now drifting towards the flies rather than the other way around. We have seen some of the most famous boat fishermen end the day without a touch when a few others have enjoyed a bonanza. What is more, they will not admit that they were fishing too fast. We have seen others come in perplexed with a single 'fluky' fish – a trout that just happened to take the fly when they had put the rod down for a few seconds to pour out some coffee. The explanation should hit them right between the eyes, but it seldom does.

It takes dedication and a firm belief that the method will work. It is especially difficult when the fishing is dour, because patience and concentration gradually evaporate as the time without any action increases. But if you believe that a static retrieve is right for the conditions, then persevere. One trick, when concentration becomes difficult, is to daydream rather than impart an unwanted movement through frustration or loss of confidence. There is nothing wrong during these periods with interspersing very slow or static retrieves with faster ones just to make sure – as long as you keep the two approaches totally separate. An unwitting combination produces a speed that is neither one thing nor the other, and seldom catches anything.

Although lake trout often announce their presence with a tug on the line, they will sometimes take and reject a static nymph in a split second. We have known days when striking at the merest suspicious twinge or movement of the line spells the difference between a 'limit' and a 'blank'. This tends to happen with the more established and educated trout. You may find yourself striking as the hook touches a patch of weed, but continuing to do so because every so often the apparent weed turns out to be alive. The deliberate strike needs to be quick yet delicate, because really savage takes will sometimes occur during the same session. This requires a strong leader or plenty of shock absorption in the tackle. On many other occasions, especially with stock fish, it is better to ignore any twitches and wait until the take develops into a more definite pull.

Strike Indicators with the Static Retrieve

One of the more controversial tricks with a static retrieve is the use of a strike indicator. This warns of any motion by producing a wake, in addition to its primary purpose of registering a take. Those using this tactic for the first time are often amazed at the number of takes that had hitherto gone unnoticed. It is absolutely deadly on those days when trout are taking and rejecting a nymph in a split second.

However, strike indicators in lakes are not the panacea that they are in rivers. River trout reject nymphs in a split second as a matter of course, whereas still-water trout do not. On many occasions, you will miss more takes by striking too quickly than you will by responding to feel with a prompt, yet measured, tightening of the line. It is not uncommon to see still-water fishermen hitting more trout when using a strike indicator, only to land far fewer.

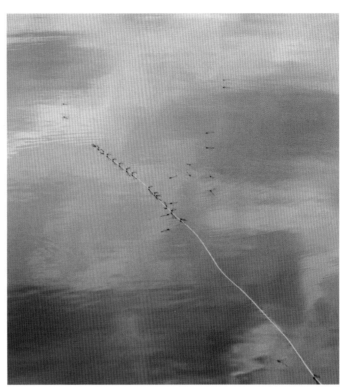

Damsels provide a natural strike indicator.

Just as in running water, a strike indicator will suspend a nymph at a fixed distance below the surface. It is remarkable how this alone will increase catch rates when the depth is right. (A sink-tip line will sometimes achieve a similar degree of success for the same reason.) Once again, though, there needs to be a word of caution, because you have to be confident that you have chosen the right depth.

It is difficult to know where to draw the line in fly-fishing ethics, and many denounce strike indicators as the infamous 'bung'. Some fisheries ban them all together, but they cannot stop anglers using a dry fly on the top dropper. That trusty old river fly, the Royal Wulff, could have been tailor-made for the purpose – and it catches a respectable number of still-water trout in its own right. It is amazing to see some of the allegedly natural imitations that appear on top droppers – large, highly visible Ethafoam creations in white and red, for example. 'They imitate roach fry or some other small fish.' We could not possibly comment!

Sink and Draw

It is often productive to allow a fly to sink between pulls. The steady pull can be anything from a few inches to a few feet, and the intervals between can vary as well. The shorter pulls may represent nymphs darting through the water. Longer pulls can convey a variety of impressions, such as a nymph making a determined ascent to the surface, or a small fish swimming through the water. In all instances, the intermittent movement may simply arouse the trout's curiosity. A fly with a lot of intrinsic mobility – from marabou herl, for example – will sink enticingly between each draw. The sinking motion becomes more pronounced with a weighted pattern. This retrieve is well suited to Dog Nobblers, which are designed to dive head first after each draw with the marabou tail fluttering seductively behind the sinking fly. It is a departure from an imitative style to one that unashamedly exploits a trout's response to movement.

The Slow Continuous Retrieve

Although a nymph or small fish may move in a series of stops and starts, as exploited by a sink and draw, it is not always easy to achieve an acceptably realistic impression. Success or failure may depend on the water conditions and the feeding habits of the trout. Whatever the explanation, it is not uncommon to catch a trout when winding in the line at the end of a session. The disproportionate number of trout caught in this way points to the value of a long, continuous movement. This is undoubtedly why the figure-of-eight retrieve is such a consistent tactic. For those who may be new to it, the finger co-ordination is more difficult to explain than to carry out, so persevere! Rather than trying to copy a series of instructions, experiment by following your own instincts to move the line continuously. It will be worth the effort. Many fishermen find that once they have acquired the knack, they will end up using the figure-of-eight more than any other type of retrieve.

Casting across the surface ripple without retrieving, from boat or bank, is a deadly technique for achieving a continuous motion as the line moves round in a gradual curve. Here the most important consideration is the direction of the strike. With a large bow in the line, a sudden lift of the rod will be inefficient

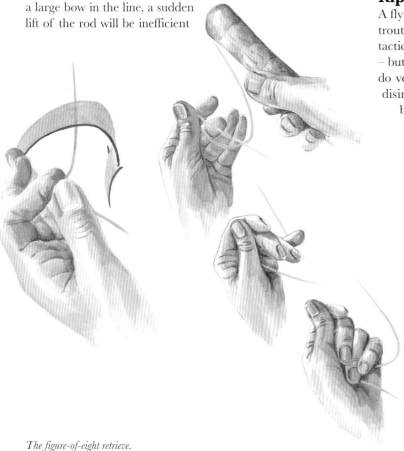

The figure-of-eight retrieve.

at setting the hook. The solution is to strike to the side, which may be totally counter intuitive, in such a way that the whole line is forced to move round in an arc. With a left to right breeze, this means moving the rod to the left, and vice versa.

The Fast Continuous Retrieve

Although slow retrieves are generally the most consistent – and certainly the most imitative for nymph fishing – there are times when trout are disinclined to feed unless given a kick start. Sometimes a faster retrieve may actually be more imitative when small fish or hatching caddis are on the menu, but there is a limit to the achievable speed when using a figure-of-eight motion. This is the time to tuck the rod under either arm, depending on preference, and exploit a technique known as 'milking the cow', 'roly-poly' or 'Cornish knitting'. Both hands pull the line, one after the other, in a repetitive motion to keep it moving as continuously as possible. This is more easily said than done, but with practice a very steady motion will ensue. One Bristol angler, Dev Stickley, used it almost exclusively to win competition after competition and a very valuable selection of prize rods. It was fascinating to watch his whole body swing round to achieve the striking movement that would normally be accomplished with the wrist. Those who are less athletic will often get away with a delayed strike by continuing to pull the line to keep it taut against the fish before grabbing hold of the rod.

Ripping It Back (Sunk Line)

A fly racing at top speed seems to arouse some basic instinct in a trout to chase its prey. We have to admit to not enjoying this tactic over prolonged periods due to the sheer exertion involved – but those with the stamina and confidence in the method often do very well indeed. It is especially appropriate when trout are disinclined to feed. Large flies, such as Sparklers and Fritz-bodied lures, are very popular and much better suited to the technique than marabou patterns. The method needs a systematic approach to count the line down for different times until the holding depth is located. If the trout are high in the water, an immediate retrieve may be necessary – and even on a high density line, the lures will remain within the first few feet of the surface.

Sometimes trout will grab the lure in the middle of the retrieve, but occasionally they will simply follow without committing themselves. When lifting off at the end of the retrieve, it is quite common to see a swirl as a fish turns away or looks around for the creature that has so suddenly disappeared. On such occasions, there needs to be a change in trajectory. One option is to stop pulling, apply a slow figure-of-eight retrieve for a few seconds, and then return to full speed.

Another, at the end of the retrieve, is to let the point fly hang a few feet down for several seconds. (This tactic often pays dividends with slower retrieves as well.) An alternative, for the more energetic, is to lift the rod high in an arc at the end of the retrieve to provide a burst of acceleration.

Ripping It Back (Floating Line)

The floating line tactic will often work when trout are looking upwards for any form of food, but it really comes to the fore when they are cruising just beneath the surface taking tiny dry flies. They easily become preoccupied, and their concentration is focused on a tiny field of vision when so high in the water. When this happens, a trout may turn to inspect a bushy pattern that disturbs the water, or a bright submerged fly that glints in the corner of its eye. Normally, it will have plenty of time to consider the options, and after following for a while will probably come to the conclusion that this strange object is best left well alone. On the other hand, a fly that sprints past its nose does not allow a lot of time for thought. The fish has to decide on impulse, and may decide to grab the fly before it can escape.

There are two approaches to fly selection that rely on attracting a surface-feeding trout's attention. A heavily palmered fly or a Muddler will advertise its presence by disturbing the surrounding water. Alternatively, a bright fly, such as a Peach Doll or Vindaloo, will have a strong visual impact. It is often a good idea to combine both attributes into a single fly – a bright orange Muddler, for example. Sometimes we have had tremendous sport by using three such flies at the same time, but it is very often the point fly that does most of the damage. This is the pattern a trout will normally see first after turning towards the flies that have just raced past.

It is also worth ripping bushy flies across the surface of lakes that are sparse in fly life. Trout in such waters often look up towards the surface, and the response can be dramatic from un-educated fish. Kielder Water in Northumberland is an example of where the recently stocked fish will come from nowhere to grab a fast pulled, bushy fly with total commitment. The established residents are less likely to be fooled, and respond more readily, for example, to a properly dressed and presented dry fly.

One of the most exciting experiences in fishing is to see a bow wave as a trout chases flies close to the surface. This will sometimes translate into a positive take, either to the attracting fly or to one of the others on the cast. There are other occasions, though, when fish after fish will follow the flies, only to turn away without any commitment. You may try various different retrieves, from ripping the flies back at full speed to a slow figure-of-eight, but to no avail. This is when the Jigger might just do the trick.

We stumbled on the Jigger by chance due to a slip of the fingers when ripping back a fly. The result was that the flies suddenly stopped moving for a split second, but the line became instantly heavy on resuming the retrieve. We have used and perfected the technique many times since then to great effect. The trick is to pull the line back as quickly as possible, and while

pulling to lift the rod at the same time to give the fly a real burst of acceleration. The trout will accelerate as well. When the rod has almost reached a vertical position, you stop the retrieve stone dead. The flies will stop too, since they have very little momentum to keep them moving against the drag of the water. But the fish will have built up a great deal of momentum and will not be able to stop so suddenly. Therefore it has two choices – to grab the fly immediately or to swim right past and miss the opportunity. A trout that makes the wrong choice is very quick to reject the fly. So it is essential to strike about a quarter of a second after stopping the line. Striking occurs with the rod already lifted, and you will invariably end up being at full stretch – but it is all worthwhile as you feel the solid resistance.

Finally, it is not always necessary to use bright or bushy flies to distract preoccupied surface-feeders. They will quite often respond to sparse nymphs that are ripped in front of them. In this case, it is better to stop the retrieve after the first couple of pulls and allow the nymphs to sink slowly. The trout may initially have been triggered into action by these jet-propelled insects, but now it sees some apparently natural food drifting in the water. There is a reasonable chance that it will commit itself at this stage.

The FTA

The polite version of the abbreviation FTA stands for Fooling Them Around – in other words teasing the trout in such a way that they cannot resist grabbing a fly that they would otherwise leave alone. It will sometimes tempt trout that have grown completely disinterested in artificial flies. We first discussed its exploitation in our previous book entitled *Success With Trout*, and it has subsequently become a widely used tactic.

Most of us will have played with a kitten by moving a piece of string. At first the kitten will pounce on the string every time, but eventually it becomes a little bored unless you add a few variations. It is exactly the same with a trout. Imagine there is one following the fly and vary the movement to tempt it into commitment. Try all sorts of variations, such as a series of rapid pulls with a delay of a couple of seconds, followed by a figure-of-eight and so on.

Anyone who visits regularly stocked waters will appreciate how the fishing becomes harder after a few days of bombardment by every possible combination of artificial fly. Initially the freshly stocked fish will grab almost anything in sight, but after a while they become more difficult to tempt. This arises either because they have seen it all before, or because they have been pricked a couple of times and grown suspicious. Now is the ideal time to convince yourself of the value of FTA by adding that bit of spice to a retrieve in order to rekindle their curiosity.

You can, of course, apply FTA throughout every retrieve, but this is not always the best tactic. An established trout that has become spooked by angling pressure is likely to keep well clear of anything that bears the remotest sign of being unnatural. This may call for exceptionally well-tied flies, the finest of leaders and probably an almost static retrieve. There is no way

FTA will sometimes induce an interested trout into commitment.

that it will fall into the trap of fancy fly motions that are designed to arouse its curiosity – though occasionally, a fly that brings out an aggressive instinct might just do the trick. These situations therefore call for just an occasional application of FTA after you have thoroughly explored an area with a more imitative approach.

Sometimes, wary trout will simply nip at an artificial fly. One of the most common mistakes is to strike at these frustrating little taps, after which the opportunity is usually lost. Continuing with a slow continuous retrieve is normally the correct tactic, which may result in a solid tightening of the line. But after severe angling pressure, not even this will work. The solution is to respond with a concerted bout of FTA immediately after a tap has occurred to trigger an impulsive response.

Denzil had his own ways of dealing with angling pressure in local hotspots. He would walk as far as he could from the area, while still remaining just in view. Since he was well known as the local expert, most of the anglers would maintain a keen interest in his movements and keep an eye on his progress. At such a distance, they could not tell and would not suspect that his bending rod was due to anything other than a trout. In fact, it was a large can of his favourite beer, chosen for its silvery sheen that was very suggestive of life as he scooped it into his net. Of course, the can of beer would not jump out of the water like a trout, but Denzil quite rightly had the reputation of being secretive, and everyone knew that he could play and land a trout with minimum commotion.

Many anglers would then leave the hot-spot and start fishing as closely as they dared to Denzil. He would deny that he had caught any decent fish, which was true, but no one would believe him. At that he would feign some mild irritation, both for the intrusion into his new-found water and for the insinuation that he was not telling the truth. So he would trail back to the original area, which was now free, while the others attacked the 'easy water' that he had just discovered. On hooking a trout, he would break all the rules and point the rod directly down the line to avoid that give-away bend. He was also quite capable of landing fish without a net.

Humphrey, on the other hand, treated his fellow anglers with greater respect. He always carried a case of superb red Rioja in his car, and was famous for his generosity in passing it around – to the extent that he would leave very little for himself. A few glasses of wine made the anglers, who had staked out the best area, very conducive to the suggestion that they should make room for Humphrey to fish in their midst. It also impaired their casting technique, which resulted in poor presentation that tended to drive the trout that little bit further out. Humphrey, by the way, was an excellent distance caster.

Retrieves in Heavily Coloured Water

Serious problems with algae, or the run-off of water over muddy fields following heavy rainfall, sometimes reduce visibility drastically – perhaps to only a few inches. Anglers often argue over the best colours, but in these situations the choice is of only secondary importance. A trout will not see a fly unless it passes virtually in front of its nose, whatever the colour. Under these conditions, you need to search for them by moving the flies or by frequently probing new areas.

Trout can, however, sense vibrations in the water from a greater distance. So it is a good idea to use a pattern, such as a Booby or Muddler, that will cause a sub-surface wake, and to move it vigorously to maximize the disturbance. Both the lack of vibration and the more restricted coverage of the lake explain why static retrieves are generally ineffective in heavily coloured water.

POINTERS TO FLY SELECTION

The choice on whether to use a nymph, dry fly or lure can be quite a teaser in itself, before even considering the next stage of breaking down the selection into individual patterns. There is no substitute for overall experience and knowledge of an individual water, but there are a few general guidelines that make the task much less of a hit and miss affair.

Surface Activity

A lot of visible movement does not necessarily point to a dry fly. It is easy in the enthusiasm of the moment to put on a dry fly after misinterpreting the rise-form, so it is worth considering a few issues before jumping to the wrong conclusion.

1. Are the fish taking right off the top? Look very carefully first, to confirm that there is some breaking of the surface. A sub-surface boil, for example, will indicate that the fish are feeding on nymphs.

2. Are they taking adults or emergers? In rough water, they are more likely to take whatever they can. A dry fly is therefore the better option because it is less likely to be swept under the waves. In calmer water, trout have much longer to pick and choose as the emerging insects struggle to break through the surface film. It is often worth fishing a combination of the two, such as a Shipman's Buzzer and a CDC emerger. If using a single fly for improved presentation, change it from one form to the other if the fish ignore it.

3. Be careful of 'red herrings'. It is very easy to assume that movement right on the surface signifies dry flies or emergers. Some of the most experienced (and more honest) fishermen will admit to having fallen into this trap at one time or another. Corixae, coming to the surface to replenish their air supply, and daphnia, situated high in the water, are two of the principal offenders. The only tell-tale sign may be a complete lack of interest in your flies when covering rising fish, rather than a rejection of the fly that would point to the wrong pattern or bad presentation. Fry feeders also break the surface, but there should be obvious clues here – fountains of scattering small fish, interest from fish-eating birds and rapid, often splashy, movement of the chasing trout.

4. Trout may be feeding on adult insects, but a dry fly may not be the best tactic. The classic example is when they become preoccupied with tiny insects and stay high in the water with a tiny window of vision. You may do much better by ripping a bright or bushy fly past their noses to cause a distraction.

No Surface Activity

Lack of surface activity does not necessarily mean that a dry fly is the wrong tactic. If there are very few natural insects on the surface and a dearth of sub-surface food, the hungry trout may keep a hopeful eye upwards. A Hopper (UK) is a good general pattern when nothing is showing, since it suggests a wide range of insects. It also has a trigger point in the legs, providing only the hackle is treated with floatant, that is visible outside the trout's window. It is also worth considering terrestrial patterns, such as dung flies or beetles, which can arrive on the water under any conditions.

Plenty of natural food on the surface without any visible activity is usually a signal to explore the depths. A Hi-D line and a lure may be the first choice in April, although it is worth putting a dark midge pupa on the dropper, which the trout will often intercept on its rise to the surface. As the water warms up, the fish are likely to move progressively upward and take a variety of patterns that represent naturally occurring nymphs. There may be a hiatus in high summer as they stay in the cooler sub-surface layers of the lake, and location of the depth where the water suddenly changes temperature can be crucial for success. This transition zone varies from a few feet to perhaps 30 ft. Nymphs are the safest tactic in clear water, but an attractor may be necessary if there are a lot of algae present. By September, the first choice will invariably be the floater with a selection of nymphs, although lures and streamers progressively come into their own as the trout seek larger offerings to build themselves up for spawning over the winter months ahead. A comprehensive tactic at this time of year is a White Lure, such as a Light Bulb, on the point, and a couple of general nymphs on the droppers.

The ultimate reward to the Panacea – a perfect brown trout (photographed alive under water).

Terrestrial Insects

Terrestrial insects are often neglected, but they provide a welcome source of food and hence a concentration of feeding fish. The best time to use them is after the sun has evaporated the morning dew from the insects' wings. Areas to look for are clumps of bushes or trees with the wind behind them. A position down-wind of a combined harvester sometimes brings superb sport. The fish may not be precisely in line with the bankside vegetation, but waiting at a point where surface currents funnel the insects. The choice of pattern should be easy. If you cannot see the flies on the water, then walk the banks and kick up the undergrowth to see what is around. The presence of cows or sheep in the nearby fields will suggest the use of a golden olive pattern to represent dung flies. In the absence of any information, black patterns are a good first choice since they cover a wide range of terrestrial insects.

Autopsies

It is worth examining the stomach contents of every trout that is despatched, because the diet can vary with location, time of day and even an individual's preferences. The location of the contents on a marrow spoon may also be important. Those insects at the tip may have been taken several hours ago, whereas those closest to the handle represent the most recent meal. The job needs to be done thoroughly by placing the contents in a small container of water to spread them out. If this is not done, all sorts of features can be missed in the closely packed mixture – the presence of legs, for example, pointing to dry flies. If there is a predominance of one type of insect, then it is worth concentrating on it. Otherwise, general patterns are the order of the day. If the fish are feeding avidly on daphnia, there should be several specimens sticking to the inside of the throat as well.

We have noticed that some nymphs turn a dull green after they have been dead for a while. Thus, care needs to be taken before deciding that green is the important colour. You should concentrate on those specimens that are still alive when placed in the container of water. They are likely to be the ones devoured recently, and hence the species on the current menu.

Fly of the Lake

Certain flies perform consistently well on selected lakes over many years. Thus, if you are not certain on fly selection, the 'fly of the lake' should remain somewhere on the cast. The middle dropper is a good position since it generally plays a less crucial role in tactics than the top dropper or point fly. You can leave the fly there all day and forget about it. To give examples from our own experiences in England, we would choose a Claret Buzzer in early summer for Chew Valley, since the trout are often tuned in to midge pupae. Rutland has a good head of upwinged flies as well as midge, and Hare's Ear nymphs (in their various forms) cover both eventualities. Finally, we would never fish Wimbleball, where the fish often look for terrestrial insects, without a black fly somewhere on the leader.

The A-Team

Stan was older than the local reservoirs where he ended up doing most of his fishing. He was a real character who would switch into the same non-stop but fascinating monologue at a moment's notice. This endeared him to the younger fishermen – particularly the wet leg story – as long as they did not have to listen to it too many times in the same month. Stan would often bemoan his age and the problems it was causing him. His wet leg occurred when he was desperate to answer a call of nature, and fumbling through his foul-weather fishing clothing had unknowingly pulled his left testicle out of his trousers by mistake.

'Give them good old-fashioned 8 lb line – they can't see it' was one of his favourite maxims, and to this he would attach a Grenadier, Claret Buzzer and Diawl Bach. Who could blame him with his failing eye-sight and dexterity? But on this rather crude and unimaginative set-up he would usually catch more than his fair share of trout. And, against immense competition, he qualified to fish for his country when he was over eighty years old.

Stan's approach may at first glance appear rather crude, but it was well thought out. He had to use thick line because of his age, but he made sure that his droppers were tied on blood knots that kept the fly well clear of the main leader. They were quite safe on the thick 8 lb line. In this way, a disadvantage of the thicker line was offset by a real plus point since there was no tendency for the dropper to wrap around the leader. He could not see the emerging flies very well, but he knew that claret midges were the most important item on the local trout's diet, and the Claret Buzzer was therefore a no-nonsense imitation of the main item of food. Many of the midges hatched into quite vivid orange adults. His palmered orange Grenadier covered the adult and emerging midges and a red sedge as well. It also produced a pronounced wake for attracting the trout. The Diawl Bach could be taken for a midge pupa, a beetle, a caddis larva and who knows what else? Yes, Stan had it all very well sussed.

If you know which insects the trout are feeding on, it should be a relatively straightforward exercise to choose the right fly. Very often, however, the still-water fisherman cannot be absolutely sure of what pattern to use. Under these conditions, it is important to take full advantage of the wide scope that three different flies on the leader can offer. It is very easy to pick each fly without any reference to the others, but then there is likely to be some important item missing from the line of attack. To get maximum effect, you should aim for a properly integrated set of flies whose qualities will complement each other. This way, your selection of flies really will be the A- rather than the B-Team.

To take an example, consider a lake where you know that the trout have been feeding recently on green midge pupae. There is no activity at the moment, but the pupae are known to rise spasmodically throughout the day. Conditions are quite bright, the water is heavily coloured and there is a moderate ripple on the surface.

Had there been some surface activity, you could quite reasonably have expected to fish three midge pupa imitations at once and taken a lot of fish. Unfortunately, since the trout are not up and looking, they are unlikely to see such patterns in the coloured water. Nevertheless, it would be very sensible to include a green midge pupa on the cast. After all, it is the current fly of the lake, and the fish are likely to switch on to it at a moment's notice – and perhaps switch off again just as quickly before you realize what has happened. So you could put a green midge pupa on the middle dropper and forget about it.

A palmered bob fly will disturb the water and draw the trout's attention to the buzzer below. It will not appear to be unnatural in the ruffled water, but the hackles should not be too bushy since there is only a moderate ripple. Although green flies have been on the recent menu, they are generally not as good as red for attracting trout near the surface. A Soldier Palmer will do nicely, since it may be taken as a hatching adult midge in addition to its powers of attraction. A scarlet or orange body would be a good choice in the heavily coloured water.

The bright conditions are crying out for a flashy fly and, since the water is coloured, gold may be more appropriate than silver on the point. The Dunkeld is eminently suitable due to its many features that are suggestive of a midge pupa. An alternative pattern for the point might be a consistent all-round nymph, such as a Stick Fly with a fluorescent green tag that stands out at depth. You should not be in too much of a hurry to change from one fly to another, but point flies are the most suitable for this purpose since there is no progressive shortening of a dropper. The point fly needs to incorporate a reasonably heavy hook to anchor the team.

So the hard part of selecting the A-Team is over. You have picked a team based on logic, rather than simply putting on what you fancy. The result will be a more confident day's fishing, and probably a lot more trout.

FISHING THE NYMPH AND WET FLY

The dominance of wet fly tactics on many still waters is partly due to the availability of sub-surface food, but there is also a historical precedent. Whereas traditional chalk-stream practitioners had concentrated on dry flies – and only the upwinged variety at that – their counterparts on the Scottish lochs and Irish loughs employed wet flies almost exclusively. Just as Skues rebelled by using nymphs on rivers, more recent devotees demonstrated beyond all question the effectiveness of dry flies on lakes. Ironically, some still-water anglers became so obsessed with the unquestionable joys of the dry fly that they lost their previously acquired nymph fishing skills.

MC with a Grafham five pounder taken on a White Sedge.

Although Wesley's all-round angling ability was not particularly impressive, he had good powers of concentration. This enabled him to be quite successful when using a team of nymphs, to the extent that he eventually qualified to represent England. Of course, the whole world had to know about it. Photographs were sent to local newspapers and a standardized letter written to all who had been foolish enough – however long ago – to have left their addresses with him. Poor old Denzil, who had failed to qualify – largely due to the ramifications of a prolonged chatting-up of a local barmaid the night before – had to listen to lectures of where he had gone wrong.

'You know, Denzil, you really should start to be more mature. One needs a clear mind in order to be able to focus on the key characteristics of the prevailing feeding habits and weather conditions. I noticed that you were moving your flies much too quickly . . .' So it went on, but Denzil had switched his mind back towards the barmaid and let all the words drift over his head.

Wesley's wife, who over the years had somehow grown immune to his presumptuous bumblings, was initially very pleased to hear the news. At least now, she would be listening persistently to a success story rather than reasons why the system, the weather and the fish had all played their part in an unfortunate series of failures. But after several weeks – and then months – even she started to complain. The last straw came on his return from the international event, when Wesley had purchased an additional England blazer badge, which he wanted sewing on to his pyjamas!

Short-lining

The traditional loch-style tactic consists of 'short-lining' three or four flies a few yards in front of a drifting boat. It is easier to work the team of flies just on or below the surface by using a long rod of up to 12 ft. A bushy fly on the top dropper (or bob) disturbs the water to bring the fish up from below. Short-lining arose as a technique for wild brown trout in Ireland and Scotland, which are more prone to rising from depth than cruising beneath the surface like the rainbows of the English reservoirs.

Few English nymph specialists who visit these lochs (and loughs) succeed with their normal tactics. This is due partly to the distribution of food, such as shrimp, which remains on the lake bed amongst the stones rather than moving in mid-water or ascending to the surface. It is therefore often necessary to distract a trout from its bottom feeding habits with a vigorous disturbance of the surface. Once attracted to the top, it will either take the bob fly or turn on one of the sleeker flies below it. Reflexes for striking into these fish have to be razor sharp – possibly because they are not so confident about taking their food close to the surface. It is very different from fishing for trout in the English and Welsh waters where the strike is often quite a leisurely affair.

The traditional winged wet flies have proved themselves over generations, and in general are more consistent for wild browns than nymph patterns. One of their great strengths is their broad appeal, without too close an imitation of any natural food item. The use of a nymph is fine during a hatch, but at other times a traditional pattern will often work much better.

The main limitation with traditional short-lining is that the bushy bob fly stands out like a sore thumb in anything less than

Working the flies.

a good ripple. The locals therefore pray for a strong wind, and some of the old protagonists will not even bother fishing in anything less than a force four. Some gillies are reluctant to take anyone out in a flat calm, and a bottle of the appropriate alcoholic nectar as a bribe is usually a very good investment. Just as many nymphs fail to impress the Scottish and Irish trout, the red Rioja often has an equally unimpressive effect on the human inhabitants. It is essential to select a top quality malt whisky to appease the Scots, noting that the cheaper, insipid malts that are popular in the English supermarkets will do more harm than good. Scottish gillies can be very selective, but without any prior local knowledge the Macallan is a good general attractor. In peaty areas, a Lagavulin might be more appropriate. In the Emerald Isle, the locals tend to be grateful for any genuine Irish whiskey – but whatever happens, do not offer them Scotch (or vice versa).

Alex was wearing a mitten on his right hand to combat a problem with blisters. One of the Scots he met at Loch Leven preferred the title of 'wee English tart wya woman's gluve'. Alex's reply, along the lines of 'it's much less tarty than wearing a skirt like some of you bl**dy lot', turned out to be somewhat unsuccessful in securing the required co-operation.

Long Lining

Although the true loch-style method has become less popular, the practice of fishing three or four wet flies is very much the norm in many still waters. There are two fundamental differences from the old style. First, the flies are cast much farther and pulled through the water with little influence from the rod. The guile comes in the method of retrieve. One cantankerous Scottish traditionalist would repeatedly yell, 'Rod up, laddie', in complete desperation at the visiting Sassenachs from south of the border. It still pays to work the flies in a loch style manner as they approach the boat, and to hold them for a few seconds before lifting off to catch those indecisive fish that appear out of the blue at the last moment. Here you will be at a disadvantage over the old traditionalists, because unless you are

as powerful as an ox, your wrists will not be able to take the strain of distance casting with a 12 ft rod. Lengths in the range from 9.5–10 ft are optimum for most people.

Second, there are absolutely no hard and fast rules about which flies to use in the team and where to fish them. The choice depends on the circumstances. You can select three bob flies, three nymphs, three wet flies, three attractors or any mixture you care to choose. You may fish a bushy fly or a Muddler on the point. It is often productive to fish a mixture of dry and wet flies on the same cast.

Short-lining on an Irish lough.

Leader Construction for Wet Flies and Nymphs

Although there is a wide variety of leader designs, with different numbers of flies, it is possible to employ a good all round set-up with a team of three sub-surface patterns to cover most eventualities. This takes account of three simple principles.

First, there is often an advantage – especially when boat fishing – in working the top dropper fly close to the surface. This is difficult to achieve if there is much more than a rod length of (virtually weightless) leader material from the end of the fly line to the top dropper. With a 4 ft long butt section, the additional length to the first dropper is therefore typically 5–6 ft.

Second, a large distance between patterns reduces the risk of a trout noticing two or more different flies moving in an unnatural, synchronized manner. It also allows you to explore a greater range of depths. The maximum separation is limited by the need to net a fish, caught on the point fly, without the top dropper snagging in the top rod ring. For a rod of 9.5 ft, and a standing angler with his arms outstretched on terra firma without the need for too many acrobatics, this maximum separation corresponds to about 15 ft.

Third, the bob fly often has the function of attracting a trout to the pattern below it – so the two flies should not be too far apart. In contrast, a point fly will invariably move more enticingly when it is free to hinge on the greatest possible length of nylon. Thus, the separation of 15 ft is best partitioned into distances of about 5 ft and 10 ft rather than into two identical lengths. Boat fishermen, who remain seated for comfort, safety and a low profile, often compromise by reducing the lengths to 5 and 8 ft respectively. An angler who is standing on a gently sloping bank, where it is possible to beach the fish, may safely increase the separation to the point fly substantially.

Several anglers step down their leader diameters from (say) 8 lb breaking strain to the top dropper, 6 lb to the middle dropper and 4 lb to the point fly. One aim is to achieve good turn-over, though in many cases – with three size 10 flies, for example – the improvement over a level leader is arguably insignificant. Nevertheless, there is a faultless logic in such a set-up for another reason. More smash takes occur on the top dropper since there is less stretch in the short length of nylon connected to the fly line – though a braided leader helps. Takes to the point fly are the least likely to result in a breakage, because there will be about 20 ft of stretchable material. Thus, a tapered leader compensates for the differences in shock absorption, so that no single fly is more vulnerable than the others to a smash take. Moreover, the all-important point fly is able to hinge more freely on the lighter nylon with reduced visibility.

It is worth mentioning a few of the many exceptions to this generic leader construction. For example, it may be necessary to use 10 ft of fluorocarbon to the first dropper if the intention is to fish nymphs deeply on a floating line. A similar length often improves catch rates on sinking lines, either by changing the trajectory slightly or by increasing the separation of the first fly from a conspicuous fly line. The use of two flies allows a greater separation for spooky fish – and a single fly might be better still. In contrast, when covering smutting fish with a tiny field of vision, there may be an increased chance of success by placing all the flies close together.

Weighted Flies

The weighting of a nymph is less crucial in still water than in rivers because there are no strong currents to sweep it over the feeding fish. An exception arises when casting across a strong wind with a floating line, since the surface motion may move the flies round to the bank before they have had a chance to reach the holding depth. Added weight also helps to get flies down quickly in front of a drifting boat. The more prestigious UK competitions ban weighted flies, but not sinking lines, and the fact that several anglers have risked disqualification for breaking this rule speaks for itself.

In most other instances, a patient angler can wait for the fly to sink to the required depth. Nevertheless, weighted flies may still bring more than their fair share of success, even when the trout are not lying very deep. First, the enticing movement of a sink and draw retrieve is more exaggerated with a weighted fly. The effect is even more potent if the weight is situated at the front to produce a diving motion, as with a Dog Nobbler. Bead-headed flies owe at least part of their success to this built-in FTA. Second, the plop of a weighted fly entering the water advertises its presence, and often causes a passing trout to turn and look. This is a good tactic for distracting fish that have become pre-occupied with very small surface insects.

Third, lake fishermen often employ three flies at the same time. A weighted point fly provides a firm anchor, which allows the team of flies to be fished over a greater range of depths. Certain anchor patterns have proved themselves to be consistently successful, such as a Montana Nymph, Green Tag Stick Fly and Green Thorax Pheasant Tail. All three incorporate a modicum of yellow or fluorescent green that turns a good pattern into a real killer when a few feet below the surface. Fishermen with a less imitative approach prefer to use a Dog Nobbler on the point.

Lightweight Nymphs

'Now down to business', echoed the guest speaker slowly and deliberately to the gathered members of the local Fly Dressers' Guild. This implied that the first stage of his talk, which had expounded his own position and importance for over 25 minutes, was now mercifully over. He pointed successively to unsuspecting members of the audience. 'At the end of the session, you, you and you should be able to tie perfect chironomid pupae that have helped me to attain my current reputation in the angling world.' Some of them sniggered, because Wesley had quite a reputation that was nothing to do with his questionable prowess as an angler.

'Most anglers tie chironomids that incorporate disproportionately exaggerated abdominal dimensions.' (Correct – in other words, like Wesley, they are too fat.) 'I have developed . . .' (questionable) '. . . an emphatically more realistic imitation, which incorporates a stripped peacock herl body. The resemblance to the natural is quite stunning.' (True.) 'In order to achieve just the right diameter, it is imperative to tie the body on a hook with a shank

Displaying the dead catch.

diameter of 0.75 millimetres.' (Perhaps – give or take a factor of two!)

To give Wesley his due, the finished product was impressive. When 'you, you and you' tried it, they caught plenty of trout that were feeding well beneath the surface. But during a rise, other people's inferior imitations would work much better, even though every one reluctantly agreed that the appearance of Wesley's nymphs was perfection itself. In trying to match the appearance of the nymph as far as possible to the natural, he had taken no account of the weight of the hook and materials used in their construction. So his nymphs would sink quickly below the feeding fish.

Slow retrieves are essential for proper imitation of many naturally occurring nymphs. The flies spend a long time in the water between casts, and therefore have plenty of opportunity to sink below the feeding trout. Any downward motion of a fly may also be obvious as an alien phenomenon when the natural nymphs are moving upwards on their journey to the surface. The imitative approach to trout feeding on nymphs near the surface must therefore be to adopt the lightest weight hooks possible. It makes no sense to fish with a lightweight hook when the fish are well down, but the lack of any visible movement can be deceptive. Trout may just be a couple of feet under the surface cruising around in the search for sub-surface food.

When trout are taking pupae of an imitable size just below the surface, it is often better to fish a team consisting exclusively of lightweight nymphs. This assumes that the wind is not too strong, because you may then need a point fly on a heavyweight hook to anchor the team. A bob fly or a brightly coloured pattern may do more harm than good. It will attract more fish, but sometimes they will repeatedly turn away without committing themselves. Small, drab and apparently uninteresting patterns will be very visible to the trout, except in heavily coloured water, and often produce really savage takes. One of the lightweight flies that we developed based on these convictions was Gerald's Midge. The subdued application of

orange, which many emerging midge pupae exhibit, provides just the right balance between attraction and imitation.

Anorexic Nymphs

For a long time we have been advocates of slimly dressed nymphs, since that is just the way that most natural insects happen to be. But nothing we had ever used came close to the patterns created by Bob Barden. Chris Ogborne commented in a magazine article that they were not just slim, but anorexic – and the name caught on. The patterns have rightly become very popular because they are unparalleled fish-takers in waters where small nymphs form the trout's staple diet.

The first reason for their development was to imitate the tiny midge pupae that proliferate in Bewl Water. The trout will often feed exclusively on these insects, and the water is sufficiently clear for sub-surface imitations to be quite visible from a respectable distance. It is not surprising that these anorexic nymphs need to be fished with a painfully slow figure-of-eight retrieve.

The second reason was to get an unweighted fly quickly down to the holding depth. This was inspired by International Rules for competition fishing, which ban additional weighting. The sink rates of bulky patterns are reduced by the buoyancy of the materials and the drag exerted by the water. The fastest sink rate occurs with a bare hook, and that is fundamentally what these patterns set out to achieve. The use of Superglue or an epoxy on some patterns assists the process by preventing the entrapment of air between the fibres. The ultimate depth also benefits from a fast-sinking leader material, for which fluorocarbons are ideal.

Graham Dean with a wild New Zealand rainbow caught on a Superglue Buzzer.

The only factor that really limits the achievable depth is the length of the leader. Bob often fishes three of them on a leader of 26 ft and a long rod of 10 ft 10 in, which means that it is just about possible to land a trout hooked on the point fly while standing at full-stretch. In principle, it is possible to reach greater depths by a leader construction that prevents the top dropper snagging in the rod tip ring when landing a trout on the point. To this end, there are three basic options.

The first is the use a single fly, providing you can avoid wind-knots. The second is to maximize the distance from the end of the fly line to the top dropper. We frequently adopt a length of 10 ft of stout (2X/8 lb) fluorocarbon material. The third option of a sink-tip or intermediate line becomes essential when you have reached the limit of your ability to get the leader to turn over satisfactorily. Faster sinking lines incorporate too much unnatural downwards motion to these sparsely dressed imitations.

At this point, we need to add a word of warning. It is very easy for a team of anorexic nymphs to sink below the feeding trout. We have known catch rates increase dramatically, for example, when reducing the length of fluorocarbon above the top dropper from 10–5 ft. A hedged-bet tactic is often the best approach, which uses a conventional, slower sinking nymph on one or more of the droppers, and anorexic nymphs below.

Superglue and epoxy buzzers, that appear in the chapter on *Great Trout Flies*, are simply thinly dressed patterns that have been sealed to prevent the ingress of air. Many other anorexic nymphs appear to incorporate a hook that is much too large for the dressing. The best way of describing them is a normal size 16 pattern tied on to a size 10. Materials, such as hare's ear, that are unsuitable for sealing, need to be tightly packed to avoid protrusions that will drag in the water or trap air.

The hook must not be too heavy to avoid unnaturally fast sink rates and a body that is insufficiently slim. We have found suitable options to be the Kamasan B175, Drennan Wet Fly Supreme and, for buzzers, the Kamasan B110. The lighter Drennan Sedge hooks are also excellent for fishing buzzers higher in the water. Nevertheless, when casting in front of a fast-drifting boat in deep water, a super-heavyweight hook on the point may be the best solution for getting down to the trout.

Finally, you really do need to concentrate to get the best results. Watch the line between the rod tip and surface like a hawk. This helps to ensure that you are not imparting any movement to the flies, which really often need to be static. It also provides an indication of a take. Sometimes trout will wrench the rod from your hand with this technique, but on other occasions you may feel nothing unless you strike at the slightest visible twitch of the line. Not surprisingly, strike indicators are very popular on those waters where they are permitted.

Wet Flies and Nymphs in a Flat Calm

General watercraft, patience and presentational skills come to the fore in the absence of any wind. The surface of the lake appears as smooth as a mirror, so that the most delicately cast line will make a disturbance that may be apparent several yards

Anorexic nymphs tied by Bob Barden.

away. Careless wading or any rocking of the boat will ensure that the fish keep their distance. Even with the greatest possible care, established fish often seem to rise just out of casting range.

It is more important than ever to rely on casting technique rather than brute force, since leaders are notoriously poor at turning over in windless conditions. A properly tapered leader will help considerably and a braided butt section will avoid unsightly coils on the surface. There is little point in using a length of (say) 20 ft to increase separation from the fly line if the nylon fails to straighten. It is better to accept a much shorter length, and redress the balance towards stealth by attaching just a single, slim-bodied fly that will cut through the air. One trick is to cast a little farther than you need, and apply a sudden brake with the fingers at the last moment. This helps the leader turn over, and is exactly the same technique used for improving presentation with shooting heads. It is arguably better to use an AFTMA 7 line and accept the slightly heavier landing, than to opt for a lighter alternative that fails to penetrate (what many anglers refer to as) 'the wall of motionless air'.

Rather than casting monotonously and keeping the fish just out of range, there is an obvious advantage in considering an alternative approach. This involves casting a floating or very slow sinking line as far as possible, and waiting for one or two minutes to allow everything to settle down. Then, and only then, should you move the line back ever so slowly with a smooth figure-of-eight retrieve that will minimize any disturbance to the water. If using a floating line, you should treat the leader to ensure it sinks to avoid any disturbance of the surface film.

You could be forgiven for assuming that takes would be very gentle in calm water, since a trout has more chance of detecting that something is not quite right. Often, however, the opposite occurs and the rod is almost wrenched out of your hand. We can only assume that the trout has had plenty of time to make up its mind, and once it has reached the decision to feed there is no immediate thought of spitting out the fly. When it first notices that something is amiss, the point of the hook may already have become embedded. It will then turn rapidly to swim away to safety, which registers as a violent take.

Point Fly Panaceas

The point fly has a great advantage over other patterns on the leader since it hinges more freely and naturally. It is also the fly that trout should see first when cruising upwind towards a drifting boat. Thus, although it is the easiest pattern to change, you should always take its selection very seriously. We therefore follow some simple rules for selecting point-fly nymphs on those occasions when the prevailing fly life is uncertain.

First, we increase our confidence of success by restricting the selection to a small number of general patterns that have proved themselves repeatedly over many years on a wide range of waters. Second, we associate each of these patterns with its own favourite water conditions. This approach is not completely fool-proof, but it gets us by for probably 90 per cent of the time.

If the fish are acclimatized to buzzers, then a Diawl Bach or Cruncher on a heavyweight hook is a good choice. For caddis, the Stick Fly takes pride of place. These patterns will often work acceptably for both categories of insect, so the selection is not too critical. Thus, there is little harm in changing from one to the other if the first choice fails to perform. In coloured water, a modicum of Phosphor Yellow will improve these patterns by providing a trigger point. A tag on the Stick Fly, and the replacement of the Cruncher by a Green Thorax Pheasant Tail, will do the trick nicely.

When there is little evidence of nymphs, the trout will not be tuned-in to either buzzers or caddis. They need something to kick them into life, and we know of nothing better than a subdued Montana Nymph, such as Dave Grove's Monty. A damsel nymph is a good alternative, since trout have a tendency to gulp down small pieces of weed. The choice between these two patterns is sometimes so difficult that we will put a damsel nymph on a dropper to keep Monty company.

Final Thoughts on Nymph Selection

When trout are feeding confidently, it is often an advantage to use an attractor pattern to bring them close to the nymph. This may involve a bushy bob fly, for example, or a sub-surface lure. However, spooky fish need treating with more respect, since they will sometimes turn away from a team of nymphs just because their suspicions have been aroused by one inappropriate pattern. One of the golden rules under these circumstances is to use a selection of flies that no trout will reject.

The patterns must therefore be as slim and as drab as the natural pupae or larvae. Good examples are a Stick Fly, Super-glue Buzzer and Diawl Bach. Many experts use such patterns exclusively, but the less adept often carry fly boxes packed with the insect-equivalents of Sumo wrestlers. 'Sumo-nymphs' may work tolerably on stock-fish, but they are hopeless for deceiving the established residents of a lake. Fluorescent materials may only be used in the sparsest of quantities to suggest life rather than to add attraction, except in heavily coloured water.

Finally, many nymphs need to remain virtually static in the water, which usually requires a floating line to prevent any downwards drag. It is possible to achieve some very respectable depths with slimly dressed patterns and a fluorocarbon leader –

John Horsey nets a Rutland rainbow.

even in front of a drifting boat in a respectable wave. You require total concentration to keep the retrieve sufficiently slow. It also takes bags of confidence to believe that the trout will pick out the drably coloured nymphs in what appears to be a wide expanse of unproductive water. Yet those who have the tenacity to stick to it will often completely outperform their less confident counterparts.

FISHING THE DRY FLY

Many of the basic principles for dry fly fishing in rivers apply to lakes as well. The differences in tactics occur due to the smaller surface currents and the propensity for still-water trout to move around in search of food.

Presentation with the Dry Fly

Lake fishermen generally have more time before surface currents remove all slack from the leader, but this quite often leads to complacency. It is surprising how few anglers even bother to consider mending or throwing a snaky profile into the line. Surface currents obviously occur in a wind, but they are also present under flat calm conditions when even the slightest drag will be apparent to the trout as an unnatural phenomenon. You can take control of the situation by a suitable choice of position. All other things being equal, it is better to fish with the wind directly behind you to remove the effect of currents. In addition, fish in such a location close to a bank are more likely to be searching for terrestrial insects that have been blown on to the water from nearby vegetation.

The speed of a river dictates the period over which the fly needs to remain afloat, and this may be as little as a few seconds. Lake fishermen, on the other hand, often need to keep their dry flies afloat for much longer, unless covering a specific rise. The old fashioned practice of greasing leaders to ensure that they float has long fallen from grace for two good reasons. First, a greased leader stands out like a ship's hawser in the surface film. Thus, you should avoid the accidental application of grease, which commonly occurs when handling the leader after adding floatant to a fly. Common sense therefore dictates that you should treat a fly just after, rather than just before, attaching it to a leader. It is good practice, even though it may be tedious, to clean your hands afterwards.

The second advantage is that the removal of grease, plus the addition of specially available compounds, helps a leader to sink. This reduces its visibility considerably since there is now no distortion of the surface film. Ideally, just a few inches next to the flies should be treated to avoid the full length of a sinking leader dragging everything down with it. You can delay this process by making the droppers as long as practicable and by avoiding fluorocarbons, which do not have a significantly reduced visibility compared with nylon when close to the surface.

If your flies do sink, it is sometimes worth figure-of-eighting them back rather than lifting them straight off the water. This increases the fishing time, reduces the risk of spooking fish and keeps you informed on the effectiveness of sub-surface tactics. It is not uncommon to realize that you should not have been fishing dry flies at all!

There is nothing seriously wrong with adopting the same spacing between a team of three flies as for sub-surface tactics. When employing a highly visible attractor pattern on the top dropper, such as a Carrot Fly, this leader construction may be optimal. It is more often the case, though, that each dry fly is there to attract a trout in its own right. This implies that the spacing should be equal in order to put the maximum separation between all the flies.

A special leader has a distinct advantage when covering fish that are cruising high in the water. Since their window of vision is small, even an expert caster will have difficulty in placing his flies with the necessary accuracy of a few inches. It is therefore worth placing the flies much closer together to increase the chances of at least one of them being seen. A separation of a couple of feet is by no means too small.

Covering Trout with the Dry Fly

Good anticipation of the direction of a cruising fish, combined with accurate casting, makes a tremendous difference to success. The need for 'forward lead' is even more important than it is for nymphs. Try to estimate the cruising speed from the distance and interval between one rise and the next. If there is a zigzagging trajectory, cast into the middle of the likely area and leave the flies there for the trout to find.

Covering fish may be exciting, but it is not always the best tactic. There are times when you will do better by just casting a team of dry flies into a general area and leaving them there patiently. Providing you understand why you are doing it, it is quite possible to summon up the will-power to resist the obvious temptation. This tactic works well when there are large numbers of trout scouring the surface for food. The chances of your flies being noticed are therefore fairly high without targeting any individual fish. The more cautious trout may spend quite a time inspecting offerings before eventually committing themselves.

Therefore, the longer your flies remain on the surface, the greater will be their chance of being taken for the real thing. This approach can also be effective when nymph fishing. The patient angler, who retrieves slowly and methodically without being distracted by rising fish, will often completely outperform his more active and alert counterpart who casts to everything that moves.

Hitting Difficult Takes with the Dry Fly

It is usual in still water to miss more opportunities to dry flies than it is to nymphs, for two main reasons. First, you can actually see a trout reject your fly at the last moment on the surface, whereas you may be completely oblivious to what is happening 2 ft down. Second, with a nymph, you generally tighten instinctively at the right time, whereas you often need to wait for a fraction of a second to allow a fish to turn on a dry fly. The duration of this delay may vary throughout the day and from one species of trout to another.

Failure to contact a taking fish often occurs when it is moving directly towards you, simply because you pull the fly straight out of its mouth. There is usually plenty of time to set the hook because the trout should feel no tension in the line at this point. This suggests waiting that little bit longer, so that you can then lift into the fish as soon as it starts to dive.

It is a frustrating experience when trout are coming short. You may have tried all the usual remedies, such as a fine degreased leader and a single small fly, but to no avail. One trick is to position the rod so that its tip is close to the water and at 90° to the fly. On seeing the rise, move the rod smoothly for a distance of only 2 or 3 ft. If the trout has taken the fly, then you should have struck successfully. If not, the fly will move gently across the water in a natural manner without leaving the surface, and remain within its reach. Quite often it will react to this stimulus by following and taking the fly.

Sometimes takes to dry flies are so violent that they result in a broken leader. The ability to deal with this varies, but some anglers just cannot avoid the inevitable smash takes. One way of overcoming this problem is to trap the line between two fingers of the rod hand, when not retrieving slack, as if holding a cigarette. The other hand lets go of the line completely. When striking, the only resistance to the fish is then the clasp of the two fingers around the line, and it is simply not possible for them to grip too tightly. The right hand therefore has its own built-in slipping clutch.

Dry Fly Patterns with Trigger Points

The inclusion of bright colours in wet flies and nymphs is a common practice, whereas dry flies usually incorporate more subdued shades to match the natural insects. The dry fly culture seems to be biased greatly towards imitation rather than stimulus. Nevertheless, trout can react just as much to stimulus on the surface as they do a few feet down. For example, the vividly bright Carrot Fly often produces the most violent takes that suggest anything other than a leisurely intent to feed. This does not necessarily mean that the trout take such flies out of aggression. The violence of the take may suggest some final commitment after being hit between the eyes by an unusual cordon-bleu midge.

The trouble with bright flies is that they tend to work occasionally rather than consistently. This suggests that it is worth experimenting with dry patterns that include just a modicum of brightness to produce a respectable trigger point. Many successful innovations include either normal or fluorescent orange, since it is a natural colour exhibited close to the wings and thorax of many hatching midge pupae. Orange also has a slightly increased range of visibility through the water from fly to fish compared with red.

A shuck case also provides a natural trigger point. Relatively few dry patterns include the discarded shuck, but it is still attached to the fly during emergence and presents a big mouthful to a hungry trout. We devised a successful yet simple trick, which involves tying in a few strands of light amber seal's fur (or substitute) behind a dry fly, such as a Shipman's Buzzer. The light amber stands out well, while being sufficiently subdued to remain within the confines of imitation.

Emergers with a Difference

We had given a lot of thought to why trout should quite happily grab Boobies with enormous lumps of Plastazote, while rejecting Suspenders so quickly. There were two possible explanations. First, their reaction to the Booby is one of curiosity, whereas in eyeing up the Suspender they are focusing clearly on a very definite food form that does not quite match up to their expectations. Second, the deliberate movement incorporated into the retrieve of a Booby gives it a more enticing appeal compared with an almost static Suspender.

The answer became clearer during one September day when fishing the English National Final in the south arm of Rutland Water. The fish were feeding right in the surface film, but after nearly three hours of fruitless experimentation JD could hardly touch them with any of our regular patterns. Then he tried the combination of a couple of lightweight nymphs on the droppers, with a 'sacrificial' Suspender on the point solely to keep them high in the water. The slow figure-of-eight retrieve took two good trout, which thumped the dropper nymphs, in the first three casts. The tactic was working like a dream, exactly as intended. Then something quite unexpected occurred.

The water seemed to go rather heavy, as if snagging in weed, but a slow lifting of the rod to free the hook connected with a 2 lb rainbow that sent the reel screaming. Fourteen rainbows came to the net during the next five hours, with about three quarters of them taking the Suspender on the point. The trick was to keep the flies moving when the line went heavy, just as when fishing the Booby, and then to lift the rod gradually into the fish to set the hook. The Suspender had successfully served its purpose of keeping the other two nymphs high in the water, but we are convinced that the tactic owed most to its bobbing action in the water. This motion has proved itself to be something that trout find hard to resist.

The technique worked on several different reservoirs during the remainder of the season – so much so that we thought we had discovered the ultimate panacea. Since that day, our close fishing acquaintances have referred to it as 'The Method'. Fortunately – for fishing would lose its interest if such tremendous successes continued – it did not work very well during the following season. Nevertheless, we frequently give it a try, and from time to time it still gives amazing sport when the trout are receptive. The reason why it remains so unpredictable is one of those mysteries that so typify the magic of fly fishing.

Dry Fly in Flat Calms

The problems of dealing with a flat calm become magnified several times over for the dry fly fisherman. Once a nymph and leader are submerged, the amount of unnatural disturbance that they will make is limited – but on the surface there is no hiding place. The visibility of a leader due to the distortion it creates in the surface film is most pronounced in a flat calm, and it is essential to treat the business end so that it sinks. Many proprietary substances exist for this purpose, but a mixture of washing up liquid and Fuller's Earth or clay works fairly well. Some leader materials need less encouragement to sink than others. They are obviously a good choice, even if they are more prone to 'smash takes', since in dry fly fishing an angler has more control over the strike than with nymphs.

Droppers sit much less naturally on the water than the point fly, since there are two adjacent strands of nylon to twist around each other. It is arguably better to tie a dropper fly directly onto the line in the New Zealand style, for example, but the leader is still more likely to be visible if connected to both ends of a fly. Getting the nylon to sink close to more than one fly is a further complication. On balance, the best solution is usually to concentrate on a single pattern and to get it right. There are exceptions for specialized tactics, such as using a dry fly to suspend a nymph just below the surface.

There is another reason why a dry fisherman's skills are truly tested in a flat calm. Emerging adult insects have difficulty in breaking through the surface film, and sometimes they take many minutes to escape. The surface acts as a trap for the emerging insects, so at any one time there are far more juicy morsels trying to break through it than there are swimming upwards through the water. So the trout may be looking for food exclusively in the surface, and will have a lot of time to inspect each offering for overall appearance and any unnatural movement.

Conventionally hackled flies do not generally work as well as sparse patterns, since every imperfection is so obvious in the mirror-like surface. Slim parachute hackled flies, such as our Panacea, are a good choice. A Shipman's Buzzer, with just enough fur to stay afloat, is one of the most consistent patterns. Emergers will often work well, providing the appendages that keep them afloat have a natural appearance. Gerald's Midge, with a teased out greased thorax, and a sparse emerger with just enough CDC to keep it suspended, are excellent patterns. The body should be compact, rather than straggly, to help it to penetrate the surface film. In some instances, a slightly heavier hook may help to achieve this objective.

JD with a wild New Zealand rainbow taken on a dry Cicada.

The CDC Suspender

Neither CDC nor Plastazote is perfect for suspending an upright emerger in the surface film is perfect. Trout will very often just sip at a Suspender and reject it in a flash. A CDC shuttlecock is more likely to provoke a solid take, but there are many occasions when the trout will reject it after seeing the unnatural profile above the surface. In both patterns, you should only incorporate enough material so that the fly remains just suspended.

In order to reduce both problems, we experimented with a fly that incorporated floatation from both sources – only half the normal amount of black Plastazote and half the normal amount of CDC. It fulfilled all our expectations. One of its first trials was from the dam wall at Farmoor, which demonstrated another very interesting behavioural aspect. It would catch a trout at 30 minute intervals without fail. We were predicting when the next take was going to come to within five minutes every time. This illustrates the way in which still-water trout will move in shoals along predefined paths. In this case they were probably moving from one end of the reservoir to the other.

The A-Team for Dry Flies

Whether covering a rising fish or simply hanging out the flies and waiting, it is worth giving careful thought to team selection. Just as for wet flies and nymphs, you need to choose a comprehensive range of colour, size and shape that will cover most eventualities. One crucial fact to establish is the most consistent food item at the current time of year. It may be aquatic or terrestrial, but once you have identified a suitable pattern to represent the 'fly of the lake', it should stay on the leader all day.

Even when you are certain of the precise details of the dry flies on the menu, it is often worth putting an emerger somewhere on the leader. It will increase the range of visibility, and may therefore attract a trout to a dry fly that would otherwise have gone unnoticed. The emerger does not have to grip the surface film. A lightweight Caretaker or Gerald's Midge on the middle dropper will happily rest a few inches under the surface if suspended by two buoyant dry flies either side of it.

The use of a Hopper (UK), with only the hackle treated to produce what John Horsey termed the 'ultimate emerger', may

When casting to rising fish in a flat calm, many experts will deliberately choose dry flies that are extremely sparse. If a fish has been covered accurately, the fly has only to stay up for a few seconds at most. Even if it starts to sink, it will only descend slowly and probably remain within the trout's field of view, providing it is tied on a lightweight hook. Moreover, as soon as it penetrates the surface, there will no longer be any restriction due to the trout's window. The use of a dry fly that slowly sinks for covering specific fish is one of the best-kept secrets.

Dry Flies for Smutting Trout

When smutting off the surface, trout invariably remain very high in the water with a tiny field of vision. Emergers therefore have an advantage, but this is not so great as you may first imagine because the trout's concentration is still focused on this tiny area. Therefore, it is a good idea to use three or four patterns that are closely spaced on the leader – as little as 18 in apart. With accurate casting, this increases the chance of at least one of them being seen.

It is often possible to cover the same fish several times, providing you are careful. You obviously must not 'line' it with an over-zealous cast, but lifting off suddenly may have the same detrimental effect. Therefore, when the flies are no longer in the right position, you should retrieve the line a good distance away from the trout before lifting it off the water.

increase the effectiveness of the team even further because those knotted legs produce an incredible trigger point. It is a good idea to choose the colour of the Hopper to match the fly of the lake, even though it may have a different size and profile. Thus, for Chew Valley in May, claret is a sensible choice due to the consistency of claret midge pupa patterns. On Wimbleball, terrestrial flies play an important role. Our first choice would then be black, to copy a Hawthorn Fly, or golden-olive if there was evidence of dung flies. Sometimes, we will fish both colours together. It is worth noting that, because much of the fly is below the surface, it will not stay up in a strong wave as well as some truly dry patterns.

Taking account of all the factors discussed in this section on dry fly fishing, we might choose the following A-Teams (starting with the top dropper) for different conditions. There are, of course, plenty of variations on the theme.

For a lake with little aquatic food and a substantial head of stock-fish: Carrot Fly or Red Hopper, golden-olive Bob's Bit and a Black Hopper.

For the same lake in a flat calm with educated fish: a single black or golden-olive Hopper.

For a coloured lake in a good wave holding midges and educated fish: red Bob's Bit or small red Hopper, crimson CDC emerger and a Shipman's Buzzer.

For a clear lake in a light ripple holding midges and educated fish: Shipman's Buzzer, CDC Suspender and a Claret Hopper.

MIXED TACTICS

Just as in rivers, you can fish a combination of nymphs and dry flies in still waters. Success depends quite crucially on the relative positions of the flies on a cast.

If the dry fly is on the point, a nymph on a dropper will remain motionless below the surface. You should be prepared to feel the take before the dry fly registers any movement. This can be quite a strange sensation.

If the dry fly is on a dropper, a nymph on the point will fish much deeper. The weight of the submerged leader, especially if using fluorocarbon, will tend to drag the dry fly under the surface. Thus, a substantially more buoyant dry fly will be needed, which will also act as an effective strike indicator.

FLY LINE SELECTION

Experience has taught us that there are three golden rules for selecting fly lines. The first is to avoid having too many different types of line, because it will only result in confusion. Many fishermen do not really appreciate at what depth they are fishing, and yet waste a considerable amount of time deliberating between two lines of quite similar density. The second is to assess the impact of the fishing method on the ultimate depth of the flies. It is possible, for example, to fish fairly close to the surface with a high density line by limiting the casting distance. In contrast, a slow sinker – or even a floater with a long leader – will reach impressive depths if cast a good distance and retrieved very slowly. The final rule is to take into account more than just the sink rate, since there is also the trajectory of the flies to consider.

The Floating Line

The floater should always be uppermost in any fly fisherman's thoughts. Even when there is no hatch of insects, trout will frequently look upwards to the surface for food. In clear water, they will rise from the depths to take an isolated dry fly that has been blown on to the surface. In coloured water, they may be cruising just a couple feet below even though there is no evidence of their presence. If a fish suddenly does give its presence away, it is possible to lift a floating line off the water immediately to cover it.

Even when the fish are remaining well down, a floating line may still be the best choice. It keeps you firmly in control since you can retrieve a nymph as slowly as necessary. Once the fly has sunk to its final depth, which increases with the length of the leader, it will remain there. On the other hand, a sinking line continues to pull the fly downwards, which often appears as an unnatural phenomenon. It is common in small waters to see Booby fishermen having most of the action in the morning before the fish grow suspicious. From then on, it is often the floating line nymph fisherman who will reap the greatest reward.

A weight forward AFTMA 6 or 7 is a good all-round compromise between delicacy and distance for most still waters. We have never noticed any significant advantage in using anything lighter. A heavier line should only be necessary when fishing large or heavy patterns, or when belting out a shooting head from the bank for maximum distance. Out of the two, an AFTMA 7 may seem a little more meaty, but its increased inertia makes it considerably better at cutting through an awkward wind.

Neutral Density Lines

The primary role of a neutral density line is to overcome the floater's problem of surface disturbance when fishing nymphs and wet flies in a flat calm. All of the leader will be submerged, thereby avoiding any surface wake, but initially the flies will be fishing no deeper than with a floating line. It is also possible to carry out a systematic search of the water with a very slow retrieve over several minutes, without the ultimate depth being governed by the length of leader (as with a floater).

We normally use two favourite flies with this tactic, seldom bothering with a middle dropper in order to increase the separation. A small imitative pattern, such as a Hare's Ear, goes on the dropper, depending on the local fly life. A Stick Fly or Pheasant Tail goes on the point in overcast conditions, but on a sunny day a size 12 Silver Invicta is mandatory. We are not sure what the Silver Invicta does to the trout, but they thump it as if possessed, and have been doing so for at least the last twenty years!

There was nothing remarkable about having a fish pond in his garden, but Reggie was not going to tarnish his reputation for eccentricity by stocking it with the usual goldfish, shubunkins or even koi carp. No – the rule was that every fish had to be caught by his own fair hand.

Wild fish, such as roach, minnows and bleak were there in abundance. There was also a small grayling, until it fell victim to Tyson the trout. But the most interesting resident was Freddie the flounder, who survived in good health at the bottom of the pond for several years.

Freddie would only eat worms. Rather than simply throwing them in, Reggie found that his pet flounder would quickly appear from the depths if he attached the worm to the end of a silvered stick. Freddie would always peck at the silver several times before taking the worm. Not only did the silver do its job as an attractor, it also provoked Freddie into nibbling it – even though it was obvious from this daily ritual that it was not a source of food.

Intermediate Lines

An intermediate line descends at roughly one inch per second, which is typically the same rate as an unweighted fly. This allows a progressive search of the layers, without pulling the nymphs downwards at an unnatural angle. Long casts with a slow retrieve will cover a considerable range of depths. It is an excellent choice for use with unweighted patterns on bright days, or on any occasion when trout tend to remain a few feet below the surface. All the flies on a leader will then have a chance to reach the fish, rather than just the point fly.

Bob Church scores with a slow-sinking line on Lough Owel.

Such lines also enable you to combat some of the undesirable effects of the wind. For example, they are useful when casting from the bank against a strong cross-current, since they will sink beneath the surface drift into the slower moving layers below. This allows the flies to sink close to where they landed on the water, rather than being swept round to the bank before reaching the holding depth. They are also perfect when boat fishing close to the surface in a big wave. A floating line would ride the peaks and troughs, whereas the intermediate cuts

though the surface motion to the likely fish holding depth just below. This also provides a more direct contact with the flies and hence more positive takes.

Finally, an intermediate line is ideal for faster retrieves at a depth of a couple of feet. This is a good tactic for fry feeders, since it maintains the flies at a depth where the trout will initially look for their prey – even though the visible signs of the ensuing chase occur close to the surface. A floating line would pull the flies up to the surface and create a wake. This might be an advantage in a good wave, but it is generally detrimental in calm water.

Floaters versus Intermediates

The decision between a floating and intermediate line is often quite marginal when fishing nymphs a few feet below the surface. Nevertheless, you can remove much of the guesswork by asking yourself a few simple questions. At the risk of repetition, it is worth spelling out the essential thought processes.

If the intention is to fish a static fly, then a floating line is likely to be the better choice since it will not impart any vertical motion. Sometimes, only one fly may hold at the appropriate depth. This pattern will merit all the attention, while the others are there principally as a bonus.

If, on the other hand, the trout are responding to even quite a slow retrieve, an intermediate line will usually produce better results. First, you can retrieve all the flies at the appropriate depth. Second, takes tend to be more positive since there is a more direct pull between line and leader. A series of missed takes on a floater might be the signal to change.

Faster Sinking Lines

Intermediate lines waste a lot of time when fish are lying deep. They are also useless in even a moderate wind for getting flies down more than a couple of feet in front of a drifting boat. Every serious still-water fisherman therefore needs to carry one of the various brands of line available that sink just about as fast as technology will allow. Some compromise may be necessary to choose a line that will at least cast respectably without tangling or landing on the water like a heap of spaghetti.

The consequences of using a fast sinking line extend beyond the simple achievement of depth. The flies will follow the line down rapidly, rather than sinking at their own natural rate. It is therefore difficult to fish imitatively in the early stages of the retrieve, and it is not uncommon to draw a blank until they start to move upwards in the water. This sudden change in direction will often trigger a response. Thereafter you can choose the rate at which the flies rise to copy the motion of an ascending nymph, and this is usually a highly productive period that requires proper concentration.

It is worth emphasizing that the effect of downwards motion becomes quite significant on any line that sinks at a rate of about 1.5 in per second or more. Thus, even some lines that are marketed as intermediates should really be considered as full-bodied sinkers. To our reckoning, the essential factor that defines an intermediate is the almost level trajectory.

At the very end of the cast, you should let the flies hang in the water before lifting off, because very often a trout will be following and unable to make up its mind. (The 'hang' is also a good tactic with floating lines – but the faster the sink rate, the more important it becomes.) You will be able to tell whether you are not holding for long enough by a boil occurring in the water after the final lift-off and the cries of 'Did you see that!' Some fishermen deliberately use a bright top dropper fly as a strike indicator, which is visible under the surface as they hold the flies stationary beneath the rod tip.

Sometimes a pronounced vertical trajectory, whether up or down, will kill the fishing stone dead. For example, trout that are boat-shy may not approach closely enough at any depth to intercept the flies on the final lift. You should therefore always remain sufficiently alert to consider the possibility of changing from a high density line (say) to a medium or even a slow sinker. An alternative tactic is to rip the flies back, which results in a fairly level and shallow trajectory. If anything, many anglers are prone to fish too deeply.

A fast-sinking line is ideal for fishing sub-surface nymphs in front of a drifting boat in a strong wind. The nymphs should only be cast about 10 yds so that the short line prevents them from sinking too far or too quickly. You can then control them throughout the retrieve with all the benefits of the final lift.

The fine diameter of a fast-sinking line results in relatively little air resistance. This means that it will shoot through the air more easily to achieve a greater casting distance than other types of line. Alternatively, the rod does not have to flex as much to propel the line over the same distance. This reduction in the required loading results in an optimum line rating that is typically about one AFTMA value higher than that quoted for the rod.

Sink-tip Lines

Sink-tips come into their own when you have to get the flies down quickly before moving them back slowly at a constant depth. This makes them ideal for nymph fishing when the fish are holding at a fixed distance below the surface. An intermediate would get the flies down to the fish more slowly before moving below them. Thus, a sink-tip has the advantage of increasing the productive fishing time.

Some of these lines with long, fast-sinking tip sections are very difficult to cast. One with a slow or medium sink-tip, such as the Air-Cel Wet Tip, will perform much better.

There is, of course, the obvious downside that the fish have to be holding at the appropriate depth dictated by the length of the sink-tip, otherwise you will miss them completely. It is therefore worth having a couple of different lengths of sink tip, and we have found that 5 and 10 ft are appropriate for most conditions. The cheapest way to do this is to attach sinking leaders, such as 'poly-tips', to the end of a floating line. You can also cover a range of depths by placing a heavy fly on the point.

One perfect application is when drifting towards boat-shy fish that are holding close to the bank. A fast-sinking line will move the flies quickly downwards, but then snag on the bottom with a slow retrieve. An intermediate line will not get the flies down far enough until the boat is on top of the fish – or, more pertinently, where they had been!

BOAT FISHING

Many tactics are fairly general to both boat and bank. When at anchor, there is really no difference, except that the boat fisherman can cover otherwise inaccessible fish in possibly deeper water with the freedom to cast in any direction. The essential departure from bank techniques is the ability to drift with the currents, which means that it is not just the flies, but also the angler, that is moving.

On one visit to Montana, we booked a day on a private lake. The local shop hired out float tubes, but there was considerable difficulty in fitting them or attaching them to the car.

'There's a small boat', we were advised (as a passing comment), 'but it'll be no use to you since it's not got an anchor.'

'We'll manage, somehow', came the immediate and gleeful reply. 'Forget the tubes.'

On the first drift, we took nine rainbows! At the time we commented on how the locals were missing out on a trick. Soon afterwards, though, we began to experiment with float tubes and began to realize what we (and the majority of British anglers) had been missing. This experience illustrated different practices on both sides of the Atlantic, but there was still one important ingredient for success on lakes anywhere in the world. Whether in a boat or tube, there are usually advantages in covering new water. There are exceptions when a fixed position is essential, such as when all the fish are moving along the same narrow channel, but without such information drifting should normally be the first choice.

When boat fishing, you should always remain seated for casting and retrieving. This is much safer since it is quite easy to overturn a small boat while standing. You also present a lower profile to the fish, which will be face to face with you on a downwind drift. It is also more ergonomically beneficial. In plain English, this means that you can relax with a gentle casting action, a confident retrieve and a glass of wine within easy reach.

Chris Klee plays a fighting rainbow on Chew Valley Lake.

The Downwind Drift

It is better to show the same fly once to completely different fish than to cover the same one repeatedly. A trout soon grows disinterested when it has seen the same fly time after time, and may become suspicious even if the patterns are changed. You therefore gain a big advantage by moving systematically from one spot to another. In a drifting boat, you do this continuously and automatically without any inconvenience.

The most widely used – and arguably the most productive – way to fish is to allow the boat to drift in its natural orientation which is broadside to the surface current. Two people can happily fish at the same time, casting in front of the boat with the wind behind them. You can, of course, cast in any other direction to cover a rising trout, but restricting routine casting to the front minimizes the chance of catching each other's lines. You can control the motion of the flies without any hindrance from the currents.

The broadside drift is ideal for a static dry fly, since you can cast straight downwind and retrieve at just the right speed to take up slack created by the movement of the boat. There are no significant cross currents on the line or leader, and hence no unnatural drag on the fly. In contrast, the surface drag will soon start to move a team of flies that is cast to the side of the boat. So, unless covering a specific fish, it is best to cast repeatedly downwind.

If you do need to cover a fish to the side of the boat, it is worth noting that the point fly is much less constrained than the droppers, since it is further from the line and attached at only one end. This results in a precious few seconds after casting during which it will not be dragged unnaturally across the surface. Thus, it is the point fly that needs to be cast into the path of a moving fish, which implies casting slightly shorter than would normally be the case. Even more important is the requirement to give plenty of 'forward lead', because trout move upwind deceptively quickly.

The flotilla sets out on Loch Leven.

Llandegfedd Reservoir yields a specimen rainbow for a delighted MC.

In rough conditions, it is still possible to keep dry flies afloat by casting them just a few yards. The water immediately in front of the boat should be considerably calmer, and there is very little line exposed to the waves to drag the flies under the surface. With this technique, there is no need to make the flies especially big and bushy. A size 14 Shipman's Buzzer, for example, will often stay afloat for long enough. The slack water in front of the

boat also attracts trout as a potential source of food, in a similar manner to calm lanes. It is rare for fish to be boat-shy in rough weather, and the small separation between fish and angler should not be a major concern. Nevertheless, they do seem to take the flies with some urgency, and you need to hold the rod at an angle that will provide plenty of cushioning against the strike.

Casting directly downwind is also a deadly technique for nymphs. This gives perfect control over the retrieve so that you can move the flies as slowly as necessary to imitate the natural insects. Nevertheless, a steady sideways drag is not such an unnatural phenomenon as it is for most dry flies. This may induce a take, and a fly moving across the ripple will intersect the paths of a greater number of trout on their upwind feeding sprees. It is certainly worth exploiting all directions.

Denzil would invariably choose the stern of a two-man boat, which gave him control of the engine. Common to most fly fishermen in the English reservoirs, he would position the boat broadside to the surface currents so that both occupants could fish directly downwind at the same time. Soon after cutting the motor, he would cast his flies as far as possible down the line of the intended drift. This resulted in a long continuous retrieve that pulled the flies round in an enticing arc. It was worth an extra couple of trout on most days.

Mid-afternoon on Lake Vyrnwy.

It takes experience to retrieve nymphs in a natural manner while compensating for the motion of a drifting boat. Getting them to move at the same speed as you would from the bank may require a great deal of concentration, especially in rough conditions. Many beginners find it almost impossible to move the flies slowly while ripping the line back, but that is exactly the hurdle they have to overcome to be successful. Ironically, many good drift fishermen, who have become used to the faster retrieve, seem to be incapable of fishing a nymph sufficiently slowly from the bank.

A drogue helps greatly in slowing down a fast-moving boat, and gives you a much better feel of the line and flies. It also lets you spend a greater time over the productive areas and creates more time for the flies to sink. The position of attachment helps to set the orientation of the boat against the waves and will also adjust the direction of drift slightly, since most boats move stern first across the wind. However, there are drawbacks. It is difficult to manoeuvre the boat quickly to intercept a moving fish, and there is the risk of losing a hooked trout if the leader tangles in the rigging. It is often not worth using a drogue with a floating line in anything less than a force four, unless you are fishing nymphs, such as Superglue Buzzers, that need to reach a considerable depth.

Drogue setting angle of drift.

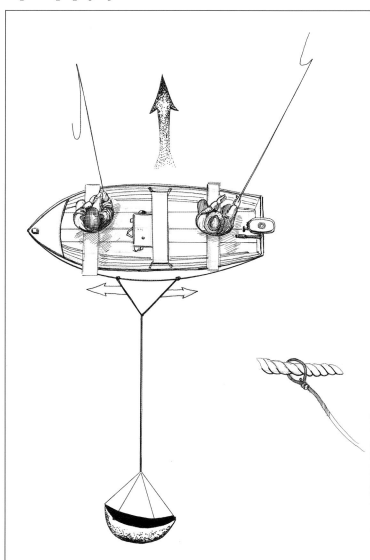

Sinking Lines from a Boat

A drogue is invaluable for controlling sinking lines even in a fairly light breeze. This is to allow the line time to sink to the trout's feeding depth before the drift of the boat has caught up with the flies. To work most effectively, a drogue needs to sink a few feet below the surface into a relatively static layer of water. Added weight on a short length of rope, however, is inefficient because the drogue will pull downwards as well as backwards. Serious boat fishermen therefore use a long rope to reduce the angle.

The lift-off with a sinking line is vital, because many trout will follow the flies to surface, only to swirl away at the last second as they leave the water. You therefore need to hold them at the end of the retrieve for several seconds – and even up to half a minute for spooky fish. Some anglers hold the top dropper close to the surface as a strike indicator. It may help to move the rod tip up and down a few times in an effort to entice them. Your concentration will improve if you always assume that there is a fish following the flies, and sometimes this is not too far from the truth.

On one very difficult and windy day, Alex had been trying a Hi-D line for some time without any success. He put the rod down to change to a reel holding a slower-sinking line with the leader still dangling in the water. (Providing you intend to keep the same leader and flies, it is quite straightforward to complete the whole operation in about a minute.) After swapping reels, he threaded the new line up through the rings to the point at which the leader was attached to the old fly line. Just when he was about to cut the knot before connecting the leader to the new line, the rod bent sharply downwards as a 4 lb rainbow took a nymph on the top dropper.

It was a strange sensation to be playing a fish attached to a reel that was sitting on the bottom of the boat, with another unconnected reel fixed to the rod. Unfortunately, the top dropper had stuck in the tip ring while changing lines, and the battle soon ended with a 'ping' and a thunderclap of bad language. This fish had probably followed the flies up and then watched them for a good minute as they dangled in the water. It was an illustration of how it can pay to hold the flies for some considerable time at the end of the cast, even though on this occasion he had done it accidentally.

Ideal conditions for setting out on Blagdon.

It is often worth casting sideways across the ripple, especially with lures. As the boat drifts forwards, a bend will progressively build up in the line. When the flies accelerate in going round this bend, a suspicious trout may suddenly lose all inhibitions and commit itself. It is more convenient with this tactic to attach the drogue to the stern in the Northampton style rather than to the middle of the boat. This causes the boat to drift bow first and gives increased freedom for two fishermen to cast their lines without impeding each other.

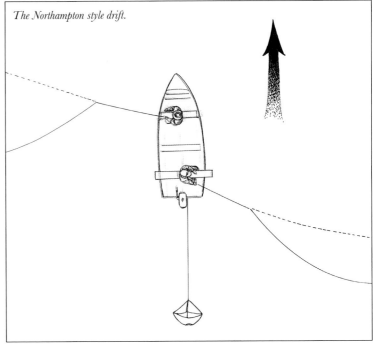

The Northampton style drift.

Shooting heads can be a liability in a boat, especially on windy days when the backing gets blown here, there and everywhere. Nevertheless, they do allow casts to be made over a much greater distance, and this gives the flies time to sink deeper. Moreover, the backing sinks much more slowly than the running line of a weight forward, so that there is a different trajectory from angler to fly. Some anglers, who use shooting heads, claim that the absence of a giant U-bend in the line is better for hitting takes.

Dog Summer Days on a Boat (Dry Flies)

Still waters are sometimes a daunting prospect on boiling hot days in high summer. The sun shines mercilessly, with not a sign of life on the flat or lightly rippled surface. Sometimes there may be enough insect life on the

surface for the occasional trout to pop its head up before returning to the deeps. On such occasions it is worth waiting patiently with a single dry fly, since droppers only increase the chances of an unnatural appearance in calm water. The last thing you want on such a difficult day, after a long patient wait, is a rejection of the fly at the last moment. Although waiting for an hour between rises may seem like an eternity, you need to remind yourself that a fish every hour is equivalent to a total of eight under the harsh daytime conditions. That is not bad by any reckoning.

Unfortunately, it is on such days that trout will often rise at extreme range deliberately to keep clear of the boat. Sometimes they will move round it in a wide arc. When this occurs, it is worth casting as far as possible and slightly to the side of the boat in anticipation. If the fish are slow to respond, the surface currents, which are all-pervasive even in a flat calm, will eventually produce some drag. This is likely to render the dry fly useless, so the best tactic may then be to choose a sacrificial buoyant pattern with a lightweight nymph about a foot behind it on the point.

Another solution to the problem is to move the boat towards a rising fish. This starts with a pull on the oars or a push from the motor, followed by a silent drift of the boat bow first. You should cast to the trout as soon as you are in range. This requires co-operation and some careful boat handling, but those who persevere often get their just reward.

Dog Summer Days on a Boat (Nymphs)

A lack of surface activity does not necessarily mean that trout will be right on the bottom of the lake. If they go too deep, oxygen levels will be seriously depleted. The actual position is a compromise between escaping from the warmer, brighter regions whilst being able to breathe comfortably. The depth will depend very much on the water clarity, its temperature and the amount of oxygenation.

In clear water, they may lie at a depth from (say) 15–30 ft, where it is sufficiently cool and oxygenated with the right light levels. Because of the competing effects of different requirements, the extent of the fish holding layer may be very narrow indeed. The water may stratify into a warm and cool layer, and large concentrations of fish will often hold station in the cool water just below this transition. Sometimes very thick surface algae extend downwards for a considerable distance, and divers have often recorded fish holding in deep positions at the exact junction between the coloured and algae-free water. As currents affect the depth of algae and the stratification, trout will move up and down accordingly.

Catching trout lying in a two foot band, say, at depths that may vary through the day from 15–30 ft, presents a challenge to any angler. Those who appreciate the trout's behaviour and have the ability to capitalize on it may do very well indeed. It is the time to use a fast-sinking line with total commitment and concentration. Confidence is a key factor, because you really have to believe that a trout at 30 ft will see a size 14 nymph in order to work the flies with the right speed and trajectory. You do not have to use a large fly or lure to attract attention, and unless small fish are on the menu, the educated trout are more likely to take a nymph.

Since nymphs do not move quickly in the water, the retrieve needs to be as slow as possible. This is difficult with a high density line since it pulls the flies down at a fair old speed. Nevertheless, you can make the most of a bad job by taking care in the positioning of the nymphs and in the retrieve. We would normally fish only a couple of flies. Two of our favourites are a Hare's Ear nymph on the dropper about 5 ft away from the end of the fly line, and a Diawl Bach about 10 ft further away on the point.

Ideally, the boat needs to be almost stationary. The technique is most easily applied while at anchor, but if the surface is virtually still there is an obvious advantage in drifting over new water very slowly to locate the fish. You should cast as far as you possibly can and allow the flies to sink for about a minute – but the optimum delay may be anything from 20–100 seconds. You may have to experiment, and it is preferable to use a watch since it will prevent you from speeding up the count through too much eagerness! Only then should you start the slowest possible figure-of-eight retrieve. It is impossible to emphasize how slow this should be – normally no more than a couple of inches per second. This requires a lot of patience, and many fishermen would fail if the speeds of their retrieves were measured.

Savage takes on the descent seem to come mostly to the point fly – perhaps because it hinges more freely away from the sinking fly line. Although the movement of the line is detrimental in moving a nymph, it does provide the necessary resistance to set the hook as a trout takes the fly. At the same time as the pull, you may see a splash as the fish motors upwards through the surface. This is exciting stuff, and the first time it happens it will bring a burst of confidence for the rest of the day.

Part way through the retrieve, the flies change their trajectory from a descent to an ascent. This often results in an induced take if it occurs in the layer of water holding the fish. If you can determine the correct countdown to achieve the right depth consistently, the results will be fantastic. Takes also come on the lift – often to the dropper fly, which moves in a more constrained ascent, being close to the fly line. This results in a sharp downwards pull, since the dropper fly is on a short leader and by now should be almost directly beneath the rod tip. A gentle upwards lift will suffice to set the hook.

The two flies have separate functions for different parts of the retrieve, and there is no need for a middle dropper. A third fly would reduce the distance between the two nymphs, thereby increasing the risk of the co-ordinated motions being noticed. This would not help the overall objective of trying to make the nymphs appear as natural as possible. Contrary to some opinion, deep water trout can be very difficult to deceive – especially the better ones.

Since trout will take on the descent and on the lift, the nymphs will cross the fish holding layer twice during each retrieve. It is therefore not essential to locate this depth, providing the initial drop of the line is sufficiently long, and the retrieve sufficiently slow, for the depth to be reached. If in doubt, you should err on the side of counting for too long. You may waste some time in fishing too deeply at first, but you will be able to correct this once you have established when the takes occur.

If the water is coloured, trout may be holding station at lesser depths. This means that you will not need to count the line down for so long, so that you should have a better chance of reaching the fish when drifting under slightly more breezy conditions. Nymphs with increased visibility will usually be more productive in the murky water. Thus, in place of a size 14 Hare's Ear or Diawl Bach for clear water, a size 10 Montana Nymph or a Pheasant Tail with a fluorescent green thorax might be the first choice. A Silver Invicta or Dunkeld can sometimes do the trick very nicely by reflecting the sun's rays – even at a modest depth – and provide an irresistible trigger point.

Dog Summer Days on a Boat (The Boils)

The aerators, which are present in many water supply reservoirs, are often the most productive places to fish in high summer. They transport cooler, oxygenated water to the surface and consequently tend to hold large numbers of fish. Unfortunately, there is no secret about 'the boils', and it is often necessary to jockey constantly for position against all the other hopefuls. Nevertheless, there is often excellent fishing about 30 yds downwind of an aerator. This is because the insects that are swept to the surface gradually drift with the current in this direction, and trout will accumulate to capitalize on the steady food supply. More importantly, they are feeding trout that will readily take a properly presented nymph or dry fly.

Echo Sounders

Those who stalk individual fish in rivers can instantly recognize a trout that is disinclined to feed by its motionless posture in the water. It is sometimes possible to spot such fish in the margins of lakes. In a crystal clear lake in Canada, we were able to observe a shoal of trout, 15 ft down, that would not turn to inspect any offering. Even tame goldfish in a garden pond will sometimes refuse to move to food thrown onto the water.

This behaviour partially explains why many fishermen's catch rates often fall substantially when first buying an echo sounder. They find a large shoal and waste hours trying different flies and tactics to no avail. Of course, there is the other possibility that they are actually targeting a shoal of coarse fish that would be unlikely to take an artificial fly – even under the most favourable conditions.

There is also the ethical question of whether echo sounders should be allowed in conjunction with fly fishing. Perhaps the best – and most defensible – approach is to use an echo sounder purely as a depth gauge to find the right contours and channels.

FLOAT TUBES

Charles Jardine is a very accomplished float tuber and a great enthusiast for passing on his knowledge and experience. It therefore came as no surprise when he offered to write this section, and we were delighted to take him up on his offer. We have simply added a few of our own initial experiences in New Zealand at the end, which reinforce some of Charles's ideas.

Overview of Tubing

For the better part of a hundred years, fisher folk have been paddling about in inner tubes. This seemingly daft behaviour began in the United States in the nineteenth century and quickly became adopted by the more eccentric 'punt gunners' for wild-fowling.

Float tubing – or the more descriptive 'belly boating' – seemed to lie dormant up to the 1960s and 70s when, again in the USA, it experienced another bout of popularity and has grown steadily since. It has now spread throughout the world, proving to be a convenient and eminently transportable way of reaching and fishing distant waters where a boat is considered impractical. Suddenly, the far, wilder shores are not so far after all.

In essence, the tube has changed very little since earlier times. An inflated lorry or truck inner tube is all it is. But nowadays the whole thing is dressed up with an outer shell – generally in tough Cordura – to incorporate pockets, back rests and a host of other angler-grabbing enticements. Indeed, some take on the appearance of a floating tackle shop, but there is a lot to be said for comfort and contentment when surrounded by water.

Increasingly, different designs and concepts are paddling into the world of the conventional tube. 'U' boats, which have horseshoe-like hulls, make getting in and out far easier. The surface-scything and faster 'V' boats offer the same ease, but with the ability to travel quickly at the mere flip of a fin due to the improved hull design.

To many anglers, the idea of float tubing is met with the same enthusiasm as say, bungee jumping with a perished rubber rope. 'Not for me', they mutter, 'but you go right ahead', with the sort of look that conjures images of strangely fastening jackets, white coats and padded cells. This lasts until they actually – in a moment of weakness – have a go in one. There are few anglers that do not, after only a few paddles, slip into a piscatorial second childhood of unbridled joy, but this makes it even more important to put safety first.

Dean Hayes enjoys the pleasures of float tubing.

Safety in the Tube

With any design, safety is the highest priority. It is remarkable just how small and insignificant you become in relation to the water, and you feel positively dwarfed by anything over fifty acres. However, float tubing is as safe as anything else involving water and fishing rods, providing due care is taken to watch the following points.

- Make certain that you always wear a CE-approved life preserver that operates both manually and automatically.
- Carry a whistle for emergencies, since it can be heard over a far greater distance than a shout.
- Ensure that your tube is inflated properly at all times. Inflate it until the wrinkles in the skin vanish, but do not overdo it. Remember, your tube can alter pressure dramatically with variations in water and air temperature, so check before entering the water. It is not a bad idea to leave the tube in the water for a while and then check the pressure and adjust accordingly.
- If you are new to tubing, do it in short bursts – three quarters of an hour at first, then progressively for longer periods.
- Do not be tempted to fish much more than 200 yds from the shore, no matter how many fish might be 'calling' to you with seductive rising sounds! Most of the fish are close in anyway. Always think about safety, and if you are 'iffy' about anything, return to the shore.
- When launching, choose a gently shelving bank that is free of mud and too much weed. Both can tip you over in a trice. A steep bank incline can be a real hazard.
- Wear neoprene waders. They will insulate you and are more buoyant and durable than other types. They must also be chest waders, otherwise you will inevitably become a mite moist!
- Some form of foot protection is desirable – boot foot waders, neoprene dive boots and 'flat' boots are a real boon.
- Whatever you do, secure the fins to your ankle by a piece of cord or purpose-designed retainers.
- Wherever possible try to launch into the wind, so if there are any problems you can just let the wind and wave action bring you ashore. I once lost just a single fin (because I had not tied it to my ankle), and spent the next twenty minutes or so going round and round in confused circles like a demented beetle. Thankfully there was a good wave, or else I might still be going round in circles in that northern Montana lake!
- If a good blow gets up while you are in the water, head for shore.
- Try not to turn quickly or make sudden backwards movements. Although it is hard to capsize a float tube due to its enormous keel (you!), it really isn't worth the risk.
- If you start to feel cold and/or tired, then get out. Cramp, no matter how fit you are, can set in at any time. Do not fool with this one.
- It is probably not a good idea to go tubing if you have a chronic heart condition. (Sorry.)
- Tubing and alcohol do not mix.
- Do not drink too much coffee or tea prior to going afloat in a tube. Peeing from a tube is a fascinating act of contortion (I am told).
- Finally, never force the issue. Safety first – always.

Tackle for Tubing

Most of the tackle that is useful from a tube parallels that used in a boat and is discussed elsewhere in the book, but there are some peculiarities. Firstly, metal nets do not float. The best designs by far are the American pan or tennis racquet styles, which not only float but allow you to land fish without giving yourself a hernia. Just select the size of aperture for the maximum size of trout expected. Make certain anything that sinks or can float away is attached.

I love using longer rods from a tube, and found 9.5 ft or 10 ft perfect for nymphing and dry work. An AFTMA 5 is my preferred choice. If you need to carry a heavier spare for sunk line work, you can get one of those metal hooked expanding, luggage retaining straps and secure it around the tube. Attach this to the left side (if you are right handed) and then jam the rod butt and reel into it, with the tip facing to the back of the tube. You will find that the rod is totally secure and can be angled to a nicety.

You will of course need all your 'bits' with you, and I suggest that you organise a filing system for the pockets that suits your requirements. When wrestling with an aggressive trout hell-bent on revenge, a rod with a will of its own, copious amounts of line and leader and two left finned feet, is not the time to start wondering where you put your priest or forceps. Get it sorted!

Speaking of which, when it rains in a tube you are going to get wet! I agree a good half of you is already immersed, but the other, upper half will need protection. A short, deep wading style rain jacket kept in the float tube's rear pouch is a sensible insurance policy. There is little need to wear a waistcoat, but if you are going to use one, make certain it is the very short style, otherwise you will experience that nasty, rising damp sensation! Another tip is to put your fly patterns into separate, floating and water-tight boxes. Do not put all your flies into one box.

Tactics for the Tube

Once you are there, togged up to the nines and safely ensconced in your floating vehicle, the possibilities are endless. There are few fly fishing styles that cannot be practised from a tube that you usually do from a boat: loch style wets, booby fishing, the 'hang', dry fly, nymphing – just about everything. Of course you will have to amend some of the techniques to suit, but whatever still-water technique you see in this learned tome can, with a tweak here and there, be applied to the tube.

However, one or two tactics spring out as being tailor made for float tubes. Most of these revolve around midge (or chironomid) fishing. Because the angler has a tendency to fin upwind or across, it makes the deadly tactic of fishing a floating line in a curve across the wind as easy as a couple of kicks with the fins. Then all that delicious, curved, tensioned line can be left either to move seductively round by wind action under its own volition or inched back by a slow figure-of-eight retrieve. Trout have a lovely habit of simply hanging themselves with this technique.

At this juncture, some of you may be wondering how on earth you should cast if you are sitting down in a tube so close to the water. In fact, it is simply with the upper body from the waist up. By doing this, the acute swaying, rocking style that is usually associated with neophytes in tubes can be avoided. Thus nullified, a stable casting platform is created. It takes a while, but practice really does make perfect.

The things to always remember when you are in your tube are: (a) you are much lower to the water than usual and therefore much harder to see, (b) you are making probably far less noise and commotion and (c) to a trout you are reminiscent of a damn great frog. Basically you are not the threat that you once were, so trout come closer. You do not have to cast as far. It's a wonderful world!

Thus, when nymph fishing, and especially when dry fly and emerger fishing, you really can have the fish almost under the rod tip – if you are careful. In fact, on one occasion when fishing a particularly intense evening rise with a Claret Hopper, I could gently fin my way to the risers, wait and then ambush them. One rainbow took so close to my tube that I actually saw the vermilion-splashed gill cover flare as it sipped in the fly. It was an astonishing experience.

There is another lovely trait regarding float tubing, and that is creeping up on them. You can literally stalk rising fish in a float tube. You have to do it backwards, of course, but you do get used to these little eccentricities after a while.

Of course, the techniques do not stop there. A float tube allows you to explore tree-lined banks, ledges and drop-offs that would simply be impossible from the bank, and distinctly difficult from a boat. But apart from the somewhat obvious instances of nymph fishing and dry fly, I have found other particularly rich seams when tubing. These include places such as dam walls or deep drop-offs, and whilst they are not traditionally floating line areas, they do suit the tube incredibly well. Tactics include a team of nymphs marched up the layers on a sunk line with a figure-of-eight retrieve, and the same method with mini lures, or (a real favourite of mine) with a Minkie or Boobie. Down the years I have tried a great many types of lines for this type of fishing, and frankly those that I have found most useful are various shooting head systems with a loop to loop join to the running line. This will effect a quick change from one line density to another in your cramped, in-tube surroundings. I also like to use various sink tips, since the floating section is very mcuh more manageable in the close confines of a tube.

You might be wondering why I keep mentioning the figure-of-eight. The reason is simply that it is so damn difficult to do anything else. Yes, you can make little downward, stripping movements, but you just try and do a thumping great one – and

at speed – and see how far you get. (Actually, you get as far as the arm rests, which is approximately eight inches away, or as far as the stripping apron which is even nearer.) An excellent remedy to this restrictive state of affairs was devised by a friend of mine, Daniel Regan. As with many good ideas, it is so simple as to make you green with envy. You simply strip upwards – not down. It is tricky to get used to at first, but with a modicum of practice it becomes utterly silken and easy to manipulate. Once mastered, you can adopt almost any speed or configuration you choose.

Experiences in New Zealand

For several years, in line with many European fly fishermen, we never really considered using these strange contraptions. Why should we, when small boats were available on most of the large lakes in the British Isles? They offered better safety, more comfort and greater speed for moving from one place to another. Even on our first trip to Montana, we managed to avoid using one at the last minute when we found that a small dinghy was available. In fact, we suffered from all the prejudices that Charles has just described.

Preparing for the assault on Lake Otamangakau.

Inevitably, it was an American (Tim Tollett) who persuaded us to have a go in the North Island of New Zealand. Most of the locals used their own boats, and we would dearly have liked to copy them. But Tim played a mean trick in getting hold of four float tubes – and it was that or nothing. On the first day, there was a strong wind and we were doubtful about going out at all – even at the sheltered end of the lake. Apprehensively, we edged carefully out into the water, and gradually the truth began to dawn about how easy it was to manoeuvre one of these strange craft. Moreover, within the first couple of hours, we had all caught rainbows in the 6 lb class.

We had always recognized that float tubes had an obvious advantage of cost and transportability over a small boat, but we soon learned that there were real fishing advantages too. First, you maintain a lower profile, which enables you to creep up on fish more easily. Second, you have greater manoeuvrability. You can turn quickly in any direction and gently move backwards to keep in direct contact with the line. You can move the line round in a curve and position yourself when playing a fish to keep it away from weed. Third, you can drift over fish much more slowly than in a boat with greater control, or remain stationary – even in a strong wind. In fact, you may often find yourself drifting against the wind rather than with it, since your fins are well below the surface currents.

In New Zealand we had access to a variety of different tubes, and certain advantages quickly became apparent. In order to avoid drifting too quickly in a strong wind, you need to choose a tube where you are effectively standing in the water so that your fins achieve the maximum possible depth. Special V-shaped designs were better for travelling across a lake, although the simple round ones were adequate. Finally, we could not get access to four good sets of fins – which is a polite way of saying that Tim had forgotten to pack them all before leaving the States. We had to take it in turns for one of us to use the only type we could obtain locally, which needed all sorts of improvised Heath-Robinson attachments to hold them in position. Good fins, where your feet fit securely inside, are essential. Force fins, with the V-shaped wedge in the ends, are best.

We shared with Tim a love of drinking just the 'occasional' beer, so he was quick to warn us that float tubing and drinking do not mix – unless you are prepared to make frequent trips to the bank. You should, of course, drink just enough fluids to avoid feeling thirsty. When sitting so low in the water, we soon experienced what Charles referred to as the rising damp sensation, even with a reasonably short waistcoat. There is really no problem in dispensing with a waistcoat altogether, and putting your fly boxes and spools inside the zipped pockets in the tube. A double-pocketed shirt is also a good idea.

One golden rule that we quickly discovered was to resist the temptation to try to move too quickly. You should stay completely relaxed with gentle movements of the fin, allowing the knees to bend. A good technique helps, but as long as you avoid trying too hard, you will have no problems – remembering that you have to move backwards. When retrieving, try to avoid any leg movements that might disturb the fish, unless you are consciously using a very gentle motion to achieve the right angle or to control the movement of the line or flies.

For the remainder of our stay in New Zealand, we had some tremendous float tubing experiences. On Lake Otamangakau, a position over one of the channels near the many weed-beds brought consistent success. We perfected the technique of looking for a boat with an echo sounder, and then paddling next to it where we could fish with a lower profile. MC used this trick on one occasion to take three large rainbows in 30 minutes. This was enough to send the frustrated and unsuccessful fisherman to motor in his expensive pride and joy to the other side of the lake. There, he recounted to JD, who was enjoying the luxury of another boat with one of the locals, about 'the old b*gg*r in the float tube' who was catching all the fish.

The next day, the old b*gg*r in the float tube hooked an enormous trout, which we estimated to be in the 15 lb class when it briefly surfaced. We all remained in the area, watching as the fight continued with the rod bent double. Spectators lined up on the bank. During this period Andrew Donaldson, wearing those 'dreaded red force-fins that seemed to attract the fish', pulled out four specimens in the 4 to 7 lb range. Then, after a timed battle of 2 hours and 20 minutes, the fish snagged in some deep weed and escaped. We still talk about the size of the fish, the duration of the struggle and the fact that the old b*gg*r in the float tube uttered not a single swear word after losing this prize specimen!

ENTICING INTRUDERS

We were once invited, along with John Horsey, to take part in a prestigious fly fishing video. The producers were fortunate in picking one of those days when the trout were feasting on tiny surface insects for prolonged periods. We commented into the microphone that it was difficult to catch them because they were cruising so high in the water with a tiny field of vision. Accurate casting was insufficient, since they were zigzagging continuously and unpredictably.

We argued the case for some highly visible concoctions to distract them, so on went the bright Peach Dolls and the hideously bright orange Vindaloos. Fish after fish bow-waved in hot pursuit, and rods bent simultaneously. But when the video was released, the editors had removed all mention of the successful patterns. There were no close-ups of fish being netted, which would have clearly shown what was happening. The producers had not dared to confront people's prejudices, in spite of the good scientific reasons why imitative flies would just not have worked.

It is true that these attractor patterns (or lures) do not usually represent any recognisable life-form. They are intruders into the trout's world, and may entice a response purely out of curiosity or aggression. Of course, white patterns may resemble small fish, black patterns may suggest leeches, and so on. If such items are on the current menu, there is the double advantage of enticement and imitation of the natural food supply. It therefore pays to bear all three motivations in mind. Apart from filling the tactical gap on those days when natural imitation fails to produce results, lure fishing adds a bit of spice and draws out a few interesting aspects of trout behaviour.

Lures do not have to be large. In fact, we have acquired most of our expertise around 'mini-lures' where the maximum length is just under an inch to meet 'International Rules'. There are good reasons for this. The same light tackle used for conventional fly fishing will easily accommodate such patterns. Moreover, a combination of an attractor pattern and nymphs on the same leader sometimes provides a comprehensive and balanced team. Even if the mini-lure fails to tempt a trout into commitment, it may attract it to the adjacent imitative flies.

All fly lines, from a floater to the fastest sinker available, are appropriate for lures of any size under the right conditions. Distraction of surface feeders obviously points to a floater, whereas a slow-sinker is often the better choice for fry or daphnia feeders. The early part of the season and very bright days in summer, when the fish tend to lie deep, usually favour fast-sinkers. Since lures tend to be rather alien phenomena, trout will often be uncertain about committing themselves and will follow for some distance. This will be obvious for surface feeders, but with a sinking line it is especially important not to lift off suddenly at the end of a retrieve. You should lift the rod gradually to an almost vertical position without pulling the top dropper out of the water, and let the flies hang for several seconds beneath the surface. It is surprising how often an invisible force suddenly pulls downwards on the rod.

Unrealistic they may be, but static lures will often produce fantastic results – providing there is plenty of movement in the wing or tail. We tie many of our patterns with wings of marabou herl or zonker rabbit fur. This is deliberate since these materials give plenty of mobility, which is most evident when the fly is virtually static. If you pull such a pattern quickly through the water, the effect is much reduced. In contrast, you will often have to pull lures without this in-built mobility much faster for any degree of success. One deadly tactic with any type of lure is to draw the line back slowly for the first half of the retrieve, and then to increase the speed or apply FTA to force it into commitment.

Basic Lure Patterns

It is always a good idea to incorporate a seductive, built-in movement into a fly to make it look alive. A simple way to achieve this is to use highly mobile materials such as marabou in the wing or tail.

The other key feature is the colour. Since lures can be rather brash in appearance, trout will often react to their first overall impression rather than examining the pattern for minutiae. Nevertheless, a credible profile is definitely an advantage, and the body should not be too bulky. Chenille is popular since it is easy to tie and comes in a good range of colours – but it has no special properties that make it an essential ingredient. You should certainly think twice about using it if there is no further mobility in the pattern from materials such as marabou. Fritz is excellent for bodies of mini-lures, since it incorporates both movement and visual contrast from its pearly fibres.

It is possible to rationalize lures (as opposed to imitative streamers) into a small selection of basic patterns. Each pattern comprises a simple body tied out of a single material, a marabou wing and perhaps a tail to add a bit of contrast. The main difference between the basic patterns is the predominant colour, which is usually black, orange, pink, white or green. These flies only take about a minute to tie and work well in spite of their simplicity. This approach saves a great deal of confusion, because a large number of variations make the task of selection unnecessarily difficult.

There are, of course, several variations that may improve these basic patterns – sometimes quite dramatically. However, it is usually more productive to think first in terms of the basic requirements, so that you can draw some simple conclusions as to when some colours will work better than others. Although it is impossible to be right all the time, this form of logical approach to selection pays handsome dividends more often than not.

We do not want to give the impression that other colours are necessarily inferior – it is simply that we have found a set of attractor patterns that will cover most circumstances. There is actually a strong case for carrying a few standby patterns in other colours – red, yellow, gold, blue or whatever takes your fancy. Such variations may come into their own when you are forced to fish for a long time in the same spot. Trout soon become used to the same unnatural fly passing in front of them time after time, and a sudden switch to another colour, size or profile will sometimes work wonders.

Black Lures

Black has always been a good choice for tempting trout over a wide range of waters and conditions and, in the absence of any other information, offers a very sensible first line of attack. There are many possible explanations. It stands out well as a sharp silhouette, irrespective of water colour or depth. Many food items are dark, and it is therefore a colour that is unlikely to raise too many alarm signals. Some creatures, such as leeches, tadpoles and many terrestrial insects, are jet black. So it is not surprising that a fly comprising no more than a black chenille body and a black marabou wing puts in a very consistent performance.

Jungle Cock Viva.

Nevertheless, there are several tricks that will improve the basic pattern. A silver rib provides extra contrast, and a fluorescent green tag transforms the pattern into a real killer. The resulting Viva is one of the best all-rounders for browns and rainbows, to which jungle cock cheeks provide an extra trigger point. We have had tremendous responses on some occasions when incorporating a small, fluorescent orange head. (The trick seems to be to use Glo-Brite Number 8, which although rather dull in the fly box, becomes transformed in the water.) For some reason, trout seem to go for the Viva out of pure aggression, and it is sometimes worth ripping the fly back through the water to try to bring out this instinct. We remember one occasion on the hallowed River Itchen when a bailiff demonstrated this to a visiting party who were becoming a little too puritanical for his liking. He first removed the point and barb from the hook. This might have been enough to stop some of the famous old names turning in their graves – though we doubt it! He then covered a wily brown trout that had failed even to turn to any of the previous potential offerings in the gin clear water. The effect was dramatic. Not only this trout, but another specimen in the same pool, swam at full speed in hot pursuit.

Concrete Bowl.

Although the Viva is a magnificent pattern, it is possible and sometimes desirable to make a few improvements. This is true in heavily fished waters where every man and his dog may have been using it, and a little extra enticement may make all the difference. Keeping to the same philosophy of black and green, the Concrete Bowl provides pulsation between the two colours. The body is a very fine Phosphor Yellow chenille, which is wound around the hook with a slight spacing between the turns. A soft black hen hackle is then tied in as a palmer in the same direction as the chenille inside the grooves. Thus, the palmer blends naturally into the fly and obscures a good proportion of the bright chenille. It also allows intermittent flashes of fluorescent green as the soft, mobile hackles move back and forth to cover and expose the body. Black marabou or soft zonker rabbit fur for the wing and tail provides additional movement and balance to the fly's appearance.

There is one final black lure that is worthy of mention, which goes by the enticing name of the Christmas Tree – for obvious reasons. It is essentially a Viva with the added trigger point of a fluorescent red throat. We tend to prefer a slight variation to the original pattern by incorporating a Phosphor Yellow tail, a flat gold tinsel rib and a fire-orange collar with no hackle. It works well as a compromise pattern that has many of the characteristics of both black and orange lures. Most importantly,

these bright materials should exist in modest amounts so that the overall impression is not overdone to achieve the right balance between visibility and 'takeability'. The pattern often out-performs the basic combination of black and green for cruising rainbows.

Orange Lures

Although browns will often succumb to the temptation, hot orange lures tend to work better for rainbows. Such patterns owe their effectiveness to high visibility rather than resemblance to any food item. They are, therefore, a good choice in coloured water or in any situation when a pattern needs to advertise its presence. Orange is a highly effective colour for distracting daphnia feeders, or for catching trout off balance that have become preoccupied with any small fly – whether on the surface or 6 ft down.

A trout's response to orange can be so strong that one of the most commonly used flies incorporates no mobility at all. The Peach Doll consists simply of a body and tail tied out of bright peach wool to give a fish like profile. Its brightness varies considerably with the light conditions. It is worth looking in your fly box as the light changes, because sometimes it appears to glow against its background – and this is the best time to use it.

One of the most striking orange lures has to be the Vindaloo. (We can claim the credit for naming this fly but not, regrettably, for inventing it.) It comprises the most fluorescent orange chenille body and marabou wing that you can possibly lay your hands on. It is so bright that any other adornments would be totally superfluous. You might think that no self-respecting trout would come near it, but they will often quite happily grab it at even the slowest of speeds when there is plenty of time for second thoughts. We have even known fish take it dry on the first cast, before the sinking line pulls it under the surface.

Vindaloo.

Humphrey had been able to spend a couple of hours by the lake each morning for the last few days. This was just what he needed before the big competition at the weekend. The tactics were obvious, since the trout were stuffed to the gills with orange-tinted daphnia. Unfortunately, this was well known, since a lot of fishermen had also been doing very well on a wide range of flies – until the Friday, that is.

On this last day the catch rates plummeted, and even the skilful Humphrey had not felt a single pull all morning. The only action had been a trout that had followed a bright orange lure almost to the surface, but there was something strange even about this. It kept at least a couple of feet away from the lure, almost as if it was escorting it away from its territory, while not daring to attack.

Humphrey's brain moved into top gear. The trout should now be getting very wary after all the recent angling pressure. The Vindaloo was so conspicuous that no trout could take another fly without noticing it first. If they had become both transfixed and alarmed by the bright orange, it might explain why nothing else was working. So he swapped the Vindaloo for something more subdued, and the response was immediate. The Viva on the point, which had failed to catch anything all morning, was now responsible for taking three out of the four trout that came to his net in the next hour.

'Humphrey's cracked it,' was the message that swept across the lake. 'But I doubt whether he'll tell us his secret.'

'He'll tell me', retorted Wesley, as he waddled towards Humphrey, confident that his position in the higher echelons of the angling world entitled him to special favours. Humphrey saw him coming, and groaned in anticipation. But quick as a flash, with his back to the pompous on-comer, he put the Vindaloo back on the top dropper.

'Now then, Humphrey. Surely not even you are going to pretend that you have been using a pupa of Limnephilus lunatus. *I suspect that your success comes from a zygoptera nymph.'*

'No. It comes from Vindaloo flashabis', replied Humphrey, using all his willpower to avoid the switch from classical to more appropriate Anglo-Saxon expressions. 'The essential ingredient is the Flashibou in the wing. It seems to be providing the most fantastic trigger point, because they wouldn't take the basic pattern.' He conveniently forgot to add that all his orange lures were tied this way, more for historical reasons than any superiority over the basic Vindaloo vulgata.

Wesley, of course, was only too eager to pass the word around. This enabled him to demonstrate his power of persuasion over Humphrey, which was far more important to him than doing well in the competition (which, in any case, was out of the question). He was also able to indulge himself in one of his pompous monologues on the demise of nymph fishing in the locality. That night, contestants were up at all hours mixing generous quantities of Flashibou into fluorescent orange marabou wings.

The next morning, apparently resigned to the fact that his secret was out, Humphrey very generously handed out the successful pattern to those unfortunate souls who pleaded with him, having only just heard about it.

Everything was going according to plan. The fishing was tough, but by midday Humphrey had taken four trout on his team of three Vivas. Most of his rivals were having problems even getting a touch, but they persevered with the same fly because it was obviously working for its originator. They also concentrated on copying every aspect of his retrieve. This was another mistake because Humphrey loved to add all sorts of variations to confuse the opposition more than the fish.

Then, at one o'clock, everything changed. The trout suddenly switched on to bright orange, thumping the Vindaloos and sending rods bending all over the lake. Even Wesley started to catch.

It took Humphrey an hour to come to terms with what was happening, by which time a few anglers had already overtaken him. He opened his fly box to take out a Vindaloo, but he had given so many away that there was now only one left. In frustration and eagerness, he tied it on to the top dropper without taking his usual care to wet and test the knot. Five minutes later he felt an almighty tug, only to feel the line go slack as a 4 lb rainbow leapt three times out of the water in an attempt to shed the hook. At last Humphrey had received his 'come-uppance' – but his reputation for honesty and generosity had now become a living legend.

Trout exhibit unpredictable behaviour towards bright orange flies. They cannot help noticing a Vindaloo before more ordinary patterns, and initially will focus their attention on it – perhaps to the exclusion of everything else. If they are not really committed to feeding, caution or indifference may win over curiosity, and they will turn away from the whole team. However, once they do embark on a feeding spree, they lose their caution and the Vindaloo becomes a devastating pattern. The message should be clear. If you are catching nothing at all with a bright orange fly somewhere on the leader – remove it. But be prepared to give it another chance later in the day.

Orange is such a good colour that it may be unwise to dismiss it completely, even if you are failing to catch any fish. A lure with a pale peach marabou wing will often provide a good compromise between attraction and subtlety. One of our favourite tactics for wary trout is to use such a mini-lure, with a pearly tinsel wound over a red silk body, on the top dropper. This needs retrieving very slowly in front of a couple of nymphs. If the trout are not actively searching for food, the added stimulus from the pulsating peach marabou sometimes makes a dramatic difference.

Pink Lures

The term 'pink' rather loosely describes lures ranging from a subdued salmon pink right through to fluorescent neon magenta. Normally pink would be our first choice in place of orange for clear rather than coloured water, although this is only a rough rule of thumb. It is wise to follow the same precautions for the brighter shades as for the orange lures.

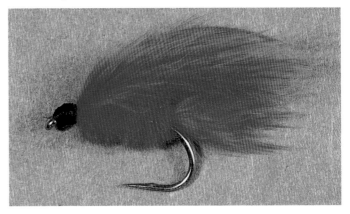

Pink Lure.

The most striking pattern – the pink equivalent of the Vindaloo – has a neon magenta marabou wing and tail and a silver body. We cannot claim that there is any reason for the metallic body in place of chenille or the existence of a tail, but this fly has worked so well for so many fishermen that we have never bothered experimenting. Some anglers use a pearl or even a holographic tinsel body, but we doubt that this makes any real difference alongside the fluorescent marabou wing.

When it comes to subdued patterns for the more sophisticated trout, the fluorescent magenta or pink wing should be toned down by adding some white marabou. There is a direct substitution of white for magenta in the tail. The magenta or pink wing is less bulky, and the deficit is made up by an additional white marabou wing tied in half-way down the body. This mixture gives a perfect compromise, which has a very enticing appearance in the water – so much so that we now very rarely bother with the more basic bright version.

White Lures

For non-imitative attractor patterns, white is an alternative to black as a good all-round colour. If forced to make a distinction, we might try white first in clear, bright conditions, and black in failing light or coloured water. However, the indisputable case for white lures is when trout are likely to feed on small fish. The basic lure incorporating just a white body and white marabou wing appears rather anaemic and unnatural. Thus, better patterns incorporate other colours for contrast, realism or attraction. Bob Church introduced two excellent fry imitators, based on a white marabou wing. The Jack Frost includes red in the tail and hackle, whereas the Appetizer incorporates contrast with an over-wing of squirrel tail.

Appetizer.

Low water towards autumn is ideal for white lures.

Specific imitations vary enormously in size and colour depending on the local population of small fish. To tackle large specimens that have an exclusive diet of 6-in fish you will invariably need a correspondingly large, purpose-designed 'seagull' and some quite beefy tackle to handle it. Dave Barker's Minkie is a superb pattern for such purposes.

Light Bulb.

The Light Bulb is usually our first choice for a general purpose white lure. It comprises no more than a white marabou wing and a Phosphor Yellow chenille body, with an optional (but unnecessary) white marabou tail. The fluorescent body gives it plenty of attraction and makes it a sensible alternative to both the Viva and Vindaloo. Since it stands out from the crowd, it is a good pattern for catching trout that are feasting on shoals of small fish. A major problem under such circumstances is getting your fly noticed, and that is unlikely to happen when the imitation is too good!

It is worth mentioning one very important point about catching fry bashers. They will often crash through the surface as they chase their prey, before returning to mop up the injured victims from the surface. During this last stage, it is sometimes possible to succeed with floating fry patterns, but it is not such a good idea to use a floating line during the chase itself. Once a trout has broken through the surface, it is already transfixed on its prey and is unlikely to be distracted. It is therefore more productive to pull the pattern through the water on a sinking line at the holding depth of the shoal. This will tempt a trout before it has selected its prey – providing your chosen imitation stands out sufficiently from the hundreds of potential victims on offer.

Green Lures

In some waters, green mini-lures are uncannily effective – especially after angling pressure when the fish have grown wary of bright colours. The reason may be due to the natural occurrence of green in many food items, such as damsel nymphs, daphnia and some midge and sedge pupae. We have also noticed short lengths of green weed, which had presumably broken free into open water, in spoonings of recently stocked fish. With the permission of a friendly fishery owner, we once rowed out to the cages in the middle of his lake and threw lengths of weed over the side. There was quite a rush to intercept them. The fish were used to the occasional green 'goodie' passing in front of them, and there would always be plenty of competition for it.

Bill Moore's Green Thing.

It is therefore always worth having a selection of green marabou lures in the fly box. A pearly tinsel wrapped over a black silk underbody adds a sophisticated green shine. We must also mention Bill Moore and his Green Thing. It is only an inch long, and not very pretty – no more than a green marabou wing with an inconspicuous lead body to get it down. Nevertheless, the retired Sergeant-Major has been scoring with it for years. You can almost hear him shouting the accompanying words as he retrieves the fly slowly through the water. 'Trout WILL grab the Green Thing. WAIT FOR IT. QUI-ICK BITE.' And they do!

Sparklers

The essential characteristic of all Sparklers is a wing comprising filaments of highly mobile plastic, such as Lureflash Mobile, with a metallic and sometimes holographic coating. They produce a sensational effect that resembles a small fish. In clear water, they will attract trout from great distances. In water thick with algae, their striking visibility will often convert a dour day into a sensational one. A mixture of gold and silver is a popular choice, but there are a variety of combinations. It is important to recognize, however, that lures incorporating these materials do not look so realistic under close examination. Therefore, whereas marabou winged lures are often effective when virtually static, Sparklers generally need to be pulled quickly through the water.

Fritz Sparkler.

One of the most consistent patterns incorporates a black Fritz body with a wing and tail of mixed gold and silver wing filaments. The body looks unnaturally bulky, but even large, established trout do not seem to mind. Moreover, we have enjoyed some marvellous fishing with this version using a slow (nymph-like) figure-of-eight retrieve.

Nobblers

It is possible to take movement one stage further than pulsation of the fibres by incorporating motion into the fly as a whole. This is the basis of Nobblers and Boobies. The inbuilt mobility gives them the quality of being able to tempt fish when nothing else will. Apart from this, they use the same materials and colours as ordinary lures, so that the same principles on fly selection apply.

Dog Nobblers were introduced to fishermen in the UK in the 1980s by Trevor Housby. The term 'dog' applied to those impossible trout that were normally considered to be a waste of time. Nobblers were such an instant success that many anglers started using nothing else. One tackle dealer even copyrighted the name! Even today, many anglers cannot resist using them all the time and, as a consequence, miss out on the joys of imitative fly fishing.

Nobblers have two key features. First, there is the weighted head – formerly a lead shot but nowadays some more environmentally friendly material. In this respect, they are no different from bead-headed flies, except there is little pretence that the weighted head has any imitative qualities. It serves no purpose other than to make the fly dive downwards. Second, unlike the bead-headed nymphs used in rivers, the downward motion exploits the mobility of a long, bushy marabou tail. As the line is pulled, the Nobbler moves forward, but at the end of the pull it sinks downwards with the marabou fibres pulsating behind it. You only have to watch the overall motion of the Nobbler in the water to appreciate why it is such a killer with its built-in FTA. This movement means that it is naturally suited to a sink and draw retrieve, but all sorts of variations are worth a try.

Like all lures, Nobblers will work in quite small sizes. Since the tail extends well behind the hook, the body can be as small as a size 14. It is easier to cast flies in the smaller sizes on light tackle if the weight of the head is not overdone. Moreover, the more gradual undulating movement from a lighter head often produces better results than a rapid dive. Some fishermen use a Nobbler as a point fly, and figure-of-eight it back very slowly with a couple of nymphs on the droppers. They are getting the best of all worlds – an attractor and an imitator used simultaneously, plus the coverage of several depths at once.

Boobies

The Booby is one of the most killing all-round patterns in existence for catching sub-surface trout. It is at its best in winter when there is no weed to snag the leader, but it will work at any time of year if such obstacles can be avoided. Success often comes much too easily, and it requires more than a little will power to return to conventional methods. Nevertheless, our friend Alan 'One-Pool' Williams has consistently won many winter competitions to prove that there is some skill to Booby fishing. He gave us some tips for this section, on the strict understanding that we did not mention his other nickname of the Booby Master. (Oops!)

Green Nobbler.

Fritz Booby.

The Booby is simply a normal marabou lure with two buoyant Plastazote 'boobs' at the head. It is therefore a complementary pattern to the Nobbler. In both cases, the weight or buoyancy at the front of the fly dictates its movement, and there is an added attraction of mobile marabou in the tail or wing. The Nobbler is pulled upwards by the retrieve and then dives due to its built-in weighting. The Booby is dragged downwards by pulls via a fast-sinking line, and then moves upwards due to its built-in buoyancy when the line goes slack. Thus, although the white versions may sometimes imitate a small fish, its success is principally due to the enticing movement induced by its two boobs at a controlled depth.

To make the most of its intrinsic qualities, this pattern requires a high density line from the bank or a stationary boat. In classic (we cannot repeat what Brian, our chalk-stream reviewer said about this adjective) Booby style, the line is allowed to sink so that it rests on the bottom before starting the retrieve. Providing the retrieve is sufficiently slow, the buoyant Booby will remain at a fixed distance above the bottom, which depends on the length of the leader. In winter, when the weed has disappeared, the leader can be as short as 6 in. The line is then retrieved in a series of short pulls, waiting after each one for a couple of seconds to allow the fly to ascend.

Apart from the obvious effects of movement, there is no better way of searching the bottom without snagging any weeds or obstacles. This enables you to reach fish that are otherwise disinclined to move about in search of food. In conditions of poor visibility, three Boobies can be fished close to the bottom at once by placing a split shot 6 in in front of each fly. (Note that split shot tend to move down the leader with frequent casting,

Booby fishing.

so you will need to check the positions frequently or tie a 'stop' knot just below each one.) The only problem with fishing multiple Boobies is their tendency to spin in the air when casting, thereby causing the leader to twist. This can be an irritation, but it is often well worth the extra inconvenience of untwisting the nylon between casts.

Takes are usually positive, although sometimes there is a series of exploratory tweaks on the end of the line in response to this unnatural phenomenon. You should not strike until these tweaks become more solid, and then you should apply a gradual lifting of the rod rather than a sudden action. Trout have a tendency to gorge these flies, so a barbless hook is important for catch and release.

We have heard anglers maintain that trout swallow Boobies simply because 'they like them so much' or because 'they are soft and compressible'. We doubt very much whether these are the reasons. It is more likely to be due to the difficulty of closing their mouths on such a mouthful, so they have to make a decision to swallow or reject. Very often a trout will mouth the back end of the fly several times while it makes its decision. This registers as a series of taps and is the cause of many missed fish due to striking too early. The chances of hooking a trout are increased by holding the rod at 90 degrees to the line rather than straight down it. The extra cushioning in the rod then allows the trout more opportunity to close its mouth on the fly and swim away.

Alex had already flattened his hat from jumping up and down on it repeatedly, and now something else had to be done. So he was starting to pull out his hair as rainbow after rainbow came to Humphrey's net. He was conscientiously copying the retrieve, fishing the same high-density line and counting for the same time before retrieving – 25 seconds measured accurately on his watch. He knew that Humphrey was using a Vindaloo Booby, for such a fly is almost impossible to disguise, and he already possessed the special tying with the Flashibou in the wing (Vindaloo flashitittibits).

'OK, I give in – yet again! Let me see the bl**dy fly. I'll buy the intercoursing drinks'. Humphrey grinned, knowing that Alex had asked the wrong question. He handed over the successful fly and changed to a black and green Booby. He proceeded to catch a couple more fish, and watched with wry amusement as the baffled comments and murmurings grew in volume and colour. Then quite an extraordinary thing happened. Perhaps it was the way that his recent exploits with the Vindaloo had backfired, or maybe an excess of Rioja had temporarily disconnected his mouth from his brain. Humphrey took genuine pity. 'Your leader's only 6 in long – it needs to be about 6 ft!'

Boobies are very successful in mid-water, sometimes enticing fish when no other method will. In the early days of experimentation, we tried a Vindaloo Booby on a 12 ft leader so that it rested on the surface as a strike indicator for the other two flies on the droppers. On the first cast a rainbow rose and took this abominable concoction dry! All you have to do is increase the length of the leader, and in this way you can fish at several different depths simultaneously. Whatever the length of the leader, the Booby is unique in providing an angler with a way to fish a fly at a fixed distance above the bottom. It is this quality as well as the intrinsic movement, that sets it in a class of its own.

We have found that the most consistent tactic is to fish with three differently coloured Boobies – orange, black and white – simultaneously at different depths. The positioning on the cast also seems to be important. An orange version goes about 6 in from the fly line to tempt the non-feeding fish that are holding station on the lake bed. A Vindaloo Booby can be fantastic, but it is often advisable to use subdued shades of orange for the more wary fish. An orange Micro Fritz body with a coral pink wing and orange boobs is an excellent all-round choice. When trout move up in the water, they are often searching for food. Thus, a Booby with a black marabou wing goes on the middle dropper about 3–4 ft away, suggesting perhaps a leech or large nymph. In coloured water we may use a fluorescent green body, but under clearer conditions black Micro Fritz is our first choice. Finally, a white Booby (Light Bulb, Jack Frost or a green Micro Fritz body) representing a small fish, goes on the point a further 5–6 ft away.

With a good ripple or current, the Booby is an ideal tactic for the lazy angler, or simply a good way to fish when taking a well earned break. The motion of the water alone can be sufficient to move the fly up and down, with the inevitable excitement as the reel starts screaming of its own accord.

We have observed suspicious trout moving backwards and forwards past an artificial fly that is dangling in the water. They do not appear to show any interest in it, but the fly is nevertheless the centre of their attention. On one occasion, when fishing from behind a bush into a clear pool, we watched a trout do this for two minutes before finally committing itself. This motion sets up currents in the water that will cause movements in soft materials such as marabou, adding to the enticement of the fly. For this reason, it is always worth holding or jiggling the flies in the water before lifting off. A respectable percentage of takes to the Booby occur right under an angler's nose.

Although Booby fishing usually involves a slow, intermittent retrieve, there are occasions when other retrieves are more productive. In heavily fished waters, a more enticing FTA approach to supplement the Booby's natural movement can pay big dividends. There are occasions when ripping the Booby back at full speed triggers a knee-jerk reaction from otherwise seemingly impossible fish. This probably results from the pronounced sub-surface wake. On one notable occasion this caught us five rainbows in an hour totalling nearly 30 lb when everything else had failed. We achieved this success by waiting for a sub-surface boil and then covering it. Another killing technique in a good wave is the use of a Booby on a floating line as if it were a Muddler.

Like all the other patterns in this chapter, the Booby does not have to be large. A normal shank size 10 hook, with 3 to 4 milli-metre boobs, is ample for most purposes – unless imitating a larger fish. Lightweight hooks are preferable to maximize the buoyancy. Marabou can form the tail, but it seems to work better as a wing that pulsates seductively when moved very slowly. Moreover, there are fewer problems with tail-nipping. If the trout have become educated, the more sophisticated Booby fisherman – if this is not a contradiction in terms – will try even smaller patterns. It is quite possible to tie these flies with tiny boobs on a size 14, lightweight hook. The end result is a pattern that is still sufficiently buoyant to be fit for the purpose, yet far less likely to raise the same degree of suspicion. These small patterns work particularly well in clear water when the trout can both spot a fly and sense danger from a greater range.

When fishing in front of a drifting boat, the boobs should be smaller than normal to help to get the fly down in the limited time available. In contrast, larger boobs may be necessary in deep water to compensate for the reduction in buoyancy due to compression of the Plastazote under the high pressure.

The boobs can be tied easily by cutting a length of Plastazote, which is more buoyant and durable than Ethafoam, with a square cross-section for ease of cutting. It is possible to buy such items with a perfectly round cross-section, but this is to tempt anglers rather than the fish. Now hold the Plastazote on top of the hook, behind the eye and at right angles to the shank, and bring the tying thread diagonally over the Plastazote from back to front. Repeat this a few times in both directions so that the centre of the Plastazote is firmly compressed on to the top of the hook. Whip finish and dab some Superglue on the thread, on the underside of the hook between the boobs, to prevent

them from twisting round the hook. Now all that remains is to shape the boobs with a pair of scissors. You do not have to achieve a work of art – trout appear to be much less fanatical about boobs than humans!

Just as with other attractors, it is possible to fish nymphs at the same time and get the best of both worlds. Moreover, the Booby gives a different trajectory to the flies. With a floating line and a conventional attractor or Nobbler on the point, the nymphs will move a fixed distance below the surface. With a sinking line and a Booby on the point, the nymphs will remain a fixed distance above the bottom of the lake, and bob up and down in a very enticing and natural manner. On the intermediate line, it makes an excellent point fly, in conjunction with two nymphs and a figure-of-eight retrieve. It slows down the rate of descent of the nymphs, and provides a variation to the normal trajectory. Two Diawl Bachs – one with and one without a red head – are good choices.

A Booby creates more of a wake than a Muddler when ripped across the waves on a floating line. With such a high-speed retrieve, the flies trailing behind have to be pretty fearsome too. Reliable favourites are a Viva on the middle dropper and a Light Bulb on the point.

Woven Nymph.

CHAPTER 8

GREAT FLY PATTERNS

RATIONALE

We resisted the temptation to give the tyings for large numbers of specific imitations, since it would not have been an honest reflection of our own expertise. Our approach is to concentrate on a limited number of patterns, and to get to know them sufficiently well to tie and fish them to maximum effect. Providing you can appreciate why particular patterns are successful, they often only need minor changes, such as a different size or colour, to tailor them to more specific requirements.

The adoption of a carefully selected set of general patterns has some very definite advantages. First, you can visit an unknown water with no visible fly life, and fish in the knowledge that there is a fair chance of choosing something that is suitable. Second, a single fly can cover more than one variety of natural insect at the same time. Third, if you use the general patterns described in this chapter, you can be confident that they will have worked over a wide variety of waters in several different countries.

This does not mean that you can choose a general pattern at random with any guarantee or even hope of success. Each one will cover only a range of species and conditions, and it is essential to tailor your choice accordingly. To some extent this requires more skill and experience than the use of exact imitations, which might be obvious from the observable fly life. It means having the determination to experiment with the patterns to get to know them better and perhaps to improve them further. There are few ways to obtain greater satisfaction in fishing than to have invented a successful general fly.

We have developed a respectable number of patterns ourselves (identified by MC and JD after the name), but the essential criterion for selection of a fly has been its proven track record. We have absolutely no reservations about including such well known patterns as the Stick Fly or Elk Hair Caddis, because they all feature so strongly in our tactics. And even with such well established flies, there are often minor variations or tricks of the trade that are not so well appreciated.

GENERAL-PURPOSE DRY FLIES AND EMERGERS

Panacea (MC and JD)

Panacea.

We had some trepidation about using such a grandiose name for one of our own creations – but why should we? We have caught trout on this fly in just about every river and lake we have visited in Great Britain and Ireland – and that constitutes quite a few! In the Western USA, it proved itself repeatedly on mighty rivers such as the Yellowstone, Missouri and Snake, spring creeks in three different States and in crystal clear lakes under the calmest of conditions. It caught rainbows in a tiny river in France where the locals had said the fish were too well educated to take an artificial fly. It has caught many trout and grayling during hatches of up-winged flies, midges and (in North America) tricos. The Panacea is one of the most consistent dry patterns that we have ever come across in both running and still water.

We are not, of course, pretending that it is always successful – but it will work on just about every type of water at one time or another. It is often our first choice of dry fly on rivers. On still waters where aquatic midge are likely to be the staple diet, we would initially opt for a more specific pattern such as Shipman's Buzzer. Nevertheless, the Panacea is always high on the list of possible substitutes.

It is an example of a parachute fly, described in the chapter entitled *Fly Tying to Catch Fish*, giving the suggestion of a dun with the shuck attached. A size 14 wide-gape hook (Kamasan B160) is the best all-round size. The tail, representative of the emptying shuck case, capitalizes on the life and movement suggested by the contrasting shades in the tip of a grizzle hackle. The tip of a second grizzle hackle provides the post, which leans forward slightly to suggest the body of an emerging adult. Three turns of a third grizzle hackle around the post, ideally from a stiff genetic cape, form the legs and keep the fly afloat.

Only the tail and the parachute hackle are normally treated with floatant. Thus, the body rests in the surface film where it is more conspicuous. However, on several occasions, it works much better with the whole body treated to ensure it rides higher on the surface. (During trico hatches, for example, we have re-vitalized the fly by drying it and then dipping it in powder after each fish.) The body is formed from 'Martin's Mix' – equal parts of black, fiery brown and light olive SLF. This is ribbed with fine pearly tinsel, stretched to keep it taut but not quite enough to turn it from green to blue.

As the need for floatation or visibility increases in the faster flowing streams, the Panacea needs adjusting accordingly – such as a white visible post in place of the grizzle hackle tip and three Microfibbets for the tail to form a better grip in the surface film.

During a session on the Snake River, Gary Willmott, who is one of the most respected local guides, uttered these immortal words: 'I hope you've got a lot of those Panacea things, because you ain't leaving this boat with all of them!'

Sail-Wing (MC and JD)

Sail-Wing.

The Sail-Wing represents a fully emerged dun as it floats ma-jestically down the stream. There are times when trout will ignore emerging adults and insist on fully matured specimens. One reason might be that emergence of the natural insects is taking place away from the fish in the reeds or weedy shallows upstream.

The body comprises a fine textured fur, such as mole or olive SLF Midge. Stripped peacock herl is a good alternative, which produces an ultra-fine, naturally ribbed effect. The wing is no more than a bunch of upright CDC fibres tied in about one third of the way down from the eye. These fibres will move enticingly in the breeze to give a wonderful suggestion of life. Two turns (at most) of a brown olive para-hackle help to keep the fly afloat and cocked with the wing vertical. Finally, the tip of a grizzle feather for the tail provides a superb trigger point. Very often, the fly will fail to catch after losing its tail.

With very small duns, it is difficult to tie a realistic, hackled dry fly on hook sizes much smaller than a size 16. Apart from the problem of manual dexterity, hackle fibres that are perfect for the larger sizes tend to become disproportionately bulky as the scale of the fly decreases. The end result may be a fly with legs that appear like tree trunks. So if there is no reaction, it is worth trying an unhackled version. It will not stay afloat for so long, but sometimes this turns out to be the only recipe for success.

We first developed this fly on a size 16 (Kamasan B400) hook with an olive body and natural grey CDC wings to represent olives emerging from the River Wylye. Since then we have tried it in various different sizes and shades with great success.

Flat-back CDC

The Flat-back CDC is another pattern that is suitable for small emerging flies due to its simplicity and lack of appendages. Whereas Sail-Wings represent the adults, this fly is an un-ambiguous emerger. As a rule of thumb, we will select an emerger if the trout are rising to insects that we cannot see. They are also good smutting patterns since the whole body is visible from all angles. Normally we will tie Flat-back CDCs on

Flat-back CDC.

wide-gape (Kamasan B160) hooks in the size range 14 to 18, but we will keep a few size 12s in reserve. Even when taking larger insects, trout sometimes prefer a pattern that has a lower profile without a post or one that represents the earlier stage of emergence.

Flat-back CDCs work consistently on rivers and lakes around the world and represent a wide variety of fly life. They therefore lend themselves to a range of body colours, but our first choice is usually a modified 'Martin's Mix' ribbed with fine, flat gold tinsel or pearly rib. For the smaller sizes, it is better using a mix of Finesse rather than the normal SLF dubbing on the Panacea. This requires an alternative of cinnamon in place of fiery brown, since the latter is not available in Finesse.

The CDC should be tied in at the head like a conventional wing and cut abruptly at the end so that it is extends above the bend of the hook. Like all tiny flies, this pattern is often more effective on the point of a fine tippet.

We have also found a weighted version of this pattern to be excellent for covering rising fish in running water. It has taken many difficult grayling for us in the chalk-streams during a hatch of Baetis. A sparse white strike indicator, about a couple of feet away, will keep the fly about a foot below the surface and will not put the fish on their guard.

Black Catch-All (MC and JD)

Black Catch-All.

It is always worth having a small black dry fly in your box to cover the many varieties of black insects. These may be aquatic species, such as reed smuts and midges, ants, beetles or a variety of terrestrial flies. (For larger insects, we tend to favour other patterns such as a Black Hopper (UK) or Bibio.) The Black Catch-All has served us well on countless occasions on rivers and lakes in several countries. It may not look much, but that should not put you off. Since black is such a natural colour which can arrive on the water at any time, it may be worth a try when nothing is showing. Trout are quite used to seeing isolated terrestrial insects arriving on the surface which are not part of a more general 'hatch'.

There are no unnatural or unnecessary appendages, so that there is very little to which trout can object. A small hook is required, such as a size 14 or 16 Kamasan B160. The tail-end of the abdomen comprises black silk, which progressively merges into a more bulky thorax of black seal's fur (or substitute). The thorax is teased out slightly to aid floatation, whereas the tail end of the fly may sink slightly to improve visibility to fish that are feeding high in the water. The wing is simply a bunch of fibres from a white cock hackle.

CDC Spinner

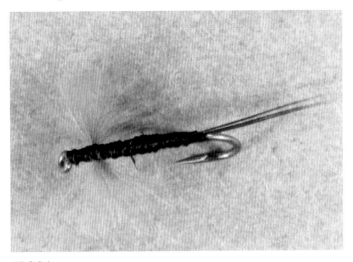

CDC Spinner.

This is a very common and simple, yet effective pattern to imitate a variety of spinners. The spent wings are simply two bunches of CDC fibres, tied at right angles to the hook just behind the eye and trimmed to shape. This gives a much softer profile than more conventional feathers. The body can be any fine-textured fur, which may be ribbed with fine wire. Stripped peacock herl makes a very enticing alternative. Two or three Microfibbet tails, which for spinners need to be about twice as long as the body, complete the pattern. Coupled with the CDC, they give the fly lots of buoyancy. There are obviously plenty of possible colour permutations for all three components of the fly to suit the naturally occurring insects.

Klinkhammer

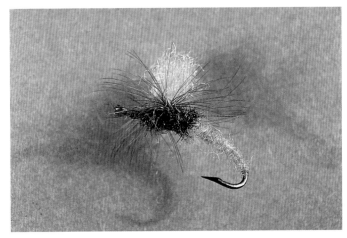

Klinkhammer.

This Hans van Klinken creation has the advantage of being an emerger that stays afloat well in the faster flowing waters. Its seductively shaped body, which is tied on a curved emerger hook, such as a Partridge GRS15ST, could represent both caddis and midge pupae. In the larger sizes, which typically correspond to a size 10 fly on a conventional hook, it presents a tasty morsel. Trout and grayling will take it quite readily on chalk-streams as well as on freestone rivers. The body consists of fur, in a range of shades, such as beige, green-olive and black, tapering towards a peacock herl thorax. A red-brown parachute hackle around a white post completes the pattern. This suspends the fly so that the abdomen, on the specially curved hook, dips beneath the surface.

HIGH PROFILE DRY FLIES (PRINCIPALLY FOR RIVERS)

Royal Wulff

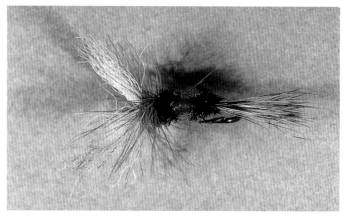

Royal Wulff.

You could be forgiven for dismissing the Royal Wulff as a fly that has no right to catch fish. Its white wings, created by splaying some white calf-tail into two sections at an angle above the hook, are crude and unnatural. The abrupt change in the middle of the body, where the bushy peacock herl gives way to a neat red band of floss silk, is more suggestive of a soldier in ceremonial uniform than of a natural insect. The elk hair in the tail is too solid to represent the sleek fibres of a dun or spinner. Then, to cap it all, there is a bushy full brown hackle at the front that ought to send alarm signals to any self-respecting trout.

That is the theory. In practice, the late Lee Wulff's creation is a fantastic general pattern that anglers use around the world with consistent and staggering success in a wide range of sizes (8 to 20). We have enjoyed great success with sizes 8–12 when terrestrial insects are in evidence, such as Heather Flies (UK), Grasshoppers (North America) and Cicadas (New Zealand). Even if they turn away, it is a wonderful indicator of whether fish are present and likely to feed if shown the right pattern. It also provides a tempting distraction when trout are preoccupied with large numbers of tiny insects. There are better imitations of many upwinged flies, such as an Adams or Grey Wulff, but even then the Royal Wulff has a couple of inbuilt advantages.

These advantages come from the white wings which increase its visibility and, along with the tail and full hackle, help it to stay afloat. Thus, it is tailor-made for the rougher, larger streams where the full hackle also gives it a prominent high profile. These properties make it ideal for use in conjunction with a trailing nymph, which is one reason why we have more

experience with the larger versions. Apart from acting as an effective strike indicator, it will attract a trout's attention or trigger it into making a closer inspection. On many occasions, especially in the rougher or rock-strewn 'pocket-waters', this dramatically increases the success rate of the nymph.

Adams

Adams.

It is impossible to ignore this fly, which is arguably the most widely used general pattern in the world to represent upwinged duns. The mixed hackles (brown and grizzle), for both the collar (or parachute in the para-Adams) and tail, give a subtle suggestion of life. One turn of each hackle is generally adequate for the collar or parachute. The grey fur body is not going to raise any alarm signals. Finally, the two grizzle hackle tips that project slightly forward as wings above the fly provide a trigger point that signals emergence.

We have enjoyed most success with this fly, in both the standard and parachute forms, in the smaller sizes from 14 to 20. It is readily available off the shelf, and we would never travel anywhere without the full range.

Humpy

Humpy.

We make no pretence that our favourite buoyant dry fly is the Royal Wulff, but the Humpy in sizes 10 to 14 provides a second line of attack by providing a different shape and a range of colours – typically black, red, lime green and yellow.

The tail comprises up to ten dark elk hair fibres. A further batch of about 20 brown elk hair fibres are used for both the back and the wings, so some care – and possibly trial and error – may be necessary. First, the cut ends of the elk hair are bound onto the hook so that they project backwards alongside the tail. Silk of the appropriate colour is then wound around the shank to form the body. The elk hair is pulled over the silk to form the back, and bound down behind the eye so that the tips form two upright wings. A few turns of badger hackle behind the wings complete the fly.

Elk Hair Caddis

Elk Hair Caddis.

We have often asked experienced river fishermen in different countries what they would choose if their fishing were restricted to half a dozen dry flies. Two flies come up repeatedly. First there is the Adams. The second is the Elk Hair Caddis. Al Troth's creation may look a bit scrappy compared to the more classical dry flies, but it is an outstandingly good pattern.

Its obvious application as a representation of an adult caddis fly dictates the body colour. The two most universally acceptable colours to keep in the fly box are cinnamon and green. A short red-game palmer, ribbed with fine gold, silver or copper wire, helps to keep the fly high in the water when static or to produce a scurrying wake when moved.

It is important to pay proper attention to the wings, since they will assume a very unnatural appearance if the fibres are too coarse or improperly bunched. They need to end just beyond the end of the body – roughly in line with the bend of the hook – and to be splayed out slightly. If the ends are cut to shape, the finish is too abrupt. Full use should be made of the naturally tapering ends of the fur, so a hair stacker is helpful. A common mistake is to use fibres that are too coarse, so it is worth shopping around for the fur from a year-old elk, which is finer

than that from a more mature animal. When tying down the wings at the head, the hair should not be trimmed but allowed to project in front of the body. It can then be fashioned to suggest the head of the fly, which is quite pronounced in the natural insect.

Since it has a high profile above the surface, it is a pattern to keep in mind for the rougher stretches of water. It is a wonderful fly for dropping first time into the riffles entering a pool, where the trout are constantly on the look out for the arrival of food. It does not seem to matter whether caddis flies are actually hatching. In practice, this is quite a general pattern, which will work in a wide variety of sizes – most commonly from size 10 to 16. A lightweight hook that is generous in the shank, such as a Kamasan B400, is ideal.

Balloon Caddis.

One special variation of this fly is Roman Moser's Balloon Caddis. The essential difference is the addition of a bright yellow Plastazote head, which imitates the gas bubble of an emerging pupa but also makes the fly visible during the fading evening light. A strip of yellow Plastazote foam, about 5 mm wide, is first bound to the hook immediately behind the eye, and then bound down again about 3 mm down the shank. This creates a ball-shaped head of foam between the two bound sections. The strip projecting forwards remains in place at this stage, whereas the strip behind the ball is trimmed as close to the binding as possible. The unpalmered fur body, which can be light olive or any suitable colour to match the natural insects, is ribbed with tying thread for extra strength. A splayed out deer (or elk) hair wing is then added. After the body and wing are in place, the strip of Plastazote is folded back over the head, tied down immediately behind it and trimmed.

Another of Roman Moser's innovative creations is the Egg-Laying Caddis. This copies the female as she raises her wings above the surface while dipping her abdomen into the water. The deer (or elk) hair wings splay out in front of the eye of the hook rather than behind it. Just behind them is a buoyant brown Plastazote thorax, which keeps the fly afloat while allowing the untreated abdomen to dip beneath the surface. The abdomen is typically brown fur, but it can be varied to suit local species.

General Purpose Ant

General Purpose Ant.

Many species of fish seem to love ants, and trout often become preoccupied with them. Most patterns are small to match the natural species. This calls for very accurate casting, persistence and perhaps a modicum of luck if a swarm alights on the surface. On such occasions, there is a good case for employing a fly that stands out from the crowd – and that is exactly what this pattern achieves, even without any natural ants on the water.

Gary Willmott, who uses the fly as a front-line general pattern on many rivers and lakes throughout western USA, attributes the original tying to René Harrop. Jeremy Herrmann has since exploited it in various parts of the world, and has consistently proved its effectiveness on the English chalk-streams.

A shaped abdomen of tightly dubbed black fur covers two thirds of a lightweight (Kamasan B400) size 12 hook. The tips from a grey cock hackle are tied in at the front of the abdomen and extend backwards. The head is a round ball of foam. In between the head and abdomen are three turns of a short red-brown cock hackle.

DRY FLIES AND EMERGERS PRINCIPALLY FOR STILL WATER

Shipman's Buzzer

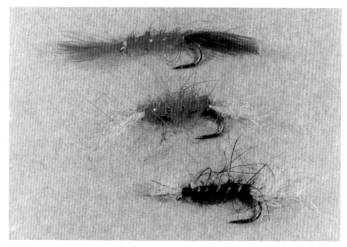

Shipman's Buzzer variations.

Although still-water trout fishing has been extremely popular in the UK for several decades, the more traditional approaches of wet flies and nymphs prevailed for a surprisingly long time. Even some of the most revered angling writers helped to propagate the myth that dry flies were for rivers, not lakes. Meanwhile, a few anglers of a more heretical nature started experimenting with dry flies, leading to an article by Dave Shipman in *Trout Fisherman* magazine that started the stampede. It is arguable that the enthusiasm then went too far. Too many good nymph and wet fly fishermen slowly lost their traditional skills as they became obsessed with dry fly techniques.

Shipman's article described a rather strange looking fly to imitate an adult midge. It had a straight body of fiery brown seal's fur, which was well teased out to help it stay afloat. The teasing also helped to give a degree of translucency, possibly giving the impression of a hatching pupa or even an empty shuck case. The flat gold tinsel ribbing was much wider than any one would use in attempting an exact imitation. There were two tufts of white wool fore and aft which helped an angler to keep sight of the fly on the water. These were far more pronounced than the breather filaments, which in any case only exist at the front end of the natural pupa.

In spite of all these apparent short-comings, this unconventional fly worked extremely well and caught large numbers of educated trout that had hitherto been uncatchable. The more innovative anglers started tying more exact patterns, and many now dismiss Dave Shipman's creation as a pioneering fly that has served its purpose. Perhaps they should explain this to the trout, because like it or not, the fly remains one of the most killing dry fly patterns in existence. It works on rivers and brooks. It has been successful in the USA, Canada, New Zealand and just about anywhere in the world. Moreover, it takes trout that have never seen a midge pupa in their lives.

Although we have stayed faithful to this basic pattern, we have incorporated a few refinements and variations. The white tufts are sparser and more natural, obtaining their added buoyancy from a number of fibrous filaments rather than too much bulk. The ideal material is white CDC, although the white fibres from the base of a hen hackle or marabou plume are also suitable. The ribbing is a fine flat gold tinsel to give a better compromise between natural and eye-catching appearances.

We also vary the body thickness according to conditions. A bushy version is fine on rough water or for better visibility when the trout are not too suspicious. But for most purposes, a much finer body will float sufficiently well and catch a greater number of fish. Shipman's Buzzer, in its most sparse form, is an excellent general pattern for a flat calm, because there are no hackles to give it an unnatural appearance in the surface film.

The most consistent hooks for general fishing are a lightweight (Kamasan B400) size 12 or 14, although there is no reason why smaller sizes should not be used to match a hatch of smaller species. As light fades in the evening, a size 10 provides a prominent silhouette against the sky when viewed from below. This trick has worked for us on several occasions when smaller sizes have failed to bring any response.

There are two other variations that we favour – the **Nephew** and the **Stripeys**. In the shade, the Nephew takes on a crimson appearance, which may not appear significantly different from the standard version. However, it obtains this colour from a mixture of claret and light orange seal's furs (or substitutes) that come to life under sunlight. The correct choice of colours is essential. If the claret is too light or the orange too hot, the two colours blend into one without any effects of contrast. The pattern will still work, but not so well.

The Stripeys have a fine fluorescent white woollen rib instead of gold tinsel and are usually tied in a size 14. The scarlet version exploits the trout's response to red and makes an ideal partner on the leader to the basic Shipman's Buzzer or Nephew. In contrast, the Black Stripey is a better fly to use at times when the natural midges are not emerging, or after a hatch when the trout are collecting the empty shuck cases. It is also worth a try on the more acidic waters where dark coloured terrestrial insects form a major part of a trout's diet.

Hopper (UK)

Amber Hopper.

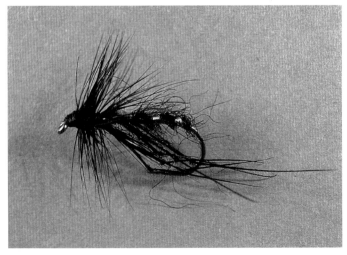

Black Hopper.

This fly is very different from the North American (Grass-) Hopper, which forms a staple diet in many regions during late summer. The only similarity is the knotted legs, which is possibly why the name was first – and inappropriately – used in England. It bears a much greater resemblance to a crane fly, and works very well as a direct imitation. Nevertheless, it is a great general pattern whenever there is a chance that fish will come to the surface, whether or not it matches any natural insects. Its seductive, knotted legs are always likely to trigger a response. The movement of these legs can prove irresistible to trout at any depth, so it is worth a try on sinking lines as well. There are two popular and successful ways to fish it, and each one requires a slightly different tying.

The first method is to ensure that both the body and legs dangle enticingly beneath the surface rather than on top of it. This also makes the fly visible outside the trout's window. This is normally our first choice when trout are feeding on emerging midge pupae. It will take fish that are surface feeding on just about anything, from adult or hatching midges or caddis to terrestrials. It works most consistently as a static fly on the point. Trout tend to turn on the Hopper and 'drown' it, so you should *usually* wait for about half a second before striking.

To achieve this 'ultimate emerger', the legs must not protrude above the body and floatant must be applied to the hackle alone. The body and/or legs can be treated with a sinkant to ensure penetration of the surface film. A medium-weight (Kamasan B170) hook will help to cock the fly into position, as will a Turle Knot (for example) that allows the nylon to pass straight through the eye to grip the shank.

Trout rejecting the static fly can sometimes be induced to take by a sudden figure-of-eight movement. Often the most successful tactic is to work a Hopper deliberately across the surface with a slow figure-of-eight retrieve. This is worth a try when trout are preoccupied with taking tiny smuts off the surface as an alternative to a more garish pattern such as a Vindaloo. On these occasions we will often fish three different coloured Hoppers on the leader at once, continuing with the retrieve after the water goes 'heavy' with a slow, progressive lift of the rod to set the hook.

The second method uses the legs to support the body on a lightweight (Kamasan B400) hook. In this case, the legs are tied deliberately to lie above the body, and, like the hackle, are treated to float. The body may remain untreated (i.e. submerged) for aquatic flies, but not on those 'terrestrial' waters where the insects do not break through the surface film. In fact, under these circumstances, there is a case for palmering the body with a short-flued, stiff genetic hackle.

All patterns should incorporate a slim fur body. The four to six knotted cock pheasant centre-tail legs (trout do not appear to count them) are splayed out for maximum attraction. Body colours should match the fly-life, and in general we have found the most consistent colours to be golden-olive, claret and black. The golden-olive Hopper is very useful as an all-purpose pattern to use in between hatches where it will imitate many terrestrial insects, such as dung flies. It even catches trout feeding on empty shuck cases, in spite of the knotted legs! Orange sometimes does particularly well on a bright sunny day.

Heather Fly.

The ribbing is usually fine gold flat tinsel on the lighter versions or pearly tinsel on the darker ones. The lighter versions use natural pheasant tail legs and a light red-brown cock hackle, but for the darker versions these materials are best dyed to match the body. Dyed red legs with a black body are deadly when Heather Flies are on the water. Two turns of a cock hackle should be the maximum under calm conditions, but up to six turns may be required to keep the fly afloat in rough or moving water.

The most consistent size is dressed on a normal shank size 10, even when the naturals are very small, with a hackle diameter of 16–18 mm. But be prepared to change down to a size 12 or even a size 14 if the larger fly is ignored or rejected.

Skeleton

Skeleton.

We have already described the advantages of including the shuck case in fly patterns. This may take the form of a few individual fibres, but the tip of a barred feather such as grizzle is arguably better. This tends to give the case a little more structure and hence that added degree of realism. In the Skeleton, you can take this effect one stage further to produce quite an enticing representation of a shuck at the back-end of the fly.

The shuck is formed from the last inch or so of a cock hackle. Ginger is a good all-round colour, but variations such as olive, black, grizzle or Greenwell's may be more appropriate for some species. The fibres closest to the tip (about half the overall length) are trimmed to form a narrow, tapered end to the shuck. The remaining fibres are bent round so that they lie along the hook shank and point towards the eye. They are then bound down at the tail-end of the shank. This produces a startling impression of segmentation caused by the gaps between the curved fibres.

The impact of this fly comes from the representation of the shuck case, so that any body can be chosen to match the natural flies. One of our favourite patterns is simply a fiery brown Shipman's Buzzer body in front of the case without any white breathers. The whole fly should be treated with floatant.

The same trick is also used to extend the length of bodies on a short-shank hook – for example, a large mayfly. In this case, instead of trimming the fibres at the tail-end, they should be treated with Floo Gloo and separated into three separate strands for the tail filaments.

Carrot Fly

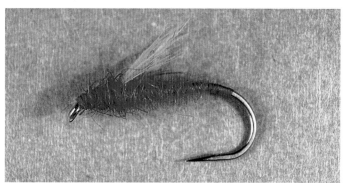

Carrot Fly.

We have mentioned in some detail how touches of fluorescent red or orange sometimes convert an ordinary dry fly into a deadly pattern. The Carrot Fly goes all the way and takes no prisoners. It is an unashamed exploitation of fluorescence that occasionally brings trout up from nowhere, catching many times more fish than less colourful patterns. On days when it is working, a novice with the advantage of this fly will totally outperform an expert – although he will not necessarily bring many fish to the net. This is because trout often take it with such commitment that you will need great presence of mind to prevent the leader breaking on impact. Sometimes, the first thing you feel is a burning of the fingers as the line accelerates into the distance.

There is one major downside to the Carrot Fly. It will often draw fish after fish that turns away from the fly never to be seen again. Thus, it has not only failed to catch anything in its own right – it has also spoiled the opportunity of catching anything on the other dry flies on the cast. When this happens the message is clear. Get rid of it!

The obvious basis of the Carrot Fly is its striking body, which is a 50/50 mix of hot orange and fluorescent red seal's furs (or substitutes). Either DFM Red or DRF fire orange will serve for the fluorescent component. The hot orange fur tones the effect down – not a lot, but it does seem to make the fly more consistent. The body on a lightweight (Kamasan B400) size 10 or size 12 hook tapers gradually, exactly as the name suggests, with the wider section towards the eye of the hook. There is a deliberate reason for this. The thin section at the rear of the fly, which is not treated to float, sinks more easily to make part of the fly visible outside the Trout's Window.

No ribbing is necessary, other than a fine red silk or nylon to hold the body in place. We do make two small concessions to natural appearance. First, a crimson seal's fur thorax gives some contrast and balance to the fly. This has to be teased out slightly to keep the fly afloat. Second, light orange hackle fibres, projecting out of the top of the fly, represent an emerging wing case.

Bob's Bit

Bob's Bit.

Bob Worts's creation is an excellent general still-water pattern that we prefer to use when there is a good ripple on the water, although we have fished with Bob when he has caught plenty of trout on it in calmer conditions. It is often tied in crimson as an adult midge imitation, but can exist in a variety of colours depending on the natural insects and the water clarity. Examples include golden olive for Dung Flies and black for Hawthorns.

The most useful all-round size is probably a size 14 tied on a lightweight (Kamasan B400) hook. The slim fur body is ribbed with fine gold wire. There are typically three turns of a red-brown throat hackle, which we prefer to cut off the bottom of the fly so that it sits better on the water. A few fibres of a light cock hackle on the top of the fly act as a wing and sighter, but this should not be overdone.

Magic Rabbit

This is a dry fly that can be quite spectacular at raising trout when retrieved in a series of twitches across the surface – or

Magic Rabbit.

sometimes even when static. In a good ripple they may murder it. In a lighter ripple, they tend to be more suspicious. We have known it raise scores of trout without a single one committing itself. When this happens, the first thing to do is to vary the retrieve to produce a surface FTA, allowing it to stop for a few seconds before twitching it again. The second thing is to forget about it altogether and try something else.

The Magic Rabbit is essentially a Palmered Shipman's Buzzer. It consists of a spiky rabbit body on a hook in the size range 10 to 14, with two small white woollen tufts added at each end. Olive green, red and fiery brown furs are good alternatives. The body is palmered with a light red-brown cock hackle and ribbed with a fine gold wire. We have found that a light Greenwell's hackle is a perfect complement to the body, but plain honey or ginger are quite adequate. It has the definite advantage of appearing the same from any angle, so that it always lands the right way up.

PFW

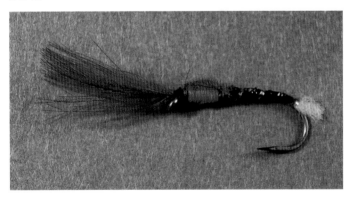

PFW variations.

This fly represents an emerger as it hangs vertically in the surface film before manoeuvring itself into a horizontal position. Although the original idea was to imitate a midge pupa, it has proved itself as a general pattern. It is a useful fly to put on a dropper to complement a dry fly on the point. This is due to its visibility outside the trout's window, as well as providing a choice of two stages of emergence. Moreover, the CDC 'shuttlecock' projects out of the water to provide the angler with a good sighting point.

An old friend of ours, Paul 'F' Weiss, did a great deal to popularize this pattern – often fishing three on a leader simultaneously. At times the fly outperformed everything else to the extent that cries of despair would come from those fishing next to him. One utterly frustrated individual used a brief but colourful adjective to describe the gentleman at his side, and the abbreviation for what he shouted has remained in the name of the fly to this day.

Trout tend not to play around with this pattern. It is all or nothing. On some days fish after fish will come to the surface only to reject it at the last minute. We can only surmise that on such occasions they are put off by the appearance of the CDC above the water. It does no harm therefore to make it as sparse and short as conditions will allow, or to use a smaller version if the rejections continue. At other times the trout take it with such conviction that the pulls on the line are absolutely savage.

The fly is simplicity itself to tie. A simple version for a midge pupa has a fine claret or black body with a fine pearly tinsel rib on a size 14 or 16 lightweight hook. In keeping with most midge pupa imitations, the abdomen may extend slightly round the bend of the hook, but this should not be overdone. A neat body material, such as floss silk, will not have any projecting strands which might grip the surface film and prevent the fly from cocking upright in the water. Even a neatly tied fur body may become teased out after a few trout have sunk their teeth into it. One highly effective pattern uses fine red holographic tinsel over ultra-fine tying silk, so that the body is hardly any thicker than a bare hook. A couple of short lengths of flat pearly tinsel as a tail are optional to represent the end of the emptying shuck case. The front end of the abdomen finishes about three quarters of the way along the shank.

Completion of the pattern involves the addition of a conventional wing case and thorax, except that the front end of the CDC wing case protrudes in front of the fly like a shuttlecock. First, bind one to three CDC feathers on to the bare shank immediately in front of the abdomen to point down the body like a conventional wing. Tie in a dubbed fur thorax to the eye, pull the CDC forward over the thorax, bind down at the eye and trim the CDC in front of the hook. The length of protruding CDC should be just sufficient to keep the fly afloat. This may vary from about 5 to 15 mm, depending on the size of the waves. The thorax can be the same colour as the body, but there is plenty of scope for experimenting with different materials.

A development of this type of fly has been to tie the CDC shuttlecock at the other end of the hook – just like a conventional tail. The fly then cocks upside down, with the point of the hook close to the surface. This does not seem to affect the catching power or the hooking capabilities, but has the advantage of preventing the fly from spinning in the air.

One version, which works well when small mayflies are present, uses hare's ear or rabbit fur with a stretched pearly rib on a size 16 or 18 hook. It has caught us many difficult trout in flat calm conditions and clear water. And as the line tightens on a seemingly impossible day, the immortal words ring out over the water – 'Paul "Fabulous" Weiss'.

NYMPHS PRINCIPALLY FOR RIVERS

River trout do not get very long to inspect a nymph, and seldom reject a fly as long as the overall profile and colour are acceptable. River anglers do not have too much time to get the fly down to the right depth. Thus appendages, such as hackles, are often absent since they add little to entice the trout while slowing down the rate of descent. Nevertheless, in spite of their simplicity, many of the patterns listed below will work quite respectably in still waters as well as in rivers.

Flashback Nymphs

Peacock Flashback.　　　　　*Hare's Ear Flashback.*

Pheasant Tail Flashback.

The best strategy for fishing a wide range of rivers is to have a single set of general nymph patterns in a range of hook sizes (10 to 16) and weights. These flies should have a few strands of the appropriate material for the tail and a progressive build-up of lead under-body towards the head so that the abdomen tapers progressively along its length.

The only extravagance we allow ourselves is to tie three different body types in hare's ear, pheasant tail and peacock herl. We have found that one of these choices may consistently, but not necessarily predictably, outperform the others on some rivers. Even then, it is important to recognize that sometimes the preference may have more to do with local fashion or another angler's prior success. In the rivers in the North Island of New Zealand, we caught all our sub-surface trout on the Hare's Ear nymph, because that is what the guide recommended. In the South Island, the peacock herl version was a real killer for all of us following Andrew Donaldson's immediate success (two five pounders in half an hour) with the fly. And at home and in North America, we have tended to use pheasant tail, simply because it has seldom let us down.

Abdomen	Rib	Thorax	Wing Case	Tail
Hare's Ear (HE)	Fine copper wire	HE	Silver or pearl	Spiky HE
Pheasant Tail (PT)	Fine copper wire	HE	Silver or pearl	PT
Peacock Herl (PH)	Fine green wire	PH	Silver or pearl	Spiky HE

You could just as easily rib the hare's ear with gold or the peacock with copper wire, use cock hackles for the tails – and so on. Many minor variations would be just as successful as these basic choices, and some might be slightly better. There is nothing special about the combinations shown above, other than the fact that we know several good anglers who have tried and tested them extensively with a high degree of success. If there is a preponderance of blue-winged olives, for example, you may quite legitimately use a rib of stretched pearly tinsel on top of the hare's ear body to give a bluish sheen to the nymph. But once you start worrying about some of the less relevant points without any firm technical basis, you run the risk of suffering from a surfeit of uncertainty that inevitably leads to confusion and reduced success.

A crucial part of the dressing is the use of flat silver or pearl tinsel for the wing case along the top of the thorax. In all but the smallest sizes, a broad tinsel is ideal. The principle behind the Flashbacks is to imitate the bubble of air that is prominent in many nymphs approaching emergence, which trout can see as reflections in the mirror outside their surface window. The transitory flash as the nymph moves in the water therefore acts as a natural trigger point.

Flashbacks were invented by Frank Schlosser and first described by him in the (New Zealand) *Flyfisher* magazine in February 1984. Soon afterwards, he showed the pattern to Tim Tollett, who took it back to North America where the idea caught on in a big way. We spent a considerable amount of time fishing with Tim and Frank in New Zealand, and shared in the considerable success from using these nymphs. They have both used Flashbacks extensively on the most spooky large trout in existence for many years, without any evidence of the extra flash raising alarm signals.

It is debatable whether to choose silver or pearl – and even Tim and Frank had different preferences. Both options seem to work comparably well, although the true pragmatist may choose a layer of pearl on top of the silver to stop himself worrying too much about the choice!

Flashback Emergers

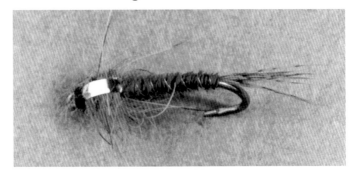

Flashback Emerger.

Emerger patterns need to give the impression of the adult about to break out from its shuck case. Thus, the thorax needs to be more bushy and the body slimmer than the Flashback nymphs. A good all-round pattern is spiky hare's ear for the thorax and pheasant tail with a copper rib for the slim, unweighted body. Some lead may be necessary in the thorax to keep the fly submerged. We have found over many years that a mottled tail feather, representing the back of the emptying shuck case, can provide an effective trigger point for emergers. Partridge brown back fibres are a good choice to match the pheasant tail body.

Bead-heads

Hare's Ear Gold-head variations.

Bead-heads, usually in gold or silver, offer an alternative to Flashbacks. They have the obvious advantage of being visible from any angle. Moreover, the weight of the bead at the front of the fly will cause the nymph to dive, which may sometimes prove irresistible. A good all-round fly consists of a body of spiky hare's ear, which tapers progressively from the tail so that it has the same diameter of the bead at the head. We originally ribbed the pattern with stretched pearly tinsel since the local trout were accustomed to feeding on blue-winged olives, and have never bothered changing it. Sometimes the fly will work even better with a sparse fluorescent reddish-orange tag in place of a hare's ear tail, and this is especially true for aggressive trout at the back-end of the season.

However, the simple addition of a bead in front of a basic river nymph produces a pattern that may look out of proportion. It is more realistic to use the bead in place of the thorax, but then some of the natural appearance is forfeited. Many good anglers, after fishing in the bright conditions prevalent in New Zealand, have commented that gold and silver headed nymphs seem to be ineffective for some of the more difficult trout.

Thus, we would recommend using Flashbacks for the more sophisticated trout, unless the amount of weight necessary to get the fly down results in a body that is unnecessarily bulky. Under these conditions, we would use a tungsten bead. This is the principle behind our Baetis Pheasant Tail nymph described below. If too much flash turns out to be a problem, then it is worth having a few patterns tied with a black tungsten bead in place of silver or gold.

Baetis Pheasant Tail (MC and JD)

Baetis Pheasant Tail.

Sawyer's Pheasant Tail was arguably the most important development in the history of nymph fishing in rivers. In omitting any legs, Sawyer achieved a pattern that cut cleanly through the water. It is so naturally 'nymphy' that there is virtually nothing to raise a trout's suspicions. Thus, it is also a highly successful general pattern for lakes.

By using more modern materials, it is possible to create a pattern of the same weight with an even slimmer body, or a heavier version having the same slender profile. It was this reasoning that led us to develop the Baetis Pheasant Tail for difficult grayling on the River Test. These fish become progressively more wary as the season progresses, and by the end of November offer as stern a challenge to any fly fisherman that we have encountered. This fly performs so consistently that JD used it almost exclusively for an entire winter season. It is

even simpler to tie than Sawyer's pioneering version, and works equally well as a general pattern in lakes where the trout have never set eyes on an agile darter.

Much of the weight comes from a very small (2 mm) gold tungsten bead on a normal shank size 14 hook, such as a Drennan Wet Fly Supreme. Wary trout and grayling seem to tolerate a gold head of this size, but if in doubt we will use a black bead in its place. This worked in New Zealand where the fly deceived a 5 lb wild brown trout feeding in clear open water little more than a foot deep. A single layer of fine lead wire (maximum diameter 0.4 mm) from the bead to just half way down the body adds a bit of extra weight. The tying silk should be used to produce an under-body with a gentle uniform taper. The tips from three reddish brown cock pheasant tail fibres are tied in to form the tail. The fibres should then be wound round the shank to form the body, ensuring that they do not overlap to maintain the slim profile. Finally, the body is ribbed with about six turns of fine copper wire. There is no hackle.

Copper John

Copper John.

We know very little about the origins of this fly, which was given to Alan 'One-Pool' Williams and Andrew Donaldson by one of George Anderson's guides on a float trip down the Yellowstone river. It did so well, that Alan gave the guide a generous $50 tip and the end of the day on behalf – he thought – of both of them. So, it appeared on the drive to the motel, had Andrew! The immediate language was colourful, the subsequent Mickey-taking from JD and Graham Knowles merciless – and the reception for the English party in the shop the next day especially friendly.

Alan gained his nickname by catching six good cutthroats out of the same pool on Slough Creek, and that evening he tied copies for the whole party. With few exceptions, it was the only nymph that all four anglers used to great effect on various rivers and spring creeks for the following ten days. It is a superb and consistent nymph, with just the right amount of weight to trail a couple of feet below a size 12 or 10 Royal Wulff (for example), without pulling the sighter fly beneath the surface.

A normal shank size 12-16 hook, such as a Drennan Wet Fly Supreme, is a good all-round option, with a small (up to 2 mm) gold head. The tail consists of two brown goose biots, angled at about 30 degrees to each other. The abdomen comprises closely wound fine copper wire, though a slightly thicker diameter may be appropriate when added weight is required. The thorax, which is about one third the length of the abdomen, consists of peacock herl with a flash-back of medium pearl tinsel. A few whisks of speckled partridge fibres extend from the head of the fly on either side, sloping downwards along about half the body. It is easier to tie these in, projecting forwards, before forming the thorax, and then to fold them backwards with the final winding of tying silk. Finally, a blob of thick Superglue or epoxy on top of the thorax allows the pearl to shine through in a very 'insecty' manner.

The Copper John is essentially a fancy version of the well-known Brassie, which on many occasions is probably equally as effective. Certainly, the fly works well without its partridge fibres after hooking a few trout. But the Copper John has caught so many fish for us, that for reasons of confidence and possibly nostalgia, we have never bothered experimenting with any further simplifications.

Gold-Headed Royal Prince

Gold-Headed Royal Prince.

This is a popular fly in the rocky streams of the western USA, and one that we would often try on arrival at any new stretch of water that might contain stoneflies. Although it has many stonefly features, it is sufficiently non-specific to perform as a general pattern. Not knowing what else to start with, JD used it on his first evening on the Beaverhead and took three good brown trout in an hour. 'But they don't work here', replied a surprised local expert, who had caught the same number of fish on the 'correct' patterns. 'That's why we never use it.' The logic should really have been the other way round. It worked during the next day too, and subsequently and consistently in English rivers for browns and rainbows. The first time that we tried it on the River Test, it accounted for a magnificent brown of over 4 lb that would never have seen a stonefly in its life.

Typically, the fly is tied on a size 10 hook, with a normal to slightly long shank. It is weighted by a single layer of closely packed lead wire coils and a gold bead at the head. There is a blood red silk collar behind the bead, which provides a trigger point, and a straightforward peacock herl body that is the foundation of many successful nymph patterns. Two brown goose biots project behind the fly at an angle of about 40 degrees to each other to form a tail. This is suggestive of a stonefly, but the overall impression is one of an edible,

non-specific nymph. Two white goose biots lie along the top of the fly, and are splayed out slightly to just beyond the end of the body. They suggest the wings of an emerging adult, but they also provide another good trigger point.

Improved (MC and JD)Killer Bug

The Killer Bug is another of Frank Sawyer's magnificent creations. He designed it specifically to catch grayling, but it will take more than its fair share of trout. Old it may be, but like his Pheasant Tail it is still one of the best nymphs in existence. It will work on lakes, but it is principally on rivers that it lives up to its name. This is because it is a slim, weighted nymph that will get down quickly through the currents.

The original pattern had a cigar-shaped body that is best suited to a normal shank size 12 hook, with the tapered end at  the tail. However, a size 14 Drennan sedge hook has a similar dimension and gives a much more seductive profile. Sawyer used an under-body of gold or copper wire, but fine lead wire is obviously preferable to obtain a slimmer body

Improved Killer Bug.

with the same ability to cut through strong currents. This can then be covered with a wire or tinsel of the appropriate colour. It is better to leave the tail-end of the fly unleaded in order to obtain a slim tapered effect.

Many references omit the most important feature of the original Chadwick's 477 wool. (A good modern substitute is Anchor Tappisserie Wool-Laine shade 9674.) There is nothing magic about the colour itself, and if simply wound around the shank it will create a very ordinary grey-fawn fly in both appearance and performance. Its value lies in the translucency that allows the under-body to shimmer through when wet. In fact, it is quite difficult to discern the existence of any wool on the body when viewing a correctly tied pattern in the water. It is therefore essential that only one strand of wool is used, or the under-body will be obliterated. It may also be worth teasing out the wool slightly before winding it in touching turns without any overlap. A fine gold or silver wire ribbing, to match the under-body, completes the fly and ensures the thin layer of wool remains in position.

The under-body shimmers through the wool more enticingly with flat gold or silver tinsel in place of the original copper or gold wire. The silver version bears a striking resemblance to a nymph in an air-filled shuck, whereas its gold counterpart exhibits an enticing, life-suggesting glow. Since it will only become apparent when the wool is wet, it is advisable to test the first fly at the bench in a glass of water to avoid tying lots of useless ones. It may be sacrilege, but like Sawyer's other famous nymph, this pattern often benefits from the addition of a gold or silver head. This can be a wrapping of flat tinsel or a small (2 mm) bead.

Scrimp (MC and JD)

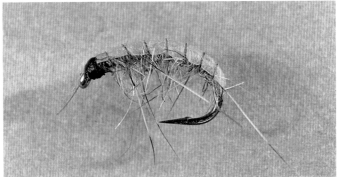

Scrimp.

Although this is a specific imitation of a shrimp or scud, depending on which side of the Atlantic you happen to be, such Crustacea are so common that they merit serious consideration at any time. Moreover, they are perfect for heavyweight patterns since the arch-shaped back will accept a great deal of lead without distorting the shape of the natural nymph. Many sizes are possible to match a wide range of natural shrimps, and we always carry a supply in the range 12 to 16 on short-shank hooks. The hooking power of this, and many other shrimp patterns, benefits from a wide gape in relation to its size. Even with such a hook, we will dress the fly short – a size 12 body, for example, on a size 10 hook. We learned this lesson from bitter experience after losing too many trout and grayling.

For unweighted patterns, it is easiest to use a curved hook to match the natural profile, but for many rivers the pattern will benefit from some additional weight. This goes on the top of the shank, thereby not compromising the hooking efficiency by reducing the gape. A conventionally shaped hook is therefore more appropriate. It is better to build up layers of lead foil on top of the shank, which are progressively shorter and wider, than to try to cram lead wire into an arched profile. Apart from the ease of the operation, the foil technique allows the lead to be more closely packed without any unwanted air gaps which will slow down the descent of the fly in the water.

We believe that this pattern scores over many of its rivals for two reasons. The first is the mixture of furs – 50% spiky rabbit and 50% fiery red SLF – which is teased out to imitate the legs. A red or orange tint is strictly only appropriate to the mating season, but this pattern seems to work almost as well in the winter. This is presumably due to the natural attraction to colours at the red end of the spectrum. A fine gold wire rib completes the fur body before tying in the second key feature – a translucent, contoured back.

Materials such as polythene lack life and realism, but a strip from a surgical glove in its place will transform the fly. A surgical glove has just the right amount of translucency rather than being totally transparent and lifeless. Moreover, it is flexible and will therefore take on a more realistic profile when ribbed with fine nylon or gold or copper wire. Note that it is the diameter of

Grayling – the lady of the stream.

the nylon that matters, not the breaking strain, and 5X is ideal for a size 12 fly. It is essential to ensure that there is a reasonable thickness of fur between the lead under-body and the surgical strip. Apart from achieving the correct colour for the back, it incorporates a soft base under the strip that allows the rib to create a contoured profile. This actually achieves segmentation, rather than simply suggesting it.

Czech Nymphs

Czech Nymph.

The Czechs are masters at fishing fast-flowing rivers, and proved it by winning the World Championship in 1996. There is no single pattern that deserves special mention, but it is worth describing imitations of the free-swimming caddis to illustrate the important features.

First, although their patterns are heavy to get down in the fast currents, they are also remarkably slim. Apart from the increased realism that this imparts, there is less drag in the water to slow down the descent. One trick is to use lead wire with a square rather than round cross-section, because the latter leaves quite a few empty pockets of air between the coils. You can achieve this by cutting strips of lead from a wine bottle top.

The immediate impression given by a free-swimming caddis larva is one of a long curvaceous creature, so it is advisable to tie the patterns on rounded size 12 or 10 hooks. The fur body needs to be slim, and although some teasing is necessary for translucency, it should be minimal. From our experiences, seal's fur (or substitute) in pale amber and light olive, and fur from the root of a hare's ear, are all successful body materials. Many patterns have a pink or orange thorax, but this is optional. It is certainly a good idea to use spiky rabbit next to the head to provide some contrast and give a suggestion of the legs. Ribbing, to provide segmentation, should be a fine wire in clear water, but in coloured conditions a flat gold tinsel will provide added attraction.

In common with our Scrimp, the back is formed from a strip of a surgical glove and ribbed with nylon of about 5X diameter. This gives a very realistic contoured profile. Caddis larvae tend to have dark backs and light under-bodies, so the surgical glove needs to be coloured with a waterproof pen. We prefer to do this on the underside where it is less prone to be washed off by the high flows of water. Rich brown is a good choice.

Green and Orange Woven Nymph (MC and JD)

Green and Orange Woven Nymph.

This all-round nymph seems to represent various food items, such as shrimp and free-swimming caddis, and combines two of the most consistent fish-catching colours in one pattern. The multi-stranded silks for the woven body can be purchased from any haberdashery shop. Suitable shades, for example, are Anchor 844 in medium olive for the back and Anchor 314 medium orange for the belly. Strips of lead wire along the sides and back produce a flattened profile, which twists in the water and fishes upside down to present an eye-catching morsel to the trout. Use of a grub-shaped hook, such as a size 10 or 12 Kamasan B110, adds to the enticement. A sparse beard hackle of speckled brown or grey partridge provides some movement in the legs. The fly works with or without a gold head on all types of river.

NYMPHS PRINCIPALLY FOR STILL WATER

The following nymphs have proved themselves consistently over a wide range of still waters. They include representations of insects, such as midges, damsels and cased caddis larvae, that tend to be more abundant in lakes than rivers. Some rely on hackle or wing movements, which often play a crucial role in enticing still-water trout.

Diawl Bach

Diawl Bach variations.

This is a Welsh fly meaning 'Little Devil', pronounced Dee-owl Bark, which has been usurped unashamedly by the English. Many consider it to represent a midge with the shuck attached, but rather perversely it usually works best when allowed to sink through the water rather than as surface fly. Perhaps it has a bit of everything in its make-up – midge and caddis pupa, beetle, shrimp and general larva.

The Diawl Bach can be fished at any speed providing it is somewhere between dead-slow and snail's pace. Too many fishermen have discarded it because they simply cannot condition themselves to fish it slowly enough. It is an ideal point fly on a floating line, or a pattern for any position on a sinking line. For a hedged bet tactic, there is no better all-round nymph for placing on the dropper when fishing an attractor on a sinking line. A Booby is an enticing companion because its buoyancy assists the nymph to move seductively in the water.

There are few flies that are as simple to tie, providing you can resist the temptation to make it too bushy. One strand of peacock herl is twisted around the straight section of the hook to form a very slim body. The body should be short, and a heavyweight sproat hook, such as a Kamasan B175, in a size 10 is ideal. The curving profile allows the long, thin tail of light red-brown cock hackle fibres to project clear of the hook shank. Remembering that the tail may represent a shuck, the fibres are best kept together rather than being allowed to splay out. The false beard hackle fibres of the same material should also be kept together.

There are several variations on the basic pattern. The use of a fine red or green holographic tinsel for the ribbing, on a size 12 hook such as a Drennan Wet Fly Supreme, is sometimes devastatingly effective. Another favourite, on a size 12-14 hook, has a red silk head and a fine red wire ribbing to suggest segmentation, although we prefer Neil West's use of fluorescent white twinkle for the rib. This suggests the air bubble associated with corixae and emerging nymphs.

Cruncher (MC and JD)

Cruncher.

We invented this fly many years ago in an attempt to improve on existing Pheasant Tail patterns, and concentrated on two key areas. First, for the body, we used fibres from the lightest cock pheasant centre tails. There is quite a large variation in the colours of these feathers, and fly tiers usually reject the lighter specimens since they lack the rich, reddish brown tints. However, if you tie a body with the light feather you will notice an impressively realistic effect of segmentation that requires no additional ribbing.

Second, we used a full Greenwell's hen hackle and tied it in such as way as to produce a 'kick'. This technique forces the base of the hackle to stand almost at right angles to the hook by butting it against the thorax. Being soft and mobile, the remainder of the hen hackle moves backwards as the fly twitches through the water, before kicking back as the line is relaxed. This kicking motion can trigger a reaction from the trout, and adds that extra bit of enticement while still retaining the natural features of a nymph. It is not surprising that a slow 'sink and draw' retrieve is usually the most successful.

The Cruncher quickly proved itself superior to many other patterns when the trout were preoccupied with tiny smuts on the surface of Chew Valley Lake. Such fish can be notoriously difficult to catch, but on this occasion it took eight trout in under an hour. From then onwards we tried it in all sorts of situations, and it has turned out to be a superb all-rounder. We gave the pattern to Jeremy Herrmann, who subsequently became the world fly fishing champion in 1995, and he quickly realized how good it was. He frequently asks for more, preferring 'our genuine articles to his inferior copies'. In truth he is trying to save himself the effort, but flattery will get him everywhere.

The Cruncher can be used as a heavyweight size 10 version on the point, but it is at its most deadly as a size 12 or 14 emerger pattern on a lightweight hook. Perversely, the heavy version tends to work better for trout that are preoccupied with surface smuts since the 'plop' as it lands on the surface helps to distract them.

The long tail of honey cock hackle fibres represents a shuck, but it improves the fly also at depth. The body is formed by winding three or four light cock pheasant centre tail fibres in the normal way along about two thirds of the shank. The use of too many fibres makes the fly unnaturally bulky. A fine silver wire ribbing, wound in the opposite direction to the body, prevents any fibres which might break in use from unwinding. Un-protected pheasant tail fibres easily disintegrate when they are crunched by a trout's teeth.

The peacock herl thorax needs to be slightly bulky at the eye of the hook so that the soft hen hackle can butt against it. You can achieve the right thickness by twisting two strands of herl together. The black colour in the Greenwell's hen hackle should extend along half the length of the fibres. (This combination usually occurs in the tip of the feather.) The dark centre blends in naturally with the dark peacock herl thorax, while the lighter ends provide contrast and mobility.

Monty

Monty.

Many of the general, still-water nymph patterns in this chapter are good choices when the fish are in the mood for feeding. When they are 'switched off', for whatever reason, there is a need to provoke them into action. Lures such as the Viva are obvious choices, but often something a little closer to their natural food is necessary. The Montana Nymph fits the bill exactly as a nymph that also packs a punch.

Irrespective of any original intention or naturally occurring species, Montana nymphs are widely used as non-specific patterns. There is enough generality in the fly to suggest the nymphs of dragonflies, stoneflies, damselflies, caddis and perhaps others. Its qualities are enhanced by the undoubted attraction of black and yellow or green to the trout, and providing this is not overdone, it still maintains a sufficiently natural profile to suggest food rather than danger.

Montana nymphs have been around for years, but this tying by Dave Grove is the best one that we have encountered. Dave is one of the best all-round fly fishermen on river and lake, and he will never go anywhere without his beloved 'Monty'.

Monty should be fished on the point with a very, very slow retrieve, since the fly will produce its own attraction with very little stimulus from an angler. One of its main attractions is its ability to catch fish that have become well spooked from repeated angling pressure. Although not designed for the purpose, it also makes an excellent top dropper fly for taking trout on the lift with a sinking line.

Large versions will often work well, but you might as well use a Viva. It is for the more 'testy' conditions that the Montana Nymph comes into its own. With this in mind, the most suitable all-round hook for catching difficult trout is a long-shank size 12. The sparse tail is about 10 mm long and uses the soft and highly mobile fur from a black zonker rabbit. The abdomen gradually tapers along its length, achieving its smooth profile from black SLF Finesse which is much finer than conventional furs. Medium silver wire forms the ribbing. The insect green SLF Finesse thorax is palmered with two to three turns of a soft black cock or black hen hackle under a pheasant tail wing case. This produces an enticing black and green pulsation in the water. (Note that the original Montana Nymph has a yellow thorax.) One trick is to wind a little bit of lead wire under the thorax so that Monty dives between the gentle pulls on the line.

Langford Damsel (MC and JD)

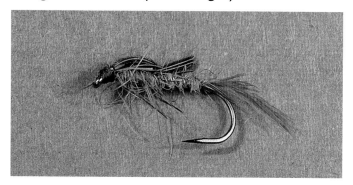

Langford Damsel.

Paul Knight runs a small fishery near the village of Steeple Langford in rural Wiltshire. There is a choice of fishing in this delightful area between a twenty acre lake and a mile stretch of the River Wylye. It is here that we have developed many fishing tactics from practical experience on the water and (of course) an essential analysis with Paul in the pub at lunch time. The Langford Damsel arose from Paul's conviction that a good general nymph pattern could work as well as many of the Nobblers than many locals were using exclusively at the time. Since developing it for Langford, it has worked in all sorts of waters throughout the world – whether damsel nymphs exist there or not. Moreover, it lies about half-way between the more imitative patterns and the Montana Nymph in its ability to pack a punch.

As its name suggests, the fly copies a damsel nymph on a size 12 or 10 long shank hook. A lightweight hook is perfect for imitating the natural, but as a general pattern the fly works very well at depth on a heavy hook or when additionally weighted with an under-body of lead wire. You will recall that green is a good general colour, and this pattern has caught lots of trout that would never have encountered a natural damsel nymph. Part of the secret of the fly's success is in the body colour which is a 75/25 mix of medium green olive and yellow seal's fur (or substitute). The yellow seems to give the fly that bit of extra life.

The tail consists of fibres of zonker rabbit fur, dyed to the same colour, which imparts a natural movement. The body is progressively tapered along two thirds of the shank and ribbed with a fine oval gold tinsel. Copper and fine flat ribbing work just as well. The wing case uses about eight fibres from a cock pheasant centre tail which are tied over a thorax of the same fur as the body. The thorax is more bulky and is teased out extensively. This gives a blurred impression of moving legs which certainly seems to pass the trout's inspection test.

Apart from imitating the natural damsel nymph on its journey to the shore, we fish it in two different ways. The heavier version makes a good point fly. The lightweight version is a good choice to fish on a leader in conjunction with other lightweight nymphs or emergers. Irrespective of depth, it performs best when moved slowly through the water, either with a figure-of-eight retrieve or with long slow draws.

Superglue Buzzer

This family of patterns represents a thinly dressed midge pupa, which is sealed by an application of Superglue. This keeps out water so that the fly will sink rapidly in conjunction with a fluorocarbon leader. They tend to work best in clear, open water where they are visible as realistic nymphs from a good distance and where a team of three flies can span a wide range of depths. A large range of successful variations exists, incorporating many colours from drab silk to sparkling red holographic tinsel. The principle we favour is to use a subdued colour scheme that a trout will find hard to reject, with the addition of a fluorescent trigger point which can increase catch rates substantially.

Superglue Buzzer variations.

The hook is quite important. A Kamasan B110, in sizes 10 and 12, has a good curved shape that makes the fly appear more alive than conventional patterns. It also has just about the right sink rate for most purposes. In spite of their name, the Drennan Sedge hooks are superbly shaped for buzzer representations. Normally, they are too light for the point fly, but are serious options for a dropper or for when the trout are higher in the water. The best tactic is to cover a range of depths.

There has been so much activity in developing minor variations to the same basic theme that several anglers often legitimately claim to have invented the same fly. One of the most consistent, which Paul Wakeham developed, consists of a black silk body with a fine silver rib. The black silk thorax has a couple of cheeks of Glo-Brite Number 4 silk that produces quite subdued wing buds. The real trigger comes from a very thin band of Glo-Brite Number 5 silk between the body and thorax. At the bench, this silk band should be just visible to prevent too much of an unnatural impact in the water.

Andy Hancock's pattern uses alternate bands of black and yellow flexi-floss and a plain black thorax. (Yellow flexi-floss on top of a black silk body produces a similar effect.) This produces a stunningly effective green and black buzzer when submerged. We have also had great success when adding the Glo-Brite trigger point and wing buds to this pattern.

Sometimes, a Superglue with Glo-Brite trigger points acts as a tremendous attractor fly that is ideally suited to the top dropper. Martin Introna produced the ultimate pattern for this tactic using Glo-Brite Number 5 throughout the entire fly with a fine pearly rib. We can vouch for its tremendous success – sometimes! The same tactic will often keep fish away from the whole team, so be prepared to change tactics quickly if there is no response.

Another highly successful pattern was created by Graham Knowles. The abdomen and thorax both use red floss silk, which becomes a deep crimson colour after adding the glue. The abdomen is ribbed with fine silver wire, and the thorax has wing buds formed from two strands of Glo-Brite Number 8 silk.

There is also a slim Glo-Brite Number 5 collar between the abdomen and thorax. This fly needs treating with caution, because sometimes the two sets of trigger points are too much for wary trout. Nevertheless, it brought us phenomenal success on the North Island lakes of New Zealand, producing savage takes from a large number of wild trout in the 5–10 lb class. One of the top local guides gave it a try after he saw the success it was bringing us, and it proceeded to transform his day's fishing.

One of our most consistent patterns for the more wary trout comprises an abdomen of red and white Flexi-floss. The black thorax, which is slightly thicker, has wing buds on both sides formed from two strands of Glo-Brite Number 4 silk. These extend from the top of the eye to the base at the back of thorax. There are also small white wool breather filaments projecting from the front.

Ideally, Superglues need to be fished statically on a floating line. It is a good idea to watch the curve in the line below the rod tip for two reasons. First, maintaining this curve in the line helps to ensure that the fly is not being moved. Second, trout will sometimes take the fly so gently that the line will twitch slightly without any feel. When fishing from a drifting boat, it is important to compensate only for the boat's motion. One trick is to use a slow-sinking line with a Superglue on a dropper and a buoyant fly, such as a Booby or Suspender, on the point. This produces a slow and reasonably natural descent, which covers a range of depths.

Nevertheless, we have caught a lot of fish when moving Superglues during a rise to keep them respectably high in the water. When conditions call for an intermediate sinking line and the trout are tuned into buzzers, we will often put one on the middle dropper. Sinking line tactics often revolve around the top dropper or point fly. You can therefore leave the Superglue in the middle and forget about it – until it reminds you of its presence by taking a respectable number of trout.

OB's Worm (MC and JD)

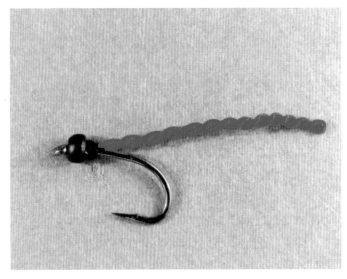

OB's Worm.

There are plenty of patterns to represent the many forms of worms, but this is one of our favourites which caught several large wild trout in New Zealand. It also hooked the enormous specimen described in the section on float tubes, which gives the essential clue to its name.

The pattern employs flexi-floss, which has the twin features of being elastic and translucent. We have had most success with red floss, but you can obviously choose any colour to suit the local species. Take a single strand, about three inches long, and (using two hands) grip each end between the finger and thumb. Then continue to twist the floss at one end until a double helix forms in the middle. When this is about an inch long, tie the two free strands (i.e. not the looped end) down securely at the head of the fly with black silk. In deep water, the fly benefits from a small tungsten black head, which also imparts a diving motion.

Stick Fly

Stick Fly variations.

The Stick Fly was probably not intended to be a general pattern, since it is a direct imitation of a cased caddis larva. The body comprises two or three strands of peacock herl, twisted around each other and then wound on to a long-shank hook, such as a Kamasan B830, in the size range 10 to 14. Although there is no visible segmentation on the cased larva, it is advisable to use a fine copper rib to strengthen the fragile fibres. A couple of turns of a red-brown cock hackle, just behind the eye, represent the busily working legs that manoeuvre the insect in its search for prey.

Since caddis are such a universally abundant source of food, the Stick Fly is a 'must' for the fly box anywhere in the world – but it also works in water that does not contain any natural larvae. Versions tied on normal shank hooks, such as a Drennan Wet Fly Supreme, are consistently successful. The Stick Fly will work over a range of depths, but ideally it is a point fly for fishing well below the surface. Weighted patterns are appropriate to lakes as well as rivers. Whether the intention is to represent a caddis larva or not, the retrieve should be kept as slow as possible.

The most common variation is a short tag of a suitable shade of fluorescent green wool, such as Phosphor Yellow or (in clear water) Signal Green. This will often convert an excellent pattern into a great one. Fluorescent red or orange tags provide good alternatives. We prefer to wrap a band of fluorescent silk around the hook in place of the wool since this increases the visibility.

Some anglers wrap the fluorescence around the throat instead of the tail. All these variations have proved themselves time and time again. In one form or another, it is deservedly the first choice of point fly for many still water anglers, and has been for the last few decades.

Sheep Creek

Sheep Creek.

This is a popular American pattern that Tim Tollett showed us in New Zealand. On the lakes there, he used virtually nothing else – and with good reason. When fished virtually statically, it represents a range of food items including caddis, damsels and snails. It is sometimes referred to as Biggs's Special, after its creator George Biggs.

The body consists of fine dark olive-green chenille. This is a dead-ringer for peacock herl, but is more robust. Perversely, the hackle, which comprises a couple of turns of a red-game cock feather, is tied at the back of the fly. Apart from this reversal of position, the pattern differs from a Stick Fly by having four to six strands of a grey mallard flank feather from the head extending over the body. This provides an added dimension that is characteristic of snails.

Hare's Ear Nymphs

Nymphs produced using the fur from a hare's ear form an in-tegral part of fly fishing in all types of water. The original **Gold-Ribbed Hare's Ear** was created in 1880 and still holds its own against modern patterns. Classically it represents the nymphs of upwinged flies, but it will also perform well as a midge pupa imitation. It is simplicity itself to tie. The body comprises dark, spiky fur from a hare's ear to form a tapered body which explodes into life at the (well teased) thorax. Three of the spiky strands are tied in first to form the tail. The rib consists of a few turns of fine flat gold tinsel. Normal sizes range from 12 to 16.

There are lots of variations possible on this basic pattern. These include dyed green-olive or golden olive fur which may be more characteristic of the prevailing species. We also tend to use spiked rabbit in place of hare's ear. We christened one of our favourite variations the **Banker**, quite simply because that it what it often turns out to be. It is a nymph that is always likely to deceive a trout. In still waters, we will often place it on the middle dropper and leave it there all day while experimenting with the point and bob flies. In rivers it provides a good member for a team of downstream wet flies.

Banker.

The Banker incorporates the advantages of a spiky rabbit body ribbed with fine gold oval tinsel. It also adds a little extra movement from a soft grey partridge hackle and a little extra zest from a modicum of fluorescence in the tail. The trick with a partridge hackle is to tie in the tip rather than the root of the feather at the head of the fly, thereby using the shortest fibres. Even then, the fibres tend to be too long for any hook smaller than a size 14. A size 12 is the perfect hook for this pattern.

The fluorescence must not detract from the realism of the fly, and for that reason we use only two short and very fine lengths of silk – one Phosphor Yellow and the other Arc Chrome. (To obtain silk that is fine enough, you may have to separate the strands.) The golden rule is to select some silk that worries you because it might be too thin, and then halve its diameter! In the fly box the fluorescent tail may hardly be visible, but in the water it converts a good pattern into a great one.

Iridescent Terror (MC and JD)

Beetles are an important source of food in many different waters, as are drowned terrestrial insects. Tom Ivens's Black and Peacock Spider is an excellent general fly for this purpose, since peacock herl has the right combination of colours. However, we have exploited modern materials to create a much stronger impression of iridescence than was achievable in the past.

A mixture of one part of dark green SLF to three parts of black seal's fur (or substitute) produces an effect that is very suggestive of beetles and terrestrial insects. This forms a slightly

Iridescent Terror.

chubby body on a size 12 hook. After ribbing with a fine flat pearly tinsel, a very thin and teased-out layer of the same body mixture is wound over the body. This partially obscures the pearly rib, so that its iridescence shimmers through the fur. We normally complete the fly with one turn of a crimson hen hackle. This imitates the red head of the common house-fly, but also adds some movement and a touch of contrast.

Clifton (MC and JD)

Clifton.

The Christmas Tree Lure is a remarkably good pattern, which seems to have a bit of everything and catches trout over a wide range of conditions throughout the season. We developed the Clifton as a scaled-down version of this famous lure for when the trout grow wary of the more precocious patterns. It is really a bridge between a lure and a nymph. We christened it one day after crossing the Clifton Suspension Bridge on our way back from Chew Valley Lake. It had just taken a dozen large trout.

The peacock herl body, on a size 10 or 12 hook, is characteristic of many nymphs such as the Stick Fly or Diawl Bach. For the same reason, it is ribbed with gold wire rather than the more flashy flat gold tinsel. There is a very short Phosphor Yellow tag, and a small fluorescent Fire Orange head. The wing is just a few strands of black marabou. If you tie one, and think about discarding it because it has lost just about all of its wing and most of its sparkle, then you have probably got the combination just right. Cast it into the water, bring it back with a slow and varied retrieve, and hang on to your rod.

Gerald's Midge (MC and JD)

Gerald's Midge.

We christened this fly in remembrance of MC's late fishing friend, Gerald Houghton. It incorporates a thorax with a 50/50 mix of orange and brown seal's fur (or substitute) that sparkles with life to suggest an emerging adult. Cock pheasant centre tail fibres form a wing case on top of the thorax. Its long tail of ginger cock fibres gives a good impression of the empty shuck that is being discarded as the adult escapes. Strictly speaking therefore, it ought to perform best when suspended in the surface film. There are two ways to achieve this. First, you can add a CDC shuttlecock, in place of the pheasant tail wing case. Second, you can add floatant to the thorax and tease it out. This will allow the fly to hang in the surface film in tricky flat calm conditions, where it is less likely to be rejected than a shuttlecock CDC. It may also keep the fly up that little bit longer in rough water after casting to a rising fish.

Although these two tactics work, we use this fly most of the time as a conventional nymph just below the surface. It may not grip the surface film, but it works very well – providing it does not sink too far. There is little doubt that it gives a better account of itself when tied on to a lightweight hook. It needs a slow retrieve such as a figure-of-eight or long slow draws, but also works very well when static. You can exploit this by tying it on the middle dropper between two dry flies when it will not sink more than a few inches. Your eyes will naturally rest on the visible dries, and it comes as quite a pleasant surprise when the line tightens before you see anything happen above the surface.

Our favourite colours are claret and a very pale green olive – almost a pale watery – both ribbed with a fine gold wire. It is important to tie the fly with a very slim body. If you are not initially worried that the fly might be too slim, then you have probably tied it too thickly. When midge pupae are on the menu, we stay faithful to at least one of these colours throughout the entire day. When upwinged flies are present, a hare's ear or rabbit body with a stretched pearly rib works very well. A good friend of ours, Bryan Archer, uses a barred teal feather for the tail of the hare's ear pattern with considerable success, adding that little bit of contrast that gives a good imitation of a shuck.

Caretaker (MC and JD)

Caretaker.

The Caretaker covers a range of emerging nymphs, and requires a lightweight size 12 hook. The jungle cock cheeks over the sides of the thorax provide a superb trigger point. They also suggest features such as wing cases, gas bubbles and breather tubes. Fur from the root of a hare's ear, or spiky rabbit, gradually tapers from nothing, at the back-end of the shank, into a thorax bursting with life. Fine flat silver ribbing touches at the tail and then progressively opens towards the thorax. This attracts trout in bright conditions and produces savage takes.

SLF Emerger

SLF Emerger.

Davy Wotton gave us some of these patterns that he developed for capitalizing on the 'aura of translucency' when a pupa is high in the water. A caddis was the ideal choice due to its striking variety of colours, natural translucency and the gas bubbles trapped within the pupal case. Moreover, a caddis offers a very tasty mouthful (a size 10 or 12 hook is ideal), and is a major source of food. The SLF Emerger is a superb fish catcher when retrieved with a sink and draw or steady figure-of-eight just beneath the surface. It will take rising trout, that do not have to be feeding on caddis, under a wide range of conditions. In heavy still-water hatches, it pays to increase the speed of retrieve. In rivers, takes will often occur on the lift at the end of the drift.

According to Davy, the pattern creates the 'translucency from within' by the split-thread dubbing technique described in the section on *Fly Tying to Catch Fish*. It incorporates a light tying thread and his own SLF dubbing in typically 'sedgy' colours, such as insect green or cinnamon. Ribbing is unnecessary to secure the body with this dubbing technique, and it would have the undesired effect of compressing the body. After tying in the dubbing, cut out a 12 mm strip of straw-coloured raffene and trim the trailing edge into a curve. Moisten it and then hold it centrally over the body so that the curved edge lines up with the back end of the body. The raffene will turn around the back and sides of the body when it is tied in position – about 2 mm from the eye of the hook. When in the water, the raffene sheath traps air to imitate the natural pupa's gas bubbles.

Three turns of a red-brown hen hackle slope back along the body. Alternatively, you can use a brown partridge hackle with the fibres drawn down and back to imitate the trailing legs. A darker coloured head (e.g. dark brown) is formed with a standard dubbing technique. At this point you can tie in two long antennae of brown mallard feathers trailing back along the body, although this does not seem to make the fly any more effective.

PALMERED SURFACE FLIES (Principally Lakes)

Palmered surface patterns make good bob flies in still water to attract upward looking trout. They sometimes work when there is no surface life, but they are obviously more imitative during a rise to buzzers or caddis, for example. As a rule of thumb, they need half a dozen turns of stiff, bushy hackles in rough water on a size 10, and a couple sparse soft hackles in a light ripple on a size 12 or 14. The softer hackled versions will often work when fished below the surface on a slow-sinking line, or as downstream wet flies in rivers.

Soldier Palmer

This is the classic top dropper fly for still waters containing midge and caddis. Body colours should match the natural insects, but in the absence of such pointers they should vary from scarlet to dark crimson, depending on whether the water is coloured or clear.

Hook: 10 to 14 normal shank
Body: Red seal's fur or substitute, teased out slightly

Soldier Palmer.

Rib:	Fine gold oval tinsel
Tail:	Optional short red tag which may be fluorescent in coloured water
Palmer:	Light red-brown (3 turns in a light ripple to 6 or more turns in a big wave)
Hackle:	Light red-brown (none in a light ripple to 6 in a big wave)

Ogborne's Fancy

Ogborne's Fancy.

Chris Ogborne's variation of the Soldier Palmer has caught so many fish for us in varied conditions and depths that it merits special mention. It has quite a few turns of hackle, but being from a soft hen feather they are not out of place in a light ripple. The fluorescent tag stands out in coloured water, but being short, it is not too severe in clear water in conjunction with the subdued body colour.

Hook: 10 normal shank
Body: Dark crimson seal's fur or substitute, teased out slightly
Rib: Fine gold oval tinsel
Tail: Short fire orange silk
Palmer: 4 turns of a hen Greenwell's
Hackle: 5 turns of a hen Greenwell's

Wingless Wickham's

Wingless Wickham's.

This variation of the traditional Wickham's Fancy provides a suitable alternative to the Soldier Palmer when fish are responding to flash. This response often occurs in bright conditions, but may also take place in the evening. It is also a very respectable imitation for small fry. A dark brown hackle gives the right degree of contrast with the light body.

Hook: 10 to 14 normal shank
Body: Flat rich gold tinsel
Rib: Fine gold oval tinsel
Tail: None, although one or two eccentrics incorporate a pink tag
Palmer: Dark brown (3 turns in a light ripple to 6 or more turns in a big wave)
Hackle: Dark brown (none in a light ripple to 6 in a big wave)

Subdued Bibio

The Bibio takes its name from the black Heather Fly (*Bibio pomonae*). The red or orange middle to the body imitates the striking colour seen on the tops of the legs of the natural insect. Whenever Heather Flies are on the menu, a bright reddish-orange provides a fantastic, natural trigger point. We tend to place the coloured fur at the tail end of the fly rather than the

Subdued Bibio.

middle. This arguably gives the artificial fly a more balanced appearance.

The Bibio is an excellent general pattern whenever dark aquatic or terrestrial flies are on the menu. Crimson fur, in place of the brighter red or orange, makes it a very consistent all-round pattern. In fact, if we had to restrict ourselves to one artificial fly for 'terrestrial' waters, this could be the one.

Hook: 10 to 14 normal shank
Body: Black seal's fur or substitute, with a short length of crimson at the back end
Rib: Fine pearl tinsel, which gives more of a 'terrestrial sheen' than gold or silver
Tail: None
Palmer: Black (3 turns in a light ripple to 6 or more turns in a big wave)
Hackle: Black (none in a light ripple to 6 in a big wave)

Although traditionally used as a wet pattern, the Bibio has proved itself to be a fantastic dry fly on many occasions. It needs to stand proud of the water to imitate some terrestrial insects. This is best achieved by dispensing with the hackle at the front, and using a stiff, genetic hackle for the palmer. The palmer needs a short flue that does not protrude further from the body than the point of the hook.

Black Pearly Palmer

The pearly body of this fly gives it a green iridescence typical of beetles and some terrestrial insects. It is therefore a classic fly on waters where such items form an important source of food. It is more of a sub-surface pattern than the other palmered flies, and therefore uses a softer hackle.

Hook: 12 to 14 normal shank
Body: Green pearly tinsel
Rib: Fine silver wire

Black Pearly Palmer.

Tail: None
Palmer: 3 turns of a soft black cock hackle
Hackle: 2 turns of a soft black cock hackle

V1 (MC and JD and Chris Ogborne)

V1.

The Grenadier is a very popular top-dropper fly when orange coloured midges are hatching. At one time every man and his dog were using it on our local Chew Valley lake, so we decided to experiment with a few variations to try to give ourselves a bit of an edge. We numbered the variations (V) in numerical order (V1, V2, etc.), and set about experimenting.

We tied the first variation more out of curiosity than design. Its body comprised an equal mix of two contrasting fluorescent materials – DRF fire orange and phosphor yellow, ribbed with a fine oval gold tinsel. The only compromise to modesty was the use of a relatively short shank size 12 hook and a drab light ginger palmered hackle. When viewed in the water, the fly stood out in an incredibly vibrant manner due to the contrasting effects of the two bright colours. The hot orange cock hackle fibres in the tail, sloping slightly downwards on the sproat hook, added to its shocking effect.

It caught fish feeding on the natural midges, but it really flourished when the trout required a little encouragement to feed. When trout were preoccupied with small surface flies, three V1s ripped across the surface would be followed by one or more bow-waves in hot pursuit. Our V1 was the forerunner of many bright flies, such as the Peach Doll and Vindaloo, which can similarly distract preoccupied trout when more conventional methods fail.

Chris Ogborne once asked JD for a V1 after seeing how effective it was when boat fishing on Grafham. He later used the idea of mixed furs to develop a more subdued variation which also proved to be a real killer. (Unfortunately, he did not change the name which has led to some confusion.) The mix of furs comprises two parts hot (but not fluorescent) orange, one part mid-orange, two parts light brown and one part yellow. The mixture is tied very, very finely on a red tying thread – so finely that the red under-body is detectable when the fly is wet. The fine gold wire ribbing gives a faint suggestion of segmentation without interfering with the impact from the body. The overall effect is one of a fly full of life, and though it employs no fluorescence, it stands out for a considerable distance. The short and sparse honey hen hackle has only one turn at the head and a further two turns down the body. At one stage we used a red woollen tail, but now we prefer to use honey hen fibres since this gives a more subtle overall effect.

The subdued V1 is an ideal top dropper fly for use with a team of nymphs to provide a bit of added enticement. Sometimes a wary trout will reject it at the last second, only to tighten the line as it takes one of the nymphs below with total commitment. When fished slowly near the surface, trout tend to turn on it as if it were a dry fly. In fact, it is often quite successful as a dry fly in its own right.

TRADITIONAL WET FLIES

It is possible that many traditional wet flies were created principally for the gratification of the fly tier or the adornment of fly boxes. We also suspect that the wings on many patterns exist for the wrong reasons ('all flies must have wings!'), since most of a trout's sub-surface feeding is to wingless aquatic nymphs. You might, therefore, be forgiven for thinking that traditional wet flies have no place in a book on modern fly fishing techniques. However, there is one inescapable fact. Some of these old, 'fuddy duddy' creations will often surpass many of the most creative modern designs over a wide range of conditions.

Whether it arose by design or trial and error, the wing is actually a rather useful appendage. It gives a contrast between the top and underside of a fly – just like many naturally occurring nymphs or small fish. Soft feathers, such as bronze mallard or teal, add movement. The hump-backed effect may suggest wing cases or, close to the surface, the profile of a nymph as it is about to break out of its pupal case.

Every self-respecting traditional pattern has a tail – probably because the fly would have appeared improperly finished without one. But many nymphs and drowned adults have tails, as do small fish. The use of translucent fibres in the tail of a pattern also represents the empty pupal case during emergence. The front hackle, which is often a false beard rather than the full variety, gives a further degree of contrast along the underside of the fly. It can imitate the legs of a nymph or an emerging adult. It may also suggest the brighter body of the emerging adult fly or the moving gill cover of a small fish.

The message should now be ringing out loud and clear. Traditional flies, in the hands of an informed user, can suggest so many different forms of food that a single fly may cover a whole host of eventualities.

Silver Invicta (Principally Lakes)

Silver Invicta.

This fly is a popular variant of the original Invicta which was invented many years ago by James Ogden of Cheltenham to imitate a hatching sedge. When sedges are hatching, both versions can be pulled quickly across the surface of the water so that the palmered hackle simulates the motion of the scurrying adult. The best tactic is to experiment with different retrieves, including long draws and short, jerky pulls.

The Silver Invicta also works during a hatch of midge pupae. In this case a much slower retrieve is recommended – either long slow draws or a steady figure-of-eight. It will also take fry feeders, when it is best fished on a slow sinking line with variable retrieves. This simulates both a slow moving fry and one that is darting for cover in fear for its life.

It is truly a general pattern which can be fished anywhere on the leader – although out of choice we would place it on the point on a floating or intermediate line. We have never really been able to explain why it can vary from being absolutely deadly to a total flop. It is for this reason that we often refer to it as the Silver Enigma, but when it is working it has no equal. On many occasions it has taken fish after fish to the exclusion of everything else on the cast. It appears to be at its most deadly in bright conditions at the end of a daytime rise, possibly because the reflection of the sunlight on the silver body rekindles the trout's desire to feed. Whatever the reason, takes under such conditions tend to be unusually savage.

That is not the end of the story. Apart from representing a wide range of food, in bright conditions it may tempt surface-moving fish which appear to ignore all other offerings thrown at them. Under these circumstances, it is worth fishing a team of three Silver Invictas and experimenting with the retrieve.

The standard text book dressing comprises golden pheasant crest fibres for the tail, a silver tinsel body (in place of yellow seal's fur in the original Invicta) with a medium red game (i.e. red-brown) palmer, gold wire or oval ribbing (depending on the size) and a false hackle of blue jay. Flat pearly is an alternative to the silver body, although the standard version would always be our first choice in bright conditions. Some anglers argue that a nickel-plated hook improves the fly. You should not be tempted to use substitute feathers for the wing, since the hen pheasant centre tail gives a perfect contrast against the silver body and provides just the right amount of movement. If you wish you can produce a very sexy upturn in the tail by wetting the golden pheasant fibres and placing them inside a wine glass to dry – but it won't catch you any more fish!

Invictas are usually tied in the size range 10 to 14, depending as always on the natural fly (or fry) life, but a size 12 is a good overall compromise for general fishing.

White Sedge (MC and JD – Principally Lakes)

White Sedge.

This is only traditional in the tying, since we invented it as recently as 1980. The combination of the fluorescent white body and orange tail is perfect for attracting trout, while the conventional hen pheasant wing and palmer give it a very natural, 'sedgy' appearance.

Hook: 12 normal shank
Body: Fluorescent white wool, tied slimly
Palmer: 3 turns of dark red-brown cock
Rib: Fine gold wire
Hackle: 2 turns of dark red-brown cock
Wing: Hen pheasant centre tail
Tail: Hot orange cock hackle fibres

Dunkeld (Principally Lakes)

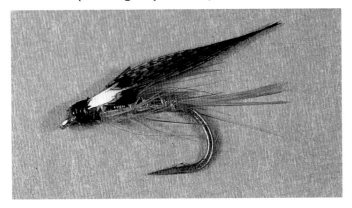

Dunkeld.

The Dunkeld takes its name from a small town in Scotland, and is one of the best known traditional flies. It was originally developed in a larger size for salmon fishing, but the smaller version has been shamelessly exploited for trout for a very long time. Most fishermen know about the fly, many have a couple in their fly boxes, but relatively few seem to appreciate what a really killing pattern it can be.

We have used it extensively over the last twenty years and experimented with it a great deal. Trial and error have convinced us that the pattern is much better suited to the intermediate and sinking lines rather than to the floater. It still works when fished near the surface of course – but so do many alternative patterns. On the sinker, it seems to have a special quality of catching fish under various conditions.

It was experiences with this fly that started us thinking that gold was a better body colour than silver in poor light conditions. The Dunkeld, at any rate, seems to perform better in coloured rather than gin-clear water. It has other features that help it to stand out under such conditions, notably the Jungle Cock cheeks and the orange beard hackle. All of these factors, although clearly visible, blend in such a natural way that it is unlikely to raise suspicions.

Its success at depth and its ability to 'stand out in a crowd' make it an ideal fly to use for daphnia-feeders. Other patterns may be more visible, but the educated trout may be more suspicious about taking them. In such situations we have often experimented with a Dunkeld on the middle dropper between two mini-lures, and it is not unknown for it to take half a dozen trout in a row. The Vindaloo or the Viva may attract the trout in the first place, but it is the Dunkeld that sometimes does the ultimate damage.

Trout feeding on midge pupa often find a Dunkeld irresistible.

To cover this eventuality, we prefer to use an eye feather from a more mature Jungle Cock cape since the older birds exhibit a very natural orange tinge. We have not found a substitute feather that achieves the same overall impression of life suggested by the genuine article. The golden body is a good representation of many caddis pupae, and the fly works tolerably well in copying a small fish. (We have even heard it argued that the Dunkeld can represent a small fish running off with a pupa in its mouth!) It is a complete sub-surface pattern which has just about everything.

It is small wonder that, when fishing the sinking line, we often put the fly on the middle dropper and leave it there all day. This is not because it necessarily works best in this position – it probably works best on the point – but it is much easier to change flies on the point without running into any problems with the length of the leader. Usually, we know from the start that this is one fly that we do not wish to substitute. It is not a fly that is ideally suited for the top dropper on a fast sinking line, where it will spend a proportionately greater amount of time on the initial descent and on the final lift. The Dunkeld seems to work best when moving with a level trajectory.

Our favourite hook is a normal shank size 10 on a reasonably heavy wire, such as a Drennan Wet Fly Supreme, to take it down. Sometimes we use a shorter shank size 8 (Drennan Traditional Wet) to increase the weight. The addition of lead to the hook shank can destroy the slim profile. Golden pheasant crest feathers provide the perfect translucent yellow tail. A bronze mallard wing gives mobility and a perfect contrast with the gold body, but it is quite acceptable to use dyed silver mallard as a cheaper substitute since it has the same mobility and a similar appearance. A rich gold tinsel gives a brighter appearance than gilt tinsels, and a ribbing of very fine gold wire helps to lengthen its life against trout's teeth. The hot orange beard hackle should not be splayed out excessively and should lie fairly close to the body to preserve the slim outline. Finally, we never use a palmered orange hackle, which so often appears on this fly. For sinking line fishing, at least, it seems to be detrimental.

Greenwell's (Rivers and Lakes)

Greenwell's.

Canon Greenwell once wrote in a letter to a friend that, at the age of 92, he had netted 100 trout in a season. He had at his disposal a superb dry fly pattern which he had inspired – even though it had actually been invented by James Wright of

Tweedside. Greenwell's Glory is still a good pattern, but it is the wet version that has pride of place in our fly boxes.

Classically it represents any olive-coloured upwinged fly on its ascent to the surface to hatch. It is therefore an excellent general pattern when fishing a team of downstream wet flies. It is one of our favourites on the Irish Loughs during a hatch of olives, where it is the perfect top dropper fly on a sink-tip or slow-sinking line in front of a drifting boat.

The wet Greenwell's can also be a superb fly when trout are feasting on small green midge pupae near the surface of still waters. Trout can be very difficult to catch under these conditions, but a single size 14 or 16 Greenwell's, moved very slowly on a long leader, will often do the trick quite nicely. This is a fly that will work consistently better in these smaller sizes in river or lake.

The most difficult part of the tying is the selection of the right colour of body silk. Traditional fly tiers used to run cobbler's wax over yellow silk to give a very realistic green/golden olive colour. We have tried this with other forms of wax, but never really come up with a colour that really looked the part. Fortunately, we once found a few spools of silk that came out to give a very natural looking fly – perhaps not as golden as the original but quite good enough. This silk only takes on the right colour when wet, so searching the shops and catalogues for a suitable shade may involve some trial and error. It is worth the effort. For reference, the photograph shows the fly with a wet body.

Otherwise, the dressing is very straightforward. A few turns of the finest gold wire rib suggest segmentation. The traditional wing consists of a translucent dun-coloured feather from a hen blackbird or starling, but CD is a good modern alternative. Fibres from a soft, light coloured Greenwell's hen cape provide the material for the tail and beard hackle. The black tips to the hackle should not be too long, and the base should be closer to honey than brown. It is better to use plain honey or ginger fibres than a hackle from an inappropriate Greenwell's cape.

SMALL FISH IMITATIONS

Many traditional wet patterns, such as the Butcher, Dunkeld and Silver Invicta, often work very well when trout are chasing small fry – as do some pretty non-descript nymphs like Pheasant Tails. There are also many purpose designed lures, including the Appetizer, Jack Frost and Jersey Herd, that are more appropriate for larger sizes, yet still remain effective on flies under an inch long. When trout are herding large numbers of fry, patterns that really stand out from the crowd have an advantage, for which the Light Bulb and Peach Doll remain firm favourites.

Sparklers

Modern materials that are both mobile and reflective have led to a series of fry imitations that often outscore their more conventional predecessors. This is because the wings stand out exceptionally well and, with care, can be tailored into good imitations of small fish. In this respect, it is advisable to tone

down the wing a little to give a more natural appearance. A good mix is pearl Lureflash Mobile with white marabou. Permutations abound, but a pattern using the same mix for the tail and an olive green Fritz body has proved itself to be very consistent.

Muddlers

Black Muddler.

The Muddler Minnow was originally devised in North America to imitate the sculpin minnow. We have caught the occasional sculpin when nymph fishing for trout. It is a small, ungainly looking fish that resembles the European bullhead (or miller's thumb). The original tying is therefore only relevant on waters where such fish provide an abundant source of food. There is no point in insisting on the precise original pattern on other waters, which form the great majority on a global perspective.

Muddlers derive most of their success from the way in which the spun deer's hair head disturbs the surface of rough water. It is a fantastic experience to see the bow wave of a chasing trout. They therefore make ideal bob flies, although they are also highly successful on the point where they will help to keep the dropper flies high in the water. It is always worth switching a Muddler from the bob to the point when follows are not translating into takes, since a fly will usually behave more naturally on the end of the leader. It is also important to experiment with the retrieve.

Muddlers also create extra disturbance on a sinking line. Sometimes trout are more responsive to disturbance below the surface than to visibility. It is a good pattern to place on a top dropper with a couple of more subdued wet flies or nymphs behind it.

There is no point in dwelling for too long on the large variety of individual variations. You simply need to tie the same size of conventional pattern on a slightly larger hook, and spin a deer's hair head on the spare section behind the eye. It is important to use a wide-gaped hook since the head may impair the hooking efficiency. Thus, you can create Soldier Muddlers, Wickham's Muddlers, Bibio Muddlers or whatever takes your fancy. In these cases, you are simply trying to add that extra disturbance to a conventionally palmered wet fly. The fly does not necessarily have to be palmered if the goal is natural imitation of a small fish rather than a skittering insect. Thus, many fry imitations, not to mention the original Muddler Minnow, have unpalmered bodies.

Muddlers are at their most killing in rough conditions where the head provides that all important wake. This does not necessarily mean that they will not work in calmer waters. We have sometimes found that they will continue to catch fish when the wind drops. Just as we are about to make a change to compensate for the conditions, another trout hammers into the Muddler. The only difference is that the fly has to be fished almost statically in calm water, whereas in a good wave it can be ripped through the water as well.

Oops!

CHAPTER 9

TRICKS OF THE TRADE

Catch and release of a big fish.

We decided to conclude the book with a few tips that did not seem to fit in with the main text. Nevertheless, they all contribute to a more effective, enjoyable or relaxed style of fishing.

Landing and Releasing Fish

When wading, be very careful while following a hooked trout along the stream. It is very easy to slip on a boulder or step into a deep gully. Make sure that there is no slack line off the reel, hold your rod high in the air, and then forget about the fish and concentrate on your own movements.

· · · · ·

Do not insert a landing net into the water until you have lifted the fish's head just above the surface. An otherwise beaten trout that sees a submerged net will often summon up enough energy to go on another run (see opposite).

· · · · ·

An old Scotsman once gave us some unusual but quite useful advice. 'Yev nay varnished ye net, Laddie.' Coating the mesh of a landing net with exterior grade polyurethane varnish prevents it from smelling (notably in a car) and from rotting. It also reduces the tendency of the net to roll over the frame when preparing to land a fish, and of hooks becoming embedded.

· · · · ·

When handling a fish, do not hold it tightly round the body. Big fish, in particular, are best held firmly by the tail. Keep it in the water, pointing upstream in a river, until it swims away under its own propulsion. You can accelerate the recovery by moving it forward through the water to increase the flow of water through its gills. After a long fight, always hold a lake-fish the right way up in the water until it swims away – otherwise it may sink upside down and not recover.

· · · · ·

If you intend to release a fish, then do not keep it out of the water for extended periods. Keep it submerged until you are ready with the camera or scales. When weighing, it is much kinder to attach a spring balance to the net and deduct the weight of the net later. Although it may seem to recover, a fish that has been out of the water for some time is likely to die over the next few hours.

Weighing fish.

When practising catch-and-release, you should always use barbless hooks to minimize the risk of injury. However, a badly de-barbed hook with a jagged contour can do more harm than good. One way to remove the barb properly is to crush it between the jaws of a fly-tying vice rather than using pliers or forceps.

• • • • •

Good Housekeeping

Replacement of the leader at some time during the day should always be a consideration, especially with pre-stretched nylon. Catching a few fish, the occasional unpicked wind knot or the removal of tangles can all contribute to leader fatigue and the loss of the fish of a lifetime.

• • • • •

Do not keep spare leaders wrapped around a card or similar flat object, since it can result in unwanted kinks. Wrap the leader round a foam cylinder or a piece of Plastazote with chamfered edges. It is also better to attach the end of the leader to the line, and then rotate the cylinder to pay out the leader from butt to tippet. This reduces the risk of a bird's nest considerably.

• • • • •

Any floatant needs to flow evenly over a fly to ensure a proper coating all round and to prevent unnatural blotchy areas where too much has been applied. This can be difficult with viscous materials, such as Gink, in cool conditions, so keep the container close to your body in your breast pocket.

• • • • •

Always use chemically sharpened hooks. More fish will be hooked and lighter nylon can be used since less force is needed to set the hook. But inspect the hook after catching a fish or snagging on an obstacle, and if damaged replace the fly or redress the point with a diamond file (better than a honing stone).

• • • • •

Droppers quickly become too short after a few changes of fly, but this can be alleviated by using an untucked half-blood knot. Undo by gripping the knot with your fingernails, pulling away from the eye of the hook. But you must use five turns when tying the knot – any fewer and the knot may slip.

• • • • •

Clear nylons have the distinct advantage of low visibility. However, the lack of colour may be at the expense of preservatives to make them survive hostile conditions such as sunlight or prolonged dampness. It is therefore essential to recognize this weakness, and to throw away a spool after perhaps as little as a couple of months in the field.

• • • • •

State of mind is essential in trout fishing. Uncertainty about an approach leads to lack of concentration and confidence, resulting in mechanical and inadequate control of the fly. If an idea is nagging away at you, do not let it impair your current tactic. Either dismiss it from your mind, or experiment with it for a fixed but adequate time, such as half an hour. Better still, get someone else sufficiently interested in the idea to try it out for you.

Those of us who are going long-sighted with age have difficulty in tying knots and attaching flies. To avoid carrying a special pair of reading glasses, it is possible to buy some stick-on bifocals for attaching to the inside of your Polaroids.

• • • • •

A nylon butt section can be attached neatly to a looped fly line. Place the end half inch of the fly line in nail varnish remover for about ten seconds, and then scrape the plastic away between two finger nails, avoiding contact between the rest of the line and the liquid. Make the exposed braid into a small loop, smear with Superglue and bind.

• • • • •

Never store conventionally hackled dry flies in, for example, a foam-lined box. Even with specially contoured Ethafoam, the base of the hackle can press against the surface and become disfigured. The fly will not land properly upright on the surface, thereby dramatically reducing the number of trout that will take it. Jeff Loud told us of a very effective method to restore the hackle by steaming the fly for a few seconds.

The effect of steaming hackles

Fly Tying

Develop your own colour code for tying threads to identify the amount of weight on a fly. This way you will be able to explore the depths in a more systematic manner, and have a point of reference for future trips to the same water. Providing the threads are not too gaudy, it will be very unlikely to be detrimental to the pattern.

• • • • •

You can reduce eye strain considerably by using a white fly tying bench or by placing a white cloth as a background to the vice.

• • • • •

Even a respectable whip finish can unwind after the fly has been used extensively. A drop of varnish on to the head after tying the fly will prevent this occurring. A dab of Superglue with a dubbing needle is even better. A drop of Superglue on a piece of card will stay workable for long enough to dab the heads of about 20 pre-tied flies.

Keep all your fly tying materials properly labelled – especially according to colour. When you discover a successful pattern, make sure that you retain a sample of the tying materials, properly labelled for future reference. Most of us can be forgetful about a successful shade, and there is a wide variation in people's perceptions. Different suppliers can show remarkable variations in what they supply as nominally the same shade.

· · · · ·

It is easy to get carried away with the huge variety of different shades of fly tying material that are available. Trout will often insist on the right general shade, but they are seldom quite as fussy as some fly tiers. Besides, there are often some quite substantial variations in the natural insects, even within the same river or lake. If in doubt, it is worth erring on the side of caution, aiming for something that is less likely to raise suspicion.

· · · · ·

When tying a wire body, an under-body of flat tinsel in the same colour will hide any imperfections in the winding. The body then appears properly segmented, without any dark patches where the tying silk shows through gaps in the coils.

· · · · ·

Basic Nous

Polaroids are invaluable for spotting trout directly or via surface disturbances, and for identifying subtle but productive calm lanes in still water. For poor light conditions, amber coloured lenses seem to work best. It is also possible to buy partially polarized glasses which let through extra light while still providing much of the advantage. Prescription Polaroids are also more comfortable than clip-ons.

· · · · ·

The stomach contents of a dead fish can be viewed much more easily and accurately by placing them into a container of water.

· · · · ·

Your hands quickly become acclimatized to the weather conditions. If the water feels warm, the wind will be chilling the surface quite effectively and discouraging flies from hatching. Dip your hand in the water, and if it feels warm perhaps you should be fishing well below the surface.

· · · · ·

When a large number of fishermen are fishing the same area, estimate the number of fish being caught per angler. It can be misleading to see a rod bending every fifteen minutes, but if there are twenty anglers in view this implies only one fish per person every five hours. Unless you know something special, pick up your rod and move on to another spot.

· · · · ·

Do not despair after an unsuccessful day's fishing when others have done much better. Eat humble pie and admit that perhaps it was not all down to bad luck. Maybe there was something lacking in your own approach or knowledge. Think carefully about what you may have been doing wrong, and use it as an opportunity for improvement. The world's best fishermen will all point to bad experiences in their careers which acted as a springboard to future success.

Many good anglers are hesitant to divulge some of their best flies and methods, which they may have spent years developing. However, at the end of a big competition, the adrenaline can loosen a successful angler's tongue considerably. Thus, whether you fish competitions or not, it is invariably worth turning up for a weigh-in to ask a few pertinent questions.

· · · · ·

If still-water trout are persistently following or swirling at a dropper fly, transfer it to the point. It is preferable to use it as the only fly on the leader. This will present the fly in a more natural manner and will often result in good, solid takes.

· · · · ·

Many river flies incorporate conspicuous white posts to improve the visibility to the angler. White is not always easy to see, especially in bright conditions. It is therefore worth taking a couple of fibre-tip pens with you on a fishing trip.

· · · · ·

When correcting for the effects of the wind in covering a fish, make greater allowances for lightweight hooks or for hackled patterns which are more prone to being blown off course.

· · · · ·

Trout can be easily spooked by a fly line landing on top of them, however delicately it may have been cast. So when fishing a new spot, start by casting a very short line to cover the fish at close range, and then progressively lengthen the leader so that all the fish in front of you can be systematically covered without disturbance.

· · · · ·

When wading across a river, it is a good idea to hold your rod horizontally above the surface. If you slip, the drag exerted by the full length of the rod on the surface will often prevent you toppling over completely. Two or more anglers can greatly reduce the risk of stumbling by linking arms.

Linking arms to cross a fast-flowing river.

EPILOGUE

At last the book is with the publisher, and we are enjoying the solitude of the River Test on a mild October morning. Suddenly the silence is broken by a string of voluminous utterings. There follows a repetitive thumping as if someone is jumping up and down on the ground – or a hat, perhaps. Alex has just lost a two pound grayling at the net.

We have treated our reviewers and advisors to a day out. Brian is visibly relieved to learn that we do not, after all, use a Woolly Bugger on the hallowed chalk-stream. But after mixing with bad company over the last year, even he has succumbed to using Boobies on the lakes. Alan shrugs off the charge of corrupting the innocent by catching some excellent grayling on tiny dry flies and nymphs. Bob, experiencing his first real taste of river fishing, is adamant that he will never use a strike indicator, which he puts on a par with the 'dreaded Bung'. We shall see.

Reggie poses for the book with his beloved composite rod of built-cane and carbon, but insists on putting a paper bag over his head first. Humphrey catches a couple of good grayling in the rough water of the hatch pool beneath us, and gives away an 'identical fly' (but without any tungsten in the silver bead). Denzil sees the fly and notices a striking resemblance to his own secret pattern – the one that he lost when fishing near Humphrey the week before.

Some things have inevitably changed over the years. The beloved Rioja now seems to have given way to Chardonnay, New World Reds and a wine with the grandiose name of Cat's Pee on a Gooseberry Bush.

Over lunch, Reggie hands out a surfeit of sandwiches. Today the choice is between runner-bean and 'ham' – though the latter has an unfamiliar colour and texture. All sorts of suggestions are offered, but Reggie will only grin. 'Mmmm – nothing wrong with it,' he protests. This time, nobody wants to take the risk.

We then read out a few carefully chosen paragraphs from the book. All the victims who are present take the references to them in good spirit, even though Humphrey does try to deny some of his dastardly deeds before questioning our parentage. But Wesley, who used his influence to obtain a sneak preview, has not turned up to pass comment. In fact, he is no longer speaking to us.

Index